P9-AES-694

WITHDRAWN
UTSA LIBRARIES

RENEWALS 458-4574

MA

AGING, COMMUNICATION, AND HEALTH

Linking Research and Practice for Successful Aging

LEA'S COMMUNICATION SERIES
Jennings Bryant/Dolf Zillmann, General Editors

For a complete list of titles in LEA's Communication Series, please contact Lawrence Erlbaum Associates, Publishers.

AGING, COMMUNICATION, AND HEALTH

Linking Research and Practice for Successful Aging

Edited by

Mary Lee Hummert
University of Kansas

Jon F. Nussbaum
The Pennsylvania State University

LAWRENCE ERLBAUM ASSOCIATES, PUBLISHERS
2001   Mahwah, New Jersey   London

Copyright © 2001 by Lawrence Erlbaum Associates, Inc.
    All rights reserved. No part of this book may be reproduced in
    any form, by photostat, microform, retrieval system, or any other
    means, without the prior written permission of the publisher.

Lawrence Erlbaum Associates, Inc., Publishers
10 Industrial Avenue
Mahwah, New Jersey 07430

Cover design by Kathryn Houghtaling Lacey

Library of Congress Cataloging-in-Publication Data

Aging, communication, and health : linking research and practice for successful aging /
    edited by Mary Lee Hummert, Jon F. Nussbaum.
        p.   cm.
    Includes bibliographical references and indexes.
    ISBN 0-8058-3379-X (cloth : alk. paper)
        1. Aged—Health and hygiene.   2. Aged—Communication.   3. Aging—Psychological
aspects.   4. Aging.   5. Health.   I. Hummert, Mary Lee.   II. Nussbaum, Jon F.
RA564.8 .A39715 2000
613'.0438–dc21   00-060980

Books published by Lawrence Erlbaum Associates are printed on acid-free
paper, and their bindings are chosen for strength and durability.

Printed in the United States of America
10   9   8   7   6   5   4   3   2   1

Library
University of Texas
at San Antonio

For our parents—
Bill and Winnie Higgins
Richard and Mary Nussbaum

Contents

Acknowledgments

The chapters in this volume grew from research presented at the Third International Conference on Communication, Aging, and Health held in Kansas City, Missouri, in May, 1996. We are indebted to the sponsors of that conference for the support that ultimately led to the publication of this volume. We extend our thanks to the Merrill Advanced Studies Center and the College of Liberal Arts and Sciences at the University of Kansas, who provided the primary support for the conference, as well as to the University of Kansas' Gerontology Center, Communication Studies Department, Office of International Studies and Programs, Center on Aging (University of Kansas Medical Center), and Hoechst Marion Roussel Pharmaceuticals.

We each received additional and much appreciated support from our respective universities during the preparation of the book manuscript. Our collaboration was greatly facilitated by a Big Twelve Faculty Exchange Fellowship awarded to Jon Nussbaum by the University of Oklahoma and a sabbatical leave awarded to Mary Lee Hummert by the University of Kansas. Mary Lee Hummert received further support during this project from National Institute on Aging/National Institutes of Health Grant R01 AG16352.

We also wish to acknowledge the people who have helped us to translate our ideas for a book into a published volume. Linda Bathgate, our editor at Lawrence Erlbaum Associates, provided invaluable support and insights throughout the publication process. Barbara Wieghaus, production editor, ensured that the copyediting and production format reinforced the content of the chapters. We greatly appreciate her attention to detail. Likewise, we are grateful to Carol and Mark Bergstrom for their efficient and comprehensive work on the index to this volume. Finally, we thank our colleagues who contributed chapters to this volume. Their willingness to share their thoughts and scholarly research on aging, communication, and health not only contributes to our knowledge within this very important area of study, but also will surely help all of us as we age and care for those who are in need of our support. We also hope that this book finds its way into the hands of those who are not academicians, and that it contributes to their quality of life as they meet the challenges and experience the many rewards of aging.

—*Mary Lee Hummert*
—*Jon F. Nussbaum*

Introduction

Successful Aging, Communication, and Health

Mary Lee Hummert
University of Kansas

Jon F. Nussbaum
Pennsylvania State University

Successful aging—each of us hopes that this term will characterize our individual experiences of growing older and the experiences of those we love. Yet what does it mean to age successfully? Simply to live a long life? To run a marathon at age 80? To get older without looking older as advertisements for cosmetics and plastic surgery suggest? To have the economic resources to retire to a life of leisure as the financial investment advertisements suggest? To live the final years of one's life surrounded by loving children, grandchildren, and great-grandchildren as in a greeting card ad? In their 1998 landmark book reporting the results of the 10-year MacArthur Foundation Study of Aging in America, physician John Rowe and psychologist Robert Kahn show that the answer is more complex. Successful aging, they argue, involves three interrelated components: "low risk of disease and disease-related disability; high mental and physical function; and active engagement with life" (p. 38). We might paraphrase this list to say that successful aging is *healthy aging—healthy body, healthy mind, and healthy relationships.*

Rowe and Kahn (1998) see these three components as hierarchically ordered in that avoiding disease and disability "makes it easier to maintain mental and physical function . . . [which] in turn enables (but does not guarantee) active engagement with life" (p. 39). Physical health is foundational in the ideal model of successful aging. Unfortunately, the physical health of the majority of older individuals today conforms not to the ideal of successful aging, but to what Rowe and Kahn label "usual aging" (p. 54).

That is, although functioning well in the present, most older persons have age-related health risk factors and diseases such as high blood pressure, osteoarthritis, hearing impairments, and so on, that increase the probability that they will develop disabilities as they get older. Given Rowe and Kahn's definition, are these individuals precluded from aging successfully? Further, with increasing age, the percentage of older adults with disabilities or conditions (e.g., Alzheimer's dementia) severe enough to require institutional living settings grows dramatically, with 1996 figures showing that 19.8% of individuals 85 and older resided in institutions (Administration on Aging, 1999). What does successful aging mean for these individuals? This book is predicated on the belief that all aspects of health—physical, cognitive, emotional—are intertwined and that they are inseparable from any notion of successful aging, and also on the belief that communication provides the essential link between health and successful aging. For example, communication affects not only the quality of medical care older persons receive and thus their ability to maintain their physical health, but also their ability to cope with the consequences of illness and disability.

THE ROLE OF COMMUNICATION IN MAINTAINING HEALTH AND ACHIEVING SUCCESSFUL AGING

Three important intellectual contributions of the preceding century demonstrate that communication is central to the lives of all individuals, regardless of age. First is the notion that language is a form of *action* (Austin, 1962; Wittgenstein, 1953), so that words carry meanings beyond their literal definitions. Second is the idea that those actions and meanings are inherently *social*, created in interaction with others (Blumer, 1969; Mead, 1934). Third is the concept that these *socially created meanings constitute our reality* (Berger & Luckmann, 1966; Schutz, 1970). These ideas are captured in Cronen, Pearce, and Harris' (1982) definition of communication as the process "through which persons co-create, maintain, and alter social order, personal relationships, and individual identities" (p. 64). Likewise, these principles underlie late 20th century theories of psychology (e.g., Harré, 1986, on the social construction of emotion; and Harré, 1991, on discursive psychology), sociology (e.g., Giddens, 1979, on structuration theory), and communication (e.g., Delia, O'Keefe, & O'Keefe, 1982, on Constructivism; Giles, Coupland, & Coupland, 1991, on Communication Accommodation Theory).

Whereas communication is important to quality of life for those of all ages, its relationship to maintaining health during the aging process deserves special attention. Certainly Rowe and Kahn's (1998) third component of successful aging—active engagement with life—requires attention to interpersonal relationships and communication, the development of close emotional ties, and effective support systems (Noels, Giles, Gallois, & Ng, chap. 11, this volume; see also Nussbaum, Pecchioni, Robinson, & Thompson, 2000, for a review of the research on interpersonal relationships and successful aging). Achieving the first two components—avoiding disease and disability, maintaining physical and mental function—however, also requires attention to communication. At the system level, access to health care can be limited for underserved rural and minority elders, but communication technologies (e.g., telemedicine) can be used to overcome those limitations (see Whitten & Gregg, chap. 1, this volume). At the interpersonal level, negative stereotypes of older persons and the aging process can act as barriers to intergenerational communication (Hummert, 1994; Hummert, Shaner, Garstka, & Henry, 1998). Such barriers can directly affect the abilities of health professionals to treat effectively the health problems of older patients and the patients' abilities to present their concerns and questions (Beisecker, 1991; Coupland & Coupland, chap. 6, this volume; Greene & Adelman, chap. 5, this volume; Greene, Adelman, Charon, & Hoffman, 1986; Greene, Adelman, Rizzo, & Friedmann, 1994; Nussbaum, Pecchioni, & Crowell, chap. 2, this volume).

Communication also influences how older individuals cope with age-related losses in physical or mental functioning so that they can "age successfully" in spite of the loss. For instance, in the Person–Environment model of aging, Lawton and Nahemow (1973) show that older persons must find the right fit between their physical and mental capabilities and their living environment. An environment that puts too much stress on those capabilities can lead to further decline and dependence, as can an environment that provides them with too few challenges (Baltes, 1996). Determining the ideal environment or modifying an existing one is often the product of decision making that involves not only an older person, but also that individual's family and physician. This decision-making process can be difficult, involving the negotiation of changing family roles and levels of dependence–independence (Cicirelli, 1992; Coupland & Coupland, chap. 6, this volume; Hummert & Morgan, chap. 8, this volume).

In addition, some age-related conditions such as hearing loss, and diseases such as dementias and strokes, directly affect individuals' ability to produce and process language, making communication itself problematic (Kemper, 1992; Ryan, 1991). Coping with these communication problems can include education and intervention programs such as the one described in relation to hearing loss by Pichora-Fuller and Carson (chap. 3, this volume). For Alzheimer's dementia, on the other hand, it may involve using language strategies to facilitate comprehension (Orange, chap. 10, this volume) or, at the latest stages of the disease, an emphasis on nonverbal communication and empathic responses to the personhood of the individual with dementia (Norberg, chap. 7, this volume).

The importance of communication to the *successful aging* of those coping with age-related losses cannot be underestimated. Heckhausen and Schulz' (1995) Life-Span Theory of Control demonstrated that individuals of all ages prefer to have primary control over their own actions and decisions, and that having primary control is strongly related to maintaining self-esteem. However, the ability to exert primary control declines with age due to age-related physical and cognitive declines (Schulz & Heckhausen, 1999). Communication, for many older individuals, may become increasingly prominent as a means of primary control, and therefore their only route to successful aging (see also Hummert & Morgan, chap. 8, this volume; Ryan & Norris, Epilogue, this volume).

INTERNATIONAL RESEARCH AGENDA
ON AGING, COMMUNICATION, AND HEALTH

Recognizing the importance of communication to successful aging, a series of international conferences have addressed the interrelationship of communication, aging, and health. The initial meeting in 1988, a Fulbright International Colloquium held at the University of Wales, was the first attempt to develop an integrated interdisciplinary framework on communication and the health of elderly persons. Key conclusions of this conference were presented in an edited volume entitled *Communication, Health, and the Elderly* (Giles, Coupland, & Wiemann, 1990). The second conference was held in Hamilton, Ontario in 1994 with the support of McMaster University's Educational Centre on Aging, the Social Sciences and Humanities Research Council of Canada, and the National Health and Research Development Program of Canada. A special issue of the journal *Health Communication* (Ryan, 1996) presented the major findings from this conference.

This book had its genesis in the Third International Conference on Communication, Aging, and Health held in 1996, with the University of Kansas' College of Liberal Arts and Sciences and the Merrill Advanced Studies Center as its primary sponsors. These chapters represent the culmination of an interdisciplinary and intercultural dialogue that began at this conference. Included are reports of empirical research generated in response to issues raised at the conference (e.g., chap. 9 by Edwards; chap. 11 by Noels et al., chap. 3 by Pichora-Fuller & Carson); essays that provide up-to-date literature reviews on traditional (e.g., physician–patient interaction, chap. 5 by Greene & Adelman; communication with those with Alzheimer's dementia, chap. 10 by Orange) and developing topics in the area (e.g., managed care, chap. 2 by Nussbaum et al.; telemedicine, chap. 1 by Whitten & Gregg); and treatises that address philosophical as well as practical considerations (e.g., chap. 7 by Norberg; Epilogue by Ryan & Norris). Mirroring the disciplinary diversity at the Third International Conference, contributors represent the fields of communication, psychology, speech pathology, audiology, public health, medicine, and nursing. They also mirror the cultural diversity at the conference, including major scholars from the United States, Canada, Great Britain, Sweden, Australia, and New Zealand.

GOALS, AUDIENCE, AND STRUCTURE FOR THIS VOLUME

In selecting the chapters for this volume, setting up its structure, and providing guidelines to the contributors, we had two goals. First, we felt that it was essential that the chapters represent the highest levels of current scholarship on communication, aging, and health so that readers could have confidence in the validity and intellectual rigor of the information presented, and so that the chapters could provide a strong foundation for future research on these important topics. Second, we wanted the chapters to address the applied implications of this research, so that the scholarship could provide practical guidance to readers dealing with these issues in their own lives. These dual goals are reflected in the subtitle for this volume, *Linking Research and Practice for Successful Aging.*

Our first goal was easily achieved, given the credentials of our contributors and their own high standards for scholarship. To address our second goal, we asked each chapter author to include a discussion of how readers—whether academics, policy makers, practitioners, older individuals, or family members—could apply the research in their own interactions. Contributors responded enthusiastically, and each chapter ends with a consideration of how the research could be used to improve readers' own communication experiences to help themselves, their clients, or their family members achieve successful aging. To further achieve our second goal, each chapter is written in a style that is accessible to educated readers in general, not just to those from the academic community.

Given its dual focus, this book meets the needs of a wide variety of audiences. These include scholars and graduate students engaged in basic and applied research on communication, aging, and health; health care practitioners—physicians, nurses, nursing home staff, public health workers, and so on—who have older clients; family members concerned with helping older relatives cope with age-related health challenges; and older individuals themselves who are committed to achieving their own experience of successful aging.

The book is divided into three parts, each of which highlights an area important to health and successful aging. Part I includes four chapters that examine developments in health care and in health communication that affect older persons. Chapters 1 and 2 focus on systemic changes to health care delivery and their potential impact on the health status of older individuals. In the first chapter, Whitten and Gregg introduce readers to telemedicine, the use of telecommunication technologies to deliver services to older patients. As these authors demonstrate, these technologies hold promise for improving health care delivery to minority and rural populations in particular. Next, Nussbaum, Pecchioni, and Crowell consider the implications of managed care for older patients and their physicians, providing insights on how both parties can build a viable physician–patient relationship within a managed care system. Chapters 3 and 4 reflect a growing emphasis on health promotion programs for older individuals (Carson & Pichora-Fuller, 1997). Such programs exist not only to help persons cope with health problems but also to encourage good health practices with a goal of identifying potential health threats before they develop into illness or disability. Pichora-Fuller and Carson (chap. 3) review the nature and pervasiveness of age-related hearing loss, detailing an ecologically oriented intervention program to improve daily communication experiences of hearing impaired individuals. This program is ecological because it addresses not only the behaviors of the hearing impaired individuals, but also the behaviors of their communication partners and aspects of the physical and social environment that could lead to improved communication. In chapter 4, Garstka, McCallion, and Toseland describe how support groups can be used to improve the health of caregivers. Further, they provide clear guidelines on implementing support groups and ensuring participation by caregivers from minority and ethnically diverse populations.

The three chapters in Part II bring provider–patient communication to the fore. Greene and Adelman (chap. 5) review the research literature on physician communication with older patients. Based on that literature, they highlight communication practices for physicians that should help them to provide individually appropriate care to older patients. In addition, they offer suggestions to older patients on ways to maximize their interactions with their physicians and to become proactive consumers of health care. Coupland and Coupland (chap. 6) take us into the examining room to observe the discourse between physicians, older patients, and accompanying family members. Such three-party interactions are quite common with older patients (Beisecker, 1989). This chapter shows how such interactions can work to the benefit of older patients or to their detriment, depending on whether the talk empowers or disadvantages the older person. The final chapter in this section, chapter 7 by Norberg, presents the reader with the most challenging of communication situations, that of professional caregivers for those with severe dementia. Norberg suggests that successful communication with those with severe dementia requires that caregivers reassess their definition of personhood, developing one that encompasses individuals who are mute and seemingly trapped within their own minds.

Part III includes four chapters that explore the relationships between family communication and health. Hummert and Morgan (chap. 8) investigate how adult children and older parents negotiate health-related decisions, such as whether to move to an assisted-living facility. Taking the views of both parents and children into consideration, they provide suggestions on how families can approach such decisions in a way that promotes the health and independence of the parent. In chapter 9, Edwards examines how communication within the family can impact the health of an older person receiving care. Using a recent empirical study, Edwards highlights those aspects of communication that lead to improved health for care receivers as well as those that seem to contribute to health declines. Chapter 10 by Orange provides a look at the effects of Alzheimer's dementia on communication within the family. Although those with severe dementia are often under the care of professionals (see Norberg, chap. 7, this volume), family members provide care for many with mild or moderate dementia. Language abilities are affected but not totally lost at these earlier stages of the disease. Orange provides specific strategies for facilitating communication with these individuals. Chapter 11 (Noels et al.) examines the relationship between intergenerational communication and the psychological health of older persons. Noels et al. add a cross-cultural perspective to the book by considering the similarities and differences in this relationship for older persons from Western and Eastern cultures.

CONCLUSIONS

This introduction has only begun the discussion of the importance of communication to health and successful aging. Each chapter continues that discussion and adds to it. In the Epilogue to this volume, Ryan and Norris integrate the contributions of the individual chapters into a single framework. Using two models of the communication and aging process, they illustrate how communication can contribute to the decline of older persons (Communication Predicament of Aging Model, Ryan, Giles, Bartolucci, & Henwood, 1986) or conversely can provide the avenue for achieving successful aging (Communication Enhancement Model, Ryan, Meredith, MacLean, & Orange, 1995). Further they not only show the necessity of linking research and practice in order to make the promise of the Communication Enhancement Model a reality, but also provide us with guidelines on forging such links.

REFERENCES

Austin, J. L. (1962). *How to do things with words.* Cambridge, MA: Harvard University Press.

Administration on Aging (1999). *Profile of older Americans: 1999.* [WWW document]. URL http://www.aoa.dhhs.gov/aoa/stats/profile/default.htm.

Baltes, M. M. (1996). *The many faces of dependency in old age.* New York: Cambridge University Press.

Beisecker, A. E. (1991). Aging and the desire for information and input in medical decisions: Patient consumerism in medical encounters. *Gerontologist, 28*(3), 330–335.

Beisecker, A. E. (1989). The influence of a companion on the doctor–elderly patient interaction. *Health Communication, 1,* 55–70.

Berger, P. L., & Luckmann, T. (1966). *The social construction of reality: A treatise in the sociology of knowledge.* New York: Doubleday.

Blumer, H. (1969). *Symbolic interactionism: Perspective and method.* Englewood Cliffs, NJ: Prentice-Hall.

Carson, A., & Pichora-Fuller, M. K. (1997). Health promotion and audiology: The community–clinic link. *Journal of the Academy of Rehabilitative Audiology, 30,* 29–51.

Cicirelli, V. G. (1992). *Family caregiving: Autonomous and paternalistic decision making.* Newbury Park, CA: Sage.

Cronen, V. E., Pearce, W. B., & Harris, L. M. (1982). The coordinated management of meaning: A theory of communication. In F. E. X. Dance (Ed.), *Human communication theory: Comparative essays* (pp. 61–89). New York: Harper & Row.

Delia, J. G., O'Keefe, B. J., & O'Keefe, D. J. (1982). The constructivist approach to communication. In F. E. X. Dance (Ed.), *Human communication theory: Comparative essays* (pp. 147–191). New York: Harper & Row.

Giddens, A. (1979). *Central problems in social theory: Action, structure and contradiction in social analysis.* Berkeley: University of California Press.

Giles, H., Coupland, N., & Coupland, J. (1991). Accommodation theory: Communication, context, and consequence. In H. Giles, J. Coupland, & N. Coupland (Eds.), *Contexts of accommodation: Developments in applied sociolinguistics* (pp. 1–68). Cambridge, England: Cambridge University Press.

Giles, H., Coupland, N., & Wiemann, J. M. (Eds.). (1990). *Communication, health, and the elderly. (Proceedings of the Fulbright Colloquium, 1988).* Manchester, England: Manchester University Press.

Greene, M. G., Adelman, R. D., Charon, R., & Hoffman, S. (1986). Ageism in the medical encounter: An exploratory study of the doctor–elderly patient relationship. *Language and Communication, 6,* 113–124.

Greene, M. G., Adelman, R. D., Rizzo, C., & Friedmann, E. (1994). The patient's presentation of self in an initial medical encounter. In M. L. Hummert, J. M. Wiemann, & J. F. Nussbaum (Eds.), *Interpersonal communication in older adulthood* (pp. 226–250). Newbury Park, CA: Sage.

Harré, R. (Ed.). (1986). *The social construction of emotion.* London: Blackwell.

Harré, R. (1991). The discursive production of selves. *Theory and Psychology, 50 ,* 51–63.

Heckhausen, J., & Schulz, R. (1995). A life-span theory of control. *Psychological Review, 102,* 284–304.

Hummert, M. L. (1994). Stereotypes of the elderly and patronizing speech. In M. L. Hummert, J. M. Wiemann, & J. F. Nussbaum (Eds.), *Interpersonal communication in older adulthood* (pp. 162–184). Newbury Park, CA: Sage.

Hummert, M. L., Shaner, J. L., Garstka, T. A., & Henry, C. (1998). Communication with older adults: The influence of age stereotypes, context, and communicator age. *Human Communication Research, 25,* 124–151.

Kemper, S. (1992). Language and aging. In F. I. M. Craik & T. Salthouse (Eds.), *Handbook of aging and cognition* (pp. 213–270). Hillsdale, NJ: Lawrence Erlbaum Associates.

Lawton, M. P., & Nahemow, L. (1973). Ecology and the aging process. In C. Eisdorfer & M. P. Lawton (Eds.), *Psychology of adult development and aging* (pp. 619–674). Washington, DC: American Psychological Association.

Mead, G. H. (1934). *Mind, self and society.* Chicago: University of Chicago Press.

Nussbaum, J. F., Pecchioni, L., Robinson, J. D., & Thompson, T. (2000). *Communication and aging.* Mahwah, NJ: Lawrence Erlbaum Associates.

Rowe, J. W., & Kahn, R. L. (1998). *Successful aging.* New York: Pantheon Books.

Ryan, E. B. (1991). Language issues in normal aging. In R. Lubinski (Ed.), *Dementia and communication: Clinical and research implications* (pp. 84–97). Toronto: B. C. Decker Publishing.

Ryan, E. B. (Ed.). (1996). Communication, aging and health (Special Issue). *Health Communication, 8(3).*

Ryan, E. B., Giles, H., Bartolucci, G., & Henwood, K. (1986). Psycholinguistic and social psychological components of communication by and with the elderly. *Language and Communication, 6,* 1–24.

Ryan, E. B., Meredith, S. D., MacLean, M. J., & Orange, J. B. (1995). Changing the way we talk with elders: Promoting health using the communication enhancement model. *International Journal of Aging and Human Development, 41(2),* 89–107.

Schulz, R., & Heckhausen, J. (1999). Aging, culture and control: Setting a new research agenda. *Journal of Gerontology, 54B,* P139–P145.

Schutz, A. (1970). *On phenomenology and social relations.* Chicago: University of Chicago Press.

Wittgenstein, L. (1953). *Philosophical investigations.* Oxford: Blackwell.

I

DEVELOPMENTS IN HEALTH CARE AND SUCCESSFUL AGING

1

Telemedicine: Using Telecommunication Technologies to Deliver Health Services to Older Adults

Pamela Whitten
Jennifer L. Gregg
Michigan State University

Health care is an important commodity in the United States because people, the consumers of health services, place a high value on health.
Health care has evolved over this century from a service accessed by a
small percentage of society to one of the biggest market sectors in the
U.S. economy. The Health Care Financing Administration (1999)
reports that the nation's total spending for health care will increase from
$1 trillion in 1996 to $2.1 trillion in 2007. Medicine in this country is
now at a crossroads of sorts. As medical innovations offer health care
providers with enhanced ways to save lives, the length of chronic illnesses and subsequent need for supporting services are likely to increase dramatically in the coming years. As a result, communities are seeking new
solutions to address accompanying issues of rising costs, improved access
to services, and acceptable levels of quality and continuity of care. New
technologies, such as telemedicine, are emerging as one approach to
address these issues.

As perhaps the most innovative technology to be introduced in the
health care arena, telemedicine has a potentially bright future. Advances
in the last decade have expanded the concept of telemedicine to include
any technology employing telecommunication technologies to deliver
health services. This can include videoconferencing on personal comput-
ers, larger room-based systems, or even on a television through regular

analog phone lines. It can also include any applications of Internet telephony such as data, voice, or audio transmitted through the Internet.

Understanding telemedicine and its applications in health is important for three reasons. First, health care in America is currently undergoing powerful changes in both the structure and delivery of medical services. For example, increasing demands for managed care (see Nussbaum, Pecchioni, & Crowell, chap. 4, this volume) are creating new relationships among physicians, patients, health care providers, insurance companies, and government agencies, indicating the need for delivery systems that allow for full participation and access for the disadvantaged. Second, recent advances in electronic telecommunications technologies present new opportunities for minimizing distances between and among caregivers, informational and educational services, and patients. Rapid growth in telecommunication programs throughout the country implies that telemedical technologies are here to stay; how they are being used to provide care for senior citizens must be understood. Third, Perednia and Allen (1995) predicted that most physicians in the United States will be directly or indirectly involved with some form of telemedicine by the year 2000. Thus, practitioners of telemedicine must understand the similarities and differences as they gradually move from their traditional medical setting to one mediated by new technologies.

As the largest consumer segment in the health industry, older Americans will simultaneously be the largest impactors of, and most impacted by, shifts in health costs and services. Taken together, these trends suggest the need for a thorough understanding of telemedicine—an important context where health providers seek to adopt and adapt new information technologies to provide quality services to patients, particularly among those who are geographically isolated. The purpose of this chapter is to examine the use of technologies to deliver medical services and health education to older persons. We focus specifically on telemedicine, the use of telecommunication technologies to provide health services, and provide an overview of telemedicine applications for older persons. Finally, we conclude by examining the potential economic and communicative consequences of telemedicine.

TELEMEDICINE AND TELECOMMUNICATION TECHNOLOGIES

Telecommunication technologies have been used for medical diagnosis, care, and education since the invention of the telephone. Telemedicine techniques, as defined previously, have been under development during the past four decades. Wittson and colleagues were the first to employ telemedicine for medical purposes in 1959 when they set up telepsychiatry consultations via microwave technology between the Nebraska Psychiatric Institute in Omaha and the state mental hospital 112 miles away (Jones & Colenda, 1997; Wittson, Affleck, & Johnson, 1961). In the same year, Montreal, Quebec, was the site for pioneer teleradiology work being done by Jutra (1959). In the 1970s, there was a flurry of telemedicine activity as several major projects developed in North America and Australia, including the Space Technology Applied to Rural Papago Advanced Health Care (STARPAHC) project of the National Aeronautics and Space Administration (NASA) in southern Arizona; a project at Logan Airport in Boston, Massachusetts, and programs in northern Canada (Dunn et al., 1980). Grigsby and Kaehny (1993) reviewed telemedicine activities undertaken prior to 1993. With the exception of the 20-year-old telemedicine program at Memorial University Hospital of Newfoundland, none of the programs begun before 1986 has survived. Although data are limited, early reviews and evaluations of these programs suggest that the equipment was reasonably effective at transmitting the information needed for most clinical uses and that users were for the most part satisfied (Conrath, Puckingham, Dunn, & Swanson, 1975; Dongier, Tempier, Lalinec-Michaud & Meunier, 1986; Fuchs, 1974; Murphy & Bird, 1974). However, when external sources of funding were withdrawn, the programs simply folded. Although Perednia and Allen (1995) suggested that the failure of these programs was caused primarily by the inability to justify these programs on a cost–benefit basis, other researchers questioned other potential issues, such as limited physician acceptance (Michaeis, 1989).

The decades of 1960, 1970, and 1980 exhibited a series of telemedicine pilot and demonstration projects. However, the 1990s have proven to be a period of rapid growth. In 1990, there were four active telemedicine programs. By 1997, there were almost 90 such programs (Grigsby & Allen, 1997). The creation of many of these programs was sparked by clinical need. For example, the program at the University of Kansas was originally proposed by rural practitioners who required access to certain medical subspecialties (Allen, Cox, & Thomas, 1992). With an area roughly equivalent to New York state, western Kansas had no local pediatric subspecialists and only a handful of adult medical specialists. The telemedicine program in Kansas was created under the premise that telemedicine could improve access to specialty medical care and thus improve the overall quality of medical care in rural areas.

In the early 1990s, new and fairly inexpensive digital technologies that could digitize and compress video, audio, and other imaging information emerged. This facilitated the transmission of information over land lines with relatively narrow bandwidths, instead of through the more expensive satellite or relatively unavailable private cable or fiber optic lines. Whereas there were only nine interactive-mediated telemedicine programs in the United States in 1992 doing a total of 1,715 consultations, by 1996 there were 69 programs doing a total of 20,000 consultations (Grigsby & Allen, 1997).

Worth noting is that a few preliminary studies indicate that telemedicine is a viable alternative for health care treatment (Perednia & Allen, 1995). Indeed, research findings related to medical efficacy and satisfaction testify to the feasibility of this alternative. For example, Allen et al. (1992) reported that "the telemedicine interaction was found to be a reasonable substitute for an on-site patient–physician encounter, in terms of patient–physician satisfaction and ability to transmit information and diagnoses" (p. 323). Technological enhancements in recent years have expanded the telemedicine paradigm. Telemedicine providers have a wide range of choices for the equipment and delivery structures they can develop for provision of care. The next section discusses these options.

Telemedicine Delivery Options: Level of Interactivity

Telemedicine analysts traditionally have looked at telemedicine services in relation to the level of interactivity inherent in the service. In the past, this often meant the amount of bandwidth available. Bandwidth simply refers to the width of a communications channel through which an audio, data, or video signal is transmitted. A traditional analog telephone line can transmit audio signals at a rate of 64 kilobits per second (kbps). This is adequate for audio transmission, but to send additional information such as video signals, additional bandwidth is needed to make the transmission smoother. Channel bandwidth can be added together to create more space in which to transmit analog and digital signals. Thus, basic rate interface ISDN would yield the equivalent of two 64 kbps channels,[1] or, a T–1 line would yield the equivalent of twenty-four 64 kbps channels.[2] This expla-

---

[1]ISDN stands for Integrated Services Digital Network. Basic Rate Interface (BRI) is designed for home or office use and allows 144 kbps over two 64 kb channels and one 16 kb signaling channel.

[2]T–1 is a digital transmission link with a capacity of 1.544 mbps (1,544,000 bits per s). It uses standard copper wires as can be found in any house, but with advanced digital voice encoding it can handle 24 voice conversations.

nation is a bit oversimplified; however, it points out that the more bandwidth available, the more signals can be sent in a faster amount of time. This is why videoconferencing on a personal computer (PC) at 128 kbps looks inferior to television signals received over cable lines into a private home; it's a matter of the bandwidth being used to transmit the signals.

Recent developments in telecommunications, however, are reshaping the way bandwidth is viewed. For example, the availability of cable modems in many mass consumer markets is reshaping perceptions of acceptable transmission speeds for downloading information from the Internet. Cable modems, which are simply modems designed for use on a television coaxial cable line, transmit at speeds at least 10 to 100 times faster than traditional dial-up modems. This means that a person can download and watch a health-related video clip off the Internet with minimal to no loading or delay time. To download a file that contains five megabytes of data, it takes 23 min using a 28.8K modem over regular phone lines; this same file takes 5 min to download if using 128 kbps and only 26 s to download with a cable modem. Many subscribers of cable modems report that they cannot go back to traditional dial-up modems (Newton, 1998). Other telecommunication technologies that read like alphabet soup (ATM,[3] DSL,[4] T–3,[5] SONET[6]) are predicted to reshape the amount of bandwidth available for telemedicine applications in the very near future. For this reason, a paradigmatic shift is taking place in the conceptual model for describing telemedicine's level of interactivity. Telemedical services for older citizens can be provided on a variety of technologies through a wide array of bandwidth options in three formats: store and forward, Internet, and synchronous interactive video.

Store and forward telemedical services are the most asynchronous of the three modalities. Asynchronous transmission means messages are not being sent at the same time. In other words, it is not interactive. In this service category, a piece of health data is collected and transmitted to a medical provider who retrieves the information, analyzes it, and responds

---

[3]ATM (asynchronous transfer mode) is high-speed transmission technology that employs high bandwidth, low delay, connection-oriented, packet-like switching and multiplexing.

[4]DSL (digital subscriber line) is the generic name for a family of evolving digital services provided by local phone companies to their subscribers, which provide up to 8 million bits per s downstream to the consumers and somewhat fewer bits per s upstream to the phone company.

[5]T–3 is a digital transmission link with a capacity of 45 mbps or 28 T–1 lines, which is capable of handling 672 voice conversations and runs over fiber optic lines.

[6]SONET (Synchronous Optical Network) is a family of fiber-optic transmission rates from 51.84 mbps to 13.22 gbps, created to provide the flexibility needed to send many digital signals with different capabilities.

when convenient. Common store-and-forward applications include teleradiology, teledermatology, and telepathology.

As the fastest growing segment of telemedicine (Allen, 1998), teleradiology technologies simply require that a digitized version of a film is transported over a telecommunication medium and retrieved by a radiologist. The radiologist examines the film and then sends correspondence regarding the diagnosis to the referring physician. This is similar to traditional radiology, except that the radiological image is transmitted in a new way. If a great deal of bandwidth is used, it can be transmitted almost instantaneously. If a small amount of bandwidth is used, it can take hours to transmit an image. The goal of the service dictates bandwidth requirements. If being used for emergency diagnoses, then obviously more bandwidth would be required.

Teledermatology is another store-and-forward application growing in use. In this case, a primary care physician can capture an elderly person's rash as a digital picture and transmit it to a dermatologist (accompanied with history and physical data information) so that a diagnosis can be made. This represents a radical shift in how a dermatologist would traditionally diagnose a rash where the patient would be present in the room with the specialist.

Internet telemedical services can be totally asynchronous or synchronous through such avenues as chat rooms where multiple participants are online discussing an issue. As noted earlier, asynchronous communication is not interactive. Synchronous communication, on the other hand, allows for real-time interaction. Internet medicine is now one of the fastest growing segments of health care (see October 21, 1998, issue of the Journal of the American Medical Association [JAMA] for an overview of this new application). Health-related services are beginning to proliferate on the Web, ranging from the simple provision of sponsored information to the actual delivery of health services and products. Steinfield, Whitten, and Kingsley (1999) identified six categories of medical services provided over the Internet, including medical equipment and supplies, clinical services, health insurance, medication, alternative medicine, and health information and continuing education.

Finally, interactive video (ITV) telemedicine services are fully synchronous. In these cases, medical care and education are conducted between two or more parties who are physically present in front of some form of ITV equipment. They can see and hear each other in real time and even share documents from which they are working. The quality of these interactions will vary with the type of equipment and transmission speeds being employed. Videoconferencing can occur on room-based systems running at very high transmission speeds or from a desktop PC at lower speeds. There are even videoconferencing technologies that can run through traditional analog phone lines. Within this category are traditional notions of telemedicine: a physician in a city treating a senior citizen located hundreds of miles away where the patient would not have access to this type of physician. In this case, medical peripheral equipment can be used to aid in the diagnosis or treatment of the patient. For example, an electronic stethoscope enables the physician to synchronously listen to heart and breath sounds while conducting the physical portion of an exam. ITV telemedical applications are also used heavily for education; health providers or community residents can access health information through classes that are transmitted over interactive video. These educational opportunities differ from satellite-downlinked events or videotapes in that they are interactive; the participant is able to ask questions or contribute to the discussion during the actual event.

The applications for store-and-forward, Internet, and ITV technologies are being developed at explosive rates. Although the role of technology is important, it is beyond the scope of this chapter to give a detailed description of all technological innovations in telemedicine. We now turn to an overview of exemplary telemedicine applications in place to deliver services to older individuals. Though not exhaustive, this overview presents the most active and compelling projects in place to date.

Telemedicine Projects for Older Persons

Since its introduction in the 1950s, telemedicine has been used for treating older patients. In the early 1970s, interactive cable was used between Mount Sinai Medical Center in New York City and a public housing highrise for older adults, allowing tenants to ask questions and participate in discussions of nutrition, exercise, chronic diseases and other health-related topics of interest to older persons (Journal of American Medical Association, 1973). Telemedicine programs have come a long way since then. Today's telemedicine programs are so diverse that it is easiest to discuss them according to the three categories of store and forward, Internet, and ITV.

Store and Forward.   As noted earlier, store-and-forward technology is the most asynchronous of the three modes of delivery. In other words, data are collected and reviewed at different times; the technology does not provide immediate feedback. Examples of store-and-forward telemedicine applications include:

• Doctors at Purdue University tested a program in the early 1990s of in-home monitoring of patients suffering from congestive heart failure. Results of the study showed that patients could easily use the system and physicians could effectively use the clinical data obtained (Patel & Babbs, 1992).

• Older patients in Virginia who had undergone hip or knee replacement surgery and were taking blood-thinning agents to prevent the formation of blood clots were taught to check their own coagulation rates at home using a home-monitoring device, then call in the readings to their health care professional. Nearly 100 percent of the participants in the study were satisfied with the process (Virtual Reality, 1998).

• Occupational therapists in Wales, currently are using electronic sensors for automated assessment of elderly patients following illness or accident (Doughty & Costa, 1997). The sensors monitor activities of daily living such as bathing, cooking, dressing, eating, and mobility and use of the stairs in the home. This system allows the therapist to note any deterioration of the patient's condition that may put the individual in an at-risk situation. Furthermore, by having the patient wear a sensor, the system is able to use simple algorithms to calculate the risk of the elderly person falling, allowing the health care staff to intervene before the fall takes place (Doughty & Cameron, 1998). This telemedicine system may allow the elderly person to return home sooner following illness or accident and allows for interventions to be made before the individual is exposed to risk of personal injury or illness.

• In Italy, the TeSAN company offers a call-center specifically tailored to the need of the elderly client. TeSAN offers three basic services for clients: (a) a personal emergency response system that allows homebound clients to call for the police, a physician, an ambulance, or other assistance, at the push of a button; (b) a careline service in which periodic proactive calls are made to subscribers to check on their status and assess their needs; and (c) a telemedicine/telemonitoring service for newly discharged hospital patients. Vital signs are taken by the patient or caregiver at the patient's home and the information is relayed to the physician (Allen, Cristoferi, Campana, & Grimaldi, 1997).

Internet.   Internet telemedical services can be asynchronous or synchronous, depending on the application. Internet applications such as chat rooms allow multiple people to participate in real-time, online discussions simultaneously.

• In Boston, two emergency department doctors opened a medical practice, called Cyberdocs (http://www.cyberdoc.com). The physicians were careful to list a copy of the degrees, certifications, and licenses for all the doctors practicing on this site. Among the services available on this site are 24-hour medical consultation and advice, prescriptions for minor ailments, and medical information services.

• Dr. Thomas Brandeisky, an ear, nose, and throat specialist from New Jersey, has a practice site (http://www.netvent.com/Doctor/consult.html) offering an online consultation on any medical topic for $9.95. Charges are billed to a credit card. This site is simple to use, and unlike other sites such as Cyberdocs, it requires no special software. Patients type in their symptoms and then literally ring a bell for service when finished. This site offers patients the chance to e-mail the office for no charge with any questions about the service.

• MoreOnline.com (http://www.moreonline.com/index_medicine. html) provides an online supermarket for consumers who want to have over-the-counter products mailed directly to their homes. Located within the supermarket is an extensive health section where consumers can purchase a wide range of over-the-counter medications including, but not limited to, analgesics, antacids, anti-diarrhea products, cold and allergy relievers, menstrual remedies, and vitamins. Clients simply load their shopping carts with these products and charge them to a credit card.

• In an attempt to improve customer service, Wal-Mart (http://www. wal-mart.com/stores/pharm_mail.shtml), a national U.S. discount store chain, offers an online service for shipment of any prescription drug within 24 hours of receipt. Customers simply e-mail their prescription (obtained by a physician) to Wal-Mart. Clients must provide the name of the medication, their doctor's name, and their doctor's phone number so that Wal-Mart can verify the prescription.

Interactive Video. Interactive video (ITV) services are fully synchronous. In this application, two or more parties are both physically present in front of the ITV equipment and can see and hear each other. Of course, the quality of the interactions depends on the equipment and transmission speeds being used.

• Recently the National Institute on Alcohol Abuse and Alcoholism (NIAAA) identified older persons as a special population at increased risk for alcoholism (Coogle, Osgood, Parham, Wood, & Churcher, 1995), and found that practitioners, caregivers, and older adults themselves were unaware of the effects of alcohol on older people. The Virginia Geriatric Education Center effectively used videoconferencing to educate service providers, older adults, and family caregivers about geriatric alcoholism. This study demonstrates that practitioners and lay people can be educated with a single outreach program and shows the feasibility of including consumers of aging services among those targeted by geriatric education programs.

• In California, MidPeninsula HomeCare and Hospice is testing personal telemedicine systems (PTS) for use by home care nurses to make video calls to patients. Nurses can listen to heart, lung, and bowel sounds with a telephonic stethoscope and monitor blood pressure and pulse with a sphygmomanometer with digital readout. The color video system allows the nurse to assess gait, medication compliance, and other parameters. Finally, a magnifying attachment allows close-up views of wounds, IV sites, and insulin syringes for dosage accuracy (Caring, 1997).

• In central Kansas inexpensive plain old telephone service (POTS)-based videoconferencing systems are installed in the homes of patients. Nurses are then able to make home health visits to patients through the telemedicine system. Initial evaluation of this program shows that it is an efficacious and satisfactory means for home health services (Whitten, Collins, & Mair, 1998).

• In France, elderly patients participated in teleconsultation with an orthopedic surgeon following surgery or traumatic injury. Patients reported favorable attitudes and a high level of satisfaction toward teleconsulting, while the surgeon expressed a satisfactory level of confidence in decision making using teleconsulting (Couturier et al., 1998). In a separate project, elderly patients in France also participated in remote psychological consultation. Although the study shows some difficulty in assessment due to hearing impairment of the patient, it demonstrates the potential for remote consultation (Montani et al., 1996).

• In Germany, elderly people are connected via a broadband video communication system to a telecare center. The system, known as the TeleCommunity, is designed to allow elderly and mobility-impaired people to live independently while reducing the demand on social service resources (Erkert, 1997). Patients reported positive satisfaction with the system and considered it an "irreplaceable enrichment to their lives." For many of the elderly clients, the system gave them a feeling of security and involvement. They reported it was important for them to know daily contact was available to them if needed.

• In Japan, videophones using full-color motion pictures and sound are used to assess at-home rehabilitation programs for the disabled elderly. Use of the videophone increased the communication abilities of older persons, stimulated the patients' attention, and improved their comprehension and expression. Furthermore, the videophone improved patients' self-esteem and sense of belonging to society (Takano, Nakamura, & Akao, 1995).

The Future.   Some projects do not fit in any of the categories mentioned. Recently, the University of Minnesota established the TeleHome Care program, which uses low-cost videoconferencing, the Internet, and monitoring devices connected to television sets to provide care for patients with heart failure, chronic obstructive pulmonary disease, or wounds (National Telecommunications and Information Administration [NTIA], 1998). This project is representative of the typical telemedical project of the future: services delivered to older persons through a mixture of available technologies.

CONSEQUENCES OF TELEMEDICINE

In attempting to understand the adoption and use of technology in health care, scholars have borrowed liberally from Rogers' (1995) classic treatise on the diffusion of innovations. Rogers' theory stipulates that the diffusion and rate of adoption for any innovation can be understood by studying its evolution through six steps. The final stage in Rogers' innovation-development process concerns the consequences of an innovation, defined by Rogers as "the changes that occur to an individual or to a social system as a result of the adoption or rejection of an innovation" (p. 150). Using technologies such as store-and-forward, the Internet, or interactive video conferencing to deliver health services to older persons will certainly impact those receiving and providing health services. Though it is too soon to have fully documented consequences, we conclude this chapter by briefly examining two categories of potential consequences, namely economic and communicative.

Economic Consequences:
Financial, Utilization, and Liability

One obvious potential consequence concerns whether telemedicine will lessen the cost of medicine because of decreased travel time and associated expenses or will, instead, serve to increase the cost of medicine as more elderly people have access to specialty care. Some in the health field are also concerned that telemedicine will add to the current preponderance of unnecessary tests. In one study (Grigsby, Burton, Kaehny, Schlenker, & Shaughnessy, 1994), medical directors expressed fear that telemedicine might be used simply to confirm impressions, thus leading to unnecessary services and costs. And, as demonstrated in this chapter, technology can enable elderly patients or their families to bypass the traditional health system and directly purchase their own health care or products. The Internet, for example, is already emerging as a means of direct purchasing power for senior citizens.

Telemedicine can also provide economic impacts by reaching older populations who face burdensome financial constraints. For example, rural older Americans have characteristics and needs that differ from their urban counterparts. They are often more isolated, have lower incomes, and have difficulty accessing health services due to transportation needs. Rural residents are more likely to stop care as a result of cost (Blazer, Landerman, Fillenbaum, & Horner, 1995). Rural residents are also less likely to obtain health care at a hospital. Even though the older population is almost universally covered by Medicare and Medicaid in the United States, substantial differences in out-of-pocket expenses, such as transportation, mean that health care is not equally accessible to all.

In addition to geography impacting economic variables, there are also gender-based disadvantages. For example, elderly women in the United States outnumber elderly men three to two. As the death of a husband often leads to acute economic changes for the surviving wife, health analysts need to consider changing needs due to economic constraints. Services available through telemedicine have the potential to impact access to health care for such economically challenged older Americans.

Among the biggest barriers to date for telemedicine are unresolved reimbursement issues. The Health Care Financing Administration currently reimburses for teleradiology services and has just implemented a rather complicated experimental scheme for ITV consults. In this reimbursement model, both a referring provider and specialist must be present during a consult, must be located within a pre-defined rural location, and must share the fee. This is obviously not an arrangement conducive to dissemination and utilization of telemedicine. Some third-party carriers (e.g., Blue Cross/Blue Shield in Kansas and Georgia) are currently reimbursing for telemedicine, yet reimbursement as a whole is still a thorny issue.

Another consequence to be monitored is how telemedicine will ultimately be utilized. What if telemedicine ultimately develops as a tool used by health care facilities to garner market share that would extend beyond the facilities' normal market areas? In Scotland, the Health Care International Hospital was created as a 260-bed telemedicine hospital in which medical consultations could occur electronically. Financed by an international consortium of investors, the hospital was developed to provide tertiary care to small, wealthy nations. This first telemedicine hospital endeavor met with financial failure, although Allen (1995) reported that potential marketing-related miscalculations, rather than any technology inadequacies, led to the demise of the hospital. Is it possible that telemedicine will be employed as a tool to simply increase market share? What if senior citizens are not perceived to be a profitable market segment? Will they be denied access to the same range of services via these technologies?

Liability and legality are additional issues confronting this innovation. If a geriatrician at the University of Michigan is treating a patient in Ohio over a telemedicine system, in which state is that geriatrician practicing medicine? In which state would a potential malpractice suit be handled? Should this geriatrician have a medical license in just one of these states or be licensed in every state in which a patient is located?

The Internet as a source for telemedicine provides its own unique legal and regulatory challenges. Currently, anyone is able to place health-related information on the Internet, and there is no regulating body to evaluate the accuracy, credibility, or quality of the health information posted there. In addition to potential problems with the quality of information on the Internet, both providers and patients will be faced with an enormous quantity of information. Some in the medical field have expressed concern that providers' liability will increase due to their easy access to a wider range of information that can be used to diagnose or treat patients (Coiera, 1997). Perhaps the enhanced access telemedicine offers for health services and information will ultimately serve to heighten expectations regarding acceptable levels of care.

Communication Consequences:
Interpersonal and Organizational

Another potential consequence of telemedicine could be a change in interpersonal relationships between patients and providers. Small scale studies performed to assess patient satisfaction with telemedicine consultations and interpersonal issues in a variety of settings throughout the world (Allen, Hayes, Sadasivan, Williamson, & Wittman, 1995; Chichton et al., 1995; Dongier et al., 1986; Jerome, 1993; Pedersen & Holand, 1995) reveal a generally positive response from patients for telemedicine. Patients agree that there are definite advantages to telemedicine including reduced waiting times, reduced costs to the healthcare system, impressions that examinations are more thorough, and excitement with the use of this new technology. Disadvantages that have been noted include nervousness about the use of the new technology, difficulty in talking to health care providers via the ITV system, a tendency to be less candid when talking to the provider via this medium, and an experience of emotional distance between users and their provider (Allen et al., 1995; Chichton et al., 1995; Pedersen & Holand, 1995; Jerome, 1993; Dongier et al., 1986).

Even though research shows that, overall, patients are satisfied with a telemedicine consult, questions remain concerning a potential society where it is an exception to be physically in the same room with a health provider. Past research has shown that provider–patient communication is a crucial element in health care (see Greene & Adelman, chap. 5, this volume). For example, Street and Wiemann (1987) demonstrated that a patient's judgement of a physician's display of warmth and interpersonal skills plays a major role in patient satisfaction. The use of telemedicine technologies will undoubtedly change the provider-patient interaction, but how? One simply has to look at social presence theory (Short, Williams, & Christie, 1976) as one potential way in which health care will "feel differently" via telemedicine. It is likely that the medium delivering the care will impact the awareness of others during a medical interaction as well as the interpersonal relationships during the interactions.

Though a limited amount of research has delved into how telemedicine impacts communication, several studies have provided evidence that telemedicine is simultaneously an effective means to provide care while still feeling different from traditional delivery modalities. For example, in one home-based telehospice project, the caregivers explained that they were initially concerned that interpersonal relations might be hampered by the technology, which would not allow them to provide the desired service. However, most reported that they could adequately care for their patients with the same level of effectiveness (Whitten, Cook, & Doolittle, 1998). Similar results in a study by Whitten, Collins, et al. (1998) found that nursing could be practiced effectively using telemedicine, despite anticipated interpersonal differences between the contexts.

Important to note is the perception that the technology is secondary in relation to the service being delivered. One subject in a telemedicine study (Mair, Whitten, May, & Doolittle, in press) stated, "I don't think the way health care is delivered is as much on the hardware as the people doing it." Yet, receiving care via telemedicine is a radically different experience than receiving care in person. One telemedicine patient explained her feeling that telemedicine can impact the way a physician–patient relationship is established through the comment, "If I had seen him (the physician) the first time on TV, I don't think we would have as good a relationship as we do" (Mair et al., in press). Another telemedicine patient captured the way telemedicine impacts the interpersonal experience through the following analogy: "well if you watch mass on TV it's certainly very good and impressive, but it's not the same as being in church" (Mair et al., in press).

Given that the nature of doctor–patient interactions may change dramatically when the open airways carry the personal histories, images, and concerns of patients, the ethical concerns inherent in these services must also be acknowledged. Yet no guidelines exist for consent and privacy issues for care delivered via this modality. Telemedicine currently taxes interpersonal relationships between practitioners and patients by asking them to work together based on good faith rather than traditional standards and legal mandates which protect a patient's privacy in traditional health delivery. It would seem probable that those patients who have positive relationships with their providers will be more comfortable with this added trust component built into the receipt of telemedical care.

Telemedicine literature to date focuses primarily on the technology itself (Caramella, Lencioni, Mazzeo, & Bartolozzi, 1994; Cook, Insana, McFadden, Hall, & Cox, 1994; Fisk et al., 1995). However, if the literal definition of telemedicine as "medicine at a distance" is accepted, then it becomes evident that one area of focus should be placed on the service or program. Unfortunately, very little research to date recognizes that organizational issues serve to make or break telemedicine programs. Even though there is increasing evidence that managerial and administrative issues play a vital role in the effectiveness and utilization of such services, few studies have attempted to document the influence and role of structure, leadership, job roles or training factors (Perednia & Allen, 1995). Research has demonstrated that organizational factors are critical determinants of success or failure of a telemedicine program (Whitten & Allen, 1995). For example, this research suggested that telemedicine programs may benefit particularly from the redefinition of roles and responsibilities of certain personnel; increasing the efficiency and decreasing the complexity of the consultation scheduling process; and clarifying and formalizing leadership and decision making.

Another recent study sought to analyze the differences and similarities between telemedical consultations and traditional medical visits (Whitten, Patterson, & Cook, 1999). In this study, physicians provided medical consults to patients via interactive video while nurses were physically present with the patient during the visit. One major difference reported by nurses was the way telemedicine changes their roles and expands their responsibilities through increased preparation time prior to the telemedicine consult and greater responsibility to educate patients afterward. One telemedicine nurse stated, ". . . as a nurse your role gets bigger. [In telemedicine consults] we spend more time with the patient before the consult for planning, and definitely after the consult making sure they understood what was said." Another nurse explained, in telemedicine consults "we are the hands for the doctor. The patients need to trust and believe in us more than in the normal setting." Other study participants expressed the feeling that telemedicine consults are more focused and that physicians tend to be more punctual and better listeners than in standard office consults.

Further, the increased preparation and planning by nurses appears to allow doctors to focus their attention more on the patient. One telemedicine nurse explained, "They (physicians) tend to take more time . . . they have to be willing to listen to the patient because if they're saying something and the patient responds, they have to stop and actually listen." Another provider stated, "Because so many people must come together for an appointment, everyone (physicians, nurses and patients) appear to be more attentive." Such research indicates that innovations in telemedicine technology need to be matched by innovations in organizational communication and structure.

CONCLUSIONS

Research has pointed out that telemedicine interactions are quite different in many ways from on-site interactions. This should not imply that they are necessarily inferior. As use of telemedicine spreads, some of the anxieties providers and patients may have regarding this mode of delivery of health care are likely to decrease. Telemedicine is an innovation with the potential to enhance communication in health care circles in innumerable ways. It is crucial that, as telemedicine expands, the importance of interpersonal and organizational issues is recognized and understood. In this way, successful implementation of telemedicine programs will be facilitated. Yet, it is important to acknowledge that some consequences of telemedicine may occur at an even higher level.

Societal consequences may also result from this innovation. If telemedicine serves to enhance access and care for elderly citizens, it may also impact their communities. There may exist communities that retain seniors who are able to contribute socially and perhaps financially due to enhanced health status. Perhaps they will be able to maintain an independent lifestyle at home for longer amounts of time due to improved access to services.

Widespread adoption of telemedicine could expand the expectations of society. Could telemedicine democratize health care by bringing specialized care to people who have difficulty getting to medical care and services? What about the very health of the older population? Is it possible that they could become healthier as a result of telemedicine services? The implementation and utilization of various telemedicine technologies pose unanswered questions, including their impact on the health care system and their feasibility. What is known is that a senior citizen can (a) log onto the Internet and purchase a prescription medication, (b) receive nursing services at home using low-end videoconferencing technologies, and (c) have, for example, chronic arthritis managed by a rheumatologist hundreds of miles away via telemedicine.

It is as difficult to provide overall advice about telemedicine as it is to provide general tips about healthcare. Telemedicine, albeit a unique way of providing care, still exists within the constraints of overarching health delivery systems. Challenges inherent in all aspects of health, ranging from managed care to provider–patient relationships to intergenerational challenges, are still present for telemedicine. However, telemedicine does add some unique dimensions to the health care encounter. For example, it is important that telemedicine providers select equipment that is user friendly for an older adult population. Health providers must also consider the context when developing a telemedicine program. Required equipment and resources will vary greatly for telemedicine services to a patient's home, a nursing home, a community mental health facility, or a rural or urban hospital. In addition the type of care being delivered will also impact decisions about equipment and bandwidth, as well as the type of health professional and technical support needed. A telehome health visit for a patient with diabetes will require a different telemedicine solution than virtual telesurgery. What is common to all of these issues is that health providers and older adults should have a basic understanding that technology can be used, when appropriate, to bring health care to people at a wide range of locations. Whereas both health providers and patients need to be sensitive to the potential interpersonal dynamics of these mediated health encounters, all parties must remember that the goal for telemedicine remains the same as that of traditional medicine: enhancing the quality of life for older adults through access to health services and education.

Rather then questioning if technology will play a major role in delivering health services, focus must be shifted to how to maximize the utilization of telemedicine technologies to bring health services to older persons. Perhaps the greatest challenge will not be related to the technology, but will instead concern age-old issues for senior citizens. For example, there are extremely complex health systems for senior citizens in many countries, and telemedicine must operate within these health systems. It remains to be seen whether these technologies will reshape these health delivery systems or whether they will instead be defined and diffused by these systems.

REFERENCES

Allen, A. (1995). Telemedicine dateline. *Telemedicine Today, 3*(1), 5.

Allen, A. (1998). The state of telemedicine today [Special issue]. *Telemedicine Today, 1998 Buyer's Guide and Directory.*

Allen, A., Cox, R., & Thomas, C. (1992). Telemedicine in Kansas. *Journal of the Kansas Medical Society, 93,* 323–325.

Allen, A., Cristoferi, A., Campana, S., & Grimaldi, A. (1997). TeSAN personal emergency response system and teleservices. *Telemedicine Today, 5*(6), 25, 33.

Allen, A., Hayes, J., Sadasivan, R., Williamson, S. K., & Wittman, C. (1995). A pilot study of the physician acceptance of tele-oncology. *Journal of Telemedicine and Telecare 1*(1), 34–37.

Blazer, D. G., Landerman, L. L., Fillenbaum, G., & Horner, R. (1995, October). Health services access and use among older adults in North Carolina: Urban vs. rural residents. *American Journal of Public Health, 85*(10), 1384–1390.

Caramella, D., Lencioni, R., Mazzeo, S., & Bartolozzi, C. (1994). Transmission of radiological images using broadband communications. *European Radiology, 4,* 377–381.

Caring. (1997, July). A global perspective: Technology in home care. *Caring Magazine,* 14.

Chichton, C., Macdonald, S., Potts, S., Syme, A., Toms, J., McKinlay, J., Leslie, D., & Jones, D. H. (1995). Teledermatology in Scotland [Letter]. *Journal of Telemedicine and Telecare 1*(3), 185.

Coiera, E. (1997). *Guide to medical informatics, the Internet and telemedicine.* London: Chapman & Hall Medical.

Conrath, D. W., Puckingham, P., Dunn, E. V., & Swanson, J. N. (1975). An experimental evaluation of alternative communication systems as used for medical diagnosis. *Behavioral Science, 20,* 296–305.

Coogle, C. L., Osgood, N. J., Parham, I. A., Wood, H. E., & Churcher, C. S. (1995). The effectiveness of videoconferencing in geriatric alcoholism education. *Gerontology & Geriatrics Education, 16*(2), 73–83.

Cook, L. T., Insana, M. F., McFadden, M. A., Hall, T. J., & Cox, G. G. (1994, May). Comparison of the low-contrast detectability of a screen-film system and third generation computed radiography. *Medical Physics 21*(5), 691–695.

Couturier, P., Tyrrell, J., Tonetti, J., Rhul, C., Woodward, V., & Franco, A. (1998). Feasibility of orthopaedic teleconsulting in a geriatric rehabilitation service. *Journal of Telemedicine and Telecare, 4*(1), 85–87.

Dongier, M., Tempier, R., Lalinec-Michaud, M., & Meunier, D. (1986). Telepsychiatry: Psychiatry consultation through two-way television: A controlled study. *Canadian Journal of Psychiatry, 31*, 32–34.

Doughty, K., & Cameron, K. (1998). Continuous assessment of the risk of falling using telecare. *Journal of Telemedicine and Telecare, 4*(1), 88–90.

Doughty, K., & Costa, J. (1997). Continuous automated telecare assessment of the elderly. *Journal of Telemedicine and Telecare, 3*(1), 23–25.

Dunn, E., Conrath, D., Acton, H., Higgins, C., Math, M., & Bain, H. (1980). Telemedicine links patients in Sioux Lookout with doctors in Toronto. *Canadian Medical Association Journal, 22*, 484–487.

Erkert, T. (1997). High-quality links for home-based support for the elderly. *Journal of Telemedicine and Telecare, 3*(1), 26–27.

Fisk, N. M., Bower, S., Sepulved, W., Garner, P., Cameron, K., Matthews, M., Ridley, D., Drysdale, K., & Wooton, R. (1995). Fetal telemedicine: Interactive transfer of real-time ultrasound and video via ISDN for remote consultation. *Journal of Telemedicine and Telecare, 1*(1), 38–44.

Fuchs, M. (1974). Provider attitudes toward STARPAHC, a telemedicine project on the Papago reservation. *Medical Care, 17*, 59–68.

Grigsby, B., & Allen, A. (1997). Fourth annual telemedicine program review. *Telemedicine Today, 5*(4), 30–38.

Grigsby, J., Barton, P. L., Kaehny, M. M., Schlenker, R. E., & Shaughnessy, P. W. (1994). *Telemedicine policy: Quality assurance, utilization review, and coverage. Analysis of expansion of access to care through the use of telemedicine and mobile health services.* (HCFA and DHHS Report 3, Contract No. 500-92-0046). Denver, CO.

Grigsby, J., & Kaehny, M. (1993). *Analysis of expansion of access to care through use of telemedicine and mobile health services: Report 1. Literature review and analytic framework.* Denver, CO: Center for Health Policy Research.

Health Care Financing Administration. (1999). *Highlights of the national expenditure projections, 1997-2007* [Online]. Available: http://www.hcfa.gov/stats/nhe-proj/hilites.mtm

Jerome, L. (1993, January). Assessment by telemedicine [Letter]. *Hospital and Community Psychiatry 44*(1), 81.

Jones, B. N., & Colenda, C. C. (1997, June). Telemedicine and geriatric psychiatry. *Psychiatric Services, 48*(6), 783–785.

Journal of the American Medical Association. (1973). Cable TV links hospital, apartments. *Journal of the American Medical Association, 226*(12), 1410.

Journal of the American Medical Association. (1998). Telemedicine [Special Issue: October 21]. *Journal of the American Medical Association, 280*(15).

Jutra, A. (1959). Teleroentgen diagnosis by means of videotape recording. *American Journal of Roentgenology, 82*, 1099–1102.

Mair, F. S., Whitten, P., May, C., & Doolittle, G. (in press). Patient perceptions of a telemedicine specialty clinic: Results from a qualitative study. *Journal of Telemedicine and Telecare.*

Michaeis, E. (1989). Telemedicine: The best is yet to come some experts say. *Canadian Medical Association Journal, 141*, 612–614.

Montani, C., Billaud, N., Couturier, P., Fluchaire, I., Lemaire, R., Malterre, C., Lauvernay, N., Piquard, J. F., Frossard, M., & Franco, A. (1996). Telepsychometry: A remote psychometry consultation in clinical geronotology: Preliminary study. *Telemedicine Journal, 2*(2), 145–150.

Murphy, R. L. H., & Bird, K. T. (1974). Telediagnosis: A new community health resource. *American Journal of Public Health, 64*, 113–119.

National Telecommunications and Information Administration. (1998). *TIIAP Award No. 27-60-98031* [Online]. Available: http://ntiaotiant1.ntia.doc.gov/cfdocs/tiiap/layout.cfm?tiiap_no=980058

Newton, H. (1998). *Newton's telecom dictionary*. New York: Miller Freeman.

Patel, U. H., & Babbs, C. F. (1992). A computer-based, automated, telephonic system to monitor patient progress in the home setting. *Journal of Medical Systems, 26*(3/4), 101–112.

Pedersen, S., & Holand, U. (1995). Tele-endoscopic otorhinolaryngological examination: Preliminary study of patient satisfaction. *Telemedicine Journal, 1*(1): 47–52.

Perednia, D. A., & Allen, A. A. (1995). Telemedicine technology and clinical applications. *Journal of the American Medical Association, 273*(6), 483–488.

Rogers, E. M. (1995). *Diffusion of innovations* (4th ed.). New York: The Free Press.

Short, J., Williams, E., & Christie, B. (1976). *The social psychology of telecommunications*. London: Wiley.

Steinfield, C., Whitten, P., & Kingsley, C. (1999). *Electronic commerce and healthcare: An overview of applications, barriers, and research issues*. Manuscript submitted for publication.

Street, R. L., & Wiemann, J. M. (1987). Patient satisfaction with physician's interpersonal involvement, expressiveness, and dominance. In M. L. McLaughlin (Ed.), *Communication yearbook 10* (pp. 591–612). Beverly Hills, CA: Sage.

Takano, T., Nakamura, K., & Akao, C. (1995). Assessment of the value of videophones in home health care. *Telecommunications Policy, 19*, 241–248.

Virtual Reality. (1998). Coagulation rates checked at home. *Telemedicine and Virtual Reality, 3*(5), 52.

Whitten, P., & Allen, A. (1995). Organizational implications of telemedicine: A study of the Kansas telemedicine program. *Telemedicine Journal, 1*(3), 203–213.

Whitten, P., Collins, B., & Mair, F. (1998). Nurse and patient reactions to a developmental telehome health system. *Journal of Telemedicine and Telecare, 4*(2), 1.1–1.9.

Whitten, P., Cook, D., & Doolittle, G. (1998). An analysis of provider perceptions for telehospice. *The American Journal of Hospice & Palliative Care, 15*(5), 267–275.

Whitten, P., Patterson, J., & Cook, D. (1999). *Understanding telemedicine: Similarities and differences between traditional and telemedical consults in providing patient care*. Manuscript submitted for publication.

Wittson, C. L., Affleck, D. C., & Johnson, V. (1961). Two-way television group therapy. *Mental Hospital, 12*, 2–23.

2

The Older Patient–Health Care Provider Relationship in a Managed Care Environment

Jon F. Nussbaum
Pennsylvania State University

Loretta Pecchioni
Louisiana State University

Tara Crowell
Miami University of Ohio

The evolution and emergence of managed health care in the United States have produced a flood of information concerning the quality of the health care delivery system. A moderate amount of this information is grounded in valid, scientific study. Other information, however, is speculative and often serves the interests of those who profit from the conclusions. This change in the health care system has primarily occurred because of the economic burden placed on those who pay for health care in this country (e.g., insurance companies, businesses, etc.). This chapter, however, is more concerned with: (a) how the emerging managed care environment changes the communicative roles of health care providers, (b) the definition of quality care as it relates to the interaction between providers and patients, and (c) most importantly, the older patient–health care provider relationship. This chapter organizes existing literature and attempts to expand the thinking of researchers, practitioners, and older patients who are concerned with how managed care influences the dynamics of the health care provider–older patient relationship so that the best quality of care may be attained.

Four propositions underline the centrality of the communication process as it relates to the influence of the managed care environment on the health care provider–elderly patient relationship:

1. There are positive opportunities for improved health care relationships within a managed care environment.
2. These improved relationships may be dependent on a reframing of what a health care provider is and does.
3. The primary care physician has been placed at the forefront of managed care. As a result, the primary care physician carries most of the relational burden for the health care side of the provider–patient relationship. This situation may provide positive relationship outcomes for both physician and older patient.
4. Research into relationship structure and development, conducted within the discipline of Communication, can illuminate the dynamics of the provider–older patient relationship.

In order to make the case that these propositions have a chance of being true, this chapter is organized into several sections. First, a brief description of the managed care environment and the possible effects that this environment may have on the older patient–health care provider relationship is presented. Second, results from empirical investigations that specifically relate to the health care provider–older patient relationship are briefly reviewed and discussed in the context of the traditional model of an appropriate, professional physician–patient relationship. Third, a discussion of several theoretical assumptions that move the definition of interpersonal and professional relationships beyond a static linear process is presented. Fourth, two specific changes in health care delivery associated with managed care—the importance of primary care providers and interdisciplinary teams to manage health care—will be considered with possible relational consequences. Finally, the communicative responsibilities for health providers, older adults, and health communication scholars who interact within or study the managed care environment are presented.

THE MANAGED CARE ENVIRONMENT

Our notion of an ideal health care environment or an ideal health care encounter is based on a combination of factors that include our own experiences with the health care system, the experience of others who tell us about their experiences with the system, impressions of health care as portrayed in the media, and a feeling of the way things should be. There was never a time in the United States that everyone had complete, open, equal, and affordable access to quality medical care. Economic status, race, gender, place of residence, age, reason(s) for needing health care, veteran status, and many other reasons generate differences in the quality of health care delivered. Each individual who enters into the health care system may have a different set of experiences and, as a result, rather different attitudes toward the system. Beyond this, the health care system has been changing for the past 30 years from a predominantly "fee-for-service" system, where a provider bills for each patient encounter or service rendered, to a managed health care system.

This change in the health care system in the United States has been motivated by spiraling medical costs and efforts to control those costs (Health Care Finance Administration, 1999). Managed care is a broad term describing health insurance products in which health care providers agree to negotiated payment levels for defined patient populations. Health care providers also agree to more aggressive utilization and quality assurance review than in traditional fee-for-service arrangements. Physician services are reimbursed in a variety of ways, ranging from discounted fee-for-service under Preferred Provider Organization (PPO) managed care insurance products to capitation under Health Maintenance Organization (HMO) products. As providers assume more financial risks, more severe restrictions are placed on patient choice to obtain services outside of the network. The "popularity" of managed care is evident in the number of individuals enrolled in these programs. In 1976, about 6 million people were enrolled in a managed care program and in 1996 that number had grown more than 10 times to 67.5 million (American Association of Health Plans, 1999). Managed care in all of its forms is now the most dominant form of health care service in the United States.

Two important structural changes have resulted from managed care: the emergence of primary care physicians and interdisciplinary teams. Primary care can be defined as medical practice based on direct contact with the patient without referral from another physician. The primary care physician serves as a "gatekeeper" for other medical services. In most managed care systems, the primary care physician is designated as responsible for providing services including evaluation and treatment of patients, as well as referral to specialty care. Patients are not allowed to "self-refer" to specialists if they want visits and treatment from the specialist covered by their insurance carrier. The role of primary care physicians and their relationships to their patients is discussed more fully later in this chapter.

The other interesting structural change in the delivery of health care that is associated with managed care, which has a particular impact on frail older patients, is the emergence of interdisciplinary health care teams (Clark, 1997). Professionals from various subdisciplines, often including physicians, nurses, physical and occupational therapists, nutrition experts, and social workers, meet within nursing homes, extended care units, assisted living facilities, hospice care units, and rehabilitation facilities to discuss the care of their older patients. Effective communication among all the professionals becomes essential within interdisciplinary meetings. These interdisciplinary teams receive more attention later in this chapter.

From the perspective of an older patient, managed care means that the older adult enters into a medical encounter that is structured quite differently from what that individual has experienced previously. The older patient may not be able to choose the specific physician or health care provider requested, may not spend as much time as desired with the physician, may not be completely aware of the payment structure for the visit or procedure, and may run into negative attitudes toward managed care held by health care providers (Farmer, 1994; Serafini, 1990; Ward, 1990). In addition, the older patient may discover more emphasis placed on routine preventative behaviors, the inclusion of numerous health care providers as active participants, a reduction in paperwork, a control of out-of-pocket expenses (perhaps only a $5 deductible for a prescription), and more egalitarian characteristics of physicians who select managed care for their practice (Serafini, 1990). Health care providers, on the other hand, are faced with possible declining revenues as a result of managed care, the possibility of spending less time with each patient, and the possibility of a redefinition of their job or profession. Each of these factors may cause relational barriers between the older patient and the health care provider (Farmer, 1994; Serafini, 1990; Ward, 1990).

The evolution of managed health care continues to have a significant impact not only on the financial reality of the business of medicine but also on the process of health care delivery. Specifically, the way health care providers interact with patients to render service is directly affected by the emergence of managed care (Greene & Adelman, 1996). It is our belief that older adults bring to the medical encounter unique characteristics that place both providers and patients into a complex and perhaps precarious interactive position. The next section briefly reviews the findings of previous research into the health care provider–older adult relationship as well as the unique characteristics that older adults bring to a medical encounter.

THE OLDER PATIENT–HEALTH CARE PROVIDER RELATIONSHIP

Excellent reviews of the rather extensive literature that reports on the results of studies looking into older patient–physician communication are quite accessible (see Beisecker & Beisecker, 1996; Beisecker & Thompson, 1995; Greene & Adelman, chap. 5, this volume). For the most part, the research points to the rather obvious conclusion that a physician's communicative competencies can affect a patient's satisfaction, compliance, and perception of health status. In addition, research has focused on the communicative skill and characteristics of the older patient in the overall outcome of the medical encounter (Haug & Ory, 1987). Older adults who are perceived to be more competent in their communicative skills not only ask more questions during the medical interaction but are more pleased with the outcome of the encounter. Further, Greene and Adelman (1996; chap. 5, this volume) have consistently stressed the importance of psychosocial talk in medical encounters. Finally, the research discusses the implications of a companion within the medical encounter and how this third party influences communication between health care providers and older patients (Coupland & Coupland, chap. 6, this volume).

Older patients have unique characteristics that set them apart from their younger counterparts. Nussbaum, Hummert, Williams, and Harwood (1995) outlined the physical, cognitive, and language changes related to aging that can influence an older person's ability to communicate effectively, which apply to medical encounters as well. In addition, factors such as the context of the medical encounter, the intergenerational nature of the medical encounter, and the presence of ageism within the encounter can affect competent physician–patient interaction (Nussbaum, 1998).

Most of the research on the provider–patient relationship has been conducted in more traditional medical settings. The managed care environment contextualizes all of the elements just mentioned in somewhat different ways that affect competent health care provider–older patient communication. The question becomes: How does the specific managed care system, which the older individual must enter into, affect the ability of that older adult and health care professionals operating within that system to communicate effectively to produce a quality relationship with a positive medical outcome?

THEORETICAL ASSUMPTIONS OF RELATIONSHIPS

The physician–patient relationship has always been assumed, at least within the medical literature, to be a very "special" relationship. Coe (1987) stated that the patient–physician relationship is "a privileged relationship, shrouded in secrecy" (p. 180). Farmer (1994) described this relationship as "almost sacred, reflecting the highest of professional ethics by physicians" (p. 27). Haug and Ory (1987) discussed the need on the part of older patients to be treated with respect and dignity. Adelman, Greene, and Charon (1991) pointed out that the current cohort of older patients prefers that the physician be more authoritarian within the medical encounter. Thus, the ideal older patient–physician relationship would be complementary with the physician being the more dominant party. Marshall (1981), however, questioned the whole notion of a patient–physician relationship given that most medical encounters last for 15 min or less. How can one possibly have any meaningful relationship in 15-min spurts?

The term *relationship* referring to the encounter between the older patient and the health care provider is often accepted without any explanation or definition. What is often missing in most discussions of the physician–patient relationship is any reference to the rich literature on relationships found within the Communication discipline (Beisecker, 1996). Scholars from many disciplines have stressed the relational dimension of human interaction, including the anthropologist Gregory Bateson (Bateson, 1958; Ruesch & Bateson, 1951), family therapist and medical doctor Carlos Sluzki (Sluzki, 1998), and psychiatrist Janet Beavin Bavelas (Bavelas, Black, Chovil, & Mullett, 1990; Watzlawick, Beavin, & Jackson, 1967). William Wilmot (1995), a communication scholar, synthesized much of this work and presented an excellent relational model of human interaction. First, relationships and communication are inextricably tied. We form and define our relationships through communicative behavior. Thus, communication is more than just providing a patient or a physician with information. The act of communicating creates and defines the relationship. Second, participants, in this case the older patient and the health care provider, create schemas about their relationships. The older patient–health care provider relationship exists in the mind of both the patient and the provider. Often, the meanings of specific words are understood or interpreted based on these relational schemas. The cognitive representation of the relationship must be communicated within the interaction if the relationship is to have a common understanding. Third, relationships must be examined within the cultural context and overall patterns of other relationships. In other words, the managed care context plays a central role in the very nature of the older adult–health care provider relationship. The context itself may be a powerful relational inhibitor or promoter. In addition, other relationships—medical, personal, and professional—affect the older patient–health care provider relationship. The most obvious examples in this context are companions who are brought to the medical encounter by the patient or other health professionals who interact with the patient during the encounter (Coupland & Coupland, chap. 6, this volume; Greene & Adelman, chap. 5, this volume).

A fourth characteristic of Wilmot's (1995) relational model is the notion that the "self" is best understood within the web of relationships. How individuals feel about themselves as older patients, as physicians, or as nurses emerges within the relationship context. Thus, the self-definition of "older patient" is dependent on behavior and thoughts within the relationships that are managed with health care providers. The same is true for physicians and nurses. What gives meaning to a label such as "physician" or "nurse" is the health care relationship.

Finally, relationships are in a continuous state of emergence. Relationships are not static, linear processes. Each communicative act and the interpretations of those acts create new definitions for the relationship. Relationships are always becoming more or less intimate, or the power dimension within the relationship is constantly being negotiated. The notion that relationships are in a continual state of emergence has received too little attention in the literature addressing patient–health care provider relationships. The constant flux of relationships calls into question any prescriptions for communicative routines by a physician or for a singular definition of the patient–physician relationship as always special and sacred.

As noted within the characteristics of Wilmot's (1995) relational model, the managed care environment causes changes in the relationships that emerge within this particular health care system. The role of the physician or nurse or older patient is different within managed care from that in the traditional fee-for-service system. Although this may seem rather obvious, most patients and health care providers have not adapted to their new relational roles. With the goal of better managing the health care of patients, managed care has enhanced the role of the primary care physician and has brought about the inclusion of a variety of health care providers as active participants in the decision-making process. The possible effects these systemic changes have on the older patient–health care provider relationship are discussed further in the next section.

THE PRIMARY CARE PHYSICIAN
AND INTERDISCIPLINARY TEAMS

As mentioned previously, the primary care physician serves as the gate-keeper for the health care system by evaluating and treating patients and referring them to specialty care when the physician deems it appropriate and necessary. It should be noted that at least 45 states include medical professionals other than physicians as primary care specialists. For instance, physician assistants and nurse practitioners are now practicing as primary care specialists by conducting routine exams and writing pre-scriptions (American Academy of Physician Assistants, 1999; Nurse Practitioner Central, 1999). The primary care physician can be trained in various specialties, including pediatrics, obstetrics, general internal med-icine, family medicine, and general practice. Geriatric medicine, which is most appropriate for the care of older patients, is considered a subspecial-ty in either family medicine or internal medicine. Typically, medical stu-dents get their formal training in geriatric medicine during a very short rotation in medical school or, after residency, in family medicine or inter-nal medicine. Those physicians interested in developing a greater under-standing of older patients and their needs can attend one of the three medical schools in the United States that have departments of geriatric medicine or serve in one of several geriatric fellowships that last up to 2 years. Training for nonphysician primary care specialists may or may not include geriatric medicine, depending on the school and the profession.

An older adult who chooses a Medicare HMO because of cost-saving benefits, such as low-cost prescriptions, eye care, and free transportation, often must first visit a primary care physician before seeing a neurosur-geon, orthopedic surgeon, cardiologist, or any other specialist. The pri-mary care physician must be on the roster of possible primary care physi-cians aligned with the Medicare HMO. If the older patient does not choose a primary care physician from the roster of possible physicians, the older patient will be assigned a primary care physician. All specialists to whom the older patient may be sent must be part of the HMO network and the primary care physician must deem the visit to the specialist appropriate. If the primary care physician sends the older adult to a specialist in the network, the visit and any medical procedures may be paid for by the HMO, but only if the HMO deems the visit or the procedures to be appropriate.

In essence, the primary care physician becomes a case manager for the older patient. The primary care physician, in consultation with the patient, the HMO or payer, the family, and other health professionals, develops a plan to achieve the optimum patient outcome. In many ways, the primary care physician serves as a key player in the continued good health of older adults. The relationship between the primary care physician and the older patient within this type of managed care system becomes quite significant. It becomes essential that both the primary care physician and the older patient are able to communicate effectively, build trust, and understand the dynamic of their unique relationship.

Beyond the structural "elevation" of primary care within the managed care environment, those working within managed care have emphasized interdisciplinary health care teams and collaborative health practices (U.S. Bureau of Health Professions, 1995). Because of the multifaceted health problems experienced by older adults and the redirection from acute and curable illnesses to maintenance of functional ability and quality of life, "interdisciplinary health care teams have gained more credibility as the 'fundamental unit of geriatric care' for frail elderly with multifaceted health problems (e.g., Tsukuda, 1990; Zeiss & Steffen, 1996)" (Clark, 1997, p. 441). At present, interdisciplinary care teams are managing the health of older patients in extended care units, nursing homes, home health services, hospice centers, and rehabilitation facilities (Clark). Approximately once a month, the team of the primary care physician, nurses, social workers, physical, occupational and recreational therapists, mental health specialists, and, at times the patient or a family member, gather to review each patient's progress. The result of the care-planning meeting is communicated to those who directly care for the patient and to the family. Clark pointed out that new interdisciplinary geriatric educational models must bridge the communication gap not only among the different health professions but also between those health professions and their older patients.

The difficulty with interdisciplinary teams operating as they are intended is the lack of interprofessional respect and a collaborative work ethic (Clark, 1997). In addition, the traditional conceptual model of medical care is suited to the understanding and management of acute and curable illness, which may not be useful for an older population of patients who are more likely to exhibit chronic illnesses (Mold, Blake, & Becker, 1991). The traditional problem-oriented approach of medical care is not as useful when: (a) the patient problem is normal physiology, (b) the process of reaching a diagnosis may cause more harm than benefit to the patient, (c) there is disagreement between the physician and patient whether there is a problem to be solved, (d) the solution to the problem is more in the control of the patient, (e) an ideal health state will never be reached again, or (f) the solution creates additional problems (Mold et al., 1991).

Mold et al. (1991) proposed a goal-oriented approach to health care with a mission to improve the quality and/or increase the quantity of life for individuals. The basic assumptions of goal-oriented health care include the following:

1. Health must ultimately be defined by each individual and therefore will be different for different individuals and at different points in time. (An individual's definition of health might therefore differ from that of the physician.)
2. An individual's health goals can best be determined through the combined efforts of that individual and his or her health care provider(s) using the special information each brings to the relationship.
3. The construction of health-related goals requires an assessment of individual strengths and resources, interests and needs, and personal values in addition to the traditional (and still very important) determination of problems.
4. Final decisions regarding prioritizing an individual's health-related goals and the amount of effort to be expended achieving them are and ultimately should be made by each individual, even if the physician is in disagreement with these decisions. Clarification of goals allows all involved parties to decide whether the relationship is likely to be beneficial and whether they want to participate in it.
5. Success for both individual and the health care provider(s) is best measured by the degree to which the individual's health-related goals are achieved. It therefore depends on the construction of goals and strategies that are both accepted and realistic (p. 47).

The physician's role in this goal-oriented process of medical care changes from that of problem solver, instructor, and enforcer to that of an equal collaborator and relational partner with the older patient and with other professionals within the interdisciplinary team. Mold et al. reasoned that this approach would result in a much stronger and closer physician–older patient relationship based on the negotiation process. For this approach to be successful, a more dynamic relationship is required: one that is based on mutual respect and sharing of personal and somewhat more intimate information. Everything from the diagnosis to the setting of achievable health-related goals would be negotiated.

This goal-oriented approach could also be helpful in the interdisciplinary team process. The traditional problem-oriented medical model currently dominates the interdisciplinary care planning process. The physician who participates in the team meetings is the most highly trained and influential member. Health-related problems for older adults, however, are often beyond the expertise of the physician. An interdisciplinary team that appreciates each profession and allows for different voices in the care of geriatric patients can not only better inform each professional but also may lead to a better care decision.

The senior author of this chapter witnessed an excellent example of how interdisciplinary teams currently operate during a recent care-planning meeting within an extended care unit of a hospital. An older man had fallen off a roof several months prior to this meeting and was recuperating from many broken bones. The nurse running the meeting called his name and each of the 12 medical professionals sitting around the room discussed how they were solving whatever problem they had defined needed a solution. The mental health person talked about the patient's current state of mind, the nutritionist talked about diet, and so on. The recreational therapist, clearly having the least status in this group, mentioned that the patient's son was taking him hunting on a weekend leave from the unit. The patient was still confined to a wheelchair and the recreational therapist was concerned about how he would hunt in a wheelchair. This produced several hunting stories from the group but eventually led to the remaining health professionals talking about what they had accomplished with their care. The older patient had communicated a goal to the recreational therapist that involved hunting. Within a goal-oriented model, the team would have leapt to hear this voice from the patient and organized their care and therapy to help the man prepare for the hunt. However, the problems being solved by the team had no voice from the patient, and neither physical nor mental preparations for the hunt were being made. In this example, the recreational therapist had the closest relationship with the patient and attempted to inform the team as to the personal health goals of the patient. Those personal goals could have been negotiated and treatment directed toward physical therapy, nutrition, and consultations with the family concerning this hunting adventure. Instead, the older patient was treated in a static, generalized manner to improve numerous and often separate indices of normal health.

RELATIONAL RESPONSIBILITIES OF HEALTH CARE PROVIDERS, OLDER PATIENTS, AND HEALTH COMMUNICATION SCHOLARS WITHIN MANAGED CARE

There is no denying that the health care delivery system is in a process of constant change. Everything from the definition of good health to exactly who should pay for health care is in a state of flux. The managed care revolution in the United States has attempted to address financial as well as social issues related to health care delivery. Many different versions of managing health care have emerged with various levels of success. However, the one consistent feature of all the different managed care systems is the move away from traditional notions of responsibility for both health care providers and patients. Simply put, physicians are losing power over much of what they controlled and patients are placed in a position that requires them to be proactive consumers to ensure they receive quality health care.

The somewhat romantic notion of the "sacred" physician–patient relationship has taken on new meanings for all interactive participants within a managed care environment. The dominant, all-knowing, quasiscientific professional who wants to rely only on test evidence is being replaced by a communicative, empathetic negotiator who must come to grips with the health priorities of the patient. At the same time, the patient can no longer just sit by submissively as if the "cost to cure" is not an issue. Older adults, who often present with more complicated, multiple, chronic illnesses that have no "cure" and yet who have been socialized to be submissive in health care encounters, may have a difficult time adapting to this changing environment.

The first responsibility for relational competence within managed care falls on both the health care provider and the older patient, and that is recognizing the importance of their relationship. Both parties need to not only believe that this relationship is "special," "sacred," and "unique," but to understand that this relationship deserves hard work. Just as any competent personal or professional relationship cannot be taken for granted, the quality of the health care provider–older patient relationship is dependent on the communicative effort of both participants. Neither participant can assume that he or she knows what is best or can read the other's mind. This need for greater communicative effort is especially true when the primary care physician must make important decisions as to whether to refer to a specialist or to include other family members in the decision-making process.

The primary care physician no longer has to make these important decisions alone. It is the responsibility of this highly trained professional with structural expert power to include others in a negotiation process to achieve quality care decisions. When an older adult assigns responsibility for decisions to the physician, the physician must work to involve the older patient in the decision as well. The primary care physician has the opportunity in such cases to reframe the relationship from a complementary one to an interdependent one. As the goal-oriented medical care model (Mold, 1995; Mold et al., 1991; Mold & McCarthy, 1995) suggests, physicians need to learn the skills necessary to actively listen to their patients and negotiate with them regarding their health-related goals. Physicians need to take the time with their patients to learn about each patient's strengths, resources, and goals. After health goals are established, the physicians need to regularly revisit previously identified goals to recognize changes in priorities or needs. Physicians need to become patient educators and advocates, providing not only information, but also encouragement and empowerment. Such a collaborative process requires on-going involvement from all parties.

In addition, if an interdisciplinary team is involved in the delivery of goal-oriented quality health care, all professionals must show respect and value the expertise of not only the other professionals but also the patient and the patient's family. Interdisciplinary teams can benefit from the unique characteristics of teams only if they bring to bear all of their members' expertise in maximizing the chances of achieving patient goals. Team meetings should focus on clarification of goals and objectives and the coordination of strategies. The synergy of teams can be realized for problem solving and goal achievement when compartmentalization of services is avoided.

Responsibility for relational competence within managed care cannot fall on only one member of the relationship, that is, the physician. Older adults must also become active participants within the patient–health care provider relationship. Literature reviews (Beisecker & Beisecker, 1996; Beisecker & Thompson, 1995; Greene & Adelman, chap. 5, this volume) provide ample evidence that older adults often do not ask enough questions or disclose pertinent information to their physicians, even though communicatively active older patients are more informed and satisfied with their care. As Greene, Adelman, Friedmann, and Charon (1994) indicated, older patients continue to prefer a physician style—one in which the physician controls the structure of the visit— that no longer exists. Greene and Adelman (chap. 5, this volume) offer useful suggestions for older patients so that they may become more involved in their health care. Older patients must be willing to actively engage the health care professionals with whom they interact.

A frequent complaint about managed care is not seeing the same primary care specialist at each visit. This lack of continuity becomes a particular detriment for older patients who have complicated medical regimens that require continuity of care for optimal treatment (Greene & Adelman, chap. 5, this volume). Older patients should request that they see the same practitioner at every visit. If older patients' requests to see the same practitioner are not met, they need to make an effort to get to know the entire staff and develop relationships with each one. Not only will this strategy reduce the possibilities of meeting a stranger at each medical encounter, but the older patient will be able to identify those individuals who provide them with the most information and can seek those individuals out, when needed. For example, if the primary care physician does not have the time to explain all the procedures or medications, the older patient will know which nurse or pharmacist will take the time to explain what each procedure or pill will accomplish. All of these relationships must be open to such discussion and negotiation.

It is also the responsibility of older patients to become more knowledgeable about their own health, to consider their personal health goals, and to learn about realistic goal setting. This knowledge must be competently communicated to all health care providers. In addition, older patients need to become more knowledgeable about the managed care system that delivers their health care and which providers are responsible for specific decisions. Good sources of information are readily available. Two useful booklets, *Checkpoints for Managed Care: How to Choose a Health Plan* and *9 Ways to Get the Most From Your Managed Health Care Plan*, are available from AARP at no cost by writing AARP Fulfillment, 601 E Street, NW, Washington, DC, 20049. Additional information about AARP can be found at their web site: www.aarp.org. The booklet, *Medicare Health Maintenance Organization, Are They Right for You?*, can be ordered for $1.00 to cover postage and handling by writing to the

Medicare Rights Center, 1460 Broadway, 8th Floor, New York, NY, 10036-7393. Additional information about the Medicare Rights Center can be found at their web site: www.medicarerights.org. The Federal government, through the Health Care Finance Administration (HCFA), also offers booklets, such as *Understanding Your Medicare Choices, Worksheet for Comparing Medicare Health Plans*, and *Learning About Medicare Health Plans*, which can be ordered at no cost by calling the Medicare hotline at 1-800-633-4227. Additional information about HCFA can be found at their web site: www.medicare.gov.

Although it seems obvious that providers and patients both have a role in improving health care within the managed care environment, Health Communication scholars have a responsibility as well. At this point in time, the excellent theoretical as well as empirical work directly related to relational theory and competent communicative behavior is all too often ignored in the medical literature and in medical education. In one of the most commonly used medical school texts, Roter and Hall (1992), a physician and a psychiatrist, argued that physicians learn interviewing skills by imitating their clinical directors, who value the collection of facts over other types of communication. Mizrahi (1986) went so far as to argue that interns and residents are trained to cure, but not to care. Medical students may actually be trained not to care or to suppress their caring in favor of moving patients through the system. Kramer, Ber, and Moore (1987) found that medical students' rejecting behaviors toward patients were minimal early in their medical school years, but increased dramatically as they patterned their behavior after their clinicians, unless both students and clinicians were made aware of and discussed the consequences of such behaviors.

Although Roter and Hall (1992) emphasized the centrality of talk within the doctor–patient relationship, they did not cite any communication scholars or journals. Although they did spend a page discussing the dynamic nature of this relationship, they devoted an entire chapter to the influence of patient characteristics on compliance and satisfaction and another to physician characteristics. Roter and Hall (1992) argued that physicians need to be better communicators and suggest the following as "critical" skills for the physician: elicit the full spectrum of patient concerns by using open-ended questions, resisting immediate follow-up, and setting priorities by negotiating an agenda and use of time; explore the significance and impact of the problem by asking explicitly for the patient's opinion, experience, understanding, and interpretation and asking explicitly for expectations; and, effectively elicit and respond to patient emotions by asking for feelings, complimenting the patient for his or her effort, legitimating the patient's feelings, and expressing accurate empathy, both verbally and nonverbally. These suggestions offer a very linear perspective of communication and ignore any discussion of developing the more dynamic aspects of the relationship.

Health care providers from nurse aides to neurosurgeons are taught that communication is important but that it is a relatively simple, linear skill. Little, if any, mention is made of the dynamic nature of relationships, the construction of relational schemas, the contextual or cultural influences on relational definitions, the "self" as best understood in the web of relationships, or that relationships develop and change over time. Unfortunately, only a small percentage of the medical profession has been exposed to communication scholarship. Appropriate texts written by or in collaboration with communication scholars (e.g., Northouse & Northouse, 1997; Ray & Donohew, 1991) are rarely used in medical schools. This fact is partially the result of health communication scholars failing to promote their empirical findings to benefit the medical profession. For example, when a medical educator or researcher goes to the library to look for literature on health care provider relationships or communication within managed care environments, the most relevant journal within the discipline of Communication, *Health Communication*, is not referenced in the medical search indexes. Health Communication scholars must be more proactive in spreading the good news and getting the attention of practitioners and consumers who can directly benefit from this knowledge.

REVISITING THE PROPOSITIONS

In the introduction to this chapter, four propositions were presented with respect to the health care provider–older patient relationship within a managed care environment. The first proposition stated that there are positive opportunities for improved health care provider–older patient relationships within managed care. Although researchers such as Greene and Adelman (1996; chap. 5, this volume) are seriously concerned that managed care systems threaten effective and compassionate medical care for the elderly, this threat does not have to become a reality. Health care workers, families, and older patients remain the main players in the delivery of care. The possibility of improving various relationships is somewhat dependent on the realization that the fee-for-service health delivery system did not produce or reinforce perfect health care provider–patient relationships. Serious barriers as well as inducements to competent relationships exist in all health care delivery systems. Inducements in managed care that would enhance competent relationships would allow sufficient time for goal negotiation and other interactions.

The second proposition stressed that improved relationships may be dependent on a reframing of what a managed care health care provider is and does. Although many health professionals do not like the role associated with or even the term "managed," inherent in such a system is the notion of interaction. Successful managing can be reframed into a process of understanding the needs of patients as well as other professionals through competent interaction. Managers of care must weigh financial considerations, the expertise of all the health professionals associated with the care of a particular patient, and the health goals of the patient and family. Managing care does not have to be an authoritarian, noninteractive process. Indeed, successful management of care should become more interactive and thus dependent on competent relationships, both with other professionals and the older patient.

The third proposition follows the second proposition by emphasizing the managing role of the primary care physician, who is placed at the forefront of the managed care delivery system. Along with this prominent role in health care delivery comes a simultaneous relational burden. This responsibility can produce positive relational outcomes for both the physician and patient. The primary care physician is the one who initially interacts with older patients and is ultimately responsible for creating an environment that is conducive to quality care. A major part of this quality care is dependent on the relationship and the use of effective communicative skills to help produce a positive physician–patient relationship. The primary care physician must realize that older patients bring with them into the encounter a complex set of individual complications, both physical and communicative. Therefore, more effort and time may be needed to build and maintain a satisfactory relationship. This effort may be time consuming at the outset, but saves time in future encounters (Greene & Adelman, chap. 5, this volume). For instance, as the relationship becomes professionally closer, the participants will not have to rehash previous discussions and both parties will be more accurate in their predictions of the others' needs and goals. Primary care physicians can embrace their new relational responsibilities as well as their new medical responsibilities within managed care. The work of physician educators like Mold (Mold, 1995; Mold et al., 1991; Mold & McCarthy, 1995), who introduced the goal-oriented model of medical care discussed earlier, places as much emphasis on developing competence in interpersonal skills as in medical skills.

The fourth proposition states that research and theory in the discipline of Communication are helpful and should be referenced in any discussion of the health care provider–older patient relationship. The work of Wilmot (1995) and other Communication scholars who have emphasized the dynamic and complex nature of relationship development and maintenance is helpful in the attempt to increase understanding of the health care provider–older patient relationship. The centrality of communicative skills and the interpretation of those communicative events within specific, cultural contexts help health care providers to better understand the emerging nature of their relationship with each older patient.

This fourth proposition calls for a move beyond the simple, static understanding of communication within health care. Most skills training within the medical literature suggests that health care provider–older patient relationships can be improved by using the correct words (e.g., "ask open-ended questions," Roter & Hall, 1992, p. 165) and gestures (e.g., "express empathy by touching the patient," p. 166). This relatively linear approach misses the most important aspects of communication within relationships. As Wilmot (1995) and Nussbaum (1998) pointed out, although relationships are tied to communication, there are no simple communicative "prescriptions" or "magic bullets" of words to ensure competent communication and, therefore, successful health care relationships. Older patients and their health care providers must understand and then actively work to build their relationship, which must include shared understandings of particular communicative acts. Each health care provider–older patient relationship possesses a unique relational dynamic that emerges over time. Both providers and older patients must strive to identify those elements of managed care that permit successful relationship development and not allow time pressures or financial imperatives to interfere with their relationship.

CONCLUSIONS

The evolution of managed care presents a variety of challenges to the maintenance of a quality health care delivery system. One of those challenges is to convince all participants within health care (professionals, older patients, and their families) that the health care provider–older patient relationship is important and can be effective within a managed care system. This chapter summarizes the theoretical writings of Communication scholars, particularly Wilmot (1995) and his relational model of human interaction, and applies this knowledge to provide a better understanding of the patient–provider relationship. Also summarized is the goal-oriented medical care approach, as outlined by Mold (Mold, 1995; Mold et al., 1991; Mold & McCarthy, 1995), which emphasizes a competent and effective health care provider–older patient relationship. This goal-oriented model is an excellent move away from the traditional problem-solving medical model, so popular prior to the evolution of managed care, and attempts to make that model fit into all medical situations. Managed care, with its emphasis on the primary care physician and interdisciplinary teams in the medical management of frail older adults, can become a health care delivery system that does not necessarily destroy the health care provider–older patient relationship. Relational responsibilities for primary care specialists, older patients, and family members may change and demand more communicative effort, but the dynamics of a closer and more open relationship will work well for both health care providers and older adults within managed care.

REFERENCES

Adelman, R. D., Greene, M. G., & Charon, R. (1991). Issues in physician–elderly patient interaction. *Ageing and Society, 11*, 127–148.

American Academy of Physician Assistants. (1999). *Job descriptions* [On-line]. Available: www.aapa.org

American Association of Health Plans. (1999). *Definitions* [On-line]. Available: www.aahp.org

Bateson, G. (1958). *Naven* (2nd ed.). Stanford, CA: Stanford University Press.

Bavelas, J. B., Black, A., Chovil, N., & Mullett, J. (1990). *Equivocal communication.* Newbury Park, CA: Sage.

Beisecker, A. E. (1996). Older persons' medical encounters and their outcomes. *Research on Aging, 18*, 9–31.

Beisecker, A. E., & Beisecker, T. D. (Eds.). (1996). *Research on Aging, 18*(1), 1–138.

Beisecker, A. E., & Thompson, T. L. (1995). The elderly patient–physician interaction. In J. F. Nussbaum & J. Coupland (Eds.), *Handbook of communication and aging research* (pp. 397–416). Mahwah, NJ: Lawrence Erlbaum Associates.

Clark, P. G. (1997). Values in health care professional socialization: Implications for geriatric education in interdisciplinary teamwork. *The Gerontologist, 37*, 441–451.

Coe, R. M. (1987). Communication and medical care outcomes: Analysis of conversations between doctors and elderly patients. In R. A. Ward & S. T. Tobin (Eds.), *Health in aging: Sociological issues and policy directions* (pp. 180–193). New York: Springer.

Farmer, R. G. (1994). The doctor–patient relationship: Quantification of the interaction. *Annals of the New York Academy of Sciences, 729*, 27–35.

Greene, M. G., & Adelman, R. D. (1996). Psychosocial factors in older patients' medical encounters. *Research on Aging, 18*, 84–102.

Greene, M. G., Adelman, R. D., Friedmann, E., & Charon, R. (1994). Older patient satisfaction with communication during an initial medical counter. *Social Science and Medicine, 38*, 1279–1288.

Haug, M. R., & Ory, M. G. (1987). Issues in elderly patient–provider interactions. *Research on Aging, 9*, 3–44.

Health Care Finance Administration. (1999). *Managed care definitions* [On-line]. Available: www.hcfa.gov

Kramer, D., Ber, R., & Moore, M. (1987). Impact of workshop on students' and physicians' rejection behaviors in patient interview. *Journal of Medical Education, 62*, 904–910.

Marshall, V. W. (1981). Physician characteristics and relationships with older patients. In M. R. Haug (Ed.), *Elderly patients and their doctors* (pp. 94–118). New York: Springer.

Mizrahi, T. (1986). *Getting rid of patients: Contradictions in the socialization of physicians.* New Brunswick, NJ: Rutgers University Press.

Mold, J. W. (1995). An alternative conceptualization of health and health care: Its implications for geriatrics and gerontology. *Educational Gerontology, 21*, 85–101.

Mold, J. W., Blake, G. H., & Becker, L. A. (1991). Goal-oriented medical care. *Family Medicine, 23*, 46–51.

Mold, J. W., & McCarthy, L. (1995). Pearls from geriatric, or a long line at the bathroom. *The Journal of Family Practice, 41*, 22–23.

Northouse, L. L., & Northouse, P. G. (1997). *Health communication: Strategies for health professionals* (3rd ed.). Englewood Cliffs, NJ: Prentice-Hall.

Nurse Practitioner Central. (1999). *Job opportunities* [On-line]. Available: www.nurse.net

Nussbaum, J. F. (1998). Physician–older patient communication during the transition from independence to dependence. *The Journal of the Oklahoma Medical Association, 91*, 1–5.

Nussbaum, J. F., Hummert, M. L., Williams, A., & Harwood, J. (1995). Communication and older adults. In B. Burelson (Ed.), *Communication yearbook 19* (pp. 1–47). Thousand Oaks, CA: Sage.

Ray, E. B., & Donohew, L. (Eds.). (1991). *Communication and health: Systems and applications.* Hillsdale, NJ: Lawrence Erlbaum Associates.

Roter, D. L., & Hall, J. A. (1992). *Doctors talking with patients/patients talking with doctors: Improving communication in medical visits.* Westport, CT: Auburn.

Ruesch, J., & Bateson, G. (1951). *Communication: The social matrix of psychiatry.* New York: Norton.

Serafini, M. W. (1990). Managed Medicare. *National Journal, 27*(15), 920–923.

Sluzki, C. (1998). Migration and the disruption of the social network. In M. McGoldrick (Ed.), *Re-visioning family therapy: Race, culture, and gender in clinical practice* (pp. 260–269). New York: Guilford.

Tsukuda, K. D. (1990). Interdisciplinary collaboration: Teamwork in geriatrics and medicine. In C. K. Cassel, D. E. Reisenberg, L. B. Sorenson, & J. R. Walsh (Eds.), *Geriatric medicine* (2nd ed., pp. 668–675). New York: Springer-Verlag.

U.S. Bureau of Health Professions (1995). *A national agenda for geriatric education: White papers.* Washington, DC: Health Resources and Services Administration.

Ward, R. A. (1990). Health care provider choice and satisfaction. In S. M. Stahl (Ed.), *The legacy of longevity* (pp. 272–290). Newbury Park, CA: Sage.

Watzlawick, P., Beavin, J., & Jackson, D. D. (1967). *Pragmatics of human communication: A study of interactional patterns, pathologies, and paradoxes.* New York: Norton.

Wilmot, W. W. (1995). *Relational communication.* New York: McGraw-Hill.

Zeiss, A. M., & Steffen, A. M. (1996). Interdisciplinary health care teams: The basic unit of geriatric care. In L. L. Carstensen, B. A. Edelstein, & L. Dombrand (Eds.), *The practice of clinical gerontology* (pp. 423–450). Thousand Oaks, CA: Sage.

3

Hearing Health and the Listening Experiences of Older Communicators

M. Kathleen Pichora-Fuller
Arlene J. Carson
University of British Columbia, Canada

Sound is essential for spoken language. It also serves a wide range of other important communicative functions (Noble, 1983; Ramsdell, 1960; Schafer, 1993, 1994; Truax, 1984). Sound connects listeners to themselves, to each other, and to many different kinds of events and objects in their acoustical world or soundscape. A *soundscape* is "an environment of sound with emphasis on the way it is perceived and understood by the individual, or by society. It thus depends on the relationship between the individual and any such environment" (Truax, 1978, p. 126). Listeners use acoustic cues to monitor and control their voices and bodies. Listeners hear the voices and sounds produced by other people, during conversation or when sharing activities, during eavesdropping, or simply because they are sharing the same physical space for otherwise independent activities. A voice, footsteps, a car horn, or even the sound pattern produced by a friend's wheelchair can inform a listener that someone is moving closer or farther away and can possibly enable the listener to identify the person. Sounds such as dog barks or alarms or sirens alert people to danger. Sounds of familiar music comfort people. A sequence of beeps signals to a cook that the coffee in the cup in the microwave has finished being reheated, or it signals to a diabetic that it is time for another dose of insulin. Time of day is cued by sounds linked to societal or institutional routines such as morning rush hour traffic. Soundscapes also vary with seasonal fluctuations in nature, for example, the summer sounds of mosquitoes buzzing or thunder and lightning during an electrical storm (Truax,

1984). Places can be identified from many features of the soundscape: dishes clattering in the dining room, pins falling in the bowling alley, birds singing in the garden, Big Ben chiming in London. Silences or interruptions in sound also convey linguistic (Jaworski, 1993, 1998) and environmental meanings (Schafer, 1994). Sounds combine with inputs from other senses in a predictable and often complementary or potentially compensatory fashion. A crunch combines with taste, texture, and smell when enjoying a fresh apple. A blind person hears sobs when tears cannot be seen. Listening—the ability to hear and interpret sound—is important for good health insofar as it supports personhood and meaningful person–person and person–environment interaction. It may be necessary for survival; it enables people to communicate using spoken language; it adds to the richness and quality of life. This chapter considers the role that listening plays in the lives of older adults.

It is widely known that auditory deficits increase markedly with age, beginning in the fourth decade. In fact, hearing loss has been identified as the most prevalent chronic disability among older adults, exceeded only by arthritis and hypertension (Binnie, 1994; Haber, 1994). Age-related hearing loss, *presbycusis*, progresses over time until there are measurable and clinically significant changes in ability to detect sound (Willott, 1991). The *audiogram* represents the results of the basic clinical hearing test and shows the lowest decibel level (loudness) of sound detected by the listener for each of eight tones differing in frequency (pitch). As shown in Fig. 3.1, the audiogram for a typical presbycusic is characterized by hearing loss for high-frequency tones and relatively little or no hearing loss for low-frequency tones. (The difference between high- and low-frequency tones corresponds roughly to the difference between consonants and vowels in language, or treble and bass notes in music.) As many as half of adults aged 75 to 79 years have some degree of audiometrically measured hearing loss (for reviews, see Kricos, 1995; Willott, 1991), as do the vast majority of those living in institutional care (Shultz & Mowry, 1995). Audiometrically measured hearing loss has also been associated with an accelerated and rapid cognitive decline in individuals with dementia (Peters, Potter, & Scholer, 1988; Uhlmann, Larson, & Koepsell, 1986; Ulmann, Larson, Rees, Koepsell, & Duckert, 1989).

In general, however, estimates of prevalence based on audiometric measures of impairment are higher than estimates based on subjective indices of handicap (Erdman, 1994) and the difference in these estimates is even more pronounced for older listeners (Lutman, 1991). For instance, in a population survey of community-living seniors, it was found

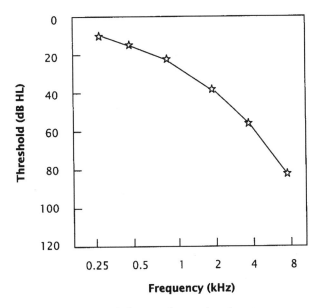

FIG. 3.1.   Audiogram of a typical presbycusic.

that one fifth reported difficulty in conversation with one person and one third reported trouble when conversing with two or more people (Regional Municipality of Hamilton–Wentworth and Hamilton–Wentworth District Health Council, 1988). The discrepancy between clinical measures of hearing loss and self-reported hearing problems highlights the need to understand how and when hearing loss influences older adults' participation in and enjoyment of everyday life (Erdman & Demorest, 1998a, 1998b). Challenges to listening may compromise learning, decision making, safety, socialization, or personal well-being. Listening, rather than hearing, is what is important to older adults.

Until recently, several issues have impeded appreciation of how changes in hearing relate to the everyday listening experiences and the quality of life of older adults. Fundamentally, it is necessary to reconcile the apparent mismatches between clinical measures of hearing and the lived experiences of listeners (Pichora-Fuller, 1997b; Pichora-Fuller, Johnson, & Roodenburg, 1998; Villaume, Brown, & Darling, 1994). These mismatches perplex all those involved: hard-of-hearing listeners, their communication partners and caregivers, and also health professionals, including audiologists. In this chapter, three interrelated issues are explored. First, how does the auditory system age and how well does the audiogram depict changes in auditory processing? Second, how well does the audiogram predict or explain an older person's ability to perform activities or participate in everyday life? Third, how effective is hearing rehabilitation for older adults? The goal of the chapter is to provide a new framework for understanding and improving the experiences of older listeners. The new framework follows a health promotion approach (Carson & Pichora-Fuller, 1997; Green & Kreuter, 1991) and is consistent with work of the World Health Organization (WHO) concerning health promotion (WHO, 1986), and the classification of impairments, activities, and participation with reference to physical and social environments (WHO, 1998).

A key notion is that *health* is more than the absence of disease—it is the ability to adapt to or cope with challenges or changes in circumstances (WHO, 1980). Based on this premise, the Ottawa Charter (WHO, 1986) stated that the purpose of health promotion is to enable people (individually or in a community) to gain greater control over the determinants of their own health. To this end, health promotion approaches emphasize the need for educational and environmental supports for actions and conditions of living conducive to health (Green & Kreuter, 1991). The era of health promotion that emerged after 1980 paralleled a shift in how impairment, disability, and handicap were conceptualized. *The International Classification of Impairments, Disabilities, and Handicaps* (ICIDH) introduced by the WHO (1980) defined *impairment* as a physical, physiological, or anatomical loss or abnormality of function, *disability* as a loss or reduction of normal ability resulting from impairment, and *handicap* as the detrimental effect that disability has on an individual's life, especially on that individual's activities and roles. Recent revisions to these classifications have resulted in both a relabeling of the concepts and a new schematization of their interrelationships as shown in Fig. 3.2. The relabeling recasts the concepts more positively to focus on function rather than dysfunction: Rather than impairments resulting from disorders or diseases, the new model considers how *health conditions* (including conditions such as pregnancy or aging that are not caused by disease or trauma) alter body functions or structures; disability is recast as *activity*; handicap is recast as *participation*. Activity refers to actual performance, as opposed to what people could or might do. Participation refers to the nature and extent of people's involvement in life situations in relation to their health conditions and activities as mediated by a complex, bidirectional, and dynamic interaction with contextual factors. In contrast to the prior model, in which impairment resulted in disability that in turn resulted in handicap, the new schematization abandons this causal view for a more interactive view

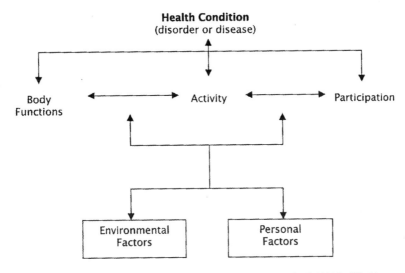

FIG. 3.2.   The model of the ICIDH-2 (1999, p. 23). Copyright © 1999 by World
Health Organization. Reprinted with permission.

and highlights the important role of context. Contextual factors include
gender, age, health issues, coping styles, social background, education, and
other conditions that influence how individuals experience a particular
impairment. Environmental factors range from physical factors such as climate and terrain to social attitudes, institutions, and laws. Contextual factors may pose barriers or act as facilitators to activities and participation.
Importantly, the emphasis has shifted from the physical limitations of the
individual to how contextual and environmental supports can be optimized to facilitate participation.

IMPAIRMENT: AUDITORY SYSTEM AGING AND BASIC CLINICAL ASSESSMENT

Most hearing losses are readily attributable to specific etiologies and sites
of lesion. These include conductive, sensori-neural and central hearing
losses. *Conductive* hearing losses are due to problems in the outer or middle ear such as wax blocking the ear canal, infection in the middle ear
possibly resulting in ruptures of the eardrum, or otosclerosis stiffening the
chain of bones in the middle ear to reduce the mechanical relay of sound
from the middle to the inner ear. Most conductive losses are remediable
by medical or surgical interventions. Common causes of *sensori-neural*
hearing losses include noise-induced or ototoxic drug damage to the hair

cells in the inner ear where neural transmission begins, or tumors on the auditory nerve along which neural transmission occurs. There are also *central* hearing losses caused, for example, by tumors in subcortical auditory areas of the brain where monaural and binaural patterns are analyzed, or by strokes affecting cortical auditory areas where specialized coding such as language processing is accomplished. Both sensori-neural and central losses are usually permanent.

In contrast to these relatively easily diagnosed conditions that can affect people across the life span, presbycusis is typically diagnosed when an older person has a high-frequency sensori-neural hearing loss with no obvious explanation for the loss other than just aging. Because presbycusis is defined by excluding other known pathologies, it does not refer to any one specific pathology and multiple sites may be affected by generalized cell loss and degeneration. Different subtypes of presbycusis have been proposed and research on differentiating subtypes is ongoing (for reviews, see Schneider, 1997; Willott, 1991). Most presbycusics have hearing loss resulting from damage to hair cells in the inner ear (sensory loss). Many also have hearing loss resulting from loss of ganglion cells and neural damage (neural loss). Still other older listeners have central losses, including some who have no clinically detectable sensori-neural loss. It is common for these various types of loss to co-exist (CHABA, 1988; Schneider & Pichora-Fuller, 2000; Willott, 1991). Chmiel and Jerger (1996) emphasized the need to recognize central as well as more peripheral forms of presbycusis, with the prevalence of central auditory processing disorders among the elderly being about 10% to 20% among a stratified random sample of the U.S. population (Cooper & Gates, 1991) but as high as 80% to 90% in a clinical population with co-occurring sensori-neural loss (Stach, Spretnjak, & Jerger, 1990). In summary, the anatomical and physiological bases for presbycusis are varied and, consequently, individuals with presbycusis may vary widely in their auditory processing abilities. It is reasonable to assume that few older adults have auditory structures and functions equivalent to those of younger adults, but the key to understanding the apparent mismatch between clinical and lived interpretations of hearing loss is to appreciate how both the auditory processing abilities and the listening experiences of older adults vary.

Unfortunately, not only are the anatomical and physiological bases for presbycusis varied, but there is also variation in the perceptual consequences associated with particular sites of lesion. Even if consideration is limited to the relationship between the simplest measure of auditory perception and the most obvious anatomical basis for sensory presbycusis, behavior is not readily predicted from anatomy. The audiogram provides highly accurate and precise information about the audibility or detectability of sounds. The hallmark of sensory presbycusis is the elevation of high-frequency thresholds of detectability. The assumed basis for this type of perceptual loss is damage to the hair cells at the base of the *cochlea* (the cells located on the basilar membrane in the inner ear where high-frequency sounds are coded). The correspondence between degree of threshold elevation and degree of hair cell loss is, however, far from straightforward. On the one hand, audiometrically measured hearing loss can result from any kind of damage to the auditory system that disrupts the transduction of sound into the normal level of biomechanical or neural activity. On the other hand, extensive hair cell damage may take place with no clinically detectable change in audiometric thresholds. A striking example of this lack of correspondence is Bredberg's (1968) finding that with as much as a 40% loss of outer hair cells in the apex of the cochlea there can be as little as only a 15 dB elevation in thresholds for low-frequency pure-tones, and that with as much as a 25% loss of outer hair cells in the base of the cochlea there can be as little as only a 20 dB elevation in thresholds for high-frequency pure-tones.

In the case of older listeners, it is especially important to realize the limitations of the audiogram as an index of impairment and to recognize that considerable physical damage may already have been done before any change is evident audiometrically. Although thresholds of detectability remain normal, other aspects of auditory processing may be affected by cell loss in the inner ear. As has already been stated, other aspects of auditory processing may also be affected by neural and central auditory system disorders that occur in conjunction with or independently of sensory disorders (Chermak & Musiek, 1997). Having good audiometric thresholds does not guarantee that an older adult will always find listening as easy as it is for a younger adult. Examples of specific auditory processing declines that are likely to be very important to listeners in everyday life, but that are not predictable from audiometric thresholds, include declines in monaural auditory temporal processing (Fitzgibbons & Gordon-Salant, 1996) and binaural processing (Grose, 1996). Further research to characterize the specific anatomical and physiological bases for these processing declines is needed to guide the development of future tests that may be more informative than the audiogram (Phillips, 1995; Schneider, 1997; Willott, 1991, 1996).

ACTIVITY AND PARTICIPATION:
BEYOND THE AUDIOGRAM

The audiogram is a measure of activity insofar as it taps a specific aspect of performance, namely, ability to detect sound. Having obtained an audiogram, an audiologist knows whether or not the person is capable of detecting any sound whose intensity and frequency characteristics are known. A sound is audible if its intensity exceeds the person's audiometric threshold in its frequency range. For example, sounds such as speech and music are composed of a broad range of frequencies (from below 100 to over 4000 Hz or cycles per second) at moderate intensity levels (about 50 dB HL or decibels referenced to normal human hearing levels). Listeners with typical presbycusic, high-frequency hearing loss are able to detect speech, even though much of the high-frequency portion (the consonant region) of the speech signal is barely audible or inaudible. Although it may be important to know what sounds are detectable because they fall within the person's hearing range, it should be obvious by now that the usefulness of the audiogram is limited in terms of its informativeness as a measure of activity.

Ability to detect sound is the simplest aspect of auditory processing. In most everyday situations, listening demands more complex perceptual and cognitive processing of suprathreshold sounds (Pichora-Fuller, 1997b). Indeed, one of the most common reports of people with hearing loss is that the voice of the talker is loud enough but that it is difficult to understand. Other common reports are that sounds seem jumbled or that it is difficult to tell where sound is coming from. Detection is necessary but not sufficient to support spoken language comprehension, music appreciation, or navigation through auditory environments. Even though a typical presbycusic listener has little difficulty detecting the presence of speech, this in no way guarantees that individual speech sounds or words are identifiable, that conversations are effortless, or that an accurate representation of the auditory world is mapped spatially. Optimal listening function in a wide range of everyday situations entails abilities such as localizing, identifying, ignoring or attending, segregating or integrating, remembering, and comprehending auditory objects or sound events and patterns (Bregman, 1990). Listening function is challenged in many everyday situations such as when multiple auditory objects are simultaneously present (e.g., many talkers at a cocktail party), when the defining sound properties are degraded during transmission in a space (e.g., high levels of reverberation or echo in a large room with highly reflective surfaces), during processing by a device (e.g., hearing aid, telephone), or because of damage to the auditory system. It is in such challenging conditions that the activities of older listeners are most severely limited.

The effects of hearing loss on the participation of older adults in everyday life may be modulated by many factors (Borg, 1998; Nespoulous, 1996; Pichora-Fuller, 1994). Such factors include the specific nature of the person's hearing-related impairments and disabilities, other impairments and disabilities such as deficits in vision or cognition (for a review, see Schneider & Pichora-Fuller, 2000), the nature of the physical environment (Hodgson, 1994), or the social environment, either at the interpersonal level (Ryan, Giles, Bartolucci, & Henwood, 1986) or the cultural level (McKellin, 1994). These nonauditory factors are likely to vary more for older adults than for younger adults. Therefore, notwithstanding the high-frequency, sensori-neural hearing loss that is typical of presbycusis and how such hearing loss contributes to real-world hearing problems, to understand more fully why older adults make the kinds of comments they do about their everyday listening experiences, it is important to see beyond the audiogram and to try to appreciate the diversity of possible factors that influence participation within a more comprehensive theoretical framework.

A crucial difference between hearing and listening is that listening is goal-driven and involves intentional and attentional influences on perception. The participation of the individual in everyday life should only be detrimentally affected if hearing problems become obstacles to achieving personal or social goals. The apparent discrepancy between objective measures of hearing and subjective reports of hearing problems can be reconciled once the focus is shifted from hearing to listening (Pichora-Fuller et al., 1998). Listening problems, but not hearing problems, are functionally significant. The shift from hearing to listening also illuminates what, until recently, have been disconcerting data suggesting that: (a) audiological services are not sought by many older adults with hearing impairment; (b) even when consultation is sought, compliance with recommended treatments is low; and (c) even when clients comply with treatments, the results are often unsatisfactory.

It is well known that there is a lag of anywhere from 8 to more than 20 years between the time a person is first aware of hearing difficulties and when professional hearing help is sought (Brink, Wit, Kempen, & Heuvelen, 1996; Getty & Hétu, 1994; Kyle, Jones, & Wood, 1985; Watson & Crowther, 1989). Gilhome Herbst, Meredith, and Stephens (1991) investigated the social implications of hearing impairment that affect seeking help in two populations of adults aged 70 years and over. One group was registered at a general medical practice in London, England (Humphrey, Gilhome Herbst, & Faruqi, 1981) and the other in Wales. In both groups, one fourth of the patients with mild hearing loss (mean loss of 35 dB HL or greater in the mid-frequency range from 1000 to 4000 Hz in the better ear) said they had not noticed any difficulty hearing. Of those who did, one fourth of the Welsh group and one third of the London group said they had never consulted their doctor about it. More than half who did consult a physician were not referred for a hearing aid assessment. Factors associated with seeking help were severity of impairment and age of onset of hearing loss before reaching retirement age. In another British study comparing adults with hearing loss who consulted physicians to those who did not, Swan and Gatehouse (1990) controlled for level of impairment, age, gender, and socioeconomic status and found that the consulters experienced greater disability (poorer speech perception ability) and greater handicap (functional problems). Similarly, a community-based study of older Dutch adults found that help seeking was positively related to the perceived seriousness of hearing problems (Brink et al., 1996). Furthermore, interviews with seniors in Quebec provided insights into various nonauditory personal and societal factors that prevent or delay seeking help (Getty, Gagné, & McDuff, 1996).

The prevailing treatment has been to get a hearing aid, with the assumption being that this device will restore function. Unfortunately, estimates suggest that only about one fourth of those whose degree of hearing loss makes them candidates for a hearing aid have one (Gabbard, 1994), and few who have one find that it overcomes all their hearing problems (Holmes, 1995). The amplification provided by hearing aids is beneficial when important sounds are inaudible; however, hearing aids also amplify unwanted background or competing sounds and, even though there have been great advances in technology over the last decade, they do not yet offer sufficiently sophisticated signal processing to mimic the processing performed by an intact auditory system (Levitt, 1993; Plomp, 1978). Thus it is not surprising that almost one third of older hearing aid wearers report that they have difficulties in everyday situations where there are multiple signals (e.g., group conversation) or background noise (Smedley & Schow, 1994). There has been a longstanding assumption that if only the amplified signal could be sufficiently improved, more people would seek help and hearing instruments would be successfully adopted by currently dissatisfied users as well as by the vast untapped market who might benefit from amplification but have never tried it. Nevertheless, the technological imperfections of hearing aids do not seem to adequately explain why this form of treatment meets with such resistance and lack of success.

Not enough research effort has been directed toward exploring what nonauditory and noninstrumental reasons related to everyday functioning might account for why so many people with measurable hearing impairments take so long to seek help and to act on treatment recommendations. The importance of social, psychological, and environmental issues in adjustment to hearing loss has received increasing attention in the last decade (Erber, Lamb, & Lind, 1996; Ross, 1997). On the one hand, unmanaged hearing loss may have an adverse effect on the physical, cognitive, emotional, behavioral, and social function of older adults (Mulrow et al., 1990). On the other hand, older adults with hearing impairment may not be handicapped if they remain able to fulfill their personal and social goals in everyday life (Garstecki & Erler, 1998; Jaworski & Stephens, 1998; Pichora-Fuller et al., 1998). Whereas the causal direction of the link between hearing loss and personal and social adjustment may be open to debate, the eventual establishment of the link between them for most older people is evident. The nature of these links needs to be better understood.

Hearing loss is associated with numerous negative aspects of personal adjustment: increased stress levels, anxiety, social withdrawal, and altered self-concepts manifested in lowered self-esteem, feelings of inferiority, insecurity, and loss of autonomy (Rousey, 1976). In a study comparing older adults with normal or impaired hearing, those with hearing impairment rated their health poorer and they were less likely to get out without help, ventured out less far, were less satisfied with their extent of mobility, had fewer friends than in the past, enjoyed life less than previously, and were more often depressed (Thomas & Gilhome Herbst, 1980). In a large-scale study of older adults, hearing, vision, and gait-balance were found to mediate the effects of intelligence on advanced activities of daily living (e.g., interpersonal communication); it was concluded that "these results suggest that sensory acuity may influence the physical and psychological resources that more directly undergrid activity participation" (Marsiske, Klumb, & Baltes, 1997, pp. 453–454). A significant association between hearing loss and cognitive dysfunction was also found in persons with dementia (Uhlmann et al., 1986, 1989).

Given the importance of sound for person–person and person–environment communication, it should be no surprise that the detrimental effects of hearing loss extend to these relationships, both at home and in

the community. Hearing loss has been found to affect intimate relationships such as those with a spouse or other family member within the same
household (Hétu, Jones, & Getty, 1993). The family member may co-
experience handicap in terms of feelings of effort, stress, isolation, negative self-image, and difficulties in interpersonal interactions. They may
become irritated at having to repeat comments, being misunderstood, or
by unwanted alterations of their shared soundscape such as playing the
television at a loud volume. Extra effort may involve added responsibilities such as always answering the telephone. Feelings of isolation and
negative self-image may arise from reduced communication, especially
intimate conversation, among all family members.

Outside the home, family members may come to act as interpreters for
the person with hearing loss. A spouse may harbor resentment arising
from restrictions imposed on the couple's social life where the spouse with
hearing loss avoids social encounters (e.g., parties) or wants to leave early.
A spouse or parent's inappropriate communication behaviors, such as
speaking too loudly or interrupting or dominating conversations, may
undermine self-image. Importantly, over time, coping with and adjusting
to hearing loss is a process that family members are engaged in with the
person with hearing loss (Hétu et al., 1993). Avoidance and control of
the social scene have been identified as two general patterns of adjustment exhibited by spouses of hard-of-hearing people (Hallberg & Carlsson, 1991). Although initial help-seeking for hearing loss is often
prompted by family members who share the process of adjustment with
the person with hearing loss, the adjustments of family members are not
usually openly discussed, negotiated, or acknowledged, a situation that
can escalate miscommunication and isolation in the family.

Relationships with friends, acquaintances, and strangers can also be
affected by hearing loss. The response of others may be to stigmatize the
person with hearing loss as a result of the person's inability to meet the
expectations associated with a role in a specified social setting (Goffman,
1963) as evidenced by the inappropriate stereotyped responses that are
common place as reactions to those with disabilities (McKellin, 1994). In
a social context, the stigma associated with hearing loss may be com-
pounded by stigma associated with ageism or sexism, with older women
with hearing loss being particularly disadvantaged. The centrality of communication in women's social roles and the multiplicity of their roles at
home and in the community (Baruch, Biener, & Barnett, 1987) seems
likely to put women at greater risk of limitations on participation due to
hearing loss; however, they are less likely to receive social support for

their communication difficulties compared to men (Erdman & Demorest, 1998b; Garstecki & Erler, 1995; Hétu et al., 1993). Persons with hearing loss may succeed in passing for normal until they decide to wear a hearing aid. A hearing aid may induce stigma by drawing unfavorable attention to the hearing loss (Smedley & Schow, 1994). The social cost of wearing a hearing aid must, therefore, be weighed against the acoustical benefits that it may provide.

Acoustic communication with respect to person–environment relationships also warrants much more careful consideration than it has received up until now. It is well known that older adults experience more difficulty communicating in noisy and reverberant conditions than in quiet conditions, and the need to improve the signal-to-noise conditions for older listeners is widely recognized (CHABA, 1988). Even though it is likely that hearing loss diminishes the quality of the soundscape for listeners with hearing loss, the person–environment aspect of participation has been largely neglected as a topic of research except in extreme cases (Pichora-Fuller, 1999). The importance of supportive environments to activity and participation is seen dramatically for frail older persons in long-term care settings. A recent study of community-living older adults with dementia also showed positive effects of hearing aid use on problem behaviors identified by caregivers, with several of these behaviors concerning person–environment responses such as searching, acting restless, pacing, and hearing things that were not there (Palmer, Adams, Bourgeois, Durrant, & Rossi, 1999).

In general, links between low-quality physical conditions of a home and poor health of residents have been found, with important implications for health and housing policy (Gitlin, 1998). Supportive environments can promote personal autonomy, independent living, and enhanced quality of life, with everyday benefits including reduction of fear and agitation, reduced risk of accidents and wandering, enhanced self-efficacy, personal control and privacy, improved orientation and awareness, enhanced comfort, enhanced social and leisure engagement, and decreased caregiver burden (Gitlin, 1998). Just as for hearing aids, the acceptance of modifications of the acoustical or listening environment also hinges on how the social acceptability of the solution trades against the functional benefits (Gitlin, 1998). Of course, others who share environments with older persons with hearing loss also have a stake in both the costs and benefits associated with environmental modifications.

Gitlin (1998) described a functional–environmental need model for the design of home modification interventions that takes into account the priority of environmental needs and the competence of the older person. Within this model, at one extreme, design for the well older person usually emphasizes safety as a prevention strategy, and at the other extreme, design for the multiply physically and cognitively impaired usually emphasizes orientation and awareness as a feature of long-term care. Optimal environments provide meaningful stimulation while minimizing noise and distractions (for a review, see Burgio & Stevens, 1998).

Environmental factors may be antecedents that trigger, and consequences that follow, problem behaviors (Burgio & Lewis, 1999). Acoustics is an important but not often studied environmental factor. Noisy environments trigger problem behaviors (Hussian & Davis, 1985) and noise-making as a form of aggression can be triggered by adverse environments (Cariaga, Burgio, Flynn, & Martin, 1991). Manipulations of the acoustical environment such as playing gentle ocean or mountain stream soundscapes over headphones have also been demonstrated to be effective in reducing verbal aggression and disruptive vocalizations (Burgio, Scilley, Hardin, Hsu, & Yancey, 1996). Further research into the effects of hearing loss on the person–environment aspects of participation holds promise for the future.

EFFECTIVENESS OF AUDIOLOGIC REHABILITATION

As with other health services based on the biophysical medical model and the notion of health as the prevention of disease, a widely recognized shortcoming of traditional rehabilitative audiology has been the focus of clinicians on hearing loss as an impairment, on the audiogram as a measure of hearing loss, and on the hearing aid as the best intervention (Ross, 1997). Fortunately, over the two decades since the definition of the concepts of *impairment, disability,* and *handicap* by the WHO (1980), this trio of concepts has altered how audiologists think about hearing loss and its consequences (Giolas, 1990; Schow & Gatehouse, 1990; Stephens & Hétu, 1991). At the same time, there has been a steady evolution in audiologic practice toward a more holistic and ecological approach to improving the everyday experiences of listeners (Carson & Pichora-Fuller, 1997; Gagné, Hétu, Getty, & McDuff, 1995; Jennings & Head, 1994; Lesner & Kricos, 1995; Pichora-Fuller & Robertson, 1994). Programs adopting an ecological approach target changes in the behaviors of the hard-of-hearing individual and their communication partners, as well as changes in the physical and social environment that would be conducive to improving listening and acoustic communication in everyday life (Carson & Pichora-Fuller, 1997; Erber, 1988; Jennings & Head, 1994; Noble, 1983). Although there is still much work to be done to improve the everyday experiences of older listeners, the outcomes of recently implemented ecologically oriented programs are encouraging. Although the potential merits of such programs seem obvious, it is important to examine their effectiveness.

We have been involved in the design and evaluation of three hearing rehabilitation programs that demonstrate a shift from traditional forms of hearing rehabilitation to more ecologically oriented programs. These programs were delivered on-site at residential care facilities because as many as 90% of elderly residents in institutional care have a hearing loss (Schow & Nerbonne, 1980) and traditional clinic-based audiologic services are known to be inadequate or inaccessible for them (Shultz & Mowry, 1995). Although the outcome of hearing aid delivery to institutionalized seniors has been studied (for a review, see Holmes, 1995), to our knowledge, others have not evaluated an on-site ecologically oriented audiologic rehabilitation program for seniors living in institutional care (Abrahamson, 1995).

The three programs discussed here were implemented in the early 1990s. They differ from each other in terms of the intensity of service provided, the qualifications and goals of the service providers, and the relative emphasis in the initial phase on service or research. It is interesting to note that all three programs were initiated by some type of community-based group of seniors and not by audiologists.

An interprofessional health subcommittee of the District Health Council of Hamilton-Wentworth, Ontario, Canada, planned the first of the three programs. Two companion health care research grants were federally funded from 1992 to 1994; one project was to implement a hearing rehabilitation program on-site at a home-for-the-aged and the other project was to conduct a formal program evaluation. One full-time audiologist was hired as the service provider and another full-time audiologist was hired as the program evaluator. This program was the most intensive and professionally dominated of the three programs, and it had the greatest emphasis on program evaluation research. The program focused on five major areas: (a) provision of hearing aids and assistive listening devices (ALDs), (b) maximization of accessibility to communication opportunities, (c) education of staff and residents, (d) training to promote use of compensatory communication strategies, and (e) drop-in audiology clinic and residents' self-help group (for a detailed description, see Jennings & Head, 1994, 1997).

The Canadian Hard of Hearing Association (CHHA) at four different sites implemented another program, "To Hear Again," in 1992 across Canada with funding obtained from the Seniors' Independence Program of Health Canada. The program undertaken by this hard-of-hearing consumer self-help and peer support organization trained hard-of-hearing seniors to act as volunteer visitors to help other hard-of-hearing seniors (Dahl, 1997). An interview-based external evaluation of the program indicated that a major benefit of the program was the positive effect that role modeling by the hard-of-hearing volunteers had on both the residents and staff of the care facilities (Carson, 1997). It was felt that the project demonstrated the relevance of CHHA's focus on partnership efforts and the importance of consumers working in cooperation with professionals.

A third program began in 1993 and has continued to evolve from the demonstration stage to being maintained as an ongoing city-wide program of the Vancouver/Richmond Health Board. This project was begun as an initiative of the Health Subcommittee of the Seniors' Advisory Committee to the City of Vancouver who obtained funding for a Community Partnership Project from the Continuing Care Program of the Ministry of Health of the province of British Columbia. The emphasis of the project was on service delivery under severe budgetary constraints. It targeted seniors unable to access traditional clinic-based programs designed for younger adults. Program delivery for this population of seniors varies somewhat in design to suit three subgroups varying in their relative independence and mobility. Level 1 services are educational and screening programs for seniors attending community center programs or living independently in designated seniors' housing. Level 2 services involve educational, screening, diagnostic, and rehabilitative services provided on-site at adult day centers or personal care housing. Level 3 services are provided in-house in continuing care facilities and involve a full range of hearing services, including planned follow-up. A hallmark of the program is its efficiency in the use of a combination of personnel, including audiologists, audiology outreach workers, regular care facility staff, and volunteers. This program has been able to incorporate the best features of the consumer-run CHHA "To Hear Again" program by involving volunteers and incorporating the key features of the audiologist-run project in Hamilton-Wentworth. Results to date suggest that this combination can be effective in reaching large numbers of hard-of-hearing seniors using relatively restricted resources (Hoek, Paccioretti, Pichora-Fuller, McDonald, & Shyng, 1997).

All three programs exemplify an ecological approach to hearing rehabilitation, but the Hamilton-Wentworth project is described in more detail because it incorporated a formal program evaluation research component. Adopting an ecological approach meant that the objectives of the program were unlike those usually set for traditional clinic-based audiologic rehabilitation and that intervention strategies and techniques were far more varied. The novelty of the program was accompanied by a need for new program evaluation methods. In a recent review of intervention research with older adults, Schultz and Martire (1998) noted that although there has been an explosion of intervention research over the last decade, the vast majority of studies still target specific health problems at the individual level. They suggested that future research should address implementing and evaluating interventions that target contexts as well as individuals. They further suggested a need for dissemination of knowledge about the practicalities of conducting intervention research. For these reasons, it is worthwhile to elaborate on the methodological challenges of evaluating an ecologically oriented hearing rehabilitation program and to report our findings.

EVALUATION OF AN ECOLOGICAL AUDIOLOGIC REHABILITATION PROGRAM

There were two main objectives of the project: (a) to determine if the program increased the scope and effectiveness of the residents' communication, and (b) to determine what specific behavioral or environmental changes accounted for any improvements in communication function that were observed. Expected overall outcomes from an effective program included a positive change in the scope of residents' participation in activities that demand communication and a positive change in the effectiveness of residents' communication during those activities. Furthermore, it was expected that overall outcomes would be accounted for by specific changes in use of hearing aids and/or ALDs, resident and staff skills in the care and handling of such prostheses, and use of compensatory communication behaviors by residents and staff. The study was designed and outcome measures were developed to tap the expected overall and specific outcomes.

Design of the Study

The project consisted of two phases, each lasting one year. In Phase 1, the measurement instruments were administered twice, at a 6-month interval, and the findings were compared to determine the extent to which there was change over a 6-month period in the absence of intervention. In Phase 2, the program was implemented and evaluated using the same measures administered to the same subjects two more times at 6-month intervals. Using this design, variability was limited to within-subject and within-site changes over time. The timing of evaluations was such that seasonal conditions between baseline and program evaluations were identical. We looked for whether or not there was a positive change (improvement or less deterioration) compared to change on the same measures during a comparable, nontreatment, preprogram period. It was important to determine how the communication experiences of the residents changed over time in the absence of treatment because their health and abilities were likely to decline such that a positive effect of the program might be observed as a stabilization rather than as an improvement in their communication experiences. Furthermore, by comparing the changes measured in Phase 1 (possibly resulting simply from our arrival at the home-for-the-aged) to changes in Phase 2, the Hawthorne effect (Suter & Lindgren, 1989, pp. 256) was controlled. Because the program was intended to alter resident and staff behaviors and the communication environment throughout the facility, it was not feasible to withhold treatment from a control group at the same facility while the program was being delivered. As using residents at a different facility as a control group would have introduced between-subject and between-site variability, we rejected this alternative design. Another feature of the evaluation was that the audiologist who administered the evaluation measures (Robertson) was not the same audiologist who delivered the service (Jennings), with each audiologist being blind to the specific activities of and the results obtained by the other.

Resident Participants.   All residents at the facility were invited to participate in the project except those who were not fluent in English, those with communication impairments other than hearing loss, or those receiving high levels of care. Residents were screened by two methods: chart review and a questionnaire given to care nurses. On the basis of information in the chart, 110 of 362 residents were considered to be eligible for the project. Of these, 95 were considered by their care nurse to have the potential to benefit from the program. Audiometric thresholds were not considered in determining the eligibility of residents for the project for several reasons: (a) The percentage of institutionalized elderly with clinically significant hearing loss has been reported to be as high as 90% (Schow & Nerbonne, 1980). (b) It was assumed that even residents with no clinically significant threshold hearing loss would experience difficulty hearing in nonideal, everyday communication situations. (c) In addition to hearing aids, the program offered a wide range of treatment options that could be advantageous regardless of degree of hearing loss.

Of the 95 eligible residents invited to participate in the project, 78 residents consented to participate. Reasons for refusing to participate included ill health, considered self to be too old, considered self to have no handicap, lack of interest, suspicions about associated costs, unwillingness to sign any document, advice of family, and satisfaction with existing hearing services. Of the 78 residents who consented to participate, 48 dropped out by the end of the second year of the study, leaving 30 who completed the program evaluation. Almost half (21) of those who dropped out did so in the first 6-month period and very few (3) dropped out in the final 6-month period. About three fourths of those who dropped out did so for reasons that were unrelated to the project itself (21 had changes for the worse in mental or physical health, 9 died, and 3 moved out of the facility). A little less than 10% dropped out because the evaluation was too demanding. Some who dropped out continued to receive services even though their participation in the formal program evaluation was discontinued. Any resident could participate in the rehabilitation program; however, only the subset that consented was involved in the formal program evaluation. Therefore, those who were evaluated should not be taken to represent the entire population of the facility, or even the subpopulation to whom audiologic services were delivered. Overall, the 30 who completed the evaluation had better and more stable health.

The majority (16) of the evaluated group had no other major health concerns besides hearing loss. Almost one third (9) had a significant visual impairment, and most of those (6) were legally blind. Other chronic health problems that coexisted with hearing loss but that were not considered to be severe enough to interfere with the participation of the affected individuals in the project were Parkinson's disease (2), multiple sclerosis (1), anxiety (1), and depression (1). Some members of the evaluated group experienced fluctuations in physical or mental health over the period of the project but these were not sufficient to cause them to drop out of the study.

The Standardized Mini-Mental State Exam (SMMSE; Molloy, Alemayehu, & Roberts, 1991) was administered to screen for cognitive deficits and to monitor for changes in cognitive function. Overall, the evaluated group was atypical in that they performed very well on the test (mean score 27/30) and remained stable over the period of the project. In contrast, almost one fourth of the drop-outs had a change in mental health, with almost all (10/11) falling to a score of 21 or less on the SMMSE. It seems that a minimal level of cognitive function, corresponding to a score of about 23/30 on the SMMSE, is sufficient to ensure meaningful participation by the resident in an audiologic rehabilitation program in which complex new skills and self-initiated behaviors must be learned. The present formal methods of program evaluation could not, however, be used to evaluate the benefit that might be realized from an appropriately structured program by those with lower levels of cognitive function (for a discussion, see Shultz & Mowry, 1995).

At the outset of the study, the mean age of the 30 residents who completed the evaluation was 85 years (range 68 to 94 years). Not surprisingly, the majority of the evaluated group (26 of 30) were women. The length of their residency in the facility ranged from 0 to 26 years, with over half having lived there at least 6 years at the start of the project. The fact that many had lived in the facility for a number of years is consistent with the impression that there was a well-established community of residents who knew each other well. According to Lubinski (1984), the prerequisites for successful communication by older adults are that the elderly person must have both the skills and motivation to communicate and that the external environment must be conducive to communication. A prevailing sense of community at the facility, which fostered and was fostered by communication, suggested these prerequisites were satisfied.

Preprogram audiometric tests were conducted to determine the hearing status of each resident in the evaluated group. Even when there was no background noise, word discrimination scores were only fair (below 80%) for about two thirds of the group (mean = 74%). Using the rule of thumb that a person with a pure-tone threshold hearing loss of at least 40 dBHL at 2000 Hz is likely to benefit from wearing a hearing aid, about half of the evaluated group were considered hearing aid candidates. The other half of the group had hearing loss above 2000 Hz but had relatively good hearing at lower frequencies. In fact, about half (16) of the evaluated group owned hearing aids at the outset of the project. Of those who had hearing aids, 15 used their hearing aid(s) at least some of the time, with most wearing them all day long, every day. Note that the evaluated group is not typical insofar as their rate and regularity of preprogram hearing aid use is much higher than that reported in previous studies, where use of amplification by the overall population of seniors living in nursing homes or retirement centers was found to be as low as 4 to 10% (Schow, 1982; Thibodeau & Schmitt, 1988), and where just over half of those with hearing aids wore them daily (Parving & Phillip, 1991).

Prior to the beginning of the project, some public telephones in the Villa were equipped with handset volume controls, and four members of the evaluated group reported using them. No other public ALDs were available (for a review of ALDs, see Pichora-Fuller, 1997a). Nine residents in the evaluated group used handset volume controls on private telephones. The only other ALDs in use prior to the program were jack-in earphones for television use that were owned, but seldom used, by two of the residents, and a one-to-one communicator that was owned, but tried only once, by one resident.

Staff Participants. The hearing rehabilitation program targeted all staff members. A subset of them participated in the formal program evaluation. At the time of each evaluation, the residents who participated in the evaluation identified the staff members who were their most regular communication partners, and these staff participated in the evaluation with the consent of their employer. The staff participants represented a cross-section of the staff from the nursing, dietary, recreation, housekeeping, and administration departments. Nearly 100 workers were evaluated at the first evaluation. With the reduction in the number of residents evaluated, there was a corresponding drop by the end of the project in the number of communication partners evaluated. Results are described only for the staff communication partners (n = 30) who participated throughout the duration of the project.

Outcome Measures

A set of outcome measures was devised to determine the impact of intervention on the scope and quality of communication in everyday activities, and to measure the knowledge and skills acquired by the residents and staff that presumably accounted for changes in their communication experiences. The measures included a questionnaire about communication in locally relevant hearing situations; a test of skill in use of hearing aids and ALDs; and the Scenarios test, which was designed to assess skill in the identification of problem sources and solutions for scenarios depicting communication difficulty.

Questionnaire About Listening Situations. Because existing questionnaires about hearing were too general for these purposes, a questionnaire was developed that was specific to situations where hearing was considered to be functionally important at the facility (Pichora-Fuller & Robertson, 1994, 1997). In a pilot study, two meetings were held, each with 15 participants: 5 residents with known hearing loss, 5 residents who were considered by staff to have good hearing, and 5 staff members. The participants were asked, "In everyday life at the Villa, when is it important for a resident to hear?" Four experts (two audiologists, a speech-language pathologist who works with older clients, and the nurse in charge of the clinic at the facility) reviewed the lists of situations generated by the participants. Ultimately, 33 situations were retained for the evaluations (see Table 3.1).

A questionnaire, developed to obtain self-report information from the residents about the scope and quality of hearing in these situations, consisted of nine basic questions: four on scope of communication, three on quality of communication, and two on use of and benefit from prostheses. The evaluation audiologist asked the questions and noted the responses during an interview held at a time and place that was convenient to the resident and when the resident was feeling well. All nine questions were asked with respect to 17 of the 33 situations (primary situations). For the

TABLE 3.1
Situations Where Hearing Was Considered to Be Important

Primary Situations	Supplementary Situations
Talking to a familiar person	Talking to strangers
Talking to a hard-of-hearing person	Talking in the lobby
Dining in the dining hall	Talking to staff during daily activities
Dining on the ward	Talking to nurses about pills
On the telephone	Informal/small group discussions
At the chapel	Listening to live music
At meetings	Dinners in the Villacourt Lounge
During the exercise program	Playing card games
Attending therapy	Playing bingo
At teas in the solarium	Bowling
At teas in the auditorium	At the beauty parlor
At tea in the tuck shop	During outings
At movies	Listening to public address system messages
Watching television	During fire drills
Listening to radio talk shows	Identifying someone by voice
Listening to taped music	Knowing that someone is approaching
Listening to taped books	

other 16 situations (supplementary situations), only two questions about scope of communication were asked.

Skill and Knowledge Regarding Devices. Skill with, and handling of, prostheses were measured using a hands-on test of skill in operating and caring for hearing aids and ALDs (Pichora-Fuller & Robertson, 1997). Residents were evaluated in each of the four evaluation periods on their own hearing aids and familiar ALDs. Their staff communication partners were evaluated during the first and final evaluation periods on devices that were used by the residents with whom they regularly communicated.

Scenarios Test. In developing the Scenarios test (adapted from Koury and Lubinski's, 1991, test of behavioral intent), we set out to measure how residents and staff perceived communication problems and the kinds of solutions that might be implemented in situations that depicted a range of messages, speakers, listeners, and environments typical of their everyday experiences (Robertson, Pichora-Fuller, Jennings, Kirson, & Roodenburg, 1997). We recognized that the interaction of individuals within a given situation might create a unique set of circumstances with associated problems and viewpoints. We were interested in developing measures that would capture changes that were important within the ecology at the facility. The 50 possible scenarios depicted in the test were constructed based on observations of life at the facility during the initial 2-month period of the project. The following are examples of the scenarios that were generated: "A group of residents are playing cards. One resident loses interest in playing because it is hard to catch what is going on"; "A resident is lying in bed feeling rather washed out with pain from arthritis and calls to ask the nurse for a Tylenol. The nurse must explain that it is not yet time for the resident's medication, but the resident has trouble understanding."

At each evaluation, the participant was asked by the evaluation audiologist to respond to six different scenarios by identifying possible sources of communication problems and then possible solutions. The six were selected randomly without replacement for each participant so that by the end of the fourth evaluation, each resident had been asked about a total of 24 different scenarios. The participant was asked: "First, name all the things you can think of that might make it hard for the resident to understand what is being said. Next, name all the things that could be done to help overcome the problem understanding what was said." The evaluation audiologist read each scenario aloud and then gave the participant a typed description of the scenario that could be read or referred to at any time. The participant was given time to respond without any prompting. When the participant stopped responding, the evaluation audiologist asked, "Can you think of anything else? Anything you can think of about the resident? Anything you can think of about someone else? Anything about the situation?"

Each response was immediately categorized as either a problem or a solution. During analysis, the problems and solutions were categorized into one of four mutually exclusive categories according to the primary component of communication that was the source of the problem: the speaker, the listener, the environment, or the message. For the solutions, the agent responsible for implementing the solution was also categorized into one of five categories: the speaker, the listener, a third party, a cooperative combination of speaker and listener, or an ambiguously stated agent. This two-way categorization of the solutions into problem source and agent was necessary because a problem arising from any given source could be solved by various possible agents; for example, the unclear speech of a speaker could be solved if the listener used a repair strategy directing the speaker to speak more clearly; background noise in the environment could be solved by either the listener, the speaker, the listener and the speaker together, or a third party taking action. The number of problems and solutions in each category was counted and the counts obtained by the residents and staff at the first and final evaluations were compared.

Results

The program had significant positive effects on the scope and the quality of the residents' participation in activities (Pichora-Fuller & Robertson, 1994). There was a significant increase in the number of activities attended by residents. There were also significant increases in the amount of time (hours/month) spent talking to familiar people, attending chapel, and participating in meetings. Residents reported significant increases in how much they understood in the chapel, when talking to a hard-of-hearing person, and on the telephone. Their satisfaction with communication on the telephone also increased significantly. In general, residents reported a high level of satisfaction with their ability to participate in situations that could be considered optional (e.g., attending meetings), although they tended to report lower levels of satisfaction for challenging communication situations that could be considered obligatory (e.g., the dining hall or chapel). We suggest that residents persisted in participating in activities that took place in difficult listening situations if they considered participation to be obligatory, whereas they participated in optional activities only if they could achieve satisfactory communication during the activity and they avoided optional activities that were communicatively too challenging or unsatisfying. Changes in degree of understanding or satisfaction with communication could be measured for activities in which the residents sustained participation, but the renewal of participation in previously abandoned activities was perhaps an even more important indicator of the effect of the program on the residents.

The positive effects of the program on scope and quality of participation in activities seem to be attributable to both the technical and behavioral aspects of the program. There was a dramatic increase in the familiarity of residents and staff with ALDs (Pichora-Fuller & Robertson, 1997). There was also significant improvement in the skills of both residents and staff in operating hearing aids and ALDs. In particular, the use of an FM system in the chapel and at meetings likely accounted for residents' reports of improvements in communication in those situations. Following no change during the preprogram period, a positive change was observed after the program began on the following measures: resident skill in operating in-the-ear hearing aids; hearing aid operation by staff; and resident and staff skill and knowledge of various ALDs that could be used for different communication needs such as telephone and television listening, listening in large rooms such as the chapel, or for one-to-one communication. Resident operation of the more difficult to handle behind-the-ear hearing aids showed a rebound in performance with a positive change observed following implementation of the program that offset the decline in performance observed during the preprogram period (see also Upfold, May, & Battaglia, 1990). Note that ability to handle hearing aids improved even though there was no significant increase in the number of residents using hearing aids as most of the residents in the evaluated group who were hearing-aid candidates were already using them before the program began. Overall, there was enhanced use of devices that had previously been used by residents as well as the successful use of new devices.

Results on the Scenarios test suggest that changes in resident and staff communication behaviors also contributed to the increases in the residents' scope and quality of participation in activities. Comparing the results obtained on the test at the first and final evaluations for residents and staff, no increase was observed in either the total number of problems or solutions generated by the staff; however, there were increases in the total number of problems and solutions generated by the residents. There were also changes in the designation of the agent responsible for the suggested solutions. Importantly, compared to the preprogram results, the distribution of solutions by agent, generated by both residents and staff at the postprogram evaluation, suggests that the residents learned to assume greater control in dealing with everyday communication problems and that the staff recognized their ability to take greater control (Robertson et al., 1997).

In summary, an ecological approach to hearing rehabilitation was found to have a positive effect on residents' participation in communication-demanding activities. These effects were attributable to a combination of technical-environmental and behavioral interventions involving both residents and the staff who were their most frequent communication partners. These effects surpassed whatever benefits had already been realized through the provision of personal hearing aids. The ecological approach provides a supportive social and physical context that not only facilitates, but also predisposes and reinforces, enhanced participation in activities.

CONCLUSIONS

A new approach to communication between audiologists and persons living with hearing loss is required to increase the success of efforts to support the everyday communication experiences of older listeners and those who participate in activities with them. The new approach must foster a larger view of presbycusis within which it is possible to translate between the views held by audiologists and those held by hard-of-hearing people and their communication partners. The extant views of presbycusis held by audiologists are biased by their professional knowledge of impairment; the views held by hard-of-hearing adults and their communication partners are formed on the basis of their lived experiences. All too frequently, the professional and the person living with a hearing loss fail to communicate to advantage about their divergent views of the importance and feasibility of the goals and options for rehabilitation. In contrast to the traditional clinical approach, a participatory health promotion approach begins with a "conversation" between the audiologist and the individual(s) or communities for whom participation in activities is compromised by hearing difficulties (Crabtree & Miller, 1994). The purpose of this exchange is to determine the needs and aspirations of those for whom the rehabilitation program is being planned (Green & Kreuter, 1991).

Only after the views of the person or community have been determined does the health professional consider how these views may or may not map onto existing technical knowledge of health issues. The program that is ultimately implemented should incorporate the use of a combination of technologies, behaviors, and environmental modifications that can achieve the functional goals of the communicators who participate in the everyday activities of interest.

REFERENCES

Abrahamson, J. (1995). Effective and relevant programming. In P. B. Kricos & S. A. Lesner (Eds.), *Hearing care for the older adult: Audiologic rehabilitation* (pp. 75–112). Boston: Butterworth-Heinemann.

Baruch, G. K., Biener, L., & Barnett, C. R. (1987). Women and gender in research on work and family stress. *American Psychologist, 42,* 130–136.

Binnie, C. A. (1994). The future of audiological rehabilitation: Overview and forecast. *Journal of the Academy of Rehabilitative Audiology Monographs, 27,* 13–24.

Borg, E. (1998). Audiology in an ecological perspective—Development of a conceptual framework. *Scandinavian Audiology, 27*(Suppl. 49), 132–139.

Bredberg, G. (1968). Cellular pattern and nerve supply of the human organ of Corti. *Acta Otolaryngologica Supplement, 236,* 1–135.

Bregman, A. (1990). *Auditory scene analysis: The perceptual organization of sound.* Cambridge, MA: MIT Press.

Brink, R. H. S. van den, Wit, H. P., Kempen, G. I. J. M., & Heuvelen, M. J. G. van (1996). Attitude and help-seeking for hearing impairment. *British Journal of Audiology, 30,* 313–324.

Burgio, L. D., & Lewis, T. (1999). Functional analysis and intervention in geriatric settings. In A. Repp & R. Horner (Eds.), *Functional analysis of problem behavior: From effective assessment to effective support* (pp. 304–317). New York: Brooks/Cole.

Burgio, L. D., Scilley, K., Hardin, J. M., Hsu, C., & Yancey, J. (1996). Environmental "white noise": An intervention for verbally agitated nursing home residents. *Journal of Gerontology: Psychological Sciences, 51B,* 364–373.

Burgio, L. D., & Stevens, A. B. (1998). Behavioural interventions and motivational systems in the nursing home. *Annual Review of Gerontology and Geriatrics, 18,* 284–320.

Cariaga, J., Burgio, L. D., Flynn, W., & Martin, D. A. (1991). A controlled study of disruptive vocalizations among geriatric patients residing in nursing homes. *Journal of the American Geriatrics Society, 39,* 501–507.

Carson, A. J. (1997). Evaluation of the To Hear Again project. *Journal of Speech-Language Pathology and Audiology, 21,* 160–166.

Carson, A. J., & Pichora-Fuller, M. K. (1997). Health promotion and audiology: The community-clinic link. *Journal of the Academy of Rehabilitative Audiology, 30,* 29–51.

CHABA (Committee on Hearing, Bioacoustics, and Biomechanics). (1988). Speech understanding and aging. *Journal of the Acoustical Society of America, 83,* 859–895.

Chermak, G. D., & Musiek, F. E. (1997). *Central auditory processing disorders: New perspectives.* San Diego, CA: Singular.

Chmiel, R., & Jerger, J. (1996). Hearing aid use, central auditory disorder, and hearing handicap in elderly persons. *Journal of the American Academy of Audiology, 7,* 190–202.

Cooper, J. C., Jr., & Gates, G. A. (1991). Hearing in the elderly—The Framingham Cohort 1983-1985: Part II. Prevalence of central auditory processing disorders. *Ear and Hearing, 12*, 304–311.

Crabtree, W. L., & Miller, B. F. (1994). Clinical research. In N. K. Denzin & Y. S. Lincoln (Eds.), *Handbook of qualitative research* (pp. 340–360). Thousand Oaks, CA: Sage.

Dahl, M. O. (1997). To Hear Again: A volunteer program in hearing health care for hard-of-hearing seniors. *Journal of Speech-Language Pathology and Audiology, 21*, 153–159.

Erber, N. P. (1988). *Communication therapy for hearing-impaired adults.* Victoria, Australia: Clavis.

Erber, N. P., Lamb, N. L., & Lind, C. (1996). Factors that affect the use of hearing aids by older people: A new perspective. *American Journal of Audiology, 5*, 11–18.

Erdman, S. A. (1994). Self-assessment: From research focus to research tool. *Journal of the Academy of Rehabilitative Audiology Monographs, 27*, 67–90.

Erdman, S. A., & Demorest, M. E. (1998a). Adjustment to hearing impairment: I. Description of a heterogeneous clinical population. *Journal of Speech, Language, and Hearing Research, 41*, 107–122.

Erdman, S. A., & Demorest, M. E. (1998b). Adjustment to hearing impairment: II. Audiological and demographic correlates. *Journal of Speech, Language, and Hearing Research, 41*, 123–136.

Fitzgibbons, P. J., & Gordon-Salant, S. (1996). Auditory temporal processing in elderly listeners. *Journal of the American Academy of Audiology, 7*, 183–189.

Gabbard, S. A. (1994). AARP's report on hearing aids. *Audiology Today, 6*, 15.

Gagné, J.-P., Hétu, R., Getty, L., & McDuff, S. (1995). Towards the development of paradigms to conduct functional evaluative research in audiological rehabilitation. *Journal of the Academy of Rehabilitative Audiology, 28*, 7–25.

Garstecki, D. C., & Erler, S. F. (1995). Older women and hearing. *American Journal of Audiology, 4*, 41–46.

Garstecki, D. C., & Erler, S. F. (1998). Hearing loss, control, and demographic factors influencing hearing aid use among older adults. *Journal of Speech, Language, and Hearing Research, 41*, 527–537.

Getty, L., & Hétu, R. (1994). Is there a culture of hard-of-hearing workers? *Journal of Speech-Language Pathology and Audiology, 18*, 267–270.

Getty, L., Gagné, J.-P., & McDuff, S. (1996, June). *Growing old with a hearing loss: What will make you seek help?* Paper presented at the Academy of Rehabilitative Audiology, Summer Institute, Snowbird, UT.

Gilhome Herbst, K. R., Meredith, R., & Stephens, S. D. G. (1991). Implications of hearing impairment for elderly people in London and in Wales. *Acta Otolaryngologica, Supplement, 476*, 209–214.

Giolas, T. G. (1990). "Measurement of hearing handicap" revisited: A 20-year perspective. *Ear and Hearing, 11*(Suppl. 5), 2–5.

Gitlin, L. N. (1998). Testing home modification interventions: Issues of theory, measurement, design, and implementation. *Annual Review of Gerontology and Geriatrics, 18*, 190–246.

Goffman, E. (1963). *Stigma: Notes on the management of spoiled identity.* New York: Simon & Schuster.

Green, L. W., & Kreuter, M. W. (1991). *Health promotion planning: An educational and environmental approach* (2nd ed.). Mountain View, CA: Mayfield.

Grose, J. H. (1996). Binaural performance and aging. *Journal of the American Academy of Audiology, 7*, 168–174.

Haber, D. (1994). *Health promotion and aging.* New York: Springer.

Hallberg, L., & Carlsson, S. (1991). A qualitative study of strategies for managing hearing impairment. *British Journal of Audiology, 25*, 201–211.

Hétu, R., Jones, L., & Getty, L. (1993). The impact of acquired hearing impairment on intimate relationships: Implications for rehabilitation. *Audiology, 32*, 363–381.

Hodgson, M. R. (1994). How the acoustical environment may alter handicap. *Journal of Speech-Language Pathology and Audiology, 18*, 220–222.

Hoek, D., Paccioretti, D., Pichora-Fuller, M. K., McDonald, M. A., & Shyng, G. (1997). Community outreach to hard-of-hearing seniors. *Journal of Speech-Language Pathology and Audiology, 21*, 199–208.

Holmes, A. (1995). Hearing aids and the older adult. In P. B. Kricos & S. A. Lesner (Eds.), *Hearing care for the older adult: Audiologic rehabilitation* (pp. 59–74). Boston: Butterworth-Heinemann.

Humphrey, C., Gilhome Herbst, K., & Faruqi, S. (1981). Some characteristics of hearing-impaired elderly who do not present themselves for rehabilitation. *British Journal of Audiology, 15*, 25–30.

Hussian, R. A., & Davis, R. L. (1985). *Responsive care: Behavioral interventions with elderly persons.* Champaign, IL: Research Press.

ICIDH-2: *International classification of functioning and disability* (1999). [Beta-2 draft, full version]. Geneva, Switzerland: World Health Organization.

Jaworski, A. (1993). *The power of silence: Social and pragmatic perspectives.* Newbury Park, CA: Sage.

Jaworski, A. (1998). Talk and silence in *The Interrogation. Language and Literature, 7*, 99–122.

Jaworski, A., & Stephens, D. (1998). Self-reports on silence as a face-saving strategy by people with hearing impairment. *International Journal of Applied Linguistics, 8*, 61–80.

Jennings, M. B., & Head, B. (1994). Development of an ecological audiologic rehabilitation program in a home-for-the-aged. *Journal of the Academy of Rehabilitative Audiology, 27*, 73–88.

Jennings, M. B., & Head, B. (1997). Resident and staff education within an ecological audiologic rehabilitation program in a home for the aged. *Journal of Speech-Language Pathology and Audiology, 21*, 167–173.

Kricos, P. B. (1995). Characteristics of the aged population. In P. B. Kricos & S. A. Lesner (Eds.), *Hearing care for the older adult: Audiologic rehabilitation* (pp. 1–20). Boston: Butterworth-Heinemann.

Koury, L. N., & Lubinski, R. (1991). Effective in-service training for staff working with communication-impaired patients. In R. Lubinski (Ed.), *Dementia and communication* (pp. 279–289). Hamilton, Ontario: B. C. Decker.

Kyle, J. G., Jones, L. G., & Wood, P. L. (1985). Adjustment to acquired hearing loss: A working model. In H. Orlans (Ed.), *Adjustment to adult hearing loss* (pp. 119–138). San Diego, CA: College-Hill Press.

Lesner, S. A., & Kricos, P. B. (1995). Audiologic rehabilitation assessment: A holistic approach. In P. B. Kricos & S. A. Lesner (Eds.), *Hearing care for the older adult: Audiologic rehabilitation* (pp. 21–58). Boston: Butterworth-Heinemann.

Levitt, H. (1993). Digital hearing aids. In G. A. Studebaker & I. Hochberg (Eds.), *Acoustical factors affecting hearing aid performance* (2nd ed., pp. 317–335). Boston: Allyn & Bacon.

Lubinski, R. (1984). The environmental role in communication skills and opportunities of older people. In C. Wilder & B. Weinstein (Eds.), *Aging and communication: Problems in management* (pp. 47–57). New York: Haworth.

Lutman, M. E. (1991). Hearing disability in the elderly. *Acta Otolaryngologica, Supplement 476*, 239–248.

Marsiske, M., Klumb, P., & Baltes, M. M. (1997). Everyday activity patterns and sensory functioning in old age. *Psychology and Aging, 12*, 444–457.

McKellin, W. (1994). Hearing and listening: Audiology, hearing and hearing impairment in everyday life. *Journal of Speech-Language Pathology and Audiology, 18*, 212–219.

Molloy, D. W., Alemayehu, E., & Roberts, R. (1991). A Standardized Mini-Mental State Examination (SMMSE): Its reliability compared to the traditional Mini-Mental State Examination (MMSE). *The American Journal of Psychiatry, 148*, 102–105.

Mulrow, C. D., Aguilar, C., Endicott, J. E., Tuley, M. R., Velez, R., Charlip, W. S., Rhodes, M. C., Hill, J. A., & DeNino, L. A. (1990). Quality-of-life changes and hearing impairment. *Annals of Internal Medicine, 113*, 188–194.

Nespoulous, J.-L. (1996). Commentary on "The analysis of conversational skills of older adults: A review of approaches" by Garcia & Orange. *Journal of Speech-Language Pathology and Audiology, 20*, 136–137.

Noble, W. (1983). Hearing, hearing impairment, and the audible world: A theoretical essay. *Audiology, 22*, 325–338.

Palmer, C. V., Adams, S. W., Bourgeois, M., Durrant, J., & Rossi, M. (1999). Reduction in caregiver-identified problem behaviors in patients with Alzheimer Disease post-hearing-aid fitting. *Journal of Speech, Language, and Hearing Research, 42*, 312–328.

Parving, A., & Phillip, B. (1991). Use and benefit of hearing aids in the tenth decade—and beyond. *Audiology, 30*, 61–69.

Peters, C., Potter, J., & Scholer, S. (1988). Hearing impairment as a predictor of cognitive decline in dementia. *Journal of the American Geriatrics Society, 36*, 981–986.

Phillips, D. P. (1995). Central auditory processing: A view from auditory neuroscience. *The American Journal of Otology, 16*, 338–352.

Pichora-Fuller, M. K. (1994). Introduction to Psycho-social impact of hearing loss in everyday life: An anthropological view [Special issue]. *Journal of Speech-Language Pathology and Audiology, 18*, 209–211.

Pichora-Fuller, M. K. (1997a). Assistive listening devices for the elderly. In R. Lubinski & D. J. Higginbotham (Eds.), *Communication technologies for the elderly: Vision, hearing, and speech* (pp. 161–202). San Diego, CA: Singular.

Pichora-Fuller, M. K. (1997b). Language comprehension in older listeners. *Journal of Speech Language Pathology and Audiology, 21*, 125–142.

Pichora-Fuller, M. K. (1999). Acoustic ecology: Concept and case study. *Canadian Acoustics, 27(3)*, 120.

Pichora-Fuller, M. K., Johnson, C. E., & Roodenburg, K. E. J. (1998). The discrepancy between hearing impairment and handicap: Balancing transaction and interaction in conversation [Special issue on intergenerational and aging issues]. *Journal of Applied Communication Research, 26*, 99–119.

Pichora-Fuller, M. K., & Robertson, L. F. (1994). Hard of hearing residents in a home for the aged. *Journal of Speech-Language Pathology and Audiology, 18*, 278–288.

Pichora-Fuller, M. K., & Robertson, L. (1997). Planning and evaluation of a hearing rehabilitation program in a home-for-the-aged: Use of hearing aids and assistive listening devices. *Journal of Speech Language Pathology and Audiology, 21*, 174–186.

Plomp, R. (1978). Auditory handicap of hearing impairment and the limited benefit of hearing aids. *Journal of the Acoustical Society of America, 63*, 533–549.

Ramsdell, D. (1960). The psychology of the hard of hearing and deafened adult. In H. Davis & S. Silverman (Eds.), *Hearing and deafness* (pp. 435–446). New York: Holt, Rinehart, & Winston.

Regional Municipality of Hamilton-Wentworth and Hamilton-Wentworth District Health Council. (1988). *Services of Seniors study—Mapping the way to the future for the elderly: Report of findings and recommendations.*

Robertson, L., Pichora-Fuller, M. K., Jennings, M. B., Kirson, R., & Roodenburg, K. (1997). The effect of an aural rehabilitation program on responses to scenarios depicting communication breakdown. *Journal of Speech-Language Pathology and Audiology, 21,* 187–198.

Ross, M. (1997). A retrospective look at the future of aural rehabilitation. *Journal of the Academy of Rehabilitative Audiology, 30,* 11–28.

Rousey, C. (1976). Psychological reactions to hearing loss. *Journal of Speech and Hearing Disorders, 36,* 382–389.

Ryan, E. B., Giles, H., Bartolucci, G., & Henwood, K. (1986). Psycholinguistic and social psychological components of communication by and with the elderly. *Language and Communication, 6,* 1–24.

Schafer, R. M. (1993). *Voices of tyranny—Temples of silence.* Indian River, Ontario: Arcana Editions.

Schafer, R. M. (1994). *The soundscape: Our sonic environment and the tuning of the world.* Rochester, VT: Destiny Books.

Schneider, B. A. (1997). Psychoacoustics and aging: Implications for everyday listening. *Journal of Speech-Language Pathology and Audiology, 21,* 111–124.

Schneider, B. A., & Pichora-Fuller, M. K. (2000). Implications of perceptual deterioration for cognitive aging research. In F. I. M. Craik & T. A. Salthouse (Eds.), *The handbook of cognitive aging* (2nd ed., pp. 155–219). Mahwah, NJ: Lawrence Erlbaum Associates.

Schow, R. L. (1982). Success of hearing aid fittings in nursing homes. *Ear and Hearing, 3,* 173–177.

Schow, R. L., & Gatehouse, S. (1990). Fundamental issues in self-assessment of hearing. *Ear and Hearing, 11*(Suppl. 5), 6–17.

Schow, R. L., & Nerbonne, M. A. (1980). Hearing levels among elderly nursing home residents. *Journal of Speech and Hearing Disorders, 45,* 124–132.

Schultz, R., & Martire, L. M. (1998). Intervention research with older adults: Introduction, overview and future directions. *Annual Review of Gerontology and Geriatrics, 18,* 1–16.

Shultz, D., & Mowry, R. B. (1995). Older adults in long-term care facilities. In P. B. Kricos & S. A. Lesner (Eds.), *Hearing care for older adults: Audiologic rehabilitation* (pp. 167–184). Boston: Butterworth-Heinemann.

Smedley, T. C., & Schow, R. (1994). Frustrations with hearing aid use: Candid observations from the elderly. *Hearing Instruments, 43,* 21–27.

Stach, B., Spretnjak, M. L., & Jerger, J. (1990). The prevalence of central presbycusis in a clinical population. *Journal of the American Academy of Audiology, 1,* 109–115.

Stephens, S. D. G., & Hétu, R. (1991). Impairment, disability and handicap in audiology: Towards a consensus. *Audiology, 30,* 185–200.

Suter, W. N., & Lindgren, H. C. (1989). *Experimentation in psychology.* Boston: Allyn and Bacon.

Swan, I. R. C., & Gatehouse, S. (1990). Factors influencing consultation for management of hearing disability. *British Journal of Audiology, 24,* 155–160.

Thibodeau, L. M., & Schmitt, L. (1988). A report on the condition of hearing aids in nursing homes and retirement centers. *Journal of the American Academy of Rehabilitative Audiology, 21,* 113–119.

Thomas, A. J., & Gilhome Herbst, K. R. (1980). Social and psychological implications of acquired hearing loss for adults of employment age. *British Journal of Audiology, 14,* 76–85.

Truax, B. (Ed.). (1978). *Handbook for acoustic ecology.* Vancouver, British Columbia: A.R.C. Publications.

Truax, B. (1984). *Acoustic communication.* Norwood, NJ: Ablex.

Uhlmann, R., Larson, E., & Koepsell, T. (1986). Hearing impairment and cognitive decline in senile dementia of the Alzheimer's type. *Journal of the American Geriatrics Society, 34,* 207–210.

Uhlmann, R. F., Larson, E. B., Rees, T. S., Koepsell, T. D., & Duckert, L. G. (1989). Relationship of hearing impairment to dementia and cognitive dysfunction in older adults. *Journal of the American Medical Association, 261,* 1916–1919.

Upfold, L. J., May, A. E., & Battaglia, J. A. (1990). Hearing aid manipulation skills in an elderly population: A comparison of ITE, BTE, and ITC aids. *British Journal of Audiology, 24,* 311–318.

Villaume, W. A., Brown, M. H., & Darling, R. (1994). Presbycusis, communication, and older adults. In M. L. Hummert, J. M. Weiman, & J. F. Nussbaum (Eds.), *Interpersonal communication in older adulthood* (pp. 83–106). Thousand Oaks, CA: Sage.

Watson, C., & Crowther, J. A. (1989). Provision of hearing aids: Does specialist assessment cause delay? *British Medical Journal, 299,* 437–439.

Willott, J. F. (1991). *Aging and the auditory system: Anatomy, physiology, and psychophysics.* San Diego, CA: Singular.

Willott, J. F. (1996). Anatomic and physiologic aging: A behavioral neuroscience perspective. *Journal of the American Academy of Audiology, 7,* 141–151.

World Health Organization (WHO). (1980). *International classifications of impairments, disabilities, and handicaps: A manual of classification relating to the consequences of disease.* Geneva, Switzerland: Author.

World Health Organization (WHO). (1986). *Ottawa Charter for Health Promotion.* Copenhagen: Author.

World Health Organization (WHO). (1998). *Towards a common language for functioning and disablement: ICIHD–2—The international classification of impairments, activities, and participation.* Geneva, Switzerland: Author.

4

Using Support Groups
to Improve Caregiver Health

Teri A. Garstka
University of Kansas

Philip McCallion
State University of New York at Albany

Ronald W. Toseland
State University of New York at Albany

The aging of the U.S. population and the high health care costs associated with chronic health conditions has spurred clinical, program development, and policy interest in ways that effectively and efficiently support informal caregivers of older persons in poor health. Family and friends provide most of the informal support elderly persons receive (National Alliance for Caregiving and the American Association of Retired Persons, 1997), and their help enables frail older adults to continue to live in community settings (Smith, Tobin, Robertson-Tchabo, & Power, 1995). There is evidence that the risk of institutionalization is reduced for older adults who have a reliable source of support and care, such as a spouse or adult child caregiver (Beisecker, Wright, Chrisman, & Ashworth, 1996; Lee & Tussing, 1998; Mittelman, Ferris, Shulman, Steinberg, & Levin, 1996; Pearlman & Crown, 1992).

The goal of most caregiving intervention research is to emphasize the positive aspects of caregiving while reducing its negative aspects. A recent review and synthesis of the caregiving literature by Kramer (1997) suggested that positive aspects of caregiving play an important role in understanding and predicting mental and physical health outcomes. However, there is also research evidence that caregiving can result in physical problems (e.g., sleeplessness, fatigue, back problems, and other somatic complaints), psychological problems (e.g., depression, anxiety, worry, guilt, and uncertainty), and social problems (e.g., isolation, work conflicts, fewer pleasurable social activities, and family strife) (Toseland & Rossiter, 1989; Toseland, Smith, & McCallion, in press). When caregivers experience these problems, the quality of the care they provide may be diminished. Thus, there is an increasing interest in assisting caregivers to locate the resources and services they need and in helping them to use positive approaches and strategies to increase their resilience to the strains imposed by caregiving.

Support group programs provide one way to reduce the stress of caregiving and to improve the psychosocial well-being of caregivers. The association between caregiver health and social support has encouraged further consideration of the potential for support groups to have a positive impact on caregiving. Indeed, a recent review by Given and Given (1998) stressed the need to examine this relationship more closely. Although there are other types of effective interventions with caregivers, such as behaviorally based interventions (Gallagher-Thompson, 1994a) or individual counseling (Toseland, Rossiter, Peak, & Hill, 1990; Toseland & Smith, 1990), this chapter focuses on support groups, reviews the health concerns of family caregivers, and describes how mutual support and psychoeducational support groups may promote healthy aging.

Despite the positive impact support groups may have, it is also known that many caregivers do not participate in such groups (Krizek, Roberts, Ragan, Ferrara, & Lord, 1999). Some groups also have trouble maintaining attendance and commitment by their members (Atkinson & Fischer, 1996; Martichuski, Knight, Karlin, & Bell, 1997; Stevens & Duttlinger, 1998). In addition, the support group experience may not be positive for all members (Galinsky & Schopler, 1994). Therefore, this chapter also describes the roles that professionals can play in referring caregivers to groups, supporting their attendance, facilitating a positive experience in the group, and ensuring that groups are available when and where they are needed.

CAREGIVER HEALTH

The health of the caregiver is an important component of the caregiving equation. Because the relationship between caregiver and care recipient is often interdependent, the caregiving process can influence the health of both parties (see Edwards, chap. 9, this volume, for a discussion of the care recipient). For example, those who provide care may find themselves without the information or resources needed to manage the needs of the care recipient. This, in turn, places strain on caregivers and adversely affects their health. Gallant and Connell (1998) modeled the relationship between the demands of caregiving for a spouse with dementia and the health behaviors of the caregiver. The results indicated that caregiving negatively influenced health-related behaviors such as exercise, sleep, weight maintenance, smoking, and alcohol consumption. Specifically, objective burden and depressive symptoms attributable to caregiving had a negative impact on behavioral health practices.

Caregivers' appraisal of their situation has been linked to other negative health outcomes. For example, Schulz et al. (1997) found that older adults who reported being under the greatest mental and physical strain as a result of caring for a spouse also reported the largest negative health outcomes in areas such as cardiovascular health. The way that caregivers appraise the health of the care recipient can affect the extent of their health care service use and how well they are able to manage the responsibilities of caregiving. Two reviews of the literature concluded that greater levels of care recipient disability may be associated with poor outcomes for both parties (McCallion, Toseland, & Diehl, 1994; Toseland, Smith, & McCallion, 1995).

Although it is clear that caregiving for an older adult by any family member involves negotiating the psychological and physical demands of the role, the nature and level of the strain experienced is affected by the caregiver–care recipient relationship. Spouses make up the single largest group of caregivers (Biegel, Sales, & Schulz, 1991; McCallion, Toseland, et al., 1994; Toseland & Rossiter, 1992) and have higher reported levels of depression than nonspouse caregivers (Schulz, Tompkins, & Rau, 1988). In addition to managing the care of their spouses' health, spouse caregivers may have to take over the responsibility of paying bills, home maintenance, and other tasks previously done by their frail spouses. In contrast, adult children do the majority of caregiving for widowed older adults (Cantor, 1994). The stresses experienced by these younger caregivers are different from those of spouse caregivers and generally involve juggling the responsibilities of caring for their own families with the responsibility of caring for an older parent.

To summarize, caregiver health may be negatively affected by caring for a frail elderly family member or spouse. However, these negative effects may be moderated by such variables as perceptions of the stress and strain of caregiving, how ill the care recipient is perceived to be, and the relationship between caregiver and care recipient. For instance, Alzheimer's family caregivers who reported more benign appraisals of stressors, used approach coping, and had greater levels of social support, were also more likely to report better mental and physical health outcomes over time than did those with more negative appraisals (Goode, Haley, Roth, & Ford, 1998). Support group interventions can help caregivers to change their appraisals of the situation, improve or enhance social support experiences, and increase the types of coping responses caregivers can use in a stressful situation (Peak, Toseland, & Banks, 1995).

SOCIAL SUPPORT AND CAREGIVING

Social support can have a positive impact on both health and the ability to cope with chronic illness (Rapp, Shumaker, Schmidt, Naughton, & Anderson, 1998). There are many forms of social support. Two broad categories are instrumental support and emotional support. Instrumental support includes task-oriented help with day-to-day needs such as housework, shopping, or transportation. Emotional support can take the form of listening, offering advice, or providing insight and assistance during times of stress or illness. Because caregivers and care recipients often report a lack of social support (Biegel, Sales, & Schulz, 1991), the type and amount of support that is given and received may influence how well caregivers cope with their situations.

Rapp et al. (1998) found that the way that caregivers established and maintained supportive relationships was significantly associated with measures of well-being. In particular, older adults who were caring for an individual with dementia reported better perceived health, less depression, more perceived benefits of caregiving, and a better quality of life when they had the ability to create and be a part of helpful social relationships. Social support is also related to a reduced risk of developing impairments in activities of daily living and related disabilities (Mendes de Leon et al., 1999). This suggests that older adult caregivers with a healthy social network may be better able to care for themselves and their loved ones.

Conversely, having inadequate social support can have a negative impact on caregiving. Inadequate social support, often in association with psychological distress or disability, has been found to be related to increased use of health care services (Kouzis & Eaton, 1998; Melamed & Brenner, 1990), institutionalization risk (Hyduk, 1996), health deterioration (Choi & Wodarski, 1996), decreased adherence to medical recommendations (Christensen et al., 1992; Sherbourne, Hays, Ordway, DiMatteo, & Kravitz, 1992), negative changes in immune function (Kiecolt-Glaser, Dura, Speicher, Trast, & Glaser, 1991), maladaptive coping responses (Manne & Zautra, 1989), and mortality (Blazer, 1982; Dalgard & Lund-Haheim, 1998; Fuhrer et al., 1999). Thus, it is clear that adequate social support is important for maintaining the health of caregivers and care recipients, and for decreasing their use of health care services.

SUPPORT GROUPS FOR CAREGIVERS

Caregivers are a diverse group of individuals with a broad range of social support needs, which can be met by a variety of groups. Recreational groups, for example, provide informal social outlets for individuals, but they do not directly address the caregiving process. For some caregivers, socializing with peers and the distraction of doing something unrelated to caregiving is beneficial. Others, however, need a group that more directly addresses their needs as caregivers (McCallion & Toseland, 1995). Mutual support groups and psychoeducational groups are two widely used forms of support groups that focus specifically on caregiving (McCallion & Toseland, 1995).

Mutual Support Groups

Mutual support groups are different from other support groups in at least three ways: (a) Support groups are often led by lay persons with caregiving experience rather than by professionals, (b) the groups are often long-term, and (c) members can attend on a flexible basis depending on their needs and the caregiving situation. To a certain extent, the level of formality of a group determines the tone and content of the discussion. As described by Toseland (1995) and McCallion and Toseland (1995), mutual support groups may be structured very informally. Caregivers in a mutual support group provide each other with understanding, empathy, information, and mutual aid. In these groups, psychological closeness results from members sharing experiences that may not be understood by noncaregivers. Through interaction, a group norm of empathetic listening, advice giving and receiving, sharing of effective coping strategies, and encouraging hope is established. In addition, the social contacts made through this type of group can help overcome the isolation of caregiving.

One beneficial psychological process that can occur within mutual support groups is social comparison. In his social comparison theory, Festinger (1954) proposed that humans have a drive to evaluate their abilities and life situations in relation to those of others. Support groups of elderly caregivers provide a context for these social comparisons and self-evaluations. Downward social comparisons are one component of this self-evaluative process (Wills, 1981), and are used in the coping process for the purpose of self-enhancement (Michinov & Monteil, 1997). These are comparisons in which people evaluate their caregiving circumstances in relation to others whose caregiving situations may be seen as worse.

Downward comparisons have been found to increase subjective well-being (Tobin, 1999; VanderZee et al.,1996). For example, a study of cancer patients revealed that when they compared themselves to a less fortunate person, 93% reported feeling that they were coping better and 96% felt they were in better health than other cancer patients (Taylor, Falke, Shoptaw, & Lichtman, 1986). Similarly, Tobin (1999) noted that the oldest-old use downward social comparisons to preserve their sense of well-being and their self-image of coping well with old age. Other types of social comparisons, such as comparing the self with those who are viewed as similar, may also be beneficial for caregivers (Pillemer & Suitor, 1996). For instance, cancer patients reported using good copers and long-term survivors as models for their own coping efforts and feeling inspired, optimistic, and hopeful as a result of such comparisons (Taylor, Aspinwall, Guiliano, & Dakof, 1993).

Caregivers within a mutual support group may use social comparisons. For example, a caregiver whose spouse has a mild case of heart disease may compare her situation with that of a group member who is caring for a spouse with cancer. As a result of this downward social comparison, she may feel relatively fortunate about her present situation. The amount of information shared about the caregiving process among members provides ample opportunity for such comparisons. Indeed, the group is structured to enable caregivers to compare and contrast their caregiving experiences. The benefits of such comparisons (e.g., feelings of relative good fortune, relief, inspiration, optimism) are a spontaneous part of the mutual support group experience and may influence the experience of members of the group. Thus, a mutual support group provides a flexibly structured group where members can exchange information and support as well as engage in comparison processes.

Mutual support groups are best suited to caregivers who are looking primarily for an outlet to vent their feelings and share their experiences. The flexibility and closeness of mutual support groups are key elements that appeal to caregivers. Also, mutual support groups are inexpensive to organize and conduct, and they can be facilitated by lay persons with experience in caregiving.

Psychoeducational Groups

With a more structured agenda than mutual support groups, the goal of psychoeducational groups is to provide caregivers with effective strategies for coping with stressful caregiving situations. These stressors may be related to the caregiving situation itself, but are often exacerbated by long-standing problems such as poor communication, family conflict, relationship difficulties, and financial hardship. The components of a psychoeducational group are generally focused on understanding the care recipient's experience: encouraging better use of informal and formal supports, improving the coping abilities of the caregiver, supporting positive attention to a caregiver's own health needs, fostering interactions and improving relationships within the family, and teaching home care and behavior management skills (McCallion, Toseland, & Diehl, 1994). Despite the similarities between caregivers in a psychoeducational group, their problems are often unique and individualized. Therefore, psychoeducational group meetings focus on the concerns of individual members who take turns presenting their problems and receiving feedback from one another.

In comparison to mutual support groups, psychoeducational groups are more likely to focus on specific goals and to use structured, short-term approaches with a well-defined agenda for each meeting. A psychoeducational group for caregivers of chronically ill spouses typically includes four primary components: education, emotion-focused coping strategies, problem-focused coping strategies, and support (Toseland, McCallion, Smith, & Bourgeois, in press). Interventions using these components have been successful with caregivers whose family members are experiencing a variety of chronic illnesses (see Labrecque, Peak, & Toseland, 1992; Toseland, 1990; Toseland, Rossiter, & Labrecque, 1989a, 1989b; Toseland, Rossiter, Peak, & Smith, 1990; Toseland, Labrecque, Goebel, & Whitney, 1992; Toseland et al., 1995). The content and approach of these components is considered next. It should be noted, however, that psychoeducational groups may incorporate additional components. Also, depending on the needs of participants, some groups may focus more on one component than another.

Educational Component.   Although mutual support groups may touch on educational health information, psychoeducational groups are more likely to impart this type of information as a formal part of the curriculum of the group. Group meetings may include a planned schedule of educational presentations to address issues participants have identified, questions and discussions, written take-home materials, and contact numbers and addresses for additional information. The educational components of psychoeducational groups can provide beneficial information about the processes of aging and health, caregivng methods, coping strategies, disease-specific information, and other content needed by caregivers. A recent review of the efficacy of interventions with families of stroke survivors, for example, found that providing information about strokes and their sequella helped reduce caregiver health problems (Korner-Bitensky, Tarasuk, Nelles, & Bouchard, 1998).

Emotion-Focused Coping Component. The emotion-focused coping component can comprise several strategies such as didactic teaching, relaxation techniques, cognitive restructuring, self-monitoring, and self-instruction. Stress Inoculation Training (SIT) developed by Meichenbaum and his colleagues (Meichenbaum, 1977, 1985; Meichenbaum & Cameron, 1983) has been used successfully in caregiver intervention programs (Barusch & Spaid, 1991; Labrecque et al., 1992; Toseland et al., 1989b; Zarit, Anthony, & Boutselis, 1987). This type of approach has also been used with individuals who are experiencing chronic health problems (Benjamin, 1989; Blanchard, 1993; Sorbi & Tellegen, 1988).

The goal of this component is to give caregivers strategies that facilitate understanding of their emotional responses to a caregiving stressor as well as to provide strategies for effective emotional regulation. As a part of the emotion-focused component, relaxation techniques may be taught. For example, Toseland et al. (1992) included a deep breathing technique in their group intervention. Members moderated their reactions to stress by consciously interrupting their usual response by using the deep breathing procedure to help slow down their cognitive processes and to use a more planned and effective coping reaction. By encouraging emotional tranquility, relaxation techniques also helped group members to more effectively manage their stress responses.

Problem-Focused Coping Component. The problem-focused coping component consists of various cognitive restructuring strategies that are used to facilitate more effective appraisals of stressful situations and to develop effective coping skills. Strategies such as self-talk, perspective-taking, and cognitive self-instruction strategies (Goldfried & Goldfried, 1980; Heinrich & Schag, 1985; Meichenbaum, 1985; Meichenbaum & Cameron, 1983) are used to teach caregivers how to recognize early stress cues and use them as signals for planning an adaptive cognitive and coping response to a stressor. For example, methods of inner dialogue or coping self-talk may help slow down cognitive processes, thereby encouraging a moderated and reasonable coping style.

Rather than discussing problems in the abstract, use of a step-by-step problem-solving approach has been shown to be an effective way of solving concrete problems (Toseland, 1977, 1990, 1995; Toseland & Rivas, 1998; Toseland, Sherman, & Bliven, 1981). A structured treatment protocol can be used to solve problems by having members (a) identify specific pressing problems, (b) assess factors that contribute to the problem or interfere with its resolution, (c) generate alternative problem-solving strategies, (d) examine the advantages and disadvantages of each potential solution, (e) discuss, specify, and cognitively or behaviorally rehearse the action plan, and (f) monitor and evaluate the action plan (Toseland, 1988; Toseland & Smith, 1990; Smith, Smith, & Toseland, 1991).

Research by Gallagher and colleagues suggested that an exclusive focus on problems, however, may increase some caregivers' sense of being overwhelmed instead of increasing their feelings of control (Gallagher-Thompson, 1994a, 1994b; Gallagher, Lovett, & Zeiss, 1989). To counteract this tendency, these researchers recommended that problem-focused strategies emphasize opportunities to learn and adapt rather than dwell on barriers and difficulties.

Support Component.   The provision of support by the group leader and other group members is also an important component of psychoeducational groups. Group leaders should strive to facilitate a supportive environment among members. Previous research has found that mutual aid and support among group members was perceived to be among the most helpful aspects of group interventions (Toseland & Rivas, 1998; Toseland & Siporin, 1986; Yalom, 1985). For example, adult child caregivers reported that the opportunity to talk about pent-up feelings and emotions about the care of their parents was one of the most helpful elements of psychoeducational groups (Toseland, Rossiter, Peak, & Hill, 1990). Thus, a benefit closely identified with mutual support groups, offering caregivers the support of others, is also a component of psychoeducational groups.

Which Support Group?

The needs of a specific caregiver will dictate whether joining a mutual support or a psychoeducational support group would be most beneficial. However, in order to adequately address the specific issues that affect caregiver health outcomes, a mutual support group may not be sufficient. Psychoeducational groups provide a much more structured environment than mutual support groups by using a problem-focused approach. They also offer specific agendas, information, and schedules. On the other hand, psychoeducational groups are more time and labor intensive and more expensive to offer. For this reason, they should be targeted to care-givers who would benefit from a focused group with specific goals that address their individual caregiving problems.

EFFICACY OF SUPPORT GROUPS
FOR ELDERLY CAREGIVERS

The efficacy of mutual support and psychoeducational groups has been examined by a number of researchers. Reviews suggest that support groups can reduce the physical, social, and psychological problems that are associated with caregiving (Bourgeois, Schulz, & Burgio, 1996; McCallion, Diehl, & Toseland, 1994; McCallion, Toseland, & Diehl, 1994; McCallion & Toseland, 1996; Toseland & McCallion, 1997). Support groups tend to be more effective than individual counseling when caregivers have social problems such as isolation or low levels of social support (Toseland, Rossiter, Peak, et al., 1990; see, however, Knight, Lutzky, & Macofsky-Urban, 1993). Group interventions can also be effective for caregivers who prefer not to participate in one-to-one or family counseling (McCallion, Toseland, & Diehl, 1994).

Mutual Support Versus Psychoeducational Groups

Numerous studies have compared different types of support group interventions (Haley, Brown & Levine, 1987; Ingersoll-Dayton, Chapman, & Neal, 1990; Lovett & Gallagher, 1988; Montgomery & Borgatta, 1989). Overall, these studies have found that group intervention is significantly more effective than no treatment, but that the different types of group intervention often appear to have equivalent effects. Indeed, in a study comparing professionally led psychoeducational groups and peer-led mutual support groups to a respite-only control condition, Toseland and colleagues (Toseland, Rossiter, Peak, et al., 1990) found that participants in both types of group interventions reported significantly greater improvement in the areas of psychological functioning, personal change, support network size, and knowledge of community resources. They also found that peer-led support groups were about as effective as professionally led support groups for most caregivers. However, peer-led mutual support groups were marginally more effective in expanding informal support networks for their participants, adding an average of four people to social networks compared to an average of three people for the professionally led groups. A review of the session tapes suggested that socializing, sharing personal experiences, and venting feelings was more prevalent in mutual support groups than in psychoeducational groups. These communication behaviors, in turn, appeared to have a positive impact on social networking among the members. (Smith et al., 1991; Toseland, Rossiter, Peak, et al., 1990).

Other research supports these merits of mutual support groups. In a study comparing 376 caregivers of Alzheimer's patients who used peer-led mutual support groups with 75 control families, Gonyea and Silverstein (1991) found that participating caregivers were more likely to use community services and that caregivers' usage of community support services was positively correlated with both the length of time they belonged to the support group and with the number of meetings they attended during the previous 12 months. Gonyea and Silverstein speculated that peer-led mutual support groups may act as socializing agents, expanding caregivers' knowledge of formal services and legitimizing their use.

Despite the increase in social network size associated with mutual support groups, Toseland, Rossiter, Peak, and Hill (1990) found that professionally led psychoeducational groups were somewhat more effective than mutual support groups in improving caregivers' psychological functioning. In comparison to participants in mutual support groups, those in professionally led groups had greater decreases in the absolute number of symptomatic disturbances (as measured by the Brief Symptom Inventory), and a greater improvement in well-being (as measured by the Bradburn Affect Balance Scale). These participants also showed greater improvement on measures of personal change. Based on analysis of the session tapes, it was concluded that professional psychoeducational group leaders were more structured in their approach, more successful in keeping participants focused on caregiving issues, and more likely to assist caregivers to formulate plans to address specific concerns than were lay leaders of mutual support groups. Toseland and colleagues noted, however, that some caregivers were resistant to both the formal structure and the active leadership of professionals in the psychoeducational groups.

Length of Support Group Interventions

Another frequently asked question is: What are the relative merits of short-term versus long-term group interventions? Research evidence is equivocal. Modest treatment gains have been found even for short-term groups (Brahce, 1989; Gray, 1983; Greene & Monahan, 1989; Haley et al., 1987; Montgomery & Borgatta, 1989; Zarit et al., 1987). There have been fewer studies of longer-term groups. There is, however, some evidence that long-term interventions are particularly effective in reducing the care recipient's inpatient and outpatient health care costs over time (Peak et al., 1995). For example, a long-term intervention by Mittelman et al. (1993, 1995, 1996) that combined individual, family, and a group component found reduced institutionalization for the care recipients. Support group interventions also have lasting effects. Whitlatch, Zarit, Goodwin, and von Eye (1995) found that a support group intervention program for caregivers lowered the rate of nursing home placement for care recipients in the year following the intervention.

Summary

On the whole, research indicates that support groups have some beneficial effects for elderly caregivers of frail elderly family members. By addressing the emotional support needs of caregivers, as well as providing training on how to manage and cope effectively with the problems that arise during caregiving, support groups can influence how caregivers experience the caregiving process. Psychoeducational support groups that present a problem-solving approach, teach effective coping and relaxation techniques, present education and information about the caregiving process, and provide an atmosphere where social support is encouraged may best meet the needs of distressed elderly caregivers.

PRACTICAL ISSUES IN DEVELOPING, IMPLEMENTING, AND MAINTAINING SUPPORT GROUPS

Both applied researchers and practitioners may become involved in the development, support, and implementation of caregiver groups. The roles and concerns of professionals are different in mutual support and psychoeducational groups. The first part of this discussion focuses on ways in which professionals may facilitate the development and implementation of mutual support groups, and the second part focuses on psychoeducational support groups.

Mutual Support Groups

One of the benefits of a mutual support group is that caregivers can receive support on their own terms rather than through a more formal professional-led group therapy protocol (Cole, Griffin, & Ruiz, 1986). Nevertheless, a professional may be involved with mutual support groups in several ways. Although the success of mutual support groups depends on caregivers assuming the majority of responsibility for initiating and maintaining the group, Toseland and colleagues have outlined ways in which a professional may help foster a successful mutual support group (Toseland & Hacker, 1982, 1985). A professional may be involved in activities that include (a) providing material support such as agency funding or meeting space; (b) linking community resources and services with caregivers and referring members to groups; (c) consulting with the group by providing information, guidance, expert knowledge, and technical assistance; (d) initiating or developing the group until members assume full responsibility; or (e) leading the support group, while encouraging members to take responsibility for the agenda and the issues that are discussed. In facilitating the growth and development of the group, professionals should bear in mind that mutual support groups have several characteristic features that tend to distinguish them from other group work services. Often, they are ongoing, long-term groups, providing caregivers with a resource they can rely on over a "career" of caregiving that may last for many years. Although some support groups decide to close their membership so that the group can grow and develop intimacy, more often participants can enter and leave as they wish in a flexible manner that meets the needs of their personal caregiving situation.

Meetings of mutual support groups are characterized by back-and-forth interaction among members. Members participate at their own pace, revitalizing, adjusting, and enhancing coping capacities that they have developed over a lifetime. During the sessions, members are encouraged to listen empathically, support each other, give and receive advice about effective coping strategies, and provide each other with hope. Members become peer models of effective coping by enabling each other to take the necessary steps to sustain and enhance their own coping capacities.

Caregivers also have the opportunity to demonstrate their wisdom and experience and to play useful and meaningful roles in helping others with their problems and concerns. With a minimum of structure, mutual support group meetings facilitate these activities.

There is often a high level of social interaction among members of mutual support groups that may be unrelated to the central concerns of the group, for example, exchanging photographs and anecdotes about grandchildren. This interaction is important too because it helps to establish a social support network among members that is often relied on between group meetings and after the group has terminated. Mutual support groups are structured to facilitate and value such interactions (McCallion & Toseland, 1995).

Psychoeducational Support Groups

Professionals play a more active role in psychoeducational groups than in mutual support groups. However, participating caregivers also have a role to play. This is particularly true when efforts are made to make groups accessible to caregivers of diverse cultures. Qualitative data from several studies suggest that the location of the group, the choice of group leader, the timing of sessions, and the range of issues addressed in the group should be developed with the input of potential group members (Henderson, Gutierrez-Mayka, Garcia, & Boyd, 1993; Toseland & Rivas, 1998). These steps are likely to promote attendance and encourage caregivers to return for subsequent sessions. Professionals should consider addressing four areas to create and maintain a psychoeducational support group's viability: (a) recruitment of group members, (b) tracking and retaining group members, (c) planning and implementing the group, and (d) development of the group and training of the leader.

Recruitment of Group Members. Identifying potential group members is a primary task for any group intervention. Personal contact is the most effective recruitment strategy, but it is more time consuming and expensive than telephone, mail, or mass media contact. Often, a multifaceted approach using several strategies yields more potential members than a single-pronged approach. Setting determines, in part, the identification and contact strategies that can be used for recruiting members. For example, if a health maintenance organization sponsors a group, participants may be solicited from the membership via letters and primary care physician referrals as was done by Toseland et al. (in press). Solicitation letters to potential group members should explain the purpose of the group, include the criteria for inclusion in the group (e.g., over 55 years of age, caregiving for a spouse with a chronic illness, etc.), and inform potential participants about the nature of the commitment. Other means of recruiting participants vary depending on the population to be reached and the context of the group. For example, phoning eligible participants from a regional Alzheimer's directory or setting up an informational booth at community events are types of activities that have been successfully used to recruit members. Some caregivers may be reluctant to request help and may feel they do not have the time to attend meetings. However, these may be the caregivers under the most stress and the most likely to benefit from support group participation. Flexible and varied strategies may be needed to reach this caregiving subpopulation.

Special attention is needed to encourage participation by caregivers from ethnically and culturally diverse populations. Aponte and Crouch (1995) indicated that the number of culturally diverse caregivers is growing rapidly. Often, the first choice of multicultural caregivers is to rely on extended family supports. In situations where such supports are absent, these caregivers may be reluctant to use support groups because they may distrust formal structures, or have cultural beliefs that one should take care of "one's own," that is, a commitment to filial piety (Lockery, 1991; Sakauye, 1989; Sung, 1995). Moreover, because of factors such as historic discrimination, legal status concerns, and alienation from services, some minority families may be uninformed about available resources such as support groups. Therefore, the most needy members of this population may receive the least service (Gratton & Wilson, 1988; Johnson, 1995; McCallion, Janicki, & Grant-Griffin, 1997). Intensive, culturally sensitive recruitment efforts can help to ensure the participation of ethnically and culturally diverse caregivers.

Ramos, Toseland, Ramos, Aquino, and Roff (1999) found that to successfully reach a Latino population of caregivers, it was first necessary to become acquainted with the community. In this case, making contacts with Latino leaders in the community was important for establishing trust and reciprocity. For example, prior to soliciting participation in a survey on caregiving, potential members were offered free services at the Latino community center such as a basic computer-training program. Having materials available in different languages and group leaders who were members of the population of interest also helped recruit group members. McCallion, Janicki, Grant-Griffin, & Kolomer (2000) have also had success by locating the intervention and the recruitment in local, community-based multicultural agencies. This strategy has the advantage of creating a new, accessible, and culturally comfortable site for support groups.

Caregivers are often overburdened by their caregiving responsibilities and may not have the resources or time available for extra activities such as attending group meetings. These barriers can be overcome. Arranging for transportation to the group meeting, scheduling times that do not conflict with work or important caregiving activities, arranging for respite care if necessary, and providing a location that is easily accessed and known to members can help foster participation. Interviews with support group members and nonattenders suggest that the greatest barrier to joining a support group is the time commitment needed to attend the group and the perceived inability to leave the care recipient unattended or with other care providers (McCallion et al., 2000; Ramos et al., 1999). Successfully locating participants for a group and ensuring ongoing attendance at meetings can result from the leader helping caregivers resolve these issues in advance.

The benefits of the group should be clearly specified to potential members. During initial contacts with potential participants, professionals must acknowledge and address the experiences of caregiving, both positive and negative, as a foundation for introducing the support group. A need for information about support services and resources can also serve as a starting point in the recruitment of many caregivers. By highlighting the shared experience of the group members and the information and strategies that would be part of the group sessions, leaders can convey what benefits (e.g., support, problem solving, knowledge of community resources, health information, etc.) would result from participation in the support group. Additionally, acknowledging the unique perspective and experience that caregivers would bring to the group encourages participation.

Tracking and Retaining Group Members.   Once a support group has been formed, it is important to track and retain its members. This is particularly relevant if the psychoeducational group is long-term in nature or multiple groups are being sponsored at the same time. Experience from operating a 12-month psychoeducational support group for HMO members suggests that regularly updating information about group members (e.g., changes of address, phone numbers, caregiving situations, etc.) helped group leaders in their efforts to encourage continued participation (Toseland et al., in press). For example, for several group members, changes in the health of care recipients imposed restrictions on the caregivers' continued participation in the group. Group leaders' awareness of this information enabled them to help caregivers continue to participate in the group. By continually updating information about members, leaders were also able to address events such as the death or institutionalization of a care recipient or drastic changes in the caregiver's own health.

Maintaining regular contact via phone and mail helps track the needs of each caregiver. Also, regular contacts by group leaders prior to the meeting can help remind caregivers of the group schedule and encourage participation. Anecdotal data from the HMO groups suggest that there were many times when a caregiver decided to discontinue the support group or to skip an important session. Contact with the group leader convinced them of the benefits of continual attendance in the group. Group leaders reported that emphasizing the important contribution each individual member makes to the group and how helpful potential members were to other caregivers in the group also helped foster positive attitudes towards continued attendance.

Planning and Implementing a Support Group. Often support group leaders are dependent on the generosity of host agencies for a site to hold the support group meeting. This may mean that the support group has a low priority for both the allocation of space and times available for the meeting. Yet, the wrong space and the wrong time for the meeting will discourage attendance. Priority should be given to providing as convenient and accessible a group meeting room as possible. Well-known buildings, community centers, or health centers are preferable. Holding group meetings in an unfamiliar neighborhood or hard to find locale discourages participation because of safety concerns and transportation availability. Once a location is selected, a comfortable, quiet, and private setting such as a conference room or small recreation room helps to ensure a positive experience for the group. Access to the building and meeting space should accommodate older adults' needs. Nearby parking, convenient restroom facilities, comfortable chairs, a table for papers and handouts, and minimal obstacles such as stairs can promote attendance.

Professionals also need to convey their belief that participants' time is valuable. A regular meeting day and time where the meeting room is reserved provides the best structure for ensuring caregivers' participation. Providing a schedule of future meetings helps group members plan ahead to accommodate their caregiving needs. Phone calls or postcard reminders of upcoming meetings inform group members of meeting times and encourage participation. However, weather, holidays, and vacations should also be taken into account when planning dates for group meetings. Contingency plans for postponed meetings should be clear and known to group members.

Leaders should develop and utilize a specific agenda completed ahead of time for each group meeting. Indeed, a manual containing the meeting schedule and the agenda and activities for each meeting ensures a consistent and coherent delivery of the intervention. Additionally, leaders should have available any materials or handouts, such as activity logs, a problem identification log, relevant health information, and lists of community resources for group members. Such steps increase the likelihood that participants will follow through on suggested strategies and approaches and that they will return for subsequent meetings.

For a psychoeducational support group, the ideal leader is a professional who is familiar with group dynamics and the health care needs of frail older persons and their caregivers. Prior to the start of a group, the leader should read all relevant material such as the program manual and obtain training on how to present key components of the intervention (e.g., problem-solving strategies) and to lead exercises (e.g., relaxation techniques). In addition, the group leader should be aware of programs and resources available for older adults in their community so that they can refer members to services they may need.

Over the course of the support group, it is important for leaders to discuss with group members their progress toward specific goals and to ensure that the problem-solving component is focused on members' specific needs. In addition, group leaders should periodically consider how well the intervention protocol has been followed. Audiotaping of meetings provides an important resource for group leaders to monitor their own leadership of the group and to identify individual caregiver concerns that they may have missed during the sessions. The use of audiotapes also facilitates outside supervision of the group leaders. Videotaping provides an even richer source of data, but is technically more difficult to do well and is more intrusive. If either method is used, the storage and use of such tapes should be discussed with participants. It is also a good idea to obtain group members' written consent before proceeding with audio- or videotaping.

CONCLUSIONS

In order for support groups to have a positive impact on caregivers, it is crucial that the groups offer benefits that are important to members. For mutual support groups, these benefits include a much needed outlet for caregivers to vent their feelings in an environment where mutual understanding and sharing is likely to occur. Older caregivers often sponta-neously report that one of the most important benefits of participating in a mutual support groups is the validation and encouragement they receive from each other and the leader (Toseland, Rossiter, Peak & Hill 1990). Indeed, relationships formed in mutual support groups often continue after meetings end.

The success of psychoeducational support groups is enhanced by practi-cal health and service information, teaching the skills necessary to balance caregiving with the older adult caregiver's own health needs, and helping caregivers arrive at more positive appraisals of their situations. Psychoedu-cational groups have at their core a practical approach to identifying key problems in the caregiving process and attempting to find realistic, positive solutions. Ensuring the success of mutual support and psychoeducational support groups requires special attention to the practical and logistical issues involved in providing this service to caregivers. As caregiving for older adults becomes further integrated into the fabric of family life, com-munity mutual support groups and psychoeducational support groups will continue to be an important part of preserving and encouraging the inde-pendence and health of older adults and their caregivers.

REFERENCES

Aponte, J. F., & Crouch, R. (1995). The changing ethnic profile of the United States. In J. F. Aponte, R. W. Rivers, & J. Wohl (Eds.), *Psychological interventions and cultural diversity* (pp. 1–18). Boston: Allyn & Bacon.

Atkinson, S. J., & Fischer, J. L. (1996). Factors affecting co-dependent's support group atten-dance. *Alcoholism Treatment Quarterly, 14*, 11–20.

Barusch, A., & Spaid, W. (1991). Reducing caregiver burden through short-term training: Evaluation findings from a caregiver support project. *Journal of Gerontological Social Work, 17*, 7–33.

Beisecker, A. E., Wright, L. J., Chrisman, S. K., & Ashworth, J. (1996). Family caregiver per-ceptions of benefits and barriers to use of adult day care for individuals with Alzheimers dis-ease. *Research on Aging, 18*, 430–450.

Benjamin, S. (1989). Psychological treatment of chronic pain: A selective review. *Journal of Psychosomatic Research, 33*, 121–131.

Biegel, D., Sales, E., & Schulz, R. (1991). *Family caregiving in chronic illness.* Newbury Park, CA: Sage.

Blanchard, E. (1993). Behavioral therapies in the treatment of headache. *Headache Quarterly, 4*, 53–56.

Blazer, D. (1982). Social support and mortality in an elderly community population. *American Journal of Epidemiology, 115*, 684–694.

Bourgeouis, M. S., Schulz, R., & Burgio, L. (1996). Interventions for caregivers of patients with Alzheimers disease: A review and analysis of content, process, and outcomes. *International Journal of Aging and Human Development, 43*, 35–92.

Brahce, C. I. (1989). The effect of a support and education program on stress and burden among family caregivers to frail elderly persons. *Gerontologist, 29*, 472–477.

Cantor, M. (1994). Family caregiving: Social care. In M. Cantor (Ed.), *Family caregiving: Agenda for the future* (pp. 1–9). San Francisco: American Society on Aging.

Choi, N. G., & Wodarski, J. S. (1996). The relationship between social support and health status of elderly people: Does social support slow down physical and functional deterioration? *Social Work Research, 20*, 52–63.

Christensen, A., Smith, T., Turner, C., Holman, J., Jr., Gregory, M., & Rich, M. (1992). Family support, physical impairment, and adherence in hemodialysis: An investigation of main and buffering effects. *Journal of Behavioral Medicine, 15*, 313–325.

Cole, L., Griffin, K., & Ruiz, B. (1986). A comprehensive approach to working with families of Alzheimer's patients. *Journal of Gerontological Social Work, 9*, 27–39.

Dalgard, O. S., & Lund-Haheim, L. (1998). Psychosocial risk factors and mortality: A prospective study with special focus on social support, social participation, and locus of control in Norway. *Journal of Epidemiology and Community Health, 52*, 476–481.

Festinger, L. (1954). A theory of social comparison processes. *Human Relations, 7*, 117–140.

Fuhrer, R., Dufoil, C., Antonucci, T. C., Shipley, M. J., Helmer, C., & Dartigues, J. F. (1999). Psychological disorder and mortality in French older adults: Do social relations modify the association? *American Journal of Epidemiology, 149*, 116–126.

Galinsky, M. J., & Schopler, J. H. (1994). Negative experiences in support groups. *Social Work Health Care, 20*, 77–95.

Gallagher, D., Lovett, S., & Zeiss, A. (1989). Interventions with caregivers of frail elderly persons. In M. Ory & K. Bonds (Eds.), *Aging and health care: Social science and policy perspectives* (pp. 167–190). London: Routledge.

Gallagher-Thompson, D. (1994a). Clinical intervention strategies for distressed caregivers: Rationale and development of psychoeducational approaches. In E. Light, G. Niederehe, & B. D. Lebowitz (Eds.), *Stress effects on family caregivers of Alzheimer's patients* (pp. 261–277). New York: Springer.

Gallagher-Thompson, D. (1994b). Direct services and interventions for caregivers: A review and critique of extant programs and a look ahead to the future. In M. H. Cantor (Ed.), *Family caregiving: Agenda for the future* (pp. 102–122). San Francisco: American Society on Aging.

Gallant, M. P., & Connell, C. M. (1998). The stress process among dementia spouse caregivers: Are caregivers at risk for negative health behavior change? *Research on Aging, 20*, 267–297.

Given, B. A., & Given, C. W. (1998). Health promotion for family caregivers of chronically ill elders. *Annual Review of Nursing Research, 16*, 197–217.

Goldfried, M., & Goldfried, A. (1980). Cognitive change methods. In F. Kanfer & A. P. Goldstein (Eds.), *Helping people change—A textbook of methods* (2nd ed., pp. 97–130). New York: Pergamon.

Gonyea, J. G., & Silverstein, N. M. (1991). The role of Alzheimer's disease support groups in families' utilization of community services. *Journal of Gerontological Social Work, 16*, 43–55.

Goode, K. T., Haley, W. K., Roth, D. L., & Ford, G. R. (1998). Predicting longitudinal changes in caregiver physical and mental health: A stress process model. *Health Psychology, 17*, 190–198.

Gratton, B., & Wilson, V. (1988). Family support systems and the minority elderly: A cautionary analysis. *Journal of Gerontological Social Work, 13*, 81–93.

Gray, V. K. (1983). Providing support for home caregivers. In M. A. Smyer & M. Gatz (Eds.), *Mental health and aging* (pp. 197–214). Beverly Hills, CA: Sage.

Greene, V., & Monahan, D. (1989). The effect of a support and education program on stress and burden among family caregivers to frail elderly persons. *Gerontologist, 29*, 472–477.

Haley, W., Brown, L., & Levine, E. (1987). Experimental evaluation of the effectiveness of group interventions for dementia caregivers. *Gerontologist, 27,* 376–382.

Heinrich, R., & Schag, C. (1985). Stress and activity management: Group treatment for cancer patients and spouses. *Journal of Consulting and Clinical Psychology, 53,* 439–446.

Henderson, J., Gutierrez-Mayka, M., Garcia., J., & Boyd, S. (1993). A model for Alzheimer's disease support group development in African-American and Hispanic populations. *Gerontologist, 33,* 409–414.

Hyduk, C. A. (1996). The dynamic relationship between social support and health in older adults: Assessment implications. *Journal of Gerontological Social Work, 27,* 149–165.

Ingersoll-Dayton, B., Chapman, N., & Neal, M. (1990). A program for caregivers in the workplace. *Gerontologist, 30,* 126–130.

Johnson, T. (1995). Utilizing culture in work with aging families. In G. Smith, S. S. Tobin, B. Robertson-Tchabo, & P. Power (Eds.), *Strengthening aging families: Diversity in practice and policy* (pp. 175–202). Newbury Park, CA: Sage.

Kiecolt-Glaser, J., Dura, J., Speicher, C., Trast, O., & Glaser, R. (1991). Spousal caregivers of dementia victims: Longitudinal changes in immunity and health. *Psychosomatic Medicine, 53,* 345–362.

Knight, B., Lutzky, S., & Macofsky-Urban, F. (1993). A meta-analytic review of interventions for caregiver stress: Recommendations for future research. *Gerontologist, 33,* 240–248.

Korner-Bitensky, N., Tarasuk, J., Nelles, J., & Bouchard, J.-M. (1998). The impact of interventions with families poststroke: A review. *Topics in Stroke Rehabilitation, 5,* 69–85.

Kouzis, A. C., & Eaton, W. W. (1998). Absence of social networks, social support and health services utilization. *Psychological Medicine, 28,* 1301–1310.

Kramer, B. J. (1997). Gain in the caregiving experience: Where are we? What next? *Gerontologist, 37,* 218–232.

Krizek, C., Roberts, C., Ragan, R., Ferrara, J. J., & Lord, B. (1999). Gender and cancer support group participation. *Cancer Practice, 7,* 86–92.

Labrecque, M., Peak, T., & Toseland, R. (1992). Long-term effectiveness of a group program for caregivers of frail elderly veterans. *American Journal of Orthopsychiatry, 62,* 575–588.

Lee, M., & Tussing, A. D. (1998). Influences on nursing home admission: The role of informal caregivers. *Abstract Book Association for Health Services Research, 15,* 55–56.

Lockery, S. (1991). Family and social supports: Caregiving among racial and ethnic minority elders. *Generations, 15,* 58–62.

Lovett, S., & Gallagher, D. (1988). Psychoeducational interventions for family caregivers: Preliminary efficacy data. *Behavior Therapy, 19,* 321–330.

Manne, S., & Zautra, A. (1989). Spouse criticism and support: Their association with coping and psychological adjustment among women with rheumatoid arthritis. *Journal of Personality and Social Psychology, 56,* 608–617.

Martichuski, D. K., Knight, B. L., Karlin, N. J., & Bell, P. A. (1997). Correlates with Alzheimer's disease caregivers' support group attendance. *Activities, Adaptation, & Aging, 21,* 27–40.

McCallion, P., Diehl, M., & Toseland, R. (1994). Support group intervention for family caregivers of Alzheimer's disease patients. *Seminars in Speech and Language, 15,* 257–270.

McCallion, P., Janicki, M., & Grant-Griffin, L. (1997). Exploring the impact of culture and acculturation on older families caregiving for persons with developmental disabilities. *Family Relations: Interdisciplinary Journal of Applied Family Studies, 46*(4), 347–357.

McCallion, P., Janicki, M., Grant-Griffin, L., & Kolomer, S. (2000). Grandparent caregivers II: Service need and service provision issues. *Journal of Gerontological Social Work, 33,* 63–90.

McCallion, P., & Toseland, R. (1995). Supportive group interventions with caregivers of frail older adults. In M. Galinsky & J. Schopler (Eds.), *Support groups: Current perspectives on theory and practice* (pp. 11–25). Binghamton, NY: Haworth.

McCallion, P., & Toseland, R. (1996). Supportive group interventions with caregivers of frail older adults. *Social Work with Groups, 18*, 11–25.

McCallion, P., Toseland, R., & Diehl, M. (1994). Social work practice with caregivers of frail older adults. *Research on Social Work Practice, 4*, 64–88.

Meichenbaum, D. (1977). *Cognitive behavior modification—An integration approach.* New York: Plenum.

Meichenbaum, D. (1985). *Stress inoculation training.* New York: Plenum.

Meichenbaum, D., & Cameron, R. (1983). Stress inoculation training: Toward a general paradigm for training coping skills. In D. Meichenbaum & M.E. Jaremko (Eds.), *Stress reduction and prevention* (pp. 115–154). New York: Plenum.

Melamed, B., & Brenner, G. (1990). Social support and chronic medical stress: An interaction-based approach. *Journal of Social and Clinical Psychology, 9*, 104–117.

Mendes de Leon, C. F., Glass, T. A., Beckett, L. A., Seeman, T. E., Evans, D. A., & Berkman, L. F. (1999). Social networks and disability transitions across eight intervals of yearly data in the New Haven EPESE. *Journals of Gerontology: Social Sciences, 54*, S162–S172.

Michinov, N., & Monteil, J. M. (1997). Upward or downward comparison after failure: The role of diagnostic information. *Social Behavior and Personality, 25*, 389–398.

Mittelman, M., Ferris, S., Shulman, E., Steinberg, G., Ambinder, A., Mackell, J., & Cohen, J. (1995). A comprehensive support program: Effect on depression in spouse-caregivers of AD patients. *Gerontologist, 35*, 792–802.

Mittelman, M., Ferris, S., Shulman, E., Steinberg, G., & Levin, B. (1996). A family intervention to delay nursing home placement of patients with Alzheimer's disease. *Journal of the American Medical Association, 276*, 1725–1731.

Mittelman, M., Ferris, S., Steinberg, G., Shulman, E., Mackell, J., Ambinder, A., & Cohen, J. (1993). An intervention that delays institutionalization of Alzheimer's disease patients: Treatment of spouse-caregivers. *Gerontologist, 33*, 730–740.

Montgomery, R., & Borgatta, E. (1989). The effects of alternative support strategies on family caregiving. *Gerontologist, 29*, 457–464.

National Alliance for Caregiving and the American Association of Retired Persons (1997, June). *Family caregiving in the U.S.: Findings from a national survey* (Final Report). Bethesda, MD: The National Alliance for Caregiving. Washington, DC: The American Association of Retired Persons.

Peak, T., Toseland, R., & Banks, S. (1995). Impact of caregiver support groups on the health care costs and utilization of care recipients. *Journal of Aging and Health, 7*, 427–449.

Pearlman, D. A., & Crown, W. H. (1992). Alternative sources of social support and their impacts on institutional risk. *Gerontologist, 32*, 527–535.

Pillemer, K., & Suitor, J. (1996). "It takes one to help one": Effects of similar others on the well-being of caregivers. *Journals of Gerontology: Social Sciences, 51*, s520–s527.

Ramos, B., Toseland, R., Ramos, V., Aquino, G., & Roff, S. (1999). *Research with Latino caregivers: Recruitment strategies and instrumentation development.* Unpublished manuscript, State University of New York at Albany.

Rapp, S. R., Shumaker, S., Schmidt, S., Naughton, M., & Anderson, R. (1998). Social resourcefulness: Its relationship to social support and wellbeing among caregivers of dementia victims. *Aging and Mental Health, 2*, 40–48.

Sakauye, K. (1989). Ethnic variations in family support of the frail elderly. In M. Goldstein (Ed.), *Family involvement in treatment of the frail elderly* (pp. 63–106). Washington, DC: American Psychiatric Press.

Schulz, R., Newsom, J., Mittlemark, M., Burton, L., Hirsch, C., & Jackson, S. (1997). Health effects of caregiving: The caregiver health effects study: An ancillary study of the Cardiovascular Health Study. *Annals of Behavioral Medicine, 19*, 110–114.

Schulz, R., Tompkins, C., & Rau, M. (1988). A longitudinal study of the psychosocial impact of stroke on primary support persons. *Psychology and Aging, 3,* 131–141.

Sherbourne, C., Hays, R., Ordway, L., DiMatteo, M., & Kravitz, R. (1992). Antecedents of adherence to medical recommendations: Results from the medical outcomes study. *Journal of Behavioral Medicine, 15,* 447–468.

Smith, G., Smith, M., & Toseland, R. (1991). Problems identified by family caregivers in counseling. *Gerontologist, 31,* 15–22.

Smith, G., Tobin, S., Robertson-Tchabo, E., & Power, P. (1995). *Strengthening aging families: Diversity in practice and policy.* Thousand Oaks, CA: Sage.

Sorbi, M., & Tellegen, B. (1988). Stress-coping in migraine. *Social Science and Medicine, 26,* 351–358.

Stevens, M. J., & Duttlinger, J. E. (1998). Correlates of participation in a breast cancer support group. *Journal of Psychosomatic Research, 45,* 263–275.

Sung, K. T. (1995). Measures and dimensions of filial piety in Korea. *Gerontologist, 35,* 240–247.

Taylor, S. E., Aspinwall, L. G., Giuliano, T., & Dakof, G. (1993). Storytelling and coping with stressful events. *Journal of Applied Social Psychology, 23,* 703–733.

Taylor, S. E., Falke, R. L., Shoptaw, S. J., & Lichtman, R. R. (1986). Social support, support groups, and the cancer patient. *Journal of Consulting and Clinical Psychology, 54,* 608–615.

Tobin, S. (1999). *Preservation of the self in the oldest years.* New York: Springer.

Toseland, R. (1977). A problem solving group workshop for older persons. *Social Work, 22,* 325–326.

Toseland, R. (1988). *An action-oriented model of practice.* Unpublished treatment manual, School of Social Welfare, State University of New York at Albany.

Toseland, R. (1990). *Group work with older adults.* New York: New York University Press.

Toseland, R. (1995). *Group work with the elderly and family caregivers.* New York: Springer.

Toseland, R., & Hacker, L. (1982). Self-help groups and professional involvement. *Social Work, 27,* 341–347.

Toseland, R., & Hacker, L. (1985). Social workers' use of self-help groups as a resource for clients. *Social Work, 30,* 232–239.

Toseland, R., Labrecque, M., Goebel, S., & Whitney, M. (1992). An evaluation of a group program for spouses of frail, elderly veterans. *The Gerontologist, 32,* 382–390.

Toseland, R., & McCallion, P. (1997). Trends in caregiving intervention research. *Social Work Research, 21,* 154–164.

Toseland, R., McCallion, P., Smith, T., & Bourgeois, P. (in press). Health education groups for caregivers in an HMO. *Journal of Clinical Psychology.*

Toseland, R., & Rivas, R. (1998). *An introduction to group work practice* (3rd ed.). New York: MacMillan.

Toseland, R., & Rossiter, C. (1989). Group interventions to support family caregivers: A review and analysis. *Gerontologist, 29,* 438–448.

Toseland, R., & Rossiter, C. (1992). Social work practice with family caregivers for frail older persons. In M. J. Holosko & P. A. Taylor (Eds.), *Social work practice in health care settings* (2nd ed., pp. 509–533). Toronto, Canada: Canadian Scholars Press.

Toseland, R., Rossiter, C., & Labrecque, M. (1989a). The effectiveness of peer-led and professionally led groups to support family caregivers. *Gerontologist, 29,* 465–471.

Toseland, R., Rossiter, C., & Labrecque, M. (1989b). The effectiveness of two kinds of support groups for caregivers. *Social Service Review, 63,* 415–432.

Toseland, R., Rossiter, C., Peak, T., & Hill, P. (1990). Therapeutic processes in support groups for caregivers. *International Journal of Group Psychotherapy, 40,* 297–303.

Toseland, R., Rossiter, C., Peak, T., & Smith, G. (1990). The comparative effectiveness of individual and group interventions to support family caregivers. *Social Work, 35,* 209–219.

Toseland, R., Sherman, E., & Bliven, S. (1981). The comparative effectiveness of two group work approaches for the development of mutual support groups among the elderly. *Social Work with Groups, 4*, 137–153.

Toseland, R., & Siporin, M. (1986). When to recommend group treatment: A review of the clinical and the research literature. *International Journal of Group Psychotherapy, 36*, 171–201.

Toseland, R., & Smith, G. (1990). The effectiveness of individual counseling for family caregivers of the elderly. *Psychology and Aging, 5*, 256–263.

Toseland, R., Smith, G., & McCallion, P. (1995). Supporting the family in elder care. In G. C. Smith, S. S. Tobin, E. A. Robertson-Tchabo, and P. W. Power (Eds.), *Enabling aging families: Directions for practice and policy* (pp. 3–24). Newbury Park, CA: Sage.

Toseland, R., Smith, G., & McCallion, P. (in press). Supporting the "family" in family caregiving. In G. Smith, S. S. Tobin, B. A. Robertson-Tchabo, & P. Power (Eds.), *Enabling aging families: Directions for practice and policy.* Newbury Park, CA: Sage.

VanderZee, K., Buunk, B., DeRuiter, J., Tempelaar, R., VanSanderen, E., & Sanderman, R. (1996). Social comparison and the subjective well-being of cancer patients. *Basic and Applied Social Psychology, 18*, 453–468.

Whitlatch, C., Zarit, S., Goodwin, P., & von Eye, A. (1995). Influence of the success of psychoeducation interventions on the course of family care. *Clinical Gerontologist, 16*, 17–30.

Wills, T. A. (1981). Downward comparison principles in social psychology. *Psychological Bulletin, 90*, 245–271.

Yalom, I. (1985). *The theory and practice of group psychotherapy* (3rd ed.). New York: Basic Books.

Zarit, S., Anthony, C., & Boutselis, M. (1987). Interventions with caregivers of dementia patients: Comparison of two approaches. *Psychology and Aging, 2*, 225–232.

II

PROVIDER–PATIENT COMMUNICATION AND SUCCESSFUL AGING

5

Building the Physician–Older Patient Relationship

Michele G. Greene
Brooklyn College

Ronald D. Adelman
Cornell University Weill Medical College

Under the current health care system, there are multiple and complex barriers for both physicians and patients to overcome in order to develop a relationship that is effective, mutually satisfying, and meaningful. This chapter briefly examines the importance of the relationship, outlines what is known about communication in the physician–older patient relationship, describes some strategies that health care professionals (physicians, in particular) and older patients may employ to help develop their relationship, and provides an actual case illustrating the significance of a meaningful physician–older patient relationship.

Researchers have clearly documented the influence of the physician–patient relationship on important patient outcomes, including adherence to therapeutic regimens, satisfaction, health status, reductions in anxiety, and appointment keeping (Roter & Hall, 1992; Stewart, 1995). For physicians, the relationship is also important. Physicians derive personal meaning from their work with patients (Suchman, Branch, & Matthews, 1995), and, despite the professional norm that espouses that physicians remain affectively neutral (Parsons, 1951), physicians' day-to-day lives are filled with encounters that affect them. As well, physicians' ability to accurately diagnose and care for patients is significantly affected by their relationship with patients (Lazare, Putnam, & Lipkin, 1995). Moreover, and what may be most compelling to some physicians, is the influence of the relationship on the likelihood of a malpractice suit (Levinson, Roter, Mullooly, Dull, & Frankel, 1997).

Although these outcomes are important, some physicians and health care managers discount the significance of both the physician–patient relationship and the communication that builds it. Often the focus in the practice of contemporary medicine is more on biomedical cures and productivity quotients than on the caring dimensions of medicine. The false dichotomy that suggests that the "science" of medicine and the "art" of medicine are independent phenomena undermines the ability of physicians to practice medicine that is both effective and compassionate. Healing, in its broadest sense, may only occur when the science and art of medicine are seen as interdependent and inextricably bound.

STUDIES OF THE PHYSICIAN–OLDER PATIENT RELATIONSHIP

As there are still few empirical investigations of the physician–older patient relationship (albeit, this number is growing), there is a tendency to extrapolate what is known about all physician–patient relationships to the physician–*older* patient relationship. The validity of this application must be questioned as there are sufficient data indicating that physician–older patient interactions differ from physician–younger patient interactions. For example, studies show that overall physician responsiveness (i.e., the quality of questioning, informing, and support) is better with younger patients than with older patients (Greene, Adelman, Charon, & Hoffman, 1986); there is less concordance on the major goals and topics of the visit between physicians and older patients than between physicians and younger patients (Greene, Adelman, Charon, & Friedmann, 1989); there is somewhat less joint decision making in visits between physicians and older patients than in visits between physicians and younger patients; physicians are less likely to be egalitarian, patient, engaged, respectful, and optimistic with older patients than with younger patients; and older patients are less assertive than younger patients (Greene, 1987).

Much of what is known about physician–older patient communication is derived from studies in which patients, their families, their doctors, or all three are interviewed or surveyed about what occurs during the medical visit. There are also studies in which physicians respond to vignettes about patients and studies in which simulated patients are employed to examine physicians' (and especially physicians in training) interviewing skills. These investigations, which provide valuable information about perceptions of physician–older patient communication and estimates about predicted behavior in real-life visits, do not provide direct evidence of what actually occurs in medical encounters. Thus, overall understanding of physician–older patient communication in natural settings is limited to the extent that perceptions and attitudes are described, but examination of actual talk is missing. In an effort to promote direct observational research in this area, the National Institute on Aging has recently funded a large empirical investigation, Assessment of Physician–Elderly Patient Transactions (ADEPT), in which 500 primary care physician–older patient interactions will be audiotaped or videotaped. This is the largest study of this cohort to date and the data, which are being analyzed using three different interactional analysis coding systems, are likely to add significantly to the body of knowledge of physician–older communication (M. A. Cook, personal communication, April, 1999).

This section briefly reviews the relatively few studies in which physician–older patient interactions were directly observed in their natural settings (e.g., hospital, office). The only studies included in this summary are those in which all patients in the sample are 60 years and over. The methods of direct observation most frequently employed were audiotaping and videotaping. The foci of the studies vary and include research on the content of discussions, the different interactional processes of the visit, the influence of a third person/companion on the visit, and the associations between interactional variables and visit outcomes. Within each section, the summaries are presented in chronological order.

Studies of Content of Physician–Older Patient Medical Encounters

Rost and Frankel (1993) examined how older patients introduced problems in follow-up medical visits. In a study of 200 diabetic patients who were 60 years and over, the researchers found over 50% of patients did not raise medical topics they were concerned about, and 60% of patients did not discuss important psychosocial issues. When patients had a shorter agenda for the visit (i.e., fewer issues to raise), it was more likely that their entire agenda would be introduced. The focus of these brief audiotaped visits (average time was 10.8 min) was largely medical (vs. psychosocial).

Waitzkin, Britt, and Williams (1994) selected two audiotaped encounters between physicians and older patients to illustrate how social problems are dealt with during routine medical visits. Overall, the researchers found that when social problems "do arise in medical encounters, the structure of discourse tends to cut off, to interrupt, and ultimately to marginalize their discussion, even though these issues may create substantial day-to-day distress" (p. 341) for the patient.

In our research, we audiotaped 81 first primary care medical visits between internists and patients 60 years and over in the general medicine clinic of a large urban hospital. The audiotapes were coded with the Multi-Dimensional Interaction Analysis (MDIA) coding system, a qualitative and quantitative approach that allows examination of the content, process, language, and behavior of interactive participants (Charon, Greene, & Adelman, 1994). In a detailed content analysis of personal habits and psychosocial talk in first visits between physicians and older patients, we found that many important subjects in these areas were infrequently discussed. The two personal habits that were least likely to be discussed were exercise (in 3.7% of visits) and sexual issues (6.2% of visits). Most likely to be discussed were diet (76.5% of visits), smoking (69.1% of visits), and alcohol (58% of visits). In the psychosocial domain, the two topics least likely to be discussed were crime and victimization (3.7% of visits) and religion (4.9% of visits). The three most frequently discussed psychosocial topics were the health care system (96.3% of visits), family and significant others (82.7% of visits), and work and leisure activities (65.4% of visits). Although physicians were more likely to initiate discussions about personal habits, older patients were more likely to raise psychosocial topics. It is important to note, however, that just to document the occurrence of talk about a specific subject does not reveal the quality of that discussion. Further work is planned to examine the quality of discourse around specific topics (Greene & Adelman, 1996a).

Studies of Interactional Processes of Physician–Older Patient Medical Encounters

In Roter's (1991) study of physicians' responses to older patients' emotional states, 83 visits of patients attending a hospital clinic specializing in geriatric care were audiotaped and coded with the Roter Interaction Analysis system. Roter found that patients rated by their physicians as anxious, depressed, or irritated were more likely to be reassured during the visit and asked open-ended questions about their emotional state by the physician. However, these patients were also less likely to receive information regarding medical issues during the visit. The study also found that patients who were rated by their doctor as depressed, emotionally dependent, and anxious were more likely to express worry during the visit and to ask the doctor for reassurance.

Coupland, Robinson, and Coupland (1994) audiotaped and observed 85 geriatric clinic visits in South Wales. The focus of their study was on the opening elements of a medical consultation and how interactive participants move from phatic talk (i.e., communication designed to help establish a relationship) to the medical work of the visit. Excerpts from selected interactions illustrate the multiple ways the expression, "How are you?" is used to establish the initial social components of the visit or to serve as a transition to medical talk.

Our study of the older patient's "presentation of self" in the medical visit and the physician's response to the patient's presentation (Greene, Adelman, Rizzo, & Friedmann, 1994), examined how the time orientation of the presentation disclosure and the level of intimacy of the disclosure influenced the physician's response, as measured with the MDIA coding system. We found that (a) physicians responded significantly better to the older patient's presentation of self when the presentations were lodged in the patients' pasts than when they focused on current life events, and (b) physicians responded somewhat better to nonintimate patient disclosures than to very intimate patient disclosures (Greene, Adelman, Rizzo, & Friedmann, 1994).

In a qualitative assessment of how physicians and older patients provide support to one another in medical visits (Greene, Adelman, & Majerovitz, 1996), we reviewed two transcripts of doctor–older patient medical visits. Overall, in the first case we found that a physician's nonsupportive approach to the patient was demonstrated through inattentive listening, perfunctory responses, no pursuit of patient-raised concerns, and topic shifts from emotional content to medical subjects. The physician in the second case demonstrated his support through actively questioning the patient about her concerns, acknowledging the patient's distress, offering tangible assistance to the patient for her problem, and providing reassurance to the patient that he would be available to her in the future. In this same investigation, we also examined a rarely studied phenomenon, namely, patient support to the physician. Using the entire sample of 81 first visits, we found that some form of patient support to the physician (usually in the form of emotional support) occurred in over 65% of first visits.

In an examination of physician responsiveness (i.e., the quality of questioning, informing and support) to different patient and physician-raised issues (Greene & Adelman, 1996b), we found that there were no differences in how physicians responded to medical topics when patients raised them compared to when the doctors initiated these discussions.

However, physicians' responsiveness was greater for personal habits topics (e.g., smoking, alcohol use, sexuality) and psychosocial topics (e.g.,
depression, family concerns, abuse) when these topics were initiated by
the physician than when they were introduced by the patient.

Studies of the Influence of a Third Person/Companion on the Medical Visit

Coe and Prendergast (1985) sought to understand the development of
coalition formation in triadic (three-person) medical encounters. The
researchers audiotaped 14 visits between physicians, patients 65 and over,
and their accompanying relative in an outpatient clinic. For comparison
purposes, in half of the visits the relative was excluded from the
encounter. The audiotapes were transcribed. Overall, Coe and Prendergast found that multiple coalitions among the three interactive participants were possible within one visit, the length of time that a coalition
existed was variable, and efforts to establish a coalition were not always
successful.

Beisecker (1989) audiotaped 21 visits between specialists in physical
medicine and rehabilitation and patients over 60 years and examined the
influence of a companion on the dynamics of the medical encounter.
Beisecker found that the presence of a companion did not influence the
length of time of the encounter. Although doctor-to-patient and patient-
to-doctor comments predominated the visits, companion-to-doctor talk
also frequently occurred. Companions' participation in the visit was most
likely during the history and final segments of the visit. As expected,
companions were relatively inactive during the physical examination
portion. Beisecker also found that interactions between patients and
companions occurred infrequently.

Hasselkus (1992) conducted a qualitative assessment of encounters
between older patients, physicians, and caregivers in a general medical or
geriatric clinic. Forty visits were audiotaped. Hasselkus found that while
the caregivers thought of themselves as colleagues of the physician in caring for the patient, the physician perceived the caregivers to be "patient-
substitutes," that is, informants providing data to the physician that the
patient may not have been able to provide. There was little discussion of
the social context of illness and care, and most of the talk was biomedical
in nature.

To examine the differences in the content and process of communication in dyadic (two-person) and triadic medical visits, we compared a

matched sample of two-person and three-person encounters (Greene, Majerovitz, Adelman, & Rizzo, 1994). We found that the content of physician talk does not appear to be different in triads and dyads, although patients are frequently referred to as "she" or "he" by the physician (which makes the patient a third party, or outsider in the interaction); patients raise fewer topics overall in triads than in dyads; patients are less responsive to topics they raise themselves and are less assertive in triads than in dyads; and there tends to be less shared laughter and joint decision making in triads than in dyads. To summarize, these studies suggest that the presence of a third person in the physician–older patient medical encounter is likely to significantly influence the interactional dynamics of visits and ultimately, the relationship that is built between the physician and the older patient. Further work on multiparty talk in geriatric care is discussed in chapter 6 (this volume) by Coupland and Coupland.

Studies Linking Physician–Older Patient Interactions With Patient Outcomes

To understand strategies that physicians may use to improve older patient's adherence with medication regimens, Coe, Prendergast, and Psathas (1984) audiotaped visits between physicians, patients, and accompanying relatives. The tapes were transcribed using an approach that examined the structure and dynamics of the encounter through assessment of the form, sequence, and content of the interactions. Three transcribed cases are discussed. Coe et al. found that polypharmacy was present in the cases reviewed and patients and relatives often did not have a complete understanding of the medications discussed, although physicians repeated information and instructions. The physician often directed conversation to the relative (rather than the patient) and relied on this individual to help manage the patient's medication regimen. Physicians tended to use language that matched the patient's level of understanding. Physicians also took into consideration the patient's daily life in determining the scheduling of the medication regimen.

Rost and Roter (1987) examined how communication between physicians and older patients influenced the likelihood of patients' recall of medication regimens and lifestyle change recommendations made during the visit. Patients in a hospital clinic specializing in geriatric care were audiotaped and coded with the Roter Interaction Analysis system. In the analysis of 83 visits, Rost and Roter found that both closed-ended questions and more informational statements were positively associated with recall of medication regimens. Discussion of patient's emotional issues was negatively associated with medication recall. Thus, in visits with emotional discussions, Rost and Roter recommended that physicians make sure to review drug regimens again at the end of a visit. In the 42 instances in which lifestyle-change recommendations were offered, physician information-giving and coders' assessment of the presence of physician and patient anger were positively associated with recall of recommendations for change in diet. Rost and Roter suggested that "information-giving in conjunction with serious affect may act to reinforce the importance of lifestyle recommendations and promote their recall" (p. 514).

To understand older patients' satisfaction with physician–patient communication, we conducted post-visit interviews and examined correlations between the coded interactions and patients' responses in the interviews (Greene, Adelman, Friedmann, & Charon, 1994). Older patients' satisfaction with the encounters was associated with greater physician support, more frequent shared laughter, a longer visit, physicians' demonstration of being engaged in the encounter, better quality physician questioning on patient-initiated topics, better quality patient informing, less patient question-asking, more frequent use of questions worded in the negative by physicians (e.g., "no chest pain, no shortness of breath?"), and more frequent use of "orientations to the visit" (i.e., letting the patient know what will be happening next during the visit). These findings suggested to us that these older patients may have preferred a communication style that is usually considered characteristic of a physician–patient relationship circa 1950, namely, a warm interpersonal style with physician control and physician-determined structure for the visit. Clearly, different groups of patients, patients at different sites, and future older patients need to be studied to determine the interactional correlates of satisfaction.

Other Studies

Most recently, we (Greene et al., 1999) examined a longitudinal series of visits between physicians and older patients during the first year and a half of their relationship to determine: (a) if there is systematic change in the communication between physicians and patients over time, and (b) how communication in the first visit influences communication in subsequent visits. Seventeen physician–older patient pairs were followed

(138 visits were audiotaped over the study period). It was found that all interactional processes (i.e., physician and patient questioning, informing, and support) and most global variables (i.e., physician egalitarianism, patience, engagement, and respect; patient assertiveness, friendliness, relaxation, and expressiveness; and encounter warmth and depth) did not systematically change over time. However, the global encounter variable, trust between the physician and the patient, increased as the physician–patient relationship continued. In addition, many of these aspects of communication in first visits were strong predictors of communication in subsequent visits. Thus, both physicians and patients may get insight into the interactional quality of their relationship at their initial meeting.

Although this research on physician–older patient interactions in natural settings is limited in some respects, the findings discussed here provide preliminary information about the content and process of communication in the physician–older patient relationship. As most of the studies (ours included) utilize small samples, different interactional coding systems, and different data collection sites and cohorts of older patients, additional methodologically sound empirical work in this area is needed. Forging the link between this research and clinical medical practice is the next important step. In the next section, we begin this effort.

STRATEGIES FOR IMPROVING THE PHYSICIAN–OLDER PATIENT RELATIONSHIP

Effective and empathic communication between the physician and the older patient is the basis for a robust physician–older patient relationship. What aspects of communication will help forge this relationship? In this section, we describe some strategies that physicians and patients may employ for developing their relationship. These recommendations are derived from our analysis of the implications of the empirical literature to date and clinical experience in geriatric care (RA). In particular we discuss: (a) non-ageist approaches to care, (b) acknowledging and supporting the "personhood" of the older patient (including life review), (c) attending to the patient's agenda, (d) confronting difficult-to-talk-about subjects, (e) sensitive methods for dealing with sensory and other functional limitations, (f) approaches to dealing with family members and others who accompany the patient to the medical visit, (g) the role of the geriatrician as the coordinator of the multidimensional aspects of the patient's care, and (h) the patient's contribution to improving the relationship.

Non-Ageist Approaches to Care

A non-ageist approach to care of older patients is essential for the development of the physician–older patient relationship (Adelman, Greene, & Charon, 1991). A non-ageist approach recognizes the extraordinary heterogeneity of the older population (Haug & Ory, 1987). Each patient (whether older or younger) must be seen as an individual, with special needs and different concerns and beliefs. By paying attention to issues such as health promotion for the older patient, the physician discards stereotypes that often (mis)guide individuals' responses to older persons. For example, health promotion concerns like smoking cessation, exercise and diet, are appropriate and important to discuss with older patients. The ageist notion that smoking may be one of an older person's few small pleasures discounts the meaning of the lives of older individuals and contributes to the continuation of a dangerous habit. Stopping smoking at any age improves health (United States Department of Health and Human Services, 1990). Although the media often treat older individuals' sexuality with humor (especially with the advent of Viagra), concerns about sexual function are real and must be addressed. Physicians who pay attention to this issue are providing non-ageist care.

Acknowledging the Personhood of the Patient

Building a relationship means getting to know the patient as a person. Through a comprehensive life history and life review of the older patient, the physician acquires this knowledge. Accessing this history may be time-consuming initially, but the pay-offs are substantial as the physician acquires information about who the patient is and acknowledges the unique "personhood" of the patient; and the patient sees that the physician is interested in him or her as more than a disease entity (Brown & Weston, 1995). Through discussions of the patient's life history, the physician develops an understanding of the patient's present life; this knowledge can greatly assist the physician in diagnosing and treating the patient's current problems. Allowing for and supporting the patient's presentation of self, that is, the patient's disclosure of his or her identity, will undoubtedly improve the relationship (Greene, Adelman, Rizzo, et al., 1994). Indeed, this process of knowing the patient is the best approach to destroying ageism: The more one knows a patient, the less the patient is relegated into a stereotype.

However, a non-ageist approach to the medical interview should not just focus on the past and the patient's history. The visit should be framed with an orientation to the present as well as to the future. Indeed, demographers provide information on the aging of the population, including the growing number of centenarians (Metropolitan Life Insurance Company, 1987), and the literature on "successful aging" presents a compelling argument for planning for the future within the context of the geriatric medical visit. For example, a non-ageist approach to the "old-old" years embraces an "anticipatory guidance" perspective, that is, allowing planning for a vital future. A primary care provider who is aware of the epidemiology of potential serious problems of older individuals may also help older patients by recommending specific preventive strategies to avoid such risks as falls and medication nonadherence and overuse.

Recently, there has been a return to medical home visits for frail elderly. These visits, which permit the physician to see the patient in the home environment, may also cement the relationship. The home visit gives the provider an unusual opportunity to examine family dynamics, functional status, living conditions, and the patient's identity. Being a visitor or guest in another's home changes the power dynamics of the medical visit and allows the patient to exert more control over the encounter (Sankar, 1986). This leveling of the interactional "playing field" may make it easier for the patient to share more intimate information and feelings with the physician.

Attending to the Patient's Agenda

Physicians often do not give patients a chance to initiate discussion of their concerns (Marvel, Epstein, Flowers, & Beckman, 1999), and patients' questions are "dispreferred" in medical interviews (Frankel, 1990; West, 1984). Compounding this lack of attentiveness, we found that physicians were more responsive to the topics they raised than to the topics that patients raised. Also, when patients are able to initiate discussion of their issues, they are not dealt with as well as when physicians raise an issue. Moreover, the patient agenda for the visit and the physician agenda for the visit may be discordant (Greene et al., 1989). Clearly, a focus on patient-raised issues or the "patient-centered" approach is called for, if the physician wishes to engage the patient in the encounter. Without such attentiveness, the relationship will be in peril (Stewart et al., 1995).

Discussing Difficult-to-Talk-About Subjects

Geriatric medicine incorporates the psychosocial realm into medical decision making. Strategies that allow psychosocial issues to naturally unfold in the encounter are essential for a comprehensive evaluation.

Older patients are likely to have multiple medical and psychosocial problems. Some of these problems may be embarrassing or uncomfortable for patients to raise. A physician who is seeking to build a relationship with older patients will make sure to create an environment in which patients feel "safe" to discuss difficult-to-talk-about subjects such as loneliness, depression, neglect and abuse, caregiver burden, fears about death, advance directives, memory loss, incontinence, and sexual dysfunction. These intimate subjects can only be discussed when patients feel that they can trust the physician. How does the physician create a safe encounter? First, physicians have to let patients know that the information which is exchanged during the medical visit is confidential. When patients understand that their privacy will be preserved, they are likely to be more disclosing. Second, physicians must strive to be nonjudgmental. Accepting patients' attitudes and behaviors, even when they are diametrically opposed to those of the physician, is key (albeit difficult to accomplish) in creating a safe setting for difficult disclosures. Third, physicians must provide continued support and encouragement to patients as they reveal their embarrassing or intimate stories. This provision of support includes allowing patients to talk without interruption, verbally acknowledging patients' distress, and being attentive to such nonverbal cues as tear-filled eyes, voice alterations, or trembling hands. Fourth, assurances that the physician will try to assist the patient by providing informational, instrumental, and/or emotional support must be offered (Greene, Adelman, et al., 1996). This support may be as basic as letting the patient know that the physician is available to listen again at their next visit or as complicated as intervening (with the patient's permission) in a case of elder abuse. Also, the physician must realize that intimate questions may need to be raised over time. Asking about do-not-resuscitate (DNR) orders at a first visit may be early for some patients. Part of the art of medicine is being sensitive to the timing of when sensitive subjects can be raised with comfort.

Awareness of Sensory and Functional Limitations

Older patients may have sensory deficits, including problems with vision, hearing, or both. They may also have problems with ambulation. When these limitations are managed in a sensitive and caring way, patients will be both relieved and grateful. For example, one physician recommends always having special hearing assistive devices available in the office (Butler, Finkel, Lewis, Sherman, & Sunderland, 1992). Medical offices must be able to accommodate wheelchairs and individuals who accompany the patient into the examining room. While such arrangements may seem obvious, in practice many offices are not designed to deal with the functional limitations that some older people have. There is a clear need for attentiveness to environmental design in geriatrics, where older patients' special needs are considered in the planning and construction of medical offices, furnishings, and equipment (Shroyer, 1994).

Dealing With Family and Significant Others

Many older individuals have multiple chronic health problems that require assistance from family members and significant others (Silliman, 1989). Thus, geriatricians must meet and talk with a patient's caregivers to assure that the patient's needs are being met. Patients may require assistance from family members or others in daily activities, maintenance of a medication regimen, or transportation for medical services. All of these needs and many others are important for the medical care and health status of the patient. In addition to discussing these tasks with family members or other caregivers, physicians must also attend to issues as diverse as caregiver burden and elder mistreatment. The geriatrician must pay attention to the patient–caregiver relationship. A well-developed working relationship between the geriatrician and the caregiver is essential for optimal care of the patient. This relationship takes on added importance when a patient is particularly frail or cognitively impaired.

Coordinating Geriatric Care

Not only must geriatricians communicate well with patients and family members or caregivers, but they must also be skilled in communicating with geriatric team members who manage the multiple, complex needs of older patients. Thus, as a team participant, the geriatrician must coordinate care and the transfer of information among the physician subspecialists, nurse, social worker, nutritionist, physical therapist, and so on. This task requires sophisticated and well-honed interpersonal skills so that integrated information is given to the patient, family, and all care providers. The development of the physician–older patient relationship is also dependent on the quality of communication that occurs within the context of the entire geriatric team (Campbell & Cole, 1987).

In addition, care for a frail elder may be provided across a continuum of services and sites. For instance, a patient who is seen in a geriatric outpatient practice may be hospitalized, then transferred to a rehabilitation center, and then transferred to a nursing home, assisted living facility, or back home. These changes, which may be traumatic for some patients, require monitoring and coordination by a member of the health care team. Models of better communication across care sites are essential to quality geriatric care.

The Older Patient's Contribution to Improving Physician–Patient Communication

Although the focus of this chapter is on the physician's role in building the physician–patient relationship, this relationship is dynamic and interactive and participants contribute in their own ways to communication in the medical encounter. Thus, in this section, we briefly discuss strategies that patients can employ to improve communication in the physician–patient relationship.

Older patients often do not raise their own important issues during the medical visit (Rost & Frankel, 1993). There are many possible explanations for why an older patient might not initiate discussion of an important subject. It is possible that the patient: (a) simply forgot to raise the issue, (b) did not think that the problem was important enough, (c) did not think the subject was appropriate to raise in a medical visit, (d) felt that other issues took precedence, (e) was discouraged from raising the topic because of the physician's response to other subjects, (f) was embarrassed about the problem, (g) feared how the physician would respond to the problem, (h) felt uncomfortable about raising the issue when a family member was present, (i) was concerned about taking up too much of the doctor's time, or (j) felt uncomfortable questioning an authority figure. Whatever the explanation, by preparing for the visit well in advance (if this is possible), many of these situations may be managed. We recommend that prior to a visit, the patient should: (a) identify his or her own agenda for the visit and write it down in a list prioritized according to the patient's level of concern; (b) prepare a list of questions and prioritize the questions; and (c) enlist the assistance of a trusted family member or friend to accompany him/her to the visit, to support the patient in getting his/her agenda addressed. During the encounter, the patient should refer to the list at the very beginning of the visit and continually refer to it during the visit. Perhaps, preparing a copy of the list for the physician would provide a definitive focus for the visit and get the important issues addressed. Also, this will allow the physician to better structure his/her time during the visit. Patients should also be prepared to take notes during the visit and ask the physician for educational materials. When information is not clearly transmitted, the physician should be asked to explain again. Although this assertive approach is difficult for some older patients, it is likely to improve patients' accurate recall of information, a prerequisite for adherence with medication and other therapeutic regimens. Also, as physicians may not be aware of hearing or vision impairments that may impede communication, the patient should inform the physician that these problems exist at the beginning of the visit.

After the visit, the older patient still has the opportunity to clarify areas of confusion or concern. Telephone calls to the doctor or nurse may be informative and extremely valuable as a patient reviews the visit and assesses subjects that require further explanation and discussion.

Older patients may have to work at getting their psychosocial concerns addressed during the visit (Greene & Adelman, 1996a; Waitzkin et al., 1994). With this mind, older patients should be reminded to specify these issues on their list of questions/concerns which they bring with them to the medical visit. Older patients should be warned, however, that when they are seen as emotionally dependent, depressed, or anxious by their doctor, they may be less likely to receive medical information during the visit (Roter, 1991). Therefore, if patients wish to discuss subjects with emotional content, they should be aware that all their medical concerns may not be adequately addressed. Although it is unfortunate that discussion of one important content area may be sacrificed for another, time constraints in current practice settings may leave physicians with few options. It may be best for both physicians and patients to think of addressing patients' multiple varied issues over several consecutive visits rather than just one hurried encounter.

There is no question that the presence of a third person in the medical encounter affects the interactional dynamics of that visit (Greene, Majerovitz, et al., 1994). It is key that the physician spend some of the visit time alone with the patient so that sensitive, private issues may be raised and addressed. This may be difficult to accomplish by the patient alone because it is the physician who structures the visit, and the patient may feel uncomfortable asking the accompanying individual to leave. If there is no time alone during the visit, the patient should call the physician to address those issues which were not discussed or express the desire to see the physician alone at their next visit.

Preliminary analysis of a longitudinal series of primary care medical visits between internists and older patients revealed that the interactional processes and global tone of the physician in the first visit was a good predictor of physician behavior in subsequent visits (Greene, Adelman, Rizzo, & Majerovitz, 1999). Thus, this small data set suggests that older patients be advised that if they are dissatisfied with a physician after the first few visits, it is not likely that there will be major changes in the physician's interpersonal style in the future. Although changing physicians is not always easily accomplished in some managed care environments and some patients find it difficult to make a change even under optimally supportive conditions, it is probably easier to search for a new provider earlier than later in the care process.

These specific and seemingly simplistic recommendations, spelled out in a volume intended for academics and clinicians, do not capture the superior interactional skills required by patients to put these suggestions effectively into practice. Older patients should not be blamed if they are unable or unsuccessful in accomplishing these tasks. The medical encounter is a complex and frequently emotional interaction. To achieve an effective and mutually satisfying medical visit is a major accomplishment for both participants.

CASE EXAMPLE

The following case illustrates how an understanding of the patient's psychosocial status and personhood directly contributes to accurate diagnosis and appropriate care. In this case, healing occurs on multiple levels.

Mr. A., a 75-year-old retired glove maker, came to the outpatient office without an appointment. He was a new patient to the practice. Because his complaint was chest pain for several days, he was seen immediately. When asked why he didn't come in earlier, he stated that he thought it was indigestion and he wasn't worried, but the symptom was getting worse and he decided to see the physician. Mr. A. denied shortness of breath and any cardiac symptoms other than left-sided chest pain. Aside from the current problem, Mr. A's prior health status was excellent. In fact, he had not seen a physician for years. He had no previous hospitalizations and was not on any medications. He stated that until recently, he walked several miles every day without shortness of breath and without chest pain.

Mr. A. was evaluated in the office and found to have normal vital signs. He was sent to the hospital emergency department (ED) for further assessment. In the ED, he was given a nitroglycerine tablet and there was no significant improvement. He was then admitted to the hospital and given a series of tests to rule out a myocardial infarction. All his tests were normal and thus, it was less likely that he had an acute cardiovascular problem.

On coming to his room 3 days after the admission, the attending geriatrician asked, "What do you think is going on?" The patient started to cry uncontrollably and told the physician that several months prior to this episode of chest pain, his sister, who he was very close to, had died. Mr. A. clearly expressed that he felt the chest pain was his heartache stemming from the loss of his sister. He hadn't mentioned this to others when asked about his personal history because he didn't think it was relevant to the medical evaluation. Mr A. explained further that he had been a prisoner in a concentration camp during World War II and his sister had been responsible for his survival. She had somehow avoided encampment and had arranged to sneak food to him during his imprisonment. He felt tremendous guilt about her death, feeling that he had not done enough for her (although he traveled a long distance to see his sister daily). He kept apologizing during this discussion about his sister, saying that physicians don't need to know this and this is not important information contributing to the work doctors do. The physician assured him that indeed it was essential to understand his psychological situation to better explain what was happening to him physiologically. Mr. A. was extremely grateful to the physician and held onto the physician's hand until the physician had to leave. Mr. A. was discharged that day (after a stress test proved to be negative) and was given a follow-up appointment with a counselor to discuss the situation. Because it was only several months since his sister's death, the patient's condition was not assessed as pathologic grief, and the doctors felt that with discussions of his past and participation in a bereavement group, Mr. A. would be able to resolve his concerns. The physicians plan to follow him closely.

The essence of geriatric medicine is in the comprehensive care of the patient. The recognition of the multidimensionality of older patients allows the geriatrician to provide effective and humane care. Without physician attention to the patient's perspective in this case, more tests may have been performed; the length of stay in the hospital would have been extended (with increased risk of iatrogenic complications); costs of care would have been greater; and most importantly, the patient would not have arrived at his own correct diagnosis. It was through the conversation with the physician that the patient was able to articulate the true cause of his problem. By creating a safe environment for the patient to verbalize his thoughts and feelings, the physician gave the patient an opportunity to access his true emotions which were present on a subconscious level. Although the relationship in this case was developed over a relatively brief time, through one office visit, a visit in the ED, and two visits in the hospital, it was enough time for this patient to recognize that the physician was accepting, nonjudgmental and empathic. The patient's reluctance to discuss his psychosocial concerns was abated by a collaborative and interpersonally astute physician.

With the threats that managed care pose to the physician–patient relationship, it is important to document that a continuing relationship is key to quality medical care. For example, to accommodate managed care, many hospitals have created "hospitalists," that is, a separate group of physicians who manage all inpatient care. The traditional primary care functions of internists, family practitioners, and geriatricians to provide continuity of outpatient and inpatient care is clearly endangered. The implications of this systemic change need to be studied. What is the impact to the physician–older patient relationship with this change in the structure of care? How are patient outcomes affected? Some of these questions are addressed by Nussbaum, Pecchioni, and Crowell (chap. 2, this volume).

This chapter reviews empirical investigations of physician–older patient communication in natural settings and attempts to draw, from this literature and the clinical experiences of one of the authors, some recommendations for building the physician–older patient relationship. The suggestions offered here must be viewed within the current context of the health care system and within the current cohort of older patients. As the system changes and as middle-aged individuals enter into the young-old cohort, we will need to revisit and reevaluate these issues. What is known and is unlikely to change is that the physician–older patient relationship has a significant impact on the lives of patients and their physicians. Medical educators must emphasize this haunting fact amid the full biomedical medical school curriculum. And practitioners, who are increasingly pressured to measure their success by assessing cost–benefit ratios, must recall the deeper meaning of their work. It is essential to urge medical educators, clinicians, researchers, and health planners to pay attention to both the caring processes of medicine and the ultimate, multilayered outcomes of care.

REFERENCES

Adelman, R. D., Greene, M. G., & Charon, R. (1991). Issues in physician–elderly patient interaction. *Aging and Society, 11*, 127–148.

Beisecker, A. L. (1989). The influence of a companion on the doctor–elderly patient interaction. *Health Communication, 1*, 55–70.

Brown, J. B., & Weston, W. W. (1995). The second component: Understanding the whole person. In M. Stewart, J. B. Brown, W. W. Weston, I. R. McWhinney, C. L. McWilliam, & T. R. Freeman (Eds.), *Patient-centered medicine: Transforming the clinical method* (pp. 44–57). Thousand Oaks, CA: Sage.

Butler, R. N., Finkel, S. I., Lewis, M. I., Sherman F. T., & Sunderland, T. (1992). Aging and mental health: Part 2. Diagnosis of dementia and depression. *Geriatrics, 47*, 49–57.

Campbell, L. J., & Cole, K. D. (1987). Geriatric assessment teams. *Clinics in Geriatric Medicine, 3*, 99–110.

Charon, R., Greene, M. G., & Adelman, R. D. (1994). Multidimensional interaction analysis: A collaborative approach to the study of medical discourse. *Social Science and Medicine, 39*, 955–965.

Coe, R. M., & Prendergast, C. G. (1985). The formation of coalitions: Interaction strategies in triads. *Sociology of Health and Illness, 7*, 237–247.

Coe, R. M., Prendergast, C. G., & Psathas, G. (1984). Strategies for obtaining compliance with medication regimens. *Journal of the American Geriatrics Society, 32*, 589–594.

Coupland, J., Robinson, J. D., & Coupland, N. (1994). Frame negotiation in doctor–elderly patient consultations. *Discourse and Society, 5*, 89–123.

Frankel, R. (1990). Talking in interviews: A dispreference for patient-initiated questions in physician–patient encounters. In G. Psathas (Ed.), *Interaction competence* (pp. 231–264). Washington DC: University Press of America.

Greene, M. G. (1987). *The physician–elderly patient relationship: An examination of the language and behavior of doctors with their elderly patients.* Final report to the AARP Andrus Foundation.

Greene, M. G., & Adelman, R. (1996a). Psychosocial factors in older patients' medical encounters. *Research on Aging, 18*, 84–102.

Greene, M. G., & Adelman, R. (1996b). *Responsiveness of physicians and older patients to self-initiated and other-initiated topics in first medical visits.* Paper presented at The Fifth Kentucky Conference on Health Communication, Lexington.

Greene, M. G., Adelman, R. D., Charon, R., & Friedmann, E. (1989). Concordance between physicians and their older and younger patients in the primary care medical encounter. *The Gerontologist, 29*, 808–813.

Greene, M. G., Adelman, R. D., Charon, R., & Hoffman, S. (1986). Ageism in the medical encounter: An exploratory study of the doctor–elderly patient relationship. *Language and Communication, 6*, 113–124.

Greene, M. G., Adelman, R. D., Friedmann, E., & Charon, R. (1994). Older patient satisfaction with communication during an initial medical encounter. *Social Science and Medicine, 38*, 1279–1288.

Greene, M. G., Adelman, R., & Majerovitz, S. D. (1996). Physician and older patient support in the medical encounter. *Health Communication, 8*, 263–280.

Greene, M. G., Adelman, R. D., Rizzo, C., & Friedmann, E. (1994). The patient's presentation of self in an initial medical encounter. In M. Hummert, J. Wiemann, & J. Nussbaum (Eds.), *Interpersonal communication in older adulthood* (pp. 226–250). Newbury Park, CA: Sage.

Greene, M. G., Adelman, R. D., Rizzo, C., & Majerovitz, S. D. (1999). *A longitudinal study of the physician–elderly patient relationship.* Unpublished manuscript.

Greene, M. G., Majerovitz, S. D., Adelman, R. D., & Rizzo, C. (1994). The effects of the presence of a third person on the physician–older patient medical interview. *Journal of the American Geriatrics Society, 42*, 413–419.

Hasselkus, B. R. (1992). Physician and family caregiver in the medical setting? Negotiation of care? *Journal of Aging Studies, 6*, 67–80.

Haug, M., & Ory, M. (1987). Issues in elderly patient–provider interactions. *Research on Aging*, 9, 3–44.

Lazare, A., Putnam, S. M., & Lipkin, M., Jr. (1995). Three functions of the medical interview. In M. Lipkin, Jr., S. Putnam, & A. Lazare (Eds.), *The medical interview: Clinical care, education, and research* (pp. 3–19). New York: Springer-Verlag.

Levinson, W., Roter, D., Mullooly, J. P., Dull, V. T., & Frankel, R. M. (1997). Physician–patient communication: The relationship with malpractice claims among primary care physicians and surgeons. *Journal of the American Medical Association*, 277, 553–559.

Marvel, M. K., Epstein, R. M., Flowers, K., & Beckman, H. B. (1999). Soliciting the patient's agenda: Have we improved? *Journal of the American Medical Association*, 281, 283–287.

Metropolitan Life Insurance Company (1987). Profile of centenarians. *Statistical Bulletin*, 68, 2–9.

Parsons, T. (1951). *The social system*. New York: Free Press.

Rost, K., & Frankel, R. (1993). The introduction of the older patient's problems in the medical visit. *Journal of Aging and Health*, 5, 387–401.

Rost, K., & Roter, D. (1987). Predictors of recall of medication regimens and recommendations for lifestyle change in elderly patients. *The Gerontologist*, 27, 510–515.

Roter, D. (1991). Elderly patient–physician communication: A descriptive study of content and affect during the medical encounter. *Advances in Health Education*, 3, 179–190.

Roter, D. L., & Hall, J. (1992). *Doctors talking with patients/Patients talking with doctors*. Westport, CT: Auburn House.

Sankar, A. (1986). Out of the clinic into the home: Control and patient–physician communication. *Social Science and Medicine*, 22, 973–982.

Shroyer, J. L. (1994). Recommendations for environmental design research correlating falls and the physical environment. *Experimental Aging Research*, 20, 303–309.

Silliman, R. (1989). Caring for the frail older patient: The doctor–patient–family caregiver relationship. *Journal of General Internal Medicine*, 4, 237–241.

Stewart, M. (1995). Effective physician–patient communication and health outcomes: A review. *Canadian Medical Association Journal*, 152, 1423–1433.

Stewart, M., Brown, J. B., Weston, W. W., McWhinney, I. R., McWilliam, C. L., & Freeman, T. R. (1995). *Patient-centered medicine: Transforming the clinical method*. Thousand Oaks, CA: Sage.

Suchman, A. L., Branch, W. T., & Matthews, D. A. (1995). The role of the medical interview in the physician's search for meaning. In M. Lipkin, Jr., S. Putnam, & A. Lazare (Eds.), *The medical interview: Clinical care, education, and research* (pp. 368–375). New York: Springer-Verlag.

United States Department of Health and Human Services (1990). *The health benefits of smoking cessation. A report of the surgeon-general*. Rockville, MD: Author.

Waitzkin, H., Britt, T., & Williams, C. (1994). Narratives of aging and social problems in medical encounters with older persons. *Journal of Health and Social Behavior*, 35, 322–348.

West, C. (1984). *Routine complications: Troubles talk between doctors and patients*. Bloomington: Indiana University Press.

6

Roles, Responsibilities, and Alignments: Multiparty Talk in Geriatric Care

Justine Coupland
Nikolas Coupland
University of Wales, Cardiff

In the provision of health care services for older people, the importance of "relationships" or "the relational dimension of professional/patient communication" scarcely needs to be argued. In terms of a multiple goals model of human communication (e.g., Tracy & Coupland, 1990), the potentially delicate and profound personal implications of illness always require professionals to attend to relational and identity goals in their interaction with patients, alongside medically oriented, instrumental goals. Indeed, we have to see relational goals as pursued in the service of the instrumental goals of medical and caring interactions (Coupland, Robinson, & Coupland, 1994; Fisher, 1991; Ragan, 1990). When patients are elderly, relational aspects of health can be even more important, for example, in cases where chronic conditions need to be "managed" rather than "cured," or when patients' social circumstances (e.g., loneliness or dependency) compound bio-medical problems.

The issue that motivates this chapter's analysis is the fact that first-line medical encounters involving older patients are often constituted by more participants than the classical "doctor–patient" pair, and that this entails a certain sort of relational complexity that deserves investigation. Indeed, studies by Beisecker (1989), Coe and Prendergast (1985), Greene, Majerovitz, Adelman, and Rizzo (1994), and Hasselkus (1992) have already shown the importance of a multiparty perspective in research on aging and medical/clinical communication (see also the review in Greene & Adelman, chap. 5, this volume). There may be practical benefits for practitioners in a close examination of how third parties feature in geriatric medical interactions, perhaps allowing them to reevaluate good practice and make more effective use of multiparty involvement as a resource. Although we touch on applied issues at the end of the chapter, as nonmedical professionals, our main ambitions are less practical and more theoretical and methodological. We believe there has been too little attention paid, in the literature on communication and aging, to the details of naturally occurring talk involving older people, and to those aspects of social relationships that talk cannot avoid constructing. In health domains, especially in social circumstances where we can inspect family members' involvement in the care of elderly patients as well as the formal institutions at work, we can build a clearer picture of how relationships impinge on health in old age. We can trace some of the values and priorities transacted in the name of "geriatric medicine,"[1] and the diversity of roles and allegiances that are central to it.

We examine a body of medical consultations at a U.K. Geriatrics Outpatients clinic, each of which involves, as principal participants, an elderly patient, a medical doctor qualified in the care of the elderly, and a third person who has accompanied the patient to the clinic. When older patients are accompanied to clinics by a friend or another family member, and when the consultation then becomes, at least in a literal sense, triadic, many relational configurations become possible. For example, the accompanying person and the doctor can enter into various sorts of confederation, perhaps with persuasive intentions, trying to gain the elderly patient's compliance with a course of treatment or an advised lifestyle change. Alternatively, family members may share in voicing the experiences of their co-present elderly relatives, validating their accounts of symptoms or troubles. Third parties may collaborate with patients in telling troubles or describing health and social changes, or they may even act as, in a sense, surrogate patients (cf. Hasselkus', 1992, remarks about "patient-substitutes").

Some of these configurations raise fundamental ethical concerns about the rights and responsibilities of health care for older people. They connect directly with the political debates that have provided the context for a good deal of sociolinguistic, social-psychological, and communication science research on aging (as represented in this volume and see, e.g., Coupland &

---

[1]We have generally tried to avoid the term *geriatrics* because of its generally pejorative uses. On the other hand, it is the term that has become established in medical domains specializing in health care for older people. It is part of the official designation of the outpatient clinic where we did our ethnographic research and collected the present body of audio-recorded data.

Coupland, 1999; Nussbaum & Coupland, 1995; Ryan & Cole, 1990). A general theme of this research has been what we might call the *communicative disenfranchisement* of older people, who can sometimes be shown to be victims of patronizing communication (e.g., Hummert, 1994; Ryan, Bourhis, & Knops, 1991) or over-accommodative talk (Coupland, Coupland, & Giles, 1991). Studies have often been driven by a desire to expose, and ideologically resist, patterns of linguistic usage that impute frailty or dependency to older people and deny them respect and autonomous control over their own decisions, values, and even experiences. "Speaking for" or "speaking past" an elderly patient can certainly be disenfranchising. It can be one form of ageist social practice, realized at the microinteractional level.

Although this perspective certainly surfaces at some points in the data, it is not the starting point for our analysis. Firstly, it would be wrong to assume that the triadic participation structure is inherently difficult² or disadvantageous to older people as patients. In the cases we consider, elderly patients have generally asked to be accompanied and have sometimes needed physical or emotional support to attend the clinic. In these ways, structuring the medical encounter as a triad of participants may be inevitable in some cases, and it may also be preferred by older people. Indeed, one of the hallmarks of geriatrics as a medical specialty is multiparty involvement with patients (Hall, Maclennan, & Dye, 1993). Care for older people very often brings

---

²Some complexities associated with triadic interaction have been commented on in the discourse and pragmatics literatures, and they have clear implications for the negotiation of relational frames. A classic difficulty in all triadic interaction, even where (as in our data) all three participants are fully ratified within the encounter, is ambiguity of inclusiveness, for example, in address. A doctor's utterance beginning with *you* may, depending on content and context, identify one or two of the other participants (in addition to the generic sense of *you* meaning "someone" or "anyone"). That is, the two hearers will each need to decide whether, at that moment, they are being framed as addressees or alternatively as over-hearers, with all that that distinction might entail. Although the speaker's direction of gaze may disambiguate intended address (and our audiotapes of course fail to record such data), there is no necessary correlation between gaze and addresseeship (Goodwin, 1981). Where a doctor's *you* address is interpretable as inclusive (addressed to both the other main participants), the relational effect may be to corral a third party into shared responsibility for a treatment regime. Where it is interpretable as exclusively addressed to a third party, the effect may be to frame the patient as excluded from such responsibility (cf. Lerner, 1996; Levinson, 1988). Comparable complexities attach to other pronoun usages. A doctor's *we* can be pragmatically inclusive of all three main participants, or of some dyad subset, or inclusive only of the doctor and his/her professional colleagues. Complexities over third-person reference (rather than address) in triadic encounters are again well known. What are the implications of a third party referring to a patient as *he* or *my father*, or to a medical or emotional problem as *his difficulty in walking* or *his depression*, in that person's presence, and how does this usage differ from second-person pronoun address (*you*) in specific circumstances? Agency, responsibility, credit or blame can be apportioned (or be assumed to be apportioned) or denied, empathy and exclusion can be signaled, very subtly by these means. Again there can be a significant impact on the relationships constructed between participants through talk.

together family members, friends, and various sorts of professionals into caring networks. Secondly, the impact of third parties on the interactional
development of these encounters is highly variable. Only certain particular
moments and interactional stances within the data conform to the disenfranchisement model. Even then, complex contextual factors qualify simple
political interpretations. There is a risk of prematurely invoking the concept
of ageism in research on aging even though ageism must remain at the top
of its political agenda. Thirdly, and implicitly in the preceding points, there
are important methodological arguments, linked to theory, for not prejudg-
ing the data. The approach we adopt in the following analyses can be called
discourse analysis or interactional pragmatics, and we set out some of its
assumptions and imperatives in the following section.

A DISCOURSE-ANALYTIC APPROACH
TO RELATIONSHIPS

Key concepts in discourse analysis are contextualization, process, and
contingency (Jaworski & Coupland, 1999). A discourse perspective considers how relationships are enacted, in particular circumstances, incre-
mentally as talk proceeds, and by virtue of participants engaging with
each other's orientations and contributions to talk. The perspective is
social constructionist, to the extent that relationships are viewed as
emerging from the processes of social interaction. Within discourse theory, relationships are not "reflected in" or "indexed by" language; relationships are inherently discursive. They are alignments manufactured in and
through acts of speaking. It is talk that generates social structure, of
which relationships are a part. There is no distinction between the social
order and the interactional order (Boden & Zimmerman, 1991).

To many, this will seem a radical theoretical position to adopt, and it
certainly requires a new reading of traditional social psychological theo-
rizing of intergroup relations (Giles & Coupland, 1991). Social psychology and communication research has held, for example, that there are
indeed regularities in the patterning of intergenerational relations, in the
sense of rather global intergroup cognitions and values, which survey
designs discern. But a discourse perspective can refine and qualify group-
level approaches and capture how relationships are actually experienced,
with all of their complexities and nuances. For example, it is important
not to homogenize social roles such as "the daughter role," "the doctor
role," or the "elderly sick role," or prejudge how people presume to fill out
these roles relate to one another. As we already suggested, it is important

not to prejudge geriatric consultation triads ethically or politically, and it is obvious in our data that many different stances and alignments are achieved. Therefore, we set out to trace the relational configurations that actually materialize in our data and better understand the sociolinguistic strategies through which participants achieve them. We want to build interpretations, based on the close examination of specific instances, of how people use the resource of multiple participation in the consultations to defend or promote their local stances and goals.

This approach necessarily sacrifices potential to generalize, in a demographic sense, about the relational processes we describe. We cannot extrapolate from our particular instances to "what most relationships are like," in geriatric medicine or intergenerationally within families. Through discourse analysis we may, on the other hand, be able to generalize about the range of contextual factors that are relevant in the process of constructing relationships in settings like ours, and to generate richer descriptions of the communicative ecology of medical consultations involving older people. From the discourse perspective, what we need to research in the area of communication, health, and the elderly is how identities, relationships, and values are constructed and managed through talk, in ways distinctive of this social situation.

We develop an approach to discourse centered on the notion of *discursive frames*. Frames, in Goffman's (1981) sense, are constellations of participants' assumptions and understandings in the light of which talk proceeds. Frames are therefore a central part of the mutuality that allows all interpersonal communication to take place. Frames too need to be seen as interactional achievements. As Goffman showed (see also Tannen & Wallat, 1993, for an illustration of frame shifting in another medical situation), participants actively negotiate frames and engineer frame shifts within ongoing talk. In an earlier analysis of other data from the geriatric medical clinic we demonstrated, for example, how doctors and patients move in and out of social frames, especially at the periphery of these encounters (Coupland, Robinson, & Coupland, 1994). We showed how social (vs. medical) frames are signaled by participants and how agreement about which frame obtains conditions the nature of talk and the inferences participants draw from it.[3] Frame

---

[3]To take an obvious case, a doctor may be expected to be positioned in a medical consultation as a medical professional, with all that this implies about speaking rights, authority, goals, constraints, and so on. This is probably the default frame for the main business of the medical encounter, unless doctors do conversational work of some sort to break this frame and propose another, perhaps one in which their talk is hearable as a "personal" (rather than a "professional") contribution. As we showed in the earlier analysis, doctors have resources to reposition themselves within these encounters, to

management can be analyzed by examining talk because frames are often marked through formal and functional elements of language. Through verbal and nonverbal markers, and conversational inferencing work linked to them, participants in triadic consultations can index and potentially impose a particular frame, that is, a particular set of understandings about how talk is being entertained. This includes framing social relationships among speakers. A frame, once established, is operative within the consultation until one or more participants move to break or modify or shift it and propose an alternative frame.

Goffman's (1981) original contribution, through the concept of framing, was to establish the multiplicity of speaking and listening roles which may be operative at any given point in a social encounter. He distinguished between categories of "listener" such as ratified versus nonratified, addressed versus unaddressed listeners. He showed that "an utterance does not carve up the world beyond the speaker into precisely two parts, recipients and nonrecipients, but rather opens up an array of structurally differentiated possibilities, establishing the participation framework in which the speaker will be guiding his delivery" (p. 137). Similarly, the role of what we call "the speaker" in fact subsumes a variety of possible "production formats" (p. 145) such as principal (information source) or animator (mouthpiece). These conceptions have been very influential in discourse analysis, and they have an obvious importance for analyzing triadic interactions. In three-party talk, participants inevitably frame themselves and others into different communicative relations, at different points; we want to assess the dominant patterns and how they are achieved.

But our particular interest is to assess the further implications of these constructed frames for the communication of care, for older patients' identities, and for geriatric medicine. Any one relational frame establishes a specific social position and identity for each participant, affecting how each is heard or silenced, validated or sidelined. Relational frames, at least in the data we are concerned with, establish not only speakership and listenership positions, but also entitlements and responsibilities. Frame analysis can therefore access some of the discourse strategies by which patients, third parties, and doctors claim positions for themselves,

---

step outside of the professional frame at specific points. This accounts for why questions of the *how are you?* sort can systematically draw either conventionally positive, phatic responses (e.g., *fine thanks*) or, on different occasions, specific, medically self-evaluative responses (e.g., *well I've been having trouble with my hip*) from patients. The negotiation of social and medical frames in medical consultations generally is pervasively required of participants.

or deny them, foist them onto others, or deny them to others. Frame con-
stitution and frame shifting, we suggest, are a key resource for doctors and
third parties in geriatric medical triads. They allow subtle and sometimes
fleeting confederations (cf. Coe & Prendergast, 1985, on "coalitions")
that can be useful ways of signaling social support. At the other extreme,
they can implement social division and disempowerment. Analysis of
frame management offers one way of capturing the diversity and fluidity
of relationships on which geriatric medical consultations are founded.

THE GERIATRICS OUTPATIENTS CONTEXT

For this analysis we select from the set of 44 triadic encounters that
appeared within the main corpus of 107 outpatient consultations. All consultations were participant-observed by a member of the research team and
transcribed using a modified version of Jefferson's transcription conventions for conversation analysis[4] (Atkinson & Heritage, 1984, ix–xvi).
    Of the 44 third parties whose presence we took to define triadic inter-
actions, 16 were patients' daughters, 3 were sons, 1 a granddaughter, 1 a
daughter-in-law, and 1 a niece. Four were residential home care assistants,
8 were the female spouses of male patients, and 6 were the male spouses
of female patients. One was a friend and 3 were sisters. Therefore, 35 of
the 44 third parties were female, and the dominant demographic pattern
is an elderly female patient mother conversing with a doctor in the presence of the patient's daughter. (Of the 107 patients we recorded alto-
gether, 73 were female and 34 male; of the 44 accompanied patients, 35
were female and 9 male.) Doctors in the data were of varying degrees of
seniority and ages. We gloss their individual demographic characteristics
at the head of each extract in the analyses to follow.
    The subset of encounters that are triadic is to some extent defined by
the patient's frailty. All 107 patients in the larger sample have been diag-

---

[4]Transcription conventions used in the following extracts are:

(.)	un-timed short pause
(1.0)	pause timed in seconds
(quietly)	informal commentary on style or context of following utterance(s)
?	indicates question function (not grammatical interrogative)
[	overlapping speech
[ ]	entirely overlapped speech
Underlining	shows unusually heavy emphasis
=	shows "latching" (utterances following each other without perceptible pause)

Line-initial numbers number the speaking turns in a particular Extract.

nosed as being, or as having been, ill according to bio-medical conceptions of health and illness. Accompanied patients are probably more frail than others. As Sidell (1995) noted,

> Disease can . . . be narrowed down to the malfunction of a particular part of the body. Medical treatment focuses on the diseased part and the tendency is to concentrate on discrete parts or organs and pay less attention to the whole or the interaction of the parts. . . . This mechanistic and disease oriented view of health inevitably paints a bleak and negative view of the prospects for health in old age. Later life is portrayed as a time of declining strength and increased frailty as organs and tissues wear out or succumb to disease and degeneration. It views individuals narrowly in terms of their bodies which are in decline as the natural consequence of growing older. (p. 4)

However, the traditional conception of illness does not adequately circumscribe the problems presented and negotiated in the data, many of which are related to depression and low morale. This places an emphasis on care and support and further highlights the importance of relationships between patient and others—not only family and friends, but also carers and medical professionals. Much of the work done by doctors and some third parties in the consultations is the construction of more supportive-seeming environments for patients.

Training texts in geriatric medicine stress the importance of a holistic orientation to older people's health, although this may not be at all unique among the medical specialities nowadays. To quote Sidell (1995) again,

> The older person is not seen as a collection of bodily ills but as a thinking, feeling, creative being who has strengths and weaknesses of body, mind and spirit. It is possible to be healthy in mind and spirit even though the body may be frail. Holism is often linked with equilibrium or a state in which bodies, minds and spirits are in harmony. (p. 6)

Support, then, is one key relational function that we need to examine in the data. What supportive and caring stances are constructed, and how are they articulated in discourse? The fact that, in our set of instances, 16 third parties are daughters and 3 others younger female relatives might imply long-term, complex, evolving relationships. Daughters who have moved into caring for their aging mothers (and, indeed, given the traditional norms of this cohort group, husbands who have moved into caring for wives) may well have experienced relational shifts and even inversions in some aspects of control and caring responsibility. As carers (if we take this as an initial expectation of their role), they may already have assumed some function within the holistic remit of the geriatric enterprise. The boundary between daughter-carers or spouse-carers and caring medics is potentially a fuzzy one, and the discourse of triadic consultations shows complex positioning of third parties in relation to home-based and institutional medical-based regimens and priorities.

The boundary between patient and carer is also complex and to some extent negotiable. Listening to the data, we sometimes ask "whose illness is it?" As Sidell (1995) wrote, "the disruption chronic illness brings to the reciprocity in social relationships requires the renegotiation of pre-illness roles" (p. 65). Chronic illness can be a "dis-ease" of the social network and forces redefinitions of social patterns and possibilities. Some of this relational reworking is achieved through framing and reframing in the discourse of the medical consultation.

A CARING SON: SPEAKING FOR

Extract 1[5] brings to the fore several of the relational issues we have already introduced.

Extract 1

Doctor H: (registrar) male, in his 30s
Patient 41: female, aged 87
Triad: with the patient's son, in his 60s
(A nurse brings the patient into the consulting room. The patient has a heart problem and diabetes. She is slightly deaf and appears very frail.)

1	Doctor:	(loudly and brightly) he<u>ll</u>o there! (3.0) (door closes) (much more quietly) hello
2	Son:	hello
3	Patient:	hello doctor
4	Doctor:	hello Mrs W__ (.) take a seat
		[
5	Son:	I'm her I'm her <u>son</u>
6	Doctor:	(slowly, clearly) Dr W____ pleased to meet you and (.) (quieter) pleased to meet you
		[
7	Patient:	(breathlessly) pleased to meet you (.) doctor

---

[5]Several of the extracts show local dialect characteristics that may be unfamiliar to readers. These include nonstandard verb morphology (e.g., *she have* for "she has" and *she do like* for "she likes").

8	Doctor:	just having a quick look at things here (referring to notes 3.0)
9	Patient:	(gasping as if in pain) oh (.) oh (.) oh
10	Doctor:	well you certainly had a (.) (louder) <u>compl</u>icated course in hospital (.) but you look quite <u>well</u> now (.) how <u>are</u> you feeling?
11	Patient:	oh I don't feel too <u>bad</u> doctor (.) but I could be <u>bett</u>er you know what I mean
12	Doctor:	what are the <u>main</u> <u>prob</u>lems?
13	Patient:	(turns to Son) (quietly) oh I don't know

                      [

14	Son:	well er it's her <u>an</u>kles doctor

                                [

15	Patient:	er my ankles have sw=
16	Doctor:	=swelled yes=
17	Patient:	=my ankles have swelled (.) see
18	Son:	er (.) I had the local doctor er doctor (.) and er he come he come and he give her some <u>wa</u>ter tablets to take
19	Doctor:	<u>right</u>=
20	Son:	=the tablets like and they dissolve in water
21	Doctor:	yes

          [

22	Son:	and she's got um (.) she's got to take it <u>twice</u> daily=
23	Doctor:	=yes
24	Son:	and he give her some tablets for the (.) <u>heart</u> like (2.0) but er sh
25	Doctor:	have they <u>helped</u>?
26	Son:	well it <u>have</u> helped (.) I don't know if they've gone down a bit (.) but they've gone

                                        [

27	Patient:	no they've <u>not</u> gone down now ((yet))
28	Doctor:	have you been short of breath? (1.0)
29	Son:	<u>yes</u> when she <u>do</u> walk a bit like doctor yes

                          [

30	Patient:	yes <u>some</u>times I do doctor
31	Doctor:	are you more short of breath than you were before hospital? (4.0)
32	Patient:	(turns to Son) oh I don't remember
33	Son:	uh?
34	Patient:	much I don't think I am

                [

35	Doctor:	OK that's alright

36	Son:	nah
37	Patient:	I don't remember much though
38	Son:	no

(3.0)

39	Doctor:	now <u>when</u> we had you in hospital we <u>did</u>n't have you on any fluid tablets (.) just the diabetic tablets and the (name of drug) are you <u>still</u> taking both of those?
40	Son:	er <u>yes</u>
41	Doctor:	right (.) and do you test your urine for sugar?

(1.0)

42	Son:	<u>no</u> I don't s (.) I didn't I didn't <u>know</u> that doctor

                                                    [

43	Patient:	no don't take ((much))

                                                      [

44	Doctor:	don't (.) nobody tests it (.) right
45	Son:	I didn't er (.) didn't know that

(36.0) (Doctor reads through case notes)

46	Doctor:	(loudly and clearly) so (.) did <u>any</u>body get a chance to talk to you about the diabetes in hospital?

(3.0)

47	Doctor:	no

                       [

48	Son:	did anybody come to you mum? (.) did anybody come to you to talk to you about your illness?
49	Patient:	I don't think so...

(After five minutes, near the end of the consultation)

50	Doctor:	we'll <u>see</u> you again Mrs W__ in <u>two</u> months
51	Patient:	two months yes
52	Doctor:	and if everything's going well then we can discharge you back to your doctor
53	Patient:	oh <u>right</u> you are

                       [

54	Son:	<u>oh</u> well
55	Doctor:	er is there <u>any</u>thing else you're worried about?=
56	Son:	=er she <u>want</u>ed to know (.) could she er is there any ch chance of going out doctor? (1.0) or is it ((unwise))?

                                                          [

57	Doctor:	<u>yes</u> she can do whatever she feels like doing
58	Son:	she can go out can she?
59	Doctor:	abso<u>lute</u>ly
60	Son:	oh that's alright then

If we look first at the general patterns of address in this extract, there is a dominant pattern of the doctor and patient doing mutual address. In the initial social or phatic sequences (up to turn 8), the doctor's two uses of *you* (in turn 6) are audibly individualized to the patient and the patient's son. The patient is hard of hearing and the quieter, second *pleased to meet you* is addressed to the son. However, once diagnostic and evaluative talk begins, the doctor's address, marked in his pronoun usage, is uniformly to the patient throughout the extract. His *yous* in turns 10, 28, 31, 39, 41, 46, 50, and 52 are all unambiguously addressed to the patient, on the evidence of content and context information (e.g., referring to her time in hospital, her state of health, and at one point mentioning her name within these turns). And if turn 55 is ambiguous in terms of address, the son's turn 56 *er she wanted to know* at least orients to it as having been exclusively addressed to his mother. Whereas at one level this pattern of address is unexceptional, at another level it has a definite ideological loading. Despite the son's presence and relatively active role within the discourse, direct address to the patient is required as part of what we might call *routine anti-ageist discourse practice* (cf. Coupland & Coupland, 1999). As we know from interview data not reported in this chapter, the doctor and his colleagues at this particular geriatrics outpatient clinic are aware that not to elicit symptoms and accounts from patients themselves, and to allocate responsibilities too freely to third parties, is potentially disenfranchising to the elderly patient.

The situation is similar to the one Silverman (1987) described in a cleft palate clinic involving adolescents and their parents, although the discursive politics of address to young people and old people in the patient role are different. Young people with facial disfigurement in the cleft palate clinic are treated as arbiters of their "feelings" about their "looks." Silverman suggested they have specific, limited rights over this nonclinical aspect of what is negotiated. In our data, the baseline assumption is that elderly patients have full rights to autonomous control over their own health decisions. All the same, in our data as in Silverman's, family members as third parties do also become significantly involved in the consultations, despite a strong tendency by doctors not to use second-person address to them. So it becomes necessary to investigate precisely what third parties contribute to the consultation and how they are positioned within the discourse, and with what relational implications.

Another characteristic of Extract 1 is that the son's talk, when he is involved, is very largely addressed to the doctor rather than to the patient herself, and this is another general feature of the 44 triadic interactions. We can list the discourse functions performed by the son's turns at talk. He focuses attention on the patient's problems (turn 14); reports aspects of the patient's previous involvement with other doctors, medicines, and treatments (turns 18, 20, 22, 24, 40, 42, 45); evaluates the success of treatment regimes (26); evaluates the patient's breathing (29); and confirms the patient's evaluative responses (36, 38). At one point, near the end of the encounter (in turn 56), the son establishes the topic of whether the patient can go out, asking a question about this on his mother's behalf. As this sequence develops he then clarifies his question (turn 58) and marks receipt and understanding of the information he has requested (60). All these discourse functions are basically information-reporting or information-requesting moves, with the doctor as their target.

The son's limited address to his mother throughout the extract is restricted to prompting her to answer a doctor's question (turns 33 and 48). With the exception of this minority set of instances, the son fills spaces in the discourse which could in principle be filled by his mother, the patient herself. At many points, and particularly when he is voicing her experiences, he is "speaking for" his mother. This is to say that a traditional doctor–patient frame for talk is maintained within the encounter, but that the patient, at various points, positions himself within that frame in place of the patient. There is therefore a general tension within the encounter. As we saw, the doctor regularly addresses the patient herself, giving her the floor to articulate her experiences, symptoms and evaluations, but it is often the son who assumes the reporting role. What does this tell us about the relationships constituted in this consultation and how we should evaluate them? Important evidence is available in local contexts of the son's reportings.

The doctor's open-ended elicitation at the end of turn 10 (*how are you feeling?*) triggers a hedged-negative response from the patient. "Not too bad" and "could be better" are two of a small set of conventional responses to "how are you?" openings in medical encounters considered in detail elsewhere (Coupland, Coupland, & Robinson, 1992; Coupland et al., 1994). At turn 12 the doctor specifies his earlier question by requesting information about the *main problems*. The patient physically orients to her son and, partly through lowered voice and partly through a further noncommittal answer (*oh I don't know*), offers the doctor's elicitation and the floor for a response to her son. After this she seems content to echo and then elaborate slightly on (turns 15 and 17) her son's response. The son then holds the floor for several turns, reporting his mother's experiences through third-person reference (*she, her*). The doctor complies with this participation frame, marking recipiency and acknowledgment of the son's information (turns 19, 21, and 23). We cannot tell whether the doctor's turn 25 question is designed for the patient or for the son, but the son clearly assumes response rights and fills out turn 26.

The patient does not retire from the conversation at this point, and in fact she interrupts her son during his turn 26 to clarify his rather hedged, uncertain response. Yet she leaves a 1-second pause after the doctor's next question (turn 28), which again provides a floor opportunity for the son. His response, in her conversational space, produces the pronominal dissonance of the doctor's patient-designed *you* (turn 28) being followed by the son's *she* (turn 29). The next few turns repeat the progression we have described, with the patient again foregoing a response (the longer pause after the doctor's turn 31) and again offering her response role to the son (turn 32). There is another instance at turn 46, where the mother's reticence to respond to the doctor's question sees the son attempting an elicitation of his own. Here he has been unable to provide the answer to the question. But more generally, the son's readiness to fill such spaces and provide quite detailed accounts of his mother's problems and activities is therefore compatible with, and at least partly occasioned by, her own reticence. This reticence is displayed not only by silence at points where the doctor has designed her to be next-speaker, but also by noncommittal responses which mark low authority to comment (e.g., *oh I don't remember, I don't remember much though, I don't think so*).

It would be difficult to conclude that the elderly patient's conversational and functional autonomy is being compromised in this extract by an "over-talking" son, and to invoke notions of ageist practice or even over-accommodation. He is certainly operating in her space, both rhetorically and experientially. We get an impression of surrogacy here, particularly when the son judges his mother's swollen ankles and shortness of breath. These assessments would normally be considered appropriate only for first-person accounts. But the son is invited into the surrogate role at crucial points. In the closing section (from turn 50), it is the son who asks whether his mother can *go out* (turn 56), following the doctor's pre-closing *is there anything else you're worried about?* On this occasion there is no pause in the mother's response space and the son's response is latched (directly adjacent to) the end of the doctor's turn. However, he prefaces his response with =er she wanted to know, which proposes that he is in any case voicing her concern, not his. He is again speaking for his mother, but the suggestion is that this is warranted by the concern being his mother's. In Goffman's (1981) terms for participation frames, the son claims to be animating concerns which she has principaled. Interestingly, the doctor is briefly drawn into third-person reference to the patient at this point (in his turn 57). But this is within a response to a question (the first in the consultation) asked by the son (turn 56), and where a response using second-person reference would have seemed inappropriate. The doctor in any case then reverts to the dominant participant design using you.

These moments of surrogate communication are interspersed with a patient–son alignment that is better described as role-shared or co-articulated. These include the echoic utterances we noted at turns 14 and 15, and the editing the patient does of her son's response at turns 26 and 27. Similarly, the answer to the doctor's question about being short of breath is jointly produced by son and patient (turns 29 and 30), with similar alignment in responses to the doctor's question about urine testing (turns 42 and 43). In the closing sequence, responses are again more evenly shared; in turns 53 and 54 it is the mother who speaks first. But the "closing sequence turns" are arguably highly reactive in any case, produced in response to information giving and confirming by the doctor, and occur as oh-prefaced change-of-state markers (Heritage, 1984). These instances do not challenge the son's generally dominant role in the discourse. It is quite possibly true that the son's conversational activity further represses the mother's involvement, which the doctor, as we saw, is keen to promote. But there is also textual evidence that the son is compensating for his mother's low involvement, and certainly that, in this interaction, she initially creates the opportunity and the need for him to be conversationally active—either with her or on her behalf.

CARING DAUGHTERS: SPEAKING WITH

Doctors seem generally more ready to design female third parties into consultation discourse than we saw with the male in Extract 1, but generally not to the extent of foregoing the principle of second-person

address to patients. All third parties and patients in the remaining
extracts we consider are female.

Extract 2

Doctor H: (registrar) male, in his 30s
Patient 37: female, aged 85
Triad: with daughter, in her 50s
(The patient and her daughter have just entered the consulting room. They have
exchanged greetings with the doctor and the doctor has gained permission to record the
consultations. The patient is a little deaf.)

1	Doctor:	good (2.0) erm (looking at patient's notes) (2.0) right I notice that we had a bit of a slow (1.0) noted a bit of a slow pulse when you were in hospital (.) have you had any problems since you've gone home?
2	Patient:	no
3	Doctor:	right (.) and (.) (to daughter) how's she been?
4	Daughter:	yeah you had a bit of er
5	Patient:	<u>oh</u>! er er=
6	Daughter:	=yeah giddy=
7	Patient:	=j j just a little (.) not not er a <u>pain</u> but (.) just a pressure (.) you know
		[ ]
8	Daughter:	((1 syll))
9	Daughter:	a pressure (.) you know in her head she (.) for a couple of days it's passed now
		[
10	Doctor:	did you actually (.) did you actually (.) be have the (.) the dizziness? (.) the=
		[
11	Patient:	no giddiness
		[ ]
12	Daughter:	no
13	Doctor:	=the sickness that you had before?
		[ ]
14	Daughter:	no
15	Patient:	no
16	Doctor:	no (.) OK (16.0) (Doctor looks at the case notes) now you had that (.) recording of the heart for twenty-four hours
17	Patient:	yes=
18	Doctor:	=that was done (.) on the six<u>teenth</u> I believe
19	Patient:	beg pardon?
20	Doctor:	(louder) you had that recording of the heart=

21	Patient:	=yes
22	Doctor:	for twenty-four hours (.) that's been done?
23	Patient:	yes
24	Daughter:	yes
25	Doctor:	you came in here and have had the tape machine on you
		[ ]
26	Daughter:	yes
27	Patient:	yes yes
28	Doctor:	unfortunately it hasn't come back to <u>us</u> yet
29	Patient:	no
30	Doctor:	it must still be being processed (.) so I'll chase that result up
31	Daughter:	mm
32	Doctor:	and I'll let your doctor know if it showed anything of concern
33	Patient:	yes

Extract 2 shows how the same doctor as in Extract 1 elicits an evaluative response from the patient's daughter early on in the consultation
with patient 37. The patient has produced a brief *no* in response to the
doctor's question in turn 1, and it is at that point that the doctor offers a
more open reformulation to the daughter, *how's she been?* Differently from
the son's talk design in Extract 1, the daughter then makes a response
which initially offers the floor back to her mother, using *you* address to
her. The account of giddiness that ensues is co-constructed by the two
women over turns 4 to 9. In fact, this pattern of role-shared response is
repeated in dealing with the doctor's next two questions (turns 11 and 12,
and 14 and 15), and later (turns 23 and 24, 26 and 27). The patient is,
this time, the primary account giver, for example, in offering the first
detailed response after the daughter's brokerage of the doctor's question
(turn 7). The daughter's main roles in the extracted talk, after facilitating
her mother's response, are to add detail to her mother's account (turn 9)
and to provide small utterances of general endorsement (turns 12, 14 and
24). A subtly different frame is constructed from the "doctor–patient
frame with patient surrogacy" of Extract 1. The third-party in Extract 2
has her own position within a more resolutely triadic structure, albeit a
subordinate position, facilitating and endorsing.

Extract 3

Doctor F: (consultant), male, in his 40s
Patient 054: female; aged 74
Triad: with daughter, in her 40s
(The patient has been describing acute pains and feelings of paralysis in her hip and arm.)

1   Doctor: it was paralysed with <u>pain</u> (.) <u>ah</u>
2   Patient: with pain from here (.) but and the sh I get pain here now till up
            in the shoulder (.) we expect it with your age I suppose
                [
3   Doctor: right (.)
            right (.) right but you <u>were</u> able to move your fingers and all that
            then
                [
4   Patient: er (.) a little bit (.) I couldn't (.) all I could do then was to do <u>that</u>
            ((you see))
                    [
5   Daughter: but the
            arm practically <u>went</u> paralysed although it was painful she couldn't use
            it at all
                                [
6   Patient: it was the arm I c
                                    [
7   Daughter: she couldn't lift it up
                                        [
8   Patient: I couldn't lift a thing
            (.) I couldn't (.) the the doctor tried as well (.) we couldn't somehow
            uh
                    [
9   Doctor: she
            couldn't lift it up because of <u>pain</u>=
10 Daughter: =no no=
                [
11 Patient: =no no=
12 Doctor: =or she couldn't lift it up because she was so weak?
                                        [
13 Patient: no I I the arth<u>ri</u>tis
                                            [
14 Daughter: she even tried to <u>hold</u>
            something and everything just went through her hand
                    [
15 Patient: and it was just dropping (.) what was it er doctor J__ said (.)
            when I came down? (.) or I overheard him telling one of them (3.0)
            he was explaining something about (.) there was no locomotion or
            something or (1 syll)
16 Doctor: right (1.0) did he think you had a <u>stroke</u>?

17   Patient: well I don't <u>think</u> so he didn't mention anything of a stroke to me
                                   [   ]
18   Doctor: no
19   Doctor: no (.) no (.) alright (.) alright

Extract 3 shows similar alignments. For example, the patient's nonverbal illustration of how her arm lacked movement in turn 4 is endorsed and verbally elaborated by her daughter in turn 5. The utterance *she couldn't lift it up* (turn 7) is both a reformulation of the patient's earlier (turn 4) *I couldn't* and a precise-timed alternative formulation of what her mother has just begun saying in turn 6. (Mother's *c* is presumably a truncated *couldn't.*) Patient and daughter jointly voice their *nos* (turns 10 and 11) in a shared response to the doctor's proposal that pain was the cause of the mother's immobility. The daughter's *everything just went through her hand* (turn 14) and her mother's *it was just dropping* (turn 15) again overlap, and are co-articulations in the further functional sense that they both offer versions of a response to the doctor's second proposal (turn 12) about weakness being the cause. "Speaking with" is a more appropriate general concept to summarize third-party contributions to Extracts 2 and 3 than "speaking for." Their talk frames them as co-narrators of their mothers' problems, symptoms, and histories, and less as discursive surrogates. They facilitate patients' own accounts as much as they contribute to them.

FORMULATING AGENCY
AND RESPONSIBILITY

All three third parties we have encountered so far undoubtedly feel they have legitimate voices in the consultations. They are family members who have witnessed, and in that sense co-experienced, at least some aspects of the health problems patients are presenting at the clinic. Many of the accounts they give, or share in giving, relate to physical and externally visible problems—swollen ankles, being breathless, giddiness, restricted movement in an arm. They may feel they have not only a right but a duty to report problems and symptoms to doctors as they have seen them. In the various ways we have examined, they stand in the place of or alongside elderly patients, offering extended informational and interpretive accounts for the doctor to assimilate and work into diagnoses and recommendations for later care.

Not surprisingly, there are instances when the third-party-as-carer role is expressed very directly in the discourse, to the extent of marking family members' agency and felt responsibility in care-taking. There are instances when this responsibility is interpreted by third parties as a mediating role between doctor and patient. The treatments and regimens that the doctor authorizes are discussed by third parties as practices they have to inculcate or police.

Extract 4

Doctor E: (professor) male, in his 60s
Patient 117: female, aged 76
Triad: with daughter, in her 50s
(The doctor is discussing the patient's need to lose weight.)

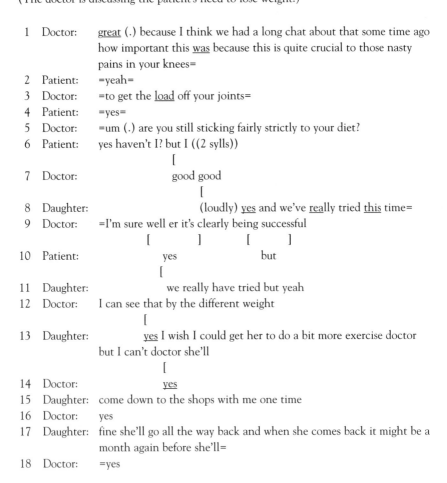

1	Doctor:	great (.) because I think we had a long chat about that some time ago how important this <u>was</u> because this is quite crucial to those nasty pains in your knees=
2	Patient:	=yeah=
3	Doctor:	=to get the <u>load</u> off your joints=
4	Patient:	=yes=
5	Doctor:	=um (.) are you still sticking fairly strictly to your diet?
6	Patient:	yes haven't I? but I ((2 sylls))
		[
7	Doctor:	good good
		[
8	Daughter:	(loudly) <u>yes</u> and we've <u>really</u> tried <u>this</u> time=
9	Doctor:	=I'm sure well er it's clearly being successful
		[ ] [ ]
10	Patient:	yes but
		[
11	Daughter:	we really have tried but yeah
12	Doctor:	I can see that by the different weight
		[
13	Daughter:	<u>yes</u> I wish I could get her to do a bit more exercise doctor but I can't doctor she'll
		[
14	Doctor:	<u>yes</u>
15	Daughter:	come down to the shops with me one time
16	Doctor:	yes
17	Daughter:	fine she'll go all the way back and when she comes back it might be a month again before she'll=
18	Doctor:	=yes

19 Daughter: make the effort to go back down again
20 Doctor: yes
21 Patient: I get so out of breath like you know walking
                                                [
22 Doctor: do you?
23 Doctor: yes
           [
24 Daughter: she perspires a lot she do
                                  [
25 Doctor: yes
                                  [
26 Patient: and er the perspiration pours off me then
                                                                      [
27 Doctor: yes yes (.) you see really what it's
           best to do is er kind of little and often (.) erm it's obvious that while your
           weight is what it is you can't do large amounts of exercise
28 Patient: no
29 Doctor: but (.) if you could do small amounts of exercise often it will help you
           greatly to get your weight down because I don't think you can
           do it wholly by diet (.) because (.) you can but it would mean such a
           restrictive diet that it would make life such a misery (.) so I think you
           should try a combination of exercise and diet and in that way you can
           eat a reasonable diet without being terri (.) over strict
           (Later, the doctor has told the patient she needs to exercise but has
           praised her at length for her weight-loss.)
30 Doctor: but in the meantime while we're er giving her medicine to treat her
           blood pressure it is important that er (.) er she (.) er continues the good
           work she's done over the past few weeks
31 Daughter: it's exercise (.) this is the problem see it's exercise (.) because she'll
           wipe a couple of dishes up (.) she will do that but after that she's up in
           the morning she sits in the armchair=
32 Doctor: =yes
33 Daughter: and unless she's going to her meetings=
34 Doctor: =yes
35 Daughter: well she's there until she goes to bed in the night (.) you know I can't
           get her active
                     [
36 Doctor: yes
37 Daughter: and she's (laughing slightly) very stubborn for me doctor (.) to try to
           get her going (smile voice) she really is
38 Doctor: well she has done well in getting eight pounds of weight down
                                 [   ]   [   ]
39 Daughter: yeah   yes

40	Doctor:	so um (.) hm (.) but nevertheless I think regular exercise=
		[
41	Daughter:	cise yes
42	Doctor:	=if you could try (.) you know (1.0) don't set yourself an impossible task though
43	Daughter:	just a little way if it's only to the corner and back
		[
44	Patient:	no
45	Doctor:	yes (.) yeah I think you've got to set yourself a reasonable aim
46	Patient:	I know when I fairly walk (clears throat) excuse me (.) when I went to walk to walk down to the shops
47	Doctor:	yes
48	Patient:	and coming back I thought I was going to <u>die</u>

Extract 4 initially shows the normative doctor–patient dyadic frame, with the doctor asking the patient (turn 5) if she has been keeping to her diet, the patient replying that she has done this (turn 6). At this point the patient looks to the daughter for confirmation *haven't I?* which overtly endorses the daughter's potential role as co-witness. The doctor's supportive endorsement in the follow-up slot (turn 7) is overlapped by an explicit marker of involvement by the daughter in the practice of maintaining the diet. She says *we've really tried this time*, reinterpreting the agency implied in the doctor's singular *you* in turn 5 as a matter of shared involvement (*we*). She repeats this in turn 11. As she elaborates on how much exercise her mother takes (another part of the regimen previously discussed), she casts herself in the causative role, relative to the walking which her mother does (or doesn't do). Her grammatical representation of their roles is very direct: *I wish I could get her to do a bit of exercise* (turn 13), and she repeats it later (*I can't get her active*, turn 35; *for me doctor (.) to try to get her going*, turn 37).

The daughter's third-person reporting on patient circumstances takes on a different quality here from the previous instances. She has established that she views her own role as causative ("getting the patient to do things"), wielding the doctor's authority by proxy. As a result, her later reporting references to her mother (e.g., *she'll go all the way back*, turn 17; *she perspires a lot*, turn 24; *she sits in the armchair*, turn 31; *she's very stubborn*, turn 37) go well beyond surrogacy and co-articulation. She is not speaking for or with the patient, but from an independent position that she assumes allows/requires her to evaluate the patient's practices as well as report on them. She is effectively exposing the patient to the doctor for her noncompliance. Note how the doctor for the most part maintains his second-person address to the patient and says very little that could be construed as supporting the daughter's construction of her own role in the triad. His main turns, after the daughter has asserted her causative role, are resolutely patient-addressed (turns 27 and 29). In the later part of the extract (at turn 38) he does reciprocate the daughter's *she* reference once, but in the context of praising the patient's achievements in the face of the daughter's earlier criticisms of her mother. He then reverts to *don't set yourself* (in turn 42, a directive that is clearly addressed to the patient herself).

THIRD-PARTY–DOCTOR CONFEDERATIONS

There are, however, radically different alignments that emerge within the data. Particularly distinctive are those events where third parties align with doctors; we consider two instances.

Extract 5

Doctor A: (registrar) male, in his 30s
Patient 059: female; aged 81
Triad: with daughter
(The patient has had a stroke which has affected her eyesight. She is depressed and reports that the antidepressants prescribed are not helping.)

1	Patient:	<u>no</u> (.) um what you (.) I can't see how those things are gonna make what you <u>think</u> (.) it's er the <u>trouble</u> I've had (.) <u>that's</u> the trouble <u>that's</u> the cause of my depression (.) nothing else...
		(The doctor acknowledges her feelings, pauses and continues)
2	Doctor:	(referring to tablets) now we find sometimes that those <u>help</u>
3	Patient:	well perhaps they <u>are</u> helping me I don't know
4	Daughter:	well <u>I</u> think I think she's better
		[
5	Doctor:	I think she's er
		[
6	Daughter:	Christmas time she just sat used to sit and sort of erm=
7	Doctor:	=I think she a little bit improved since
		[
8	Daughter:	she didn't want to do things (.) yes
9	Doctor:	since I saw you last time
10	Daughter:	<u>yes</u>
		(2.0)

11 Doctor: how do <u>you</u> think things are going?
12 Patient: (sighs) (2.0) well sometimes I feel alright and sometimes (.) I feel
                (.) er oh it's not what the hell's er living in when you put the <u>news</u> on
                what do you get? (.) it's <u>all</u> trouble here and (.) everywhere in the world
                is is <u>misery</u> and trouble (.) you think what the <u>hell's</u> the good of living
                (.) in a world like this?
13 Daughter: you could do with a good <u>laugh</u> couldn't you? (chuckles)
14 Patient: (laughs slightly) <u>yes</u> yeah (3.0)
15 Daughter: well you went on <u>ho</u>liday didn't you had a week's holiday
                         [   ]
16 Patient: there's nothing to <u>laugh</u> at
                (nearing the end of the consultation)
17 Doctor: but er (.) I think things are <u>OK</u> and I think they'll im<u>prove</u>
18 Patient: mm
19 Doctor: OK?
20 Patient: well what the hell do I ex<u>pect</u> (.) I must be <u>mad!</u>
21 Daughter: (chuckles)
22 Doctor: (sounding amused) I don't think you're mad
23 Patient: (laughs) I'm just a crabby old=
24 Daughter: =a thirty year old er brain inside an <u>eighty</u> year old (laughs)
                                                              [
25 Doctor: that's right
                (.) it's frustrating isn't it?
26 Patient: I can't <u>get on</u>
                [
27 Daughter: oh but she's much better ((than she says))
28 Doctor: she <u>is</u> better?
29 Daughter: <u>yes</u>
30 Doctor: OK
31 Patient: yes (sounding heartfelt) <u>thanks</u> ever so much
32 Doctor: <u>that</u>'s alright (2.0) look <u>after</u> yourself...

In the first transcribed turn of Extract 5, the patient is expressing her
frustrations about taking the antidepressant medication she has been prescribed. She is putting the case to the doctor that her depression relates
to her past personal troubles, and will not respond to drugs. If, once again,
we begin by examining pronoun-indexed address and reference, we see a
relational pattern develop early in the extract that is very untypical of the
data as a whole. The daughter embarks on third-person reference, *she*, in
turn 4. The doctor and the daughter then maintain mutual *she* through
turns 5, 6, 7, and 8, and it returns, in the closing sequence of the consultation, in turns 27 and 28. As we commented earlier, second-person

address is the ideologized norm at the clinic, and this suggests that the switch must be strategically linked to local circumstances.

The mutuality of third-person reference is important in itself. It allows the doctor and the daughter (who instigates it) to articulate a shared stance, a confederation. The stance is to argue that the patient's morale has in fact improved over time, to counter the patient's own account that her depression is not responding to drug treatment. Doctor and third party are attempting to "talk the patient up." They cast her in the discourse role of overhearer, albeit intended overhearer. This is an instance of Goffman's "byplay" that is, "subordinated communication of a subset or ratified participants" (1981, p.134). What's more, it is a particular form of collusive byplay because the doctor and daughter make quasidyadic, quasiobjective evaluations of the patient's progress, but of course within her hearing. The strategy positions the patient as a nonaddressed observer of an apparently neutral assessment of her improving circumstances. However transparent the participation framework device is, it may be responsible for the patient's more positive self-assessment at least at the onset of turn 12.

Another key aspect of the relational framing of this extract is the daughter's willingness to do second-person address (with or without the *you* pronoun) to her mother, which again contrasts with the normal design of triads in the data. At turn 13, the daughter suggests *you could do with a good laugh couldn't you*, and similarly in turn 15, probably also in turn 24. These turns have a strongly non-institutional quality in their ideational focus (having a laugh, going on holiday) and perhaps in their denial of age-salience (turn 24). Because morale and "talking up" define their main local objectives, the daughter and the doctor have an investment in breaking clinic norms, which are themselves mainly driven by doctor's institutional authority and interactional control for the purposes of orderly symptom-getting, evaluation, decision making, and so on (Silverman, 1987). But this normative institutional order is redundant at this moment. Doctor and third party need to present themselves in "ordinary observer" roles at this moment, presenting "what anyone would observe" about the patient's improving situation. A further indication of how the institutional frame has lapsed is the patient's repeated self-talk within the extract. In turns 1, 12, 16, 20, 23, and 26, her talk is not obviously designed as addressed to either of the other participants. The utterance *what really do I expect (.) I must be mad* (turn 20) expresses her own response to a self-designed evaluative question. Similarly, her use of *you* in turn 12 is, in context, clearly non-second-person.

Extract 5's relational confederation is no doubt positively motivated. The doctor collusively enters the confederation because it is potentially in the patient's interest to do so. In contrast, an instance from a different interaction shows a third party seeking collusion with a senior doctor much more destructively.

Extract 6

Doctor E: (professor), male, in his 60s
Patient 115: female, aged 75
Triad: with daughter
(The patient has been describing pins and needles in her leg when she tries to walk. The transcript begins about 5 minutes into the consultation, during which the daughter has said very little, while the doctor and patient discuss symptoms and medication another doctor has so far prescribed.)

1	Patient:	now when I first went there (.) he told me to take <u>them</u> (puts the second bottle of pills down on the table)
		[
2	Daughter:	(irritatedly) put them all on the <u>table</u>
3	Patient:	for the high blood pressure right?
4	Doctor:	yes
5	Patient:	then they (.) it couldn't bring the blood down so he told me to take <u>those</u> with it (puts a bottle of pills on the table) (.) right?
6	Doctor:	yes
7	Patient:	they're a different colour doctor=
8	Doctor:	=yes=
9	Patient:	but um they're the same thing...
		(Several minutes later the doctor has finished taking the history.)
10	Doctor:	no (.) right okay fine (.) right would you like to pop onto the couch (.) we'll pull the curtain around you and we'll come and have a little look at you
11	Daughter:	it'll be alright don't worry (.) (to doctor) if I wasn't here she wouldn't speak at all (laughs slightly)
12	Doctor:	(laughs slightly) yes (.) they do get a bit nervous don't they? (.) strange places
		[
13	Daughter:	yeah they do ((get a bit))
		(20.0) (The doctor goes through notes and nurse can be heard helping the patient to get undressed)
14	Daughter:	she's a <u>worrier</u>

15 Doctor: pardon?
16 Daughter: she is a worrier
17 Doctor: yes (.) gets a bit <u>an</u>xious does she?
                (15.0)
18 Daughter: she's not quite sure whether she's got an<u>gi</u>na or no this is what ((could
                be))
                                                                            [
19 Doctor: yes well we'll
                sort all that out (.) yes now (3.0) yes it's difficult when you know (.)
                when one's not quite certain what <u>is</u> wrong (.) then people get much
                more <u>an</u>xious about (.) er
20 Daughter: I think when you get to her age you get a bit confused actually
                                        [   ]
21 Doctor: yes   yes
22 Doctor: well it's difficult if we're (.) you know sometimes somebody's
                conditions need a little bit of treatment (.) her blood pressure does (.)
                her doctor really was quite right (.) I mean to chop and <u>change</u> things
                because
                                                            [
23 Daughter: ((he tried to regulate
                it))
24 Doctor: it takes a little time sometimes to get the blood pressure <u>under</u> adequate
                control and you <u>do</u> often need to chop and change the tablets a<u>round</u> to
                get it just right=
25 Daughter: =well this is what I tried to explain really=
26 Doctor: =because you don't want it <u>too</u> low and yet you don't want to leave it
                (.) <u>high</u> and you can't give the exact dose first time round because you
                usually start on <u>very</u> small doses and work it up <u>slow</u>ly and often you
                need to add another tablet to kind of po<u>ten</u>tiate it and it's always safer
                to do it bit by bit and <u>slow</u>ly
27 Daughter: and this is what I tried to explain but (.) when they get to their age they
                think well why are they <u>do</u>ing it=
28 Doctor: =yes
29 Daughter: they don't know
30 Doctor: yes (.) well it <u>is</u> very difficult to understand of <u>course</u> (.) (moving
                across the room to the examination cubicle; to Patient) fine here we
                are <u>right</u> dear

At turn 10 of Extract 6 the doctor and the patient's daughter remain at
the doctor's desk while the patient, out of earshot, moves to a cubicle with
a nurse who will help her to get undressed. The daughter then instigates a
discussion with the doctor about her mother's emotional, bio-medical and

cognitive condition, some of it clearly stereotype-driven and age-prejudicial. Within turn 11, the daughter frame-switches from addressing her
mother to commenting about her mother to the doctor. The switch is
marked stylistically (cf. Tannen & Wallett's, 1993, discussion of "register
shifting"). The mother is reframed by this switch, from ratified second-person addressee to non-ratified third-party subject. But the relational definitions attached to this switch in participation framework are radical. The
mother's constructed addressee role as "a recipient of endearment" (*it'll be
alright don't worry*) is reconfigured, within the turn, as "nervous or incompetent old person" (*if I wasn't here she wouldn't speak at all (laughs slightly)*).
It is worth repeating that until this point in the consultation, the talk has
been largely dyadic in doctor–patient address. In the terminology of communication accommodation theory (Coupland et al., 1991), we might
suggest that the patient is both over-accommodated and under-accommo-
dated within a single turn at talk (11). The social identity imputed in that
part of the turn where she is addressed is wholly restructured in the later
part where she is nonaddressed subject.

The daughter's slight laugh at the end of that same turn, in the context of the imputation she makes that her mother is nervous or incompetent, is important to reading its relational effect. The laughter gives her
utterance a collusive quality, and it is interesting that the doctor echoes
the laugh at the beginning of his turn, seeming to agree to collude. His
utterances in turn 12 do agreement (*yes*), and accounting (*they do get a bit
nervous don't they? (.) strange places*). He implies that the patient's nervousness is attributable to the circumstances of the clinic (*strange places*)
but also, surprisingly, to her group membership (*they*), which must refer to
elderly people or elderly patients. Even if we interpret the doctor's strategy as being to minimize the daughter's imputation of nervousness/
incompetence by accounting for it, he nevertheless uses a way of referring
to her which is age-group based and de-individualizing. Because the
daughter agrees in similar terms (turn 13), doctor and daughter have now
entered a relational frame where they, as "younger people," are jointly
evaluating the patient in intergroup terms. This pattern again runs directly counter to the anti-ageist ideology of the clinic, where age-group-
directed reference is generally considered age-prejudicial. The clinic
commits itself to "treating patients as individuals."

While the patient remains out of earshot (from mid-turn 11 to mid-
turn 30), the daughter tries to construct further forms of collusion with
the doctor, inviting him to endorse several of her own typological per-

ceptions and even diagnoses of her mother. She suggests to the doctor that her mother is *a worrier* (turns 14, 16), that her "confusion" is typical of old people (20). She implies (in turn 27) that older people lack understanding (*when they get to their age they think well why are they doing it . . . they don't know*, turns 27, 29). The doctor does discursive work throughout this sequence to withdraw from the constructed collusion. Most of his turns propose reformulations of the daughter's typologies. For example, he proposes an individuated characterization (*gets a bit anxious*, turn 17) in place of the daughter's group label (*a worrier*, turn 14); and similarly in reformulating the daughter's *when you get to her age* (turn 20) with *somebody's conditions* (turn 22). He works to retrieve a medical context for evaluating the patient's circumstances, in place of the daughter's age-referenced generalizations.

THE "CHAUFFEURING" MODEL
OF MEDICAL TRIADS

Several different dimensions of frame structure are being negotiated simultaneously in these extracts. We have focused on the construction and negotiation of frames that establish participants in specific relationships to one another, concentrating on the social roles constructed by or for elderly patients, and by or for third parties, that is, the family members accompanying elderly patients to the clinic.

The framing of third parties' participation in the consultation discourse and of their alignments to patients and doctors is obviously highly variable, across and within the extracts we have examined. Their roles and alignments are not "given" by the institutional or intergenerational structure of the encounters themselves. They are actively proposed, and in some cases resisted, by participants. We can ask whether third-party participation, as lived out in the data, is consistent with what has been called *a chauffeur role* (e.g. Silverman, 1987). Silverman developed a rather literalist interpretation of the chauffeur role in medical/clinical interactions, in his analysis of pediatric outpatient interactions (involving babies or very young children). He considered a direct analogy between accompanying a young child to a pediatric clinic and "what happens when a motorist takes a car to a garage workshop" (p. 35), where the third party equates to the motorist, the doctor to the mechanic, and the patient to the car. With important caveats about the "deeper moral and emotional basis" in the medical case, Silverman saw some power in the analogy. It allowed him, he said, to appreciate a distinction between "fault-repairing" and "servicing" events, parallelled by clinical visits that are symptom-specific and those that are asymptomatic (check-up visits). In the first set, parents as chauffeurs may expect doctors to assume responsibility for "fixing" problems, and they themselves will be relatively inactive in the discourse. In the second set, medical and other processes will be more negotiable, and Silverman expects third-parties to be more conversationally active as a result.

The direct analogy clearly does not capture anything of the complexity of our own data. There is no clear division between symptomatic and asymptomatic instances in our data. Very few elderly patients at the clinic we observed have no medical or social problems of any degree of severity to report. Elderly patients are not "chauffeured" in anything resembling the same sense as babies or young children might be, and we have commented on the dominant ideology at the clinic that patients should be arbiters of their own health decisions and outcomes. But could an alternative analogy based on the concept of chauffeuring be useful, at least in mapping out some of the relationships between patients and third parties framed in our data? If we see a chauffeur as a "mobilizer" (providing the service of moving another person from one position to another, discursively as well as physically), then some third parties' communication, and the relational positions constructed through it, do seem to fall within the scope of the concept. Chauffeurs, after all, have to be "front seat drivers" but they are also in the service of those people they mobilize, and they may adopt relatively powerless or powerful roles. Some third parties, notably the daughter in Extract 4, represent their caring role as a causative one, mobilizing patients to comply with courses of treatment or lifestyle changes doctors have recommended ("getting the patient to do something"). This daughter positioned herself as having a powerful role to play, in many respects relegating her mother to a powerless "back seat," despite exposing her mother to the doctor for her passivity in sitting there. The Extract 6 daughter, seen as a chauffeur, positioned her mother as one of a set of elderly "nondrivers," firmly denying her access to the "front seat." Other third parties are less assertive in their chauffeuring roles. They exchange decisions about route and speed with their parents, variously deciding for them (as surrogate patients) and sitting alongside them, negotiating with them, making some of the relevant decisions about speed and route, as what we called "co-articulators."

The chauffeuring analogy is still inadequate, however, because it fails to indicate how important the multiparty context is for understanding all the relationships constructed in the data—even those constructed in what appear to be simple dyadic exchanges (e.g., when daughters and doctors talk out of earshot of elderly patients). The Extract 6 daughter, for example, would be better described as seeking to assert her front-seat chauffeuring position in the eyes of "a driving instructor" (if this is at all a plausible analogy for the doctor). Her ageist construction of "the back-seat elderly client" is far more adverse when the client cannot hear her talk. The patient in Extract 1 is, over many sequences of talk, not involved in "steering" or "navigation," when her son shows himself quite enthusiastic to talk on her behalf. The Extract 5 daughter and doctor (viewed as chauffeur and instructor) actively remove themselves from the front seat to the back seat, to chat about the mother's improving driving competence. They try to boost her driving confidence and encourage her to resume a driving position (achieve greater control over her emotional life).

The data we have considered show that social roles in the care of elderly people are interdependent and, at least to some extent, negotiable. For example, we can see how the "back seat" role becomes natural or even inevitable when another person moves, communicatively, to take driver's seat. But even then, participants are able to negotiate a set of particular stances that vary, in terms of the chauffeuring metaphor, between "front seat co-driver" (navigating, deciding on route and speed) and "back-seat passenger" (a passive role whose occupant takes little or no role in decision making or responsibility). It certainly appears that these roles are products of communication practices. "Chauffeurs," "passengers," and "instructors" can and do reconstruct their roles during their (consultative) journeys.

HEALTH, AUTONOMY, AND AGING

The data raise some wider questions about dependency and autonomy in old age, and we hope that our analyses—specific as they are—will help to crystallize discussion of them by patients and practitioners alike. We suggested earlier that our subsample of patients who are accompanied by third parties are likely to be more dependent than those who are not. But how is dependency, and how is autonomy, constituted in these medical consultations? In one of its senses, dependency is an economically based concept. In the context of aging it often points to the absence of a full or legitimizing contribution to the social system. It is, alternatively, definable in physical terms. But the way we have approached our data, through frame analysis, emphasizes the social and communicative senses of dependency, and in these senses we are all (inter)dependent social actors (cf. Bytheway & Johnstone, 1990). The elderly patients in our data are neither fully dependent nor fully autonomous social actors, and in fact the same is true for third parties and doctors. Yet the data clearly show how framing strategies in talk can construct wide-ranging levels and dimensions of dependency that might well have effects beyond the consultations themselves.

We have commented quite extensively on pronoun-marked address in the data. But we showed how address, most obviously by doctors to patients in medical interactions, frames far more than addresseeship in Goffman's sense. It is one of the means by which rights and responsibilities are acknowledged and, in a wider sense, constructed. When a doctor organizes talk through direct address to the patient, that talk carries the presumption of autonomous representation and judgement of self, and potential to be involved in determining one's health outcomes. We saw in the clinic data that doctors not only tend to use second-person address to patients but that they often re-impose this pattern when it has been broken by third-party involvement, for example, speaking for patients, and so claiming response floor. Similarly, third-person reference to patients in these interactions frames more than non-addresseeship or Goffman's role of auditor or over-hearer. Third-person reference (by doctors and even by third parties) is at least potentially silencing and repressive of rights. In the local dynamics of doctors' talk, there is a fairly consistent pattern of attempted empowerment, and resistance to disenfranchisement. The anti-ageist ideology of the clinic is partly realized through the doctors' preferences for managing conversation.

In contrast with the clinic's overarching ideology, two extracts stand out as moments when talk does recycle ageist values: Extracts 4 and 6. For example, in 4, when the patient briefly brings her daughter into the conversation (at turn 6) to confirm that she has been keeping to her diet, a series of disenfranchising moves by the daughter begins. Persistent third-person reference to her co-present mother carries a consistent theme of complaint to the doctor about her mother. The daughter portrays herself as overseeing an uncooperative charge; she silences her mother's self-arbitering role in the clinic proceedings. But we have tried to present more detailed accounts of these disenfranchising events than is typically managed in research into communication and aging. We have suggested that the "surrogate patient" roles constructed by and for third parties in Extract 2 (and perhaps even in Extract 1) are not simple instances of "over-talking." There is a form of role complementarity in each—in 1 because the elderly patient on several occasions cedes her reporting rights at crucial moments to her son, and in 2 because there is obvious sharing of the reporting tasks between the patient and her daughter. Whatever the wider implications of "talking for" and even of "talking with" elderly people, as general communicative styles, there is local evidence in the discourse that these particular speaker-pairs have fashioned frameworks that meet their own priorities and preferences. The often-heard prescription to "avoid talking for an older person" is of course well motivated, but it skates over important factors in the local dynamics of communication, to which we all need to be sensitive.

If our sample is representative, third-party presence in geriatric medical consultations is a relatively common occurrence (just over 40% in our data), and when third parties are present, they do tend to be active in the consultation proceedings. Beisecker suggested that companions are most active in the early (history-taking) and late (negotiation of treatment) parts of the consultation, and this is consistent with our own data. Our analyses of specific instances suggest that this triadic structure should not be seen, in itself, as either a positive or a negative design feature. We have emphasized the variety of relational effects that can be achieved through it. We have indicated how doctors can sometimes use the third party as a resource when history-taking or when discussing treatment regimes and lifestyle changes, as well as moments when ageist assumptions and stances surface. Looked at most broadly, the data provide striking evidence of how providing health care for older people often is, and often needs to be, a collaborative and multiparty process. Doctors' work often involves negotiating aspects of patients' age and health identities, including patients' depression and morale, their physical symptoms, and the usually hidden details of personal and social routines. We usually define these to be "intimate" and "personal" concerns, and expect them to fall within individuals' autonomous control. We view doctors as having privileged access to these personal concerns, for limited periods and purposes, and under the stringent constraints of the Hippocratic oath. Analysis of the discourse of triadic involvement makes us reconsider these assumptions, even when third parties are close family members and doing co-articulation rather than usurping patients' rights.

The circumstances of old age, in specific cases, blur the boundary between the individual and the social network, and it may be that the western cult of individualism clouds our ethical judgments about aging. It remains crucial to respect and police the autonomy of elderly people where it can exist, and to do this at the microinteractional level as well as in social policy and law. But, earlier, we mentioned the view that health problems in old age often need to be seen as a "dis-ease" of the social network, and many of the problems negotiated in the data involve older people's experiences of increasing frustration and incapacity within their social lives. It is not surprising that under these circumstances, medical consultations take on qualities of therapeutic initiatives, and that doctors need to work with family members to provide social as well as medical support. In many ways, a multiparty perspective is a more natural framework for research on aging than the standard dyadic model that drives much of communication theory and everyday thinking about the medical encounter.

REFERENCES

Atkinson, J., & Heritage, J. (1984). *Structures of social action: Studies in conversational analysis*. Cambridge, UK: Cambridge University Press.

Beisecker, A. L. (1989). The influence of a companion on the doctor–elderly patient interaction. *Health Communication, 1*, 55–70.

Boden, D., & Zimmerman, D. (1991). *Talk and social structure*. Cambridge, UK: Polity Press.

Bytheway, B., & Johnstone, J. (1990). On defining ageism. *Critical Social Policy, 29*, 27–39.

Coe, R. M., & Prendergast, C. G. (1985). The formation of coalitions: Interaction strategies in triads. *Sociology of Health and Illness, 7*, 237–247.

Coupland, J., Coupland, N., & Robinson, J. (1992). "How are you?": Negotiating phatic communion. *Language in Society, 21*, 201–230.

Coupland, J., Robinson, J., & Coupland, N. (1994). Frame negotiation in doctor–elderly patient consultations. *Discourse and Society 5*, 1, 89–124.

Coupland, N., & Coupland, J. (1999). Aging, ageism and anti-ageism: Moral stance in discourse. In H. Hamilton (Ed.), *Language and communication in old age* (pp. 177–208). New York: Garland.

Coupland, N., Coupland, J., & Giles, H. (1991). *Language, society and the elderly: Discourse, identity and ageing*. Oxford, UK: Blackwell.

Fisher, S. (1991). A discourse of the social: Medical talk, power talk, oppositional talk. *Discourse and Society, 2*(2), 157–182.

Giles, H., & Coupland, N. (1991). *Language: Contexts and consequences*. Milton Keynes, UK: Open University Press.

Goffman, E. (1981). *Forms of talk*. Oxford, UK: Blackwell.

Goodwin, C. (1981). *Conversational organization: Interaction between speakers and hearers*. New York: Academic Press.

Greene, M. G., Majerovitz, S. D., Adelman, R. D., & Rizzo, C. (1994). The effects of the presence of a third person on the physician–older patient medical interview. *Journal of the American Geriatrics Society, 42*, 413–419.

Hall, M. R. P., Maclennan, W. J., & Dye, M. D. W. (1993). *Medical care of the elderly* (3rd ed.). Chichester, UK: Wiley.

Hasselkus, B. R. (1992). Physician and family caregiver in the medical setting? Negotiation of care? *Journal of Aging Studies*, 6, 67–80.

Heritage, J. (1984). A change-of-state token and aspects of its sequential placement. In J. M. Atkinson & J. Heritage (Eds.), *Structures of social action: Studies in conversational analysis* (pp. 299–345). Cambridge, UK: Cambridge University Press.

Hummert, M. L. (1994). Stereotypes of the elderly and patronizing speech. In M. L. Hummert, J. M. Wiemann, & J. F. Nussbaum (Eds.), *Interpersonal communication in older adulthood: Interdisciplinary research* (pp. 162–184). Newbury Park, CA: Sage.

Jaworski, A., & Coupland, N. (Eds.). (1999). *The discourse reader*. London: Routledge.

Lerner, G. H. (1996). On the place of linguistic resources in the organisation of talk-in-interaction: Second-person reference in multi-party conversation. *Pragmatics*, 6(3), 281–294.

Levinson, S. C. (1988). Putting linguistics on a proper footing: Explorations in Goffman's concepts of participation. In P. Drew & A. Wootton (Eds.), *Erving Goffman* (pp. 161–227). Oxford, UK: Polity Press.

Nussbaum, J., & Coupland, J. (Eds.). (1995). *Handbook of communication and aging research*. Mahwah, NJ: Lawrence Erlbaum Associates.

Ragan, S. (1990). Verbal play and multiple goals in the gynecological examination. *Journal of Language and Social Psychology*, 9, 67–84.

Ryan, E. B., & Cole, R. (1990). Perceptions of interpersonal communication with elders: Implications for health professionals. In H. Giles, N. Coupland, & J. Wiemann (Eds.), *Communication, health and the elderly* (pp. 172–91). Manchester, UK: Manchester University Press.

Ryan, E. B., Bourhis, R. Y., & Knops, U. (1991). Evaluative perceptions of patronizing speech addressed to elders. *Psychology and Aging*, 6, 442–450.

Sidell, M. (1995). *Health in old age: Myth, mystery and management*. Buckingham, UK: Open University Press.

Silverman, D. (1987). *Communication and medical practice: Social relations in the clinic*. London: Sage.

Tannen, D., & Wallat, C. (1993). Interactive frames and knowledge schemas in interaction: Examples from a medical examination/interview. In D. Tannen (Ed.), *Framing in discourse* (pp. 57–76). Oxford, UK: Oxford University Press.

Tracy, K., & Coupland, N. (Eds.). (1990). *Multiple goals in discourse*. Clevedon, UK: Multilingual Matters.

7

Communication in the Care of People With Severe Dementia

Astrid Norberg
Umeå University, Sweden

Human beings dwell in their own world. Sometimes the places where they live are given the meaning of a home. Homes are not only certain physical locations but also symbolize the matching of the concrete and abstract arenas of their lives (Kelly, 1975). Interviews with healthy people aged between 2 and 102 years have shown that the essence of feeling at home is a feeling of being connected to significant others, significant things, significant places, significant activities, oneself, and transcendence (Zingmark, Norberg, & Sandman, 1995). During various phases of life, a person is given a home, creates a home, shares a home, and offers a home. It is important to be welcomed into a home (Marcel, 1982).

Being at home in the world is related to a sense of integrity (Zingmark et al., 1995). At home you feel whole. Erikson (1982) described how throughout their lives people pass through a series of phases and struggle to achieve an experience of trust, autonomy, initiative, industry, identity, intimacy, generativity, and integrity (wholeness and meaning). Communication is essential for both connectedness and integrity.

How the phenomenon communication is understood depends on how life is understood. This chapter is based on an understanding of human life as a mystery and suffering as an experience of being homeless. I argue that as people with dementia gradually lose their ability to communicate, they experience suffering that derives from a feeling of being disconnected, disintegrated, and homeless. As a result, communication with people with severe dementia should be based on a consoling communion between carers and patients.

ONTOLOGY

The understanding of life that grounds this chapter is expressed in the writings of the French philosopher Gabriel Marcel (1963, 1965a, 1973), who differentiated between problem and mystery. A problem is something we meet, whereas a mystery is something in which we are involved. That is, we can never confront a mystery as a whole in front of us as we can a problem. The question "Who am I?" leads from problem to mystery. In dealing with an illness such as Alzheimer's dementia, cure belongs to the realm of problem, whereas consolation belongs to the realm of mystery.

Marcel (1963) thought that deep in human beings there is a global feeling of a *we*, a universal family. When at home with oneself one can welcome the other into one's home, that is, to the sacred dimension. All people recognize a sacredness in life, even those who do not belong to any church and who reject all ritualism (Marcel, 1973). A mother's adoration of her child and the phenomenon *respect* as the recognition of the dignity of others are examples of the experience of sacredness. Life, according to Marcel (1973), is "as it were, surprised in its center; and must it not be said that this center is revealed only to love" (p. 113). Weil (1962) wrote about the sacred in people: "At the bottom of the heart of every human being, from earliest infancy until the tomb, there is something that goes on indomitably expecting, in the teeth of all experience of crimes committed, suffered, and witnessed, that good and not evil will be done to him [sic]. It is this above all that is sacred in every human being" (p. 10).

COMMUNICATION

Communication understood from the perspective of mystery is thus concerned with how to relate to such things as suffering and death and how carers can meet the person with severe dementia in his or her world. Communication from the perspective of problem concerns how we communicate about things that can be solved. In this chapter communication is addressed mainly from the perspective of mystery. However, mystery and problem can be kept totally apart only in theory. Therefore communication with those with Alzheimer's dementia as a problem must sometimes be touched on (see Orange, chap. 10, this volume).

SUFFERING FROM DEMENTIA

Suffering from severe dementia means losing one's sense of being at home (Zingmark, Norberg & Sandman, 1993) and integrity (wholeness and meaning; Ekman, Robins Wahlin, Norberg, & Winblad, 1993; Kihlgren, Hallgren, Norberg, & Karlsson, 1994, 1996). Feeling homeless and experiencing oneself as dis-integrated imply real suffering. Very few writers have addressed the issue of suffering in relation to people with dementia. Harlan (1993), writing about the therapeutic value of the arts, however, stated that art can provide "a small window into this private world of suffering and bewilderment" (p. 102). The carer may listen to the patient while artwork is being produced. Art can help consolidate the sense of self. Suffering has been described as a loss of the sense of connectedness (Younger, 1995), a kind of alienation (Cassell, 1991). Weil (1968) described a special kind of suffering that she called affliction. Affliction, she wrote, is "a device for pulverizing the soul, . . . a state of extreme and total humiliation, . . . the death of the soul" (p. 190). Affliction takes possession of the soul and marks it; it is "an uprooting of life" and a social degradation; it is "a destruction of personality" (p. 190). It seems reasonable to suggest that suffering from dementia may sometimes be experienced as affliction.

Suffering as Feeling Homeless

Suffering alienates the sufferers from themselves—*This sick individual is not me!*— and suffering alienates the sufferers from others—*This individual is not my father, as I knew him!* There is a risk of our turning away from the stranger. Suffering alienates sufferers from their ultimate source of meaning. Thus feeling at home seems to be the opposite of suffering, or suffering seems to be a kind of homelessness. The sense of not being connected, that is, being homeless, is often evident in the wandering behaviors of people with severe dementia. They may be on their way home looking for their small children or their parents (Zingmark et al., 1993).

Suffering as Dis-Integration

Cassell (1991) described suffering as "brought about by an actual or perceived threat to the integrity or continued existence of the whole person" (p. 24). The person with severe dementia becomes more and more vulnerable and feels threatened not only by the outside but also by his or her own psyche. The suffering person with severe dementia needs caring that promotes a sense of being at home and being a whole person. In other words, the suffering person requires consolation.

Suffering From Being Degraded

The term *dementia* means *without soul* (de mens, i.e., out of mind; Jenkins & Price, 1996). Jenkins and Price wrote that dementia was defined in 1726 in *Blanchard's Physical Dictionary* as "anoea, . . . extinction of the imagination and judgement" (pp. 84–85). Reviewing the literature, Midence and Cunliffe (1996) described severe dementia as "a total intellectual, motor, and behavioral disintegration," reminding readers that dementia has been seen as "the funeral without end, . . . the loss of self, . . . the death before death" (p. 591). Asplund and Norberg (1993) found that professional carers responding to a picture of a person with severe dementia and to a picture of an infant, saw the former as painful, apathetic, suffering, weak, afraid, sad, cold, dark, rough, and ugly, whereas they saw the infant positively. These negative associations with the dementia construct have led to medicalization, stigmatization, and objectification of people with dementia (Herskovits, 1995).

The language of dementia care contains several words that are consistent with the concept *de-mentia*. For example, the term *behavioral disturbance* is often used in a way that implies that the behavior of a person with dementia does not express experience, that is, it is without any meaning (e.g., Tariot et al., 1995). A patient with severe dementia who cries may be called a screamer and no one asks what the cry means. Metaphorically speaking, the patient is treated as if she or he is without a soul. Conversely, if an infant cries, we do not say that he or she exhibits a behavioral disturbance. Instead, we ask: What does the cry mean? Is the baby hungry, wet, or lonely?

Considering that this is the dominant view of people with dementia, it is not surprising that there have been so few studies about how people with dementia experience their world. Personhood and self are important concepts in studying the experiences of people with severe dementia because both phenomena seem deeply affected by the progression of the disease. Various criteria have been suggested for describing personhood, including consciousness, reasoning, self-motivating activity, capacity to communicate, self-concept, and self-awareness (Warren, 1973). McCurdy (1998) criticized this rational-self-consciousness model of personhood because it designates personhood as something that a person possesses, a quality added to one's being, when in fact personhood is one's being.

Neisser's (1988) description of five kinds of self (ecological, interpersonal, extended, private, and conceptual) is an example of a rational-self-consciousness model of personhood. Jenkins and Price (1996) argued that each of these kinds of self is affected by dementia. The ecological self that is linked to the body and physical space is affected when dementia leads to a distorted perception of the body. The interpersonal self that is involved in emotional rapport with others is affected when communication and morale decline. The extended self is related to being in time, drawing on memories, and anticipating future events, and is affected by the declines in memory associated with dementia. The private self, connected to experiences during life, is affected by the erosion of identity as the illness progresses. The conceptual self is affected by the loss of roles and status experienced by the person with dementia. According to this model of personhood, then, individuals with severe dementia lose their personhood as the disease erodes each of these five kinds of self. Yet it is my belief, derived from empirical studies (Ekman et al., 1993; Jansson, Norberg, Sandman, Athlin, & Asplund, 1993; Kihlgren et al., 1994, 1996; Norberg, Melin, & Asplund, 1986), that even those with severe dementia retain their essential personhood, but that personhood is being ignored (Normann, Asplund, & Norberg, 1999). It is necessary to find a definition of personhood that acknowledges the personhood of those with severe dementia.

Suffering From Poor Environments

The performance of people with severe dementia varies with environmental pressure (see, e.g., Corcoran & Gitlin, 1991). The physical and psychological care environment can influence the competence displayed by a person with dementia. People with severe dementia may be deprived of the possibility of utilizing their full competence in a poor environment. Sandman, Norberg, and Adolfsson (1988), for example, videotaped a group of people with moderate and severe dementia during meals. The behavior of this group changed dramatically when the carers switched from wearing uniforms to wearing everyday attire. Group members behaved much more properly and increased their interaction when the clothing of the staff suggested a noninstitutional setting than when it conformed to the institutional one.

Suffering From Communication Difficulties

Problems of memory, language, perception, attention, and comprehension make verbal and nonverbal communication difficult for people with severe dementia (American Psychiatric Association [APA], 1994; see also Orange, chap. 10, this volume). Asplund, Jansson, and Norberg (1995) used the FACS (Facial Action Coding System; Ekman & Friesen, 1978) to analyze videotaped facial expressions of four patients with severe dementia of the Alzheimer type. The FACS is a technique to identify distinct facial movements such as lid, jaw, eye, and brow movements. These are combined to form facial action units (AUs), which can be related to emotional reactions such as anger, happiness, sadness, and surprise (Ekman & Friesen). As a previous study (Asplund, Norberg, Adolfsson, & Waxman, 1991) had shown that complete AUs could not be identified in patients with severe dementia, Asplund et al. (1995) used incomplete AUs in their assessments of videotaped patient faces during various activities, including morning care, listening to music, rocking in a rocking chair, eating, and listening to the carer reading aloud. The FACS coding identified very few emotional expressions in the patients.

However, the researchers also used an unstructured naturalistic method to identify emotions. This method corresponded to the way in which carers might try to identify emotions, that is, by considering context, vocalizations, their knowledge of the person's general behavior, and so on, as opposed to a strict focus on isolated facial movements. Researchers saw significantly more expressions of emotion using this naturalistic method than the modified FACS method. Asplund et al. (1995) suggested that these results provide evidence that those with severe dementia do experience and communicate affect, but that interpreting that affect requires an understanding of and a history of interaction with either a particular patient or other similar patients.

There are other reports, as well, that people with severe dementia of the Alzheimer type express a range of affective signals (e.g., Magai, Cohen, Gomberg, Malatesta, & Culver, 1996). Preserved nonverbal language in severe dementia is therefore important as the patients' sole avenue of communication with others. Sensitivity to these nonverbal cues may assist carers in providing optimal care, increasing, for example, their ability to detect patients' discomfort (Hurley, Volicer, Hanrahan, Houde, & Volicer, 1992). Emotional problems of those with severe dementia—such as lability, intrusiveness, and catastrophic reactions—have been described (Haupt, 1996) and interfere particularly with the relationship aspects of communication. In the final stage of the disease, people with severe dementia may be mute, making communication extremely difficult (Norberg et al., 1986).

LIVING WITH DEMENTIA

Living in Two Worlds

The person with dementia may seem to live in another world than the carer. Hellzén, Asplund, Gilje, Sandman, and Norberg (1998) reported on a man with severe complicated dementia who showed progressive deterioration, increased motor activity, oral and sexual activity, and destructive and aggressive actions. During moments of lucidity, he indicated that he felt this was not an authentic expression of his "real" self. He experienced a splintered world. The world of the person with severe dementia may appear to be a calm and safe place where the patient should be allowed to dwell, but it can also appear to be an awful and frightening place from which the patient should be rescued.

Miesen (1993) hypothesized that people with severe dementia function on two levels: On one level they are aware of their situation, and on another level they are not. For example, a colleague's observation notes described the following incident. A woman with severe dementia was searching for her husband. A nurse approached the woman and said, "It's no use searching for your husband; he's dead." The woman was upset and replied, "Of course, I know that he's dead, but I also know that he is alive!" And she kept searching for him. One reason that these two levels of awareness seem to exist for those with dementia is related to their loss of recent memory. The inability to recall recent experiences may mean having to use memories of past experiences to communicate about present ones. For instance, the person with severe dementia may ask the carer in a soft voice: "You are my mother, aren't you?," thus telling the carer that he or she feels loved and cared about in the present by casting the carer in the mother role (Norberg, 1994).

Ingression

People with severe dementia have been seen as regressing to a state that in many respects resembles that of infancy (Hurley et al., 1992). They may, for instance, exhibit attachment-seeking behavior (Wright, Hickey, Buckwalter, & Clipp, 1995). Berg Brodén (1992) suggested that the term *ingression* would be a more appropriate term than *regression* to describe this adult use of early behavior. The phenomenon of ingression can be understood through the metaphor of the Russian doll, a large hollow wooden doll with increasingly smaller dolls nested within it. Like the nested dolls, the adult person can be conceptualized as being composed of layers of experiences. There is a nucleus of early experiences and abilities encased in layers developed later (Norberg, 1996). The impairments suffered by people with severe dementia particularly affect those abilities added at later stages of development. As a result, these individuals must rely on early abilities, such as nonverbal behavior, for communication.

Episodes of Lucidity

Sometimes people with severe dementia appear to be fully in the here and now, both lucid and highly verbal. Episodes of lucidity have been documented in videotapes of interactions between patients with severe dementia and carers (Ekman et al., 1993; Jansson et al., 1993; Kihlgren et al., 1994, 1996; Norberg et al., 1986), observation studies (e.g., Hallberg, Holst, Nordmark, & Edberg, 1995; Häggström, Jansson, & Norberg, 1998; Zingmark et al., 1993), audio-recorded interactions (e.g., Edberg, Nordmark Sandgren, & Hallberg, 1995; Hallberg, Norberg, & Johnsson, 1993). Normann, Asplund, and Norberg (1998) analyzed formal carers' narratives about 92 episodes of lucidity in people with severe dementia. The narratives shared a common framework. The episodes seemed to occur spontaneously when the carers were acting in close proximity to the patient. The carers who reported these experiences also seemed to share a personhood-oriented perspective (Kitwood & Bredin, 1992) toward their patients. That is, they did not make demands on them and regarded them as valuable human beings whose behaviors are meaningful expressions of their experiences. Other authors have reported similar accounts of episodes of lucidity (e.g., Bleathman & Morton, 1992; Bright, 1992; Gibson, 1994; Kitwood & Bredin, 1992; Sabat & Harré, 1992).

CONFIRMATION

Several philosophers and researchers have emphasized the importance of confirmation in relationships between people. Büber (1957) stated that all people wish to be confirmed as who they are, and even as who they can become. It seems reasonable to suggest that people with severe dementia need to be confirmed as the people they are as well as the people they were. Watzlawick, Bavelas, and Jackson (1967) too saw confirmation as an important aspect of communication. Cissna and Sieburg (1981, p. 259) wrote that confirmation is giving the other the message: "To me, you exist! We are relating! To me, you are significant! Your way of experiencing your world is valid!" Dis-confirming communication, in contrast, may well add to the suffering of people with severe dementia by treating them as objects not people (Athlin, Norberg, Asplund, & Jansson, 1989).

CONSOLATION

People who suffer need consolation. The phenomenon labeled *consolation* has a long history. It was a special term in Greek and Roman philosophy, an antidote to suffering (Duclow, 1979), and in the Middles Ages epistles and dialogues on consolation were recognized as a humanist genre (Strohl, 1989). Consolation means a shift of focus from the sufferer to the in-between, the belonging, feeling at home, communion (Marcel, 1982; Söderberg, Gilje, & Norberg, 1999). Consolation is a kind of healing, a form of renewal. It concerns relationship, relatedness and connection, the reestablishment of relationship to and within oneself and to others (cf. Duclow, 1979; Marcel, 1982).

Several authors who have written about consolation have emphasized that consolation is based in communion. The term *communion* was at first a religious term (Vidich & Hughey, 1988) but has gradually acquired an additional secular meaning (Vest, 1987). Communion in this sense is reciprocal love, and entering deeply into communion gives hope. When one is in despair, everything lacks meaning; the person loses any sense of integrity. Being hopeful means grasping the "substance of life" (Marcel, 1965b, p. 10). Communion enables one to hope and reveals a sacredness beyond itself (Marcel, 1973).

Communion between carers and those with dementia can occur even if the parties relate to different conceptions of the current time and space. Persons with severe dementia may believe, for instance, that they are in their childhood homes with their parents, while to the carers, the patients and they are in a nursing home in the present. The important prerequisite for communion seems to be a shared affective state, rather than a shared cognitive interpretation of the physical environment (cf. Norberg, 1994; Stern, 1985).

Another important dimension of consolation is dialogue that leads to a shift of perspective (MacIntyre & Ricoeur, 1970). This is a healing dialogue

(Duclow, 1979), a confirming dialogue in which the sufferer feels that he or she has been acknowledged as a unique and valuable person (Normann et al., 1998). Thus consolation involves both communion and communication. Nonverbal communication may play an important role in consolation. When analyzing videotaped social dancing among people with dementia, Bengtsson and Ekman (1997) found that social dance seemed to facilitate communication and communion between the patients and their carers.

Consoling People With Severe Dementia

Promoting an Experience of "Being at Home." After 1½ years of participant observation at a group home for people with moderate and severe dementia, Zingmark et al. (1993) reported that in undemanding and calm situations, residents behaved as if they felt completely "at home." Zingmark et al. saw the resulting connection between the patients and carers as a deep contact involving full acceptance of the other and with no demands being made of the other. It could be labeled *communion* (cf. Ekman & Norberg, 1993).

Promoting an Experience of Integrity. Kihlgren et al. (1994, 1996) found that when carers applied the Erikson (1982) theory of eight stages of development in order to promote the experience of integrity (wholeness and meaning) in people with moderate or severe dementia, the patients appeared to be much more integrated and even disclosed a competence and strength that they had previously not exhibited. Ekman et al. (1993) reported similar findings from a study of bilingual immigrants with severe dementia. These patients revealed competence in interaction that reflected an experience of integrity. This occurred mainly in interactions with bilingual carers. According to Ekman et al., the patients seemed to react more to the melody of the speech rather than to its content, much as infants react to the tone of their mothers' voices (cf. Fernald, Taeschner, Dunn, & Papousek, 1989). Ekman and Norberg (1993) wrote that carers and patients appeared to be in communion with each other. That is, they displayed a mutual symbolic understanding through their use of humor, singing, eye contact, and touch. There was a synchrony between the parties that conveyed mutual liking.

Understanding People With Severe Dementia. There are reports that suggest that carers can sometimes understand the messages of people with severe dementia. Athlin, Norberg, and Asplund (1990) drew on Pawlby's (1977) theory about imitative interaction between mothers and their infants to understand how carers can communicate with those with severe dementia. Pawlby's theory states that the mother imitates her infant and imputes meaning to his or her cues. When the mother acts as if the infant's cues are comprehensible, the infant feels that what he or she communicates has a meaning. According to Athlin et al., carers may similarly impute meaning to incomprehensible communicative cues from patients, creating a feeling of contact with the carer on the part of the patient. Likewise, Jansson et al. (1993) interpreted carers' understanding of patients with severe dementia as starting from a conviction that there is a meaning in the patients' communicative cues. Carers see the situation as a narrative in which the patient's meaning is implicit. As a result, carers actively fill in the missing pieces in the puzzle of communication with their patients. Consistent with this view, Zingmark et al. (1993; see also Häggström et al., 1998) found that carers at a group dwelling interpreted the communications of people with severe dementia about past time and places as revealing messages about emotions related to the present. Patients and carers were observed to move very flexibly in "time" and "space," an observation reported by other researchers as well (e.g., Norberg, 1994).

Häggström and Norberg (1996) studied some female carers who seemed to be especially able to communicate with residents with moderate or severe dementia. In other words, these carers seemed to understand the residents as well as to be understood by them. When asked to reflect on their communication with the residents, the carers frequently used a mother metaphor to explain their actions and feelings. They talked about themselves as daughters of mothers, as mothers of children, and they talked about their relationships with residents as that of mothers and children.

It seems reasonable to suppose that the carers chose the mother metaphor in order to express an experience that was difficult to verbalize in institutional caregiving terms. The use of a mother metaphor should not be seen as an argument that only females can be effective carers. It seems reasonable that female carers who are also mothers would use this metaphor. Male carers would probably have used a father metaphor. My interpretation is that the use of the mother metaphor highlights the carers' feeling of responsibility for residents' welfare that is engendered by the almost total dependency of persons with severe dementia. Ruddick (1990) equated maternal thinking with attentive love. The close contact between mother and infant and the mother's constant attentiveness to the infant's needs may explain mothers' sensitivity to their infants' emotions and communication (Callery, 1977; Stern, 1985). The use of the mother metaphor by carers (Häggström & Norberg, 1996) may be an indicator that maternal thinking on the part of the carers may also account for their ability to attune to the emotions of residents with severe dementia (Häggström et al., 1998; Zingmark et al., 1993) and to interpret their communicative cues (Jansson et al., 1993).

BEING A CONSOLING CARER OF PEOPLE WITH SEVERE DEMENTIA

Being in communion with people with severe dementia presupposes that the carers can also cope with sharing negative, sometimes horrifying, affective states in order to console the suffering person. Weil (1968) wrote that suffering can evoke a sense of tender pity while affliction evokes a "shock of horror," and people "shiver and recoil. . . . To put oneself in the place of someone whose soul is corroded by affliction, or in near danger of it, is to annihilate oneself" (pp. 71–74). The afflicted can only be reached through a certain kind of attention called love. Harm sharpens an individual's thirst for good; and if the wound is deep, the thirst is for good in its purest form, that is, love. Consoling nursing care presupposes carers who can be in communion with sufferers and bring about a connection to light, goodness, beauty, and life. This type of care emphasizes being more than doing (Söderberg et al., 1999).

In interviews (Jansson & Norberg, 1992), consoling carers related experiences such as the death of a mother that fit the definition of *limit* experiences (Jaspers, 1994). Limit experiences touch people deeply and force them to change their outlook on life. That is, limit experiences put people in contact with the sacred sphere of life. Obviously, in order to be able to help people with severe dementia achieve experiences of beauty, goodness, light, and life—that is, the sacred sphere—carers need these experiences themselves. They need to feel at home with themselves to be able to welcome others and offer them a home. In fact, consoling carers have emphasized that they strive to create a homelike atmosphere (Häggström et al., 1998; Häggström & Norberg, 1996). It seems reasonable to suggest that this atmosphere of a home is an important prerequisite for the experience of being at home among people with severe dementia as well as among carers.

Some carers see caring for people with severe dementia as meaningless work. Others consider it not only as very meaningful work, but also as rewarding work, asserting that they get so much from the patients. Asked what he gets from people with severe dementia, one carer said, "When I see a patient sitting in his chair and I can see how he suffers from pain, and I can help him to bed, and I see how he relaxes and falls asleep I feel I have received a gift." The gift is, of course, being able to help another human being. Such carers talk about patients with respect as valuable human beings, and they seem proud of their work. It appears that the carers' perceptions of the patients are of the utmost importance. If they see patients as valuable persons, then their work of caring for patients is important. In turn, care providers' own sense of worth is bolstered (Norberg 1996). This orientation to care can only exist when people, even people with severe dementia are considered *we*, the in-between in the sacred sphere of life.

CONCLUSIONS

Suffering from severe dementia means having difficulties communicating. For example, it means having to use memories of past experiences to communicate about present ones. Suffering from severe dementia may mean losing one's sense of being at home and integrity (wholeness and meaning). Feeling homeless and experiencing oneself as dis-integrated imply real suffering. Another important source of suffering is carers' dis-confirming communication, which conveys that they regard the person with severe dementia as de-mented, that is, without a soul, not as a person.

During episodes of lucidity people with severe dementia show that they still have a soul; although it is often hidden, they are still persons, still conscious beings. An episode described in Norberg et al. (1986) demonstrates this phenomenon. A woman with severe dementia had been lying curled up in a fetal position and had not spoken for 2 years. Even when we tried to reach her by playing music and using massage, we were able to elicit only two types of response: an increase or decrease of eye blinking and mouth movements. No other reactions could be identified. At one meal, the patient, who was being spoon-fed, swallowed the wrong way and coughed. When she could breathe again, the care provider said with delight: "Now it is OK!" "Yes," the woman answered, "I think so too." The nurse lifted the glass and showed it to the woman saying, "You have some milk left." "Yes, I can see that," the patient answered, "but I wish to save it." After this exchange, the woman remained silent for another year before she died.

Like this silent woman, all people with severe dementia need confirming communication; they need to get the messages: "To me, you exist! We are relating! To me, you are significant! Your way of experiencing your world is valid!" (Cissna & Sieburg, 1981). Due to difficulties of communication at the verbal level, confirmation can sometimes only be given as consolation, through communion, that is, sharing of emotions, participating in the mysterious realm of life. The importance of this consoling care for those who may not be able to respond must be emphasized. To illustrate, I offer some comments of a man with severe dementia. During an episode of lucidity the man told his carer, "My life would have been without any meaning, had it not been for all the kindness that I met. All kindness I meet makes my life meaningful. I still enjoy it!" This man described the importance of consoling care. Consoling care requires carers who can be in communion with sufferers and, in doing so, bring about for those sufferers a connection to light, good, beauty, and life.

REFERENCES

American Psychiatric Association. (1994). *Diagnostic and statistical manual of mental disorders*. (4th ed.). Washington, DC: Author.

Asplund, K., Jansson, L., & Norberg, A. (1995). Expressive facial behaviour in patients with severe dementia of the Alzheimer type (DAT). A comparison between unstructured naturalistic judgements and analytic assessment by means of the Facial Action Coding System (FACS). *International Psychogeriatrics, 7*, 527–534.

Asplund, K., & Norberg, A. (1993). Caregivers' reactions to the physical appearance of a person in the final stage of dementia as measured by semantic differentials. *International Journal of Aging and Human Development, 37*, 205–215.

Asplund, K., Norberg, A., Adolfsson, R., & Waxman, H. (1991). Facial expressions in severely demented patients. A stimulus–response study of four patients with dementia of the Alzheimer type. *International Journal of Geriatric Psychiatry, 6*, 599–606.

Athlin, E., Norberg, A., & Asplund, K. (1990). Caregivers' perceptions and interpretations of severely demented patients during feeding in a task assignment care system. *Scandinavian Journal of Caring Sciences, 4*, 147–156.

Athlin, E., Norberg, A., Asplund, K., & Jansson, L. (1989). Feeding problems in severely demented patients seen from task and relationship aspects. *Scandinavian Journal of Caring Sciences, 3*, 113–121.

Bengtsson, L. P., & Ekman, S. L. (1997). Social dancing in the care of persons with dementia in a nursing home setting: A phenomenological study. *Scholarly Inquiry for Nursing Practice: An International Journal, 11*, 101–118.

Berg Brodén, M. (1992). *Psykoterapeutiska interventioner under spädbarnsperioden* [Psychotherapeutic interventions during the period of infancy]. Trelleborg, Sweden: Förlagshuset Swedala.

Bleathman, C. I., & Morton, I. (1992). Validation therapy: Extracts from 20 groups with dementia sufferers. *Journal of Advanced Nursing, 17*, 658–666.

Bright, R. (1992). Music therapy in the management of dementia. In G. Jones & B. M. L. Miesen (Eds.), *Caregiving in dementia. Research and applications* (pp. 162–180). London: Routledge.

Buber, M. (1957). Distance and relation. *Psychiatry, 20*, 97–104.

Callery, P. (1997). Maternal knowledge and professional knowledge: Co-operation and conflict in the care of sick children. *International Journal of Nursing Studies, 34*, 27–34.

Cassell, E. J. (1991). Recognizing suffering. *Hastings Center Report, 21*, 24–31.

Cissna, K. N. L., & Sieburg, E. (1981). Patterns of interactional confirmation and disconfirmation. In C. Wilder-Mott & J. H. Weakland (Eds.), *Rigor & imagination. Essays from the legacy of Gregory Bateson* (pp. 253–281). New York: Praeger.

Corcoran, M., & Gitlin, L. N. (1991). Environmental influences on behaviour of the elderly with dementia: Principles for intervention in the home. *Occupational Therapy in Geriatrics, 9*, 5–20.

Duclow, D. F. (1979). Perspective and therapy in Boethius's Consolation of Philosophy. *The Journal of Medicine and Philosophy, 4*, 334–343.

Edberg, A. K., Nordmark Sandgren, Å., & Hallberg, I. R. (1995). Initiating and terminating verbal interaction between nurses and severely demented patients regarded as vocally disruptive. *Journal of Psychiatric Nursing, 2*, 159–167.

Ekman, P., & Friesen, W. V. (1978). *Facial Action Coding System: A technique for the measurement of facial movement.* Palo Alto, CA: Consulting Psychologist Press.

Ekman, S. L., & Norberg, A. (1993). Characteristics of the good relationship in the care of bilingual demented immigrants. In S. L. Ekman (Eds.), *Monolingual and bilingual communication between patients with dementia diseases and their caregivers* (pp. 139–158). Umeå, Sweden: Umeå University.

Ekman, S. L., Robins Wahlin, T. B., Norberg, A., & Winblad, B. (1993). Relationship between bilingual demented immigrants and bilingual/monolingual caregivers. *International Journal of Aging and Human Development, 37*, 37–54.

Erikson, E. H. (1982). *The life cycle completed: A review.* New York: Norton.

Fernald, A., Taeschner, T., Dunn, J., & Papousek, M. (1989). A cross language study of prosodic modifications in mothers' and fathers' speech to preverbal infants. *Journal of Child Language, 16*, 477–501.

Gibson, F. (1994). What can reminiscence contribute to people with dementia? In J. Bornat (Ed.), *Reminiscence reviewed, perspectives, evaluations, achievements* (pp. 46–60). Buckingham, England: Open University Press.

Häggström, T., Jansson, L., & Norberg, A. (1998). Achieving an understanding of people with moderate and severe Alzheimer's disease. *Scholarly Inquiry for Nursing Practice, 12*, 239–266.

Häggström, T., & Norberg, A. (1996). Maternal thinking in dementia care. *Journal of Advanced Nursing, 24*, 431–438.

Hallberg, I. R., Holst, G., Nordmark, Å., & Edberg, A. K. (1995). Cooperation during morning care between nurses and severely demented institutionalized patients. *Clinical Nursing Research, 4*, 78–104.

Hallberg, I. R., Norberg, A., & Johnsson, K. (1993). Verbal interaction during the lunch-meal between caregivers and vocally disruptive demented patients. *American Journal of Alzheimer's Care and Related Disorders & Research, 8*, 26–32.

Harlan, J. E. (1993). The therapeutic value of art for persons with Alzheimer´s disease and related disorders. *Recreation, Leisure and Chronic Illness, 6*, 99–106.

Haupt, M. (1996). Emotional lability, intrusiveness and catastrophic reactions. *International Psychogeriatrics, 8*, 409–414.

Hellzen, O., Asplund, K., Gilje, F., Sandman, P. O., & Norberg, A. (1998). From optimism to pessimism. A case study of a psychiatric patient. *Journal of Clinical Nursing, 7*, 360–370.

Herskovits, E. (1995). Struggling over subjectivity: Debates about the "self" and Alzheimer's disease. *Medical Anthropology Quarterly, 9*, 146–164.

Hurley, A. C., Volicer, B. J., Hanrahan, P. A., Houde, S., & Volicer, L. (1992). Assessment of discomfort in advanced Alzheimer patients. *Research in Nursing and Health, 15*, 369–377.

Jansson, L., & Norberg, A. (1992). Ethical reasoning among registered nurses experienced in dementia care. Interviews concerning the feeding of severely demented patients. *Scandinavian Journal of Caring Sciences, 6,* 219–227.

Jansson, L., Norberg, A., Sandman, P. O., Athlin, E., & Asplund, K. (1993). Interpreting facial expressions in patients in the terminal stage of the Alzheimers Disease. *Omega, 26,* 319–334.

Jaspers, K. (1994). Limit situations. In E. Ehrlich, L. H. Ehrlich, & G. B. Pepper (Eds.), *Karl Jaspers: Basic philosophical writings* (pp. 96–104). NJ: Humanities Press. (Original work published 1932)

Jenkins, D., & Price, B. (1996). Dementia and personhood: a focus for care? *Journal of Advanced Nursing, 24,* 84–90.

Kelly, D. A. (1975). Home as a philosophical problem. *The Modern Schoolman, 52,* 150–167.

Kihlgren, M., Hallgren, A., Norberg, A., & Karlsson, I. (1994). Integrity promoting care of demented patients. Patterns of interaction during morning care. *International Journal of Aging and Human Development, 39,* 303–319.

Kihlgren, M., Hallgren, A., Norberg, A., & Karlsson, I. (1996). Disclosure of basic strengths and basic weakness in demented patients during morning care, before and after staff training. Analysis of video-recordings by means of the Erikson theory of "eight stages of man." *International Journal of Aging and Human Development, 43,* 219–233.

Kitwood, T., & Bredin, K. (1992). Towards a theory of dementia care: Personhood and well-being. *Aging and Society, 12,* 269–287.

MacIntyre, A., & Ricoeur, P. (1970). *The religious significance of atheism.* New York: Columbia University Press. (Original work published 1969)

Magai, C., Cohen, C., Gomberg, D., Malatesta, C., & Culver, C. (1996). Emotional expressions during mid- to late-stage dementia. *International Psychogeriatrics, 8,* 383–395.

Marcel, G. (1963). *The existential background of human dignity.* Cambridge, MA: Harvard University Press.

Marcel, G. (1965a). *Being and having.* London: Collins, The Fontana Library. (Original work published 1935)

Marcel, G. (1965b). *Homo viator. Introduction to a metaphysic of hope.* London: Harper & Row. (Original work published 1951)

Marcel, G. (1973). *Tragic wisdom and beyond.* Evanston, IL: Northwestern University Press. (Original work published 1935)

Marcel, G. (1982). *Creative fidelity.* New York: Crossroad. (Original work published 1964)

McCurdy, D. B. (1998). Personhood, spirituality and hope in the care of human beings with dementia. *The Journal of Clinical Ethics, 9,* 81–91.

Midence, K., & Cunliffe, L. (1996). The impact of dementia on the sufferer and available treatment interventions: An overview. *The Journal of Psychology, 130,* 589–602.

Miesen, B. M. L. (1993). Alzheimer's disease, the phenomenon of parent fixation and Bowlby's attachment theory. *International Journal of Geriatric Psychiatry, 8,* 147–153.

Neisser, U. (1988). Five kinds of self knowledge. *Philosophical Psychology, 1,* 35–59.

Norberg, A. (1994). Ethics in the care of elderly with dementia. In R. Gillon (Ed.), *Principles of health care ethics* (pp. 721–732). Chichester, NH: Wiley.

Norberg, A. (1996). Caring for demented people. *Acta Neurologica Scandinavica, 165,* 105–108.

Norberg, A., Melin, E., & Asplund, K. (1986). Reactions to music, touch and object presentation in the final stage of dementia. An exploratory study. *International Journal of Nursing Studies, 23,* 315–323.

Normann, K., Asplund, K., & Norberg, A. (1998). Episodes of lucidity in people with severe dementia as narrated by formal carers. *Journal of Advanced Nursing, 28,* 1295–1300.

Normann, K., Asplund K., & Norberg A. (1999). The attitude of registered nurses towards patients with severe dementia. *Journal of Clinical Nursing, 8,* 353–359.

Pawlby, S. J. (1977). Imitative interaction. In H. R. Scaffer (Ed.), *Studies in mother–infant interaction* (pp. 203–224). London: Academic Press.

Ruddick, S. (1990). *Maternal thinking. Towards a politics of peace.* London: The Women's Press.

Sabat, S. R., & Harré, T. (1992). The construction and deconstruction of self in Alzheimer's disease. *Ageing and Society, 12,* 443–461.

Sandman, P. O., Norberg, A., & Adolfsson, R. (1988). Verbal communication and behaviour during meals in five institutionalized patients with Alzheimer-type dementia. *Journal of Advanced Nursing, 13,* 571–578.

Söderberg, A., Gilje, F., & Norberg, A. (1999). Transforming desolation into consolation: The meaning of being in situations of ethical difficulty in intensive care. *Nursing Ethics, 6,* 357–373.

Stern, D. N. (1985). *The interpersonal world of the infant.* New York: Basic Books.

Strohl, J. E. (1989). Luther's "Fourteen Consolations." *Lutheran Church Quarterly, 3,* 169–182.

Tariot, P. N., Mack, J. L., Patterson, M. B., Edland, S. D., Weiner, M. F., Fillenbaum, G., Blazina, L., Teri, L., Rubin, E., Mortimer, J. A., et al. (1995). The behavior rating scale for dementia of the consortium to establish a registry for Alzheimer's disease. *American Journal of Psychiatry, 152,* 1349–1357.

Vest, J. H. C. (1987). The philosophical significance of wilderness solitude. *Environmental Ethics, 9,* 303–330.

Vidich, A. J., & Hughey, M. W. (1988). Fraternization and rationality in global perspective. *Politics, Culture, and Society, 2,* 242–256.

Warren, M. (1973). On the moral and legal status of abortion. *The Monist, 57,* 43–61.

Watzlawick, P., Bavelas, J. B., & Jackson, D. D. (1967). *Pragmatics of human communication. A study of interactional patterns, pathologies and paradoxes.* New York: Norton.

Weil, S. (1962). Human personality. In R. Rees (Ed. & Trans.), *Selected essays 1934–1943* (pp. 9–34). London: Oxford University Press.

Weil, S. (1968). *On science, necessity, and the love of God.* New York: Oxford University Press.

Wright, L. K., Hickey, J. V., Buckwalter, K. C., & Clipp, E. C. (1995). Human development in the context of aging and chronic illness: The role of attachment in Alzheimer's disease and stroke. *International Journal of Aging and Human Development, 41,* 133–150.

Younger, J. B. (1995). The alienation of the sufferer. *Advances in Nursing Science, 17,* 53–72.

Zingmark, K., Norberg, A., & Sandman, P. O. (1993). Experience of at-homeness and homesickness in patients with Alzheimer's disease. *The American Journal of Alzheimer's Care and Related Disorders and Research, 8,* 10–16.

Zingmark, K., Norberg, A., & Sandman, P. O. (1995). The experience of being at home throughout the life span. Investigation of persons aged from 2 to 102. *International Journal of Aging and Human Development, 41,* 47–60.

III

FAMILY COMMUNICATION AND SUCCESSFUL AGING

8

Negotiating Decisions in the Aging Family

Mary Lee Hummert
University of Kansas

Melanie Morgan
University of Louisville

One of the most important relationships in the aging family and one for which communication becomes especially critical is that between an adult child and an older parent. In fact, Mancini (1989) wrote that, "perhaps the most enduring of all bonds is the parent–child bond" (p. 3). No other relationship lasts as long or has the same capacity for mutual influence as that of parent and child (Mancini & Blieszner, 1989). Throughout the life span, the parent–child relationship experiences many changes as its members shift between states of dependence, independence, and interdependence (Horowitz, Silverstone, & Reinhardt, 1991). This negotiation between independence and dependence is an area of particular interest to aging families as older parents are faced with a growing number of situations in which they find themselves dependent on others, often their children (Cicirelli, 1992). How families approach the decision making required by these situations can have profound implications for the psychological and physical health of the parents as well as the quality of the relationships among family members (Lieberman & Fisher, 1999).

In this chapter we consider how families handle this decision-making process. We begin with an overview of the research on adult child–older parent relationships and communication within those relationships. Next we discuss the special challenges to parent–child communication of making decisions with implications for the independence/dependence of the parent (e.g., to drive or not to drive, to remain in one's own home or move to assisted living). We conclude with some ideas on how family members can best negotiate such decisions so that the parent's simultaneous needs for help (dependence) and a sense of personal control (independence) can be met, and with some suggestions for future research on this topic.

ADULT CHILD–OLDER PARENT
RELATIONSHIPS

A prominent myth regarding older adulthood is that it is a time of isolation where one can expect little assistance from family members (Cicirelli, 1992; Mancini, 1989; Mancini & Blieszner, 1989; Nussbaum, Thompson, & Robinson, 1989). Research has negated this myth, showing that adult children have frequent contact with their parents and provide help to their parents when needed (Cicirelli, 1981, 1989; Lye, 1996; Norris & Tindale, 1994; Rossi & Rossi, 1990). Frequent contact is maintained even when large geographical distances separate children and parents. Lawton, Silverstein, and Bengston (1994), for example, found that 60% of adult children have weekly contact with their mothers while 20% have daily contact. Similarly, Troll, Miller, and Atchley (1979) reported that approximately 75% of the older parents in their study had face-to-face contact with their children on a weekly or semiweekly basis. This contact is often associated with some type of assistance to the parent, particularly in terms of instrumental aid (e.g., driving, shopping) and emotional support (Mancini & Blieszner, 1989). According to Cicirelli (1992), "the majority of elderly depend on help from adult children and other family members more than help from any other source" (p. 8).

Another myth is that parents and adult children have low quality relationships with the result that the contact they have is dissatisfying for both parties. Again, research shows otherwise. Quality of relationship between adult children and their parents has been assessed in a variety of ways: using a single item measure (Aguilino, 1994) and using scale measures (Amato & Booth, 1991); assessing feeling of closeness and attachment (Cicirelli, 1983; Rossi & Rossi, 1990) and assessing amount of disagreement, strain, and dissatisfaction (Aldous, 1987; Umberson, 1992). Regardless of the type of instrument used or approach taken, results show that the majority of adult children and parents report close relationships and are satisfied with the quality of the relationship (Lye, 1996; Mancini & Blieszner, 1989).

Communication in Adult Child–Older Parent Dyads

Few studies have explored communication within the context of the aging family (Weigel & Weigel, 1993; Norris, Powell, & Ryan, 1996). Gerontological studies reveal how frequently parents and their adult children interact, but tell us very little about the messages that are exchanged within these dyads. In the family communication literature, the adult child–older parent dyad has been neglected as a focus of study. For instance, communication within the aging family is not addressed in a recent review of the family communication literature (Fitzpatrick & Badzinski, 1994), even as a direction for future research. The exception to this pattern is in the study of family communication with persons with dementia (see Orange, chap. 10, this volume), where the emphasis is on how families meet the challenges of communicating with individuals whose language skills are declining. Recent studies (Hummert & Morgan, 1999; Morgan & Hummert, 2000; Norris et al., 1996; Pecchioni, 1999; Weigel & Weigel, 1993), however, have considered communication between older parents and adult children in more general terms.

Weigel and Weigel (1993) surveyed 71 intergenerational farm families. Each family consisted of an older father, mother, son, and daughter-in-law. Each family member was given the family communication satisfaction scale, which was adapted from Olson and Wilson's (1982) Family Satisfaction Scale. The scale measures family members' satisfaction with the communication within their intergenerational family system. Perceptions of communication problems were measured using an 8-item subscale of the Farm Family Strain Scale (Weigel, Weigel, & Blundall, 1987).

Weigel and Weigel (1993) found that the older parents had much more favorable perceptions of the communication that occurred in the family than did their sons and daughter-in-laws. The parents were also more satisfied overall with the communication that occurred between family members. Adult sons and their spouses perceived more communication problems within the intergenerational family context and had lower communication satisfaction than did parents. Problems identified involved influence attempts, conflicts, and negative criticism.

Norris et al. (1996) explored family communication patterns by manipulating filial anxiety through two scenarios in which older women were depicted in critical situations of dependency. One situation concerned a 75-year-old mother who had recently suffered a ministroke from which she had completely recovered, and the struggle the family members felt regarding their mother's autonomy and independence and their desire to protect her from harm. The second scenario described a 75-year-old mother who provides care to her husband who suffers from mild dementia. The mother in this scenario insists on cooking the family Christmas dinner, although her children feel that it is too much for her to handle with the burden of caring for their father.

Participants were presented with both of the scenarios and asked to describe how they thought the situations would be realistically resolved. Participants reported that they would expect disagreement in these discussions, with the children controlling decision making and using a communication style that conveyed low levels of respect to their mother. The authors concluded that the participants' responses are evidence for a family-based example of the Communication Predicament of Aging Model (Ryan, Giles, Bartolucci & Henwood, 1986).

The Communication Predicament of Aging Model (Ryan et al., 1986; Ryan & Norris, this volume) is grounded in Communication Accommodation Theory (Giles, Coupland, & Coupland, 1991), which seeks to explain conversational behaviors as accommodations or adaptations to other interactants' styles and particular communication needs. According to Ryan et al., a predicament occurs in communication with older individuals when the accommodations are based on negative stereotypes of aging rather than the actual communicative competence of those individuals. These accommodations to the stereotype rather than to the person have been termed overaccommodations. In communication with older individuals, overaccommodations to negative stereotypes have been associated with patronizing talk (Ryan et al., 1986; Ryan, Hummert, & Boich, 1995; Hummert, Shaner, Garstka, & Henry, 1998; Hummert & Ryan, in press). Patronizing talk to older persons is characterized by such linguistic adaptations as the use of simple clauses, short sentences, and diminutives, as well as by such paralinguistic adaptations as speaking loudly, speaking slowly, and using exaggerated intonation (Ryan et al., 1995). It may also involve restricted communication topics and attempts to assume control over the older person (Ryan et al., 1995; Hummert & Ryan, 1996). In the Norris et al. (1996) study, family members expected to overaccommodate to negative age stereotypes by being overly directive and discouraging joint decision making. This family communication predicament of aging is driven, we believe, by the interplay between the older parent's simultaneous needs for independence and assistance and the adult child's desire to help/protect the parent by adopting a paternalistic role (Hummert & Morgan, 1999; Morgan & Hummert, 2000).

DEPENDENCY IN OLDER ADULTHOOD
AND ITS CHALLENGES TO FAMILY COMMUNICATION

The family is essential in the negotiations of dependency described by Norris et al. (1996), as this is where we first learn to become independent. Independence is one of the most important skills a family can teach its young members. As Clark (1969) argued, "only by being independent can an American be truly a person, self-respecting, worthy of concern, and the esteem of others" (p. 59). According to Baltes (1996), Western cultures value independence and self-reliance to such a degree that they become the "imperative" (p. 7). Dependency is something to be outgrown and is not sanctioned. She asserts, however, that there are situations in which a society will tolerate dependency and in some cases elect to relieve certain individuals of the burdens of independence. One of these situations is older adulthood.

Aging is viewed as a time of decline and disability both physically and mentally. Because of this negative view of aging, we, as a society, tolerate dependency in older adulthood and often relieve our older family members from some of the burdens related to independence. Just as young adults negotiate the move from dependence to independence within the family, it is also within the family that older adults begin to re-negotiate their level of independence and to make decisions in response to the challenges of aging (Cicirelli, 1992). Adult children play a significant role in that re-negotiation. Consider the following excerpt from an interview with a married couple aged 79 and 75 who have three middle-aged daughters living in another city (Hummert & Morgan, 1999). The interviewer has asked whether the couple does their own yardwork. Transcription conventions used in this and subsequent excerpts are: (( )) double parentheses for pauses, laughter, etc.; [[two left brackets to indicate that speakers began to talk simultaneously; [ ] closed brackets around text of completely overlapping utterances; and ( ) single parentheses around comments inserted by authors.

Interview 2, Excerpt 1

1	Wife:	Part of it. Our children wanted us to hire some help. We need, we need to keep moving. If we sit down we'll get so we can't move. We have so much shrubbery. That's one of our big jobs during the spring years—is to get out there and trim all that shrubbery. Forty some bushes. Big ones. ((laughter)) And then the leaves collect. We have to rake them out at least twice a year. And ah, it gets to be quite a job. We can only do so much every time but we keep plugging at it.
2	Interviewer:	So, they're concerned about you doing all the yardwork?
3	Wife:	They think we try to do too much. Yeah, they . . .
4	Interviewer:	How do you know that?
5	Husband:	[We have a boy . . .]
6	Wife:	[They said so.]
7	Husband:	They said so.
8	Interviewer:	Who said so?
9	Wife:	Ummm. . . Both L. and B. (two of the couple's daughters) said we should hire somebody to come in and help us, but we said as long as we could do it we wanted to try and keep doing it ourselves.

In this excerpt, the wife's comments reveal how her daughters encouraged their parents to give up the physically demanding task of caring for their yard. She notes (turn 3) that the daughters are concerned about their parents "doing too much," a concern which seems warranted when the couple reveals later in the interview that the husband has a heart condition. However, to this couple, doing the yardwork is important to their physical health because it keeps them "moving" (turn 1). The wife's comments detailing the extent of the care required to maintain their yard (turn 1) also display pride in their accomplishments. Although this is "quite a job," they "keep plugging at it" until it's finished. Doing the yardwork also seems to contribute to their psychological health by reinforcing their personal sense of competence. By qualifying her assertion about their desire to do the yardwork alone with the phrase "as long as we could do it" (turn 9) the wife does acknowledge that they may need help at some time in the future.

While relief from a time-consuming and tiring task such as yardwork is inviting, this couple seems aware that such relief has its costs. As Baltes (1996) stated, "such protection often results also in disempowerment and paternalism, consequences at the root of the conflict between dependency and personal control, autonomy, and competence" (p. 7). The difficulty for many older individuals and their families is that the vagaries of life and health place them at the center of this conflict between dependency and autonomy.

The Paradoxical Relationship Between Dependence and Independence in Aging Families

Cicirelli (1992) defined dependency in older adulthood as no longer being able to satisfy one's needs or wants by him or herself. Using psychological terms, dependency can also be seen as the loss of primary control strategies (Heckhausen & Schultz, 1995; Schultz & Heckhausen, 1999). Blenkner (1965) divided these dependencies into four areas: economic, physical, mental, and social. Economic dependency occurs because of a lack of finances and is usually related to retirement. Physical dependencies are characterized by diminished energy, poor health and slowed reflexes. Mental dependencies are related to deterioration in memory and loss of orientation while social dependencies are related to loss of roles, status, and power. As dependency in one of these areas increases, it creates a paradoxical situation for older parents and their children: Maintaining the parent's independence in other areas requires assistance from the children.

As mentioned earlier in this chapter, adult children have frequent contact with their parents and provide help to their parents when needed (e.g., Rossi & Rossi, 1990). Our research (Hummert & Morgan, 1999) suggests that much of this support is directed towards maintaining the independence of a parent with chronic health problems. For instance, one woman described the extensive help that she, her immediate family, and her siblings were providing to their mother, aged 82, who had suffered a stroke. This help included a sister coming to the mother's home daily to arrange medications, do wash, and so forth; a brother doing finances; and the interviewee's husband and college-age daughter spending their spring break vacations caring for their mother-in-law/grandmother. The interviewer responded:

Interview 6, Excerpt 1

1 Interviewer: So it's almost like um you're trying to help her maintain the lifestyle
                  she had before.
2 Daughter: [[we're trying
3 Interviewer: [[and she wants to maintain that lifestyle.

4   Daughter: Yeah, we're trying to let her be as independent as she possibly can. Um,
                   And, you know, feel worthwhile and be happy . . .

The extensive aid provided to the mother by this daughter and her siblings were designed to maintain the mother's "independence." Another
interviewee (Hummert & Morgan, 1999) commented directly on how
her 94-year-old mother is independent, yet also dependent on her daughter for transportation.

Interview 1, Excerpt 1

1   Interviewer: She's 94?
2   Daughter: Um Hum. She's a very independent lady. She makes all her own decisions.
3   Interviewer: ((laughs))
4   Daughter: Except, ah, she calls on us ((laughs)) when she gets a little stuck, but ah,
                   she did have to give up her car so she doesn't drive anymore, which
                   sort of took some of her freedoms away . . .

Later in the interview when asked whether not driving was a problem
for her mother, the daughter replied:

Interview 1, Excerpt 2

1   Daughter: Not at all, because we were still picking her up and ah, going in and out
                   nearly every day. So I don't think, no. We were, she was, in a way she
                   was very dependent and yet in another way she wants to be independ-
                   ent. So that's kind of a conflict for older people. They still want to be
                   independent but they can't be.

In Excerpt 1, this interviewee clearly characterizes her mother as
independent, but then quickly qualifies this assertion with "except when
she gets stuck" due to not driving. Her comments in Excerpt 2 show that
she sees her mother's simultaneous needs for support and independence
as a typical conflict experienced by older people. Further, she is quite
willing to provide the support that makes her mother's independence
possible.

The excerpts from these two interviews illustrate the paradoxical relationship between independence and dependence experienced by many
older individuals and their families. Although the families are often willing
to provide the support necessary to maintain their parents' independence,
the process itself may affect interactional patterns within the family.

Effects of Dependency on Family Interaction

Changes in interactional patterns usually accompany the provision of support by adult children to their parents (Cicirelli, 1992). These changes in interactional patterns eventually lead to changes in established interpersonal relationships due to shifts in power and role status. In the following excerpt from our interview study (Hummert & Morgan, 1999), a middle-aged daughter describes how dependency changed her relationship with her 89-year-old widowed father:

Interview 10, Excerpt 1:

1 Daughter: Oh, obviously since I've been an adult, I mean I've been here and he's been there. So we were visitors in each other's homes when we had contact with each other and now, it's more a daily basis and that changes the tenor of things. Um, in some respect, I've seen him at his worst and he knows it, I mean, when he's been the most emotionally strained. And that changes a person's relationship, you know. Dad is Dad, Dad is the strong one, Dad is the one who provides, Dad is all kinds of things. Daddy is easily the, the um, I won't say the center of that whole family because that isn't really the case but he was the oldest male among the first seven of the kids. And he was always viewed as the most sensible, he's the one who arranged funerals when there wasn't another immediate family member that, you know, he was kind of the cornerstone in some ways. Um, ((pause)) and he's not playing that role in my life now, if that means anything, if there's a certain amount of role reversal going on. Ah, and he takes it pretty well. He would really like to do things and we've tried to allow, like he wants to repaint the trim on the porch, that'll, I think that'll be all right although he's not sure if he can, well we'll just see what he can manage and what he can't we'll see that it gets done or we'll do it ourselves, which would be the faster way, but in a sense it's almost feeling with again he wants to try his wings. He still wants to do something and make himself useful to somebody. And I think that's part of what he's feeling is that he's not very useful to anybody. He can't do those things that he did that made him useful.

As this daughter's comments indicate, she and her father have in effect reversed their roles as parent and child. Although she qualifies this statement with the aside "if that means anything," it is clear from her extended account that this shift is quite meaningful and—to an extent—disturbing to her. The role reversal is accomplished even in the language used to describe her father's efforts to remain useful: She has tried to "allow" him to do things; and the father is trying "his wings," just like a baby bird (Hummert & Morgan, 1999). It is equally evident in this excerpt that the daughter is sensitive to her father's need to remain as independent as possible, and that she wishes to support his efforts in that direction.

Like this daughter, many adult children have a difficult time balancing familial shifts in power and roles and often find themselves in situations where they are struggling to balance the autonomy needs of their parents with their own paternalism needs to protect their parents (Baltes, 1996; Cicirelli, 1992). At the same time parents are struggling to reconcile their own need for independence with their need for assistance in some areas of their lives.

DECISION MAKING AS NEGOTIATION

Adult children have a great deal of influence regarding decision making over important areas in their parent's lives (Cicirelli, 1992). This influence is even greater for widowed parents (Pratt & Jones-Aust, 1993). As older adults begin to experience age-related health problems, families confront decisions regarding living arrangements, transportation issues, health care, and financial concerns. The interactions that constitute the decision-making process may be characterized as problematic (Coupland, Wiemann, & Giles, 1991). They are problematic because the family members may have conflicting needs for (and beliefs in) autonomy and paternalism that must be negotiated as part of the process (Cicirelli, 1992).

Autonomy and Paternalism

"Personal autonomy means having the capacity to make and execute deliberated decisions to satisfy needs and attain goals in a manner consistent with one's values" (Cicirelli, 1992, p. 14). Exercising personal autonomy or primary control is important for maintaining one's psychological health at all ages (Heckhausen & Schulz, 1995). However, even when older individuals have the capacity to make and execute decisions, they may not do so. There may be internal constraints (e.g., negative self-stereotyping) or external constraints (e.g., pressure from significant others, financial constraints) that impede a person's ability to exercise autonomy.

While adult children may be aware of the importance of personal autonomy to their parents, they may feel an equally strong need to exercise paternalism. According to Cicirelli (1992), paternalism includes a concern for the welfare or happiness of the parent, a belief that the child knows best what would be most beneficial (or least harmful) to the parent, and a conviction that the child has the moral right and responsibility to intervene to protect the parent, even if that requires going beyond persuasion. In paternalism, the well-being of the parent has priority over his or her autonomy. The assumptions that constitute paternalism imply that the child is more competent than the parent in this situation.

Pecchioni (1999) translated Cicirelli's (1992) theory into interaction styles. She interviewed 36 mother–daughter dyads, asking them to discuss how they would handle a situation in which the mother became increasingly debilitated. All mothers in the study were currently healthy. Three interaction styles emerged, one in which the mother dominated the discussion (analogous to Cicirelli's complete autonomy), another in which the mother and daughter jointly participated in the discussion (analogous to shared autonomy), and a third in which the daughter dominated (analogous to paternalism). About 25% of the daughters dominated the discussion, which could only occur with the collaboration of the mothers. Pecchioni suggested that these discussion patterns reflect the type of decision-making style that the women may adopt when faced with an actual health crisis for the mother. As she concluded, these results indicate that paternalism and autonomy may be embedded within long-term family communication practices.

Politeness theory (Brown & Levinson, 1987) can provide a framework for understanding the negotiation of autonomy and paternalism within aging families. Politeness theory asserts that interactants in any communicative encounter are concerned about the presentation of their own identity or face and the identity or face of others. Face is made up of two components, negative face or the right "to freedom of action and freedom from imposition" (Brown & Levinson, p. 66) and positive face or the desire that one's self concept be accepted by and approved of by others.

In interactions between aging family members where increased dependency is salient, issues of face become crucial. Anytime children seek to confront an aging parent about declines in abilities or to offer advice about these declines they are potentially committing a face threatening act (FTA). For example, in aging families the topic of driving is often an area of conflict and concern. Older adults wish to remain independent and view driving as a key component in maintaining their independence (Lustbader & Hooyman, 1994). Persson (1993) asserted that driving is one of the most important instrumental activities of daily living for maintaining independence. Comments made by older adults in our interview study (Hummert & Morgan, 1999) reflect this theme of independence (autonomy) and driving. The 94-year-old woman (Hummert & Morgan, Interview 3), whose daughter was quoted earlier, said of her decision to stop driving, "That was pretty bad when you have to sell your car, you don't have any way to go. It's kind of hard, you know, you think, well, you're depending on somebody else all the time, and that's kind of hard to do." An 85-year-old man (Hummert & Morgan, Interview 8) said of others in his retirement complex, "We've had three people here that have had cars and they give them up and sold them and they have to depend on the bus. Well when you get up to 90, there's one coming 93 or 4 and he just felt like he wasn't capable of driving. You could make something happen, you know." When the interviewer agreed that it would be "pretty hard" to think that one had caused an accident, the man continued "Yeah, it would. Hard to give up the car, too." These statements underscore the conflict many older adults feel about their declining ability to drive effectively and their desire to remain independent.

This area seems to be rather difficult terrain to cross for the aging family. Addressing driving in family conversations involves threats to the face of the parent. As the interview with the 85-year-old man quoted earlier continued, the following exchange occurred:

Interview 8, Excerpt 1

1	Interviewer:	Have your daughters ever said anything to you about you driving?
2	Man:	Oh yeah.
3	Interviewer:	What do they say?
4	Man:	They don't like me driving.
5	Interviewer:	Why?
6	Man:	They say I can't see.
7	Interviewer:	Because you can't see?
8	Man:	That's what they say.
9	Interviewer:	Oh that's what they say. And what do you think?
10	Man:	I told them I see fine. Well I've had cataracts, ya know, I've had a little trouble before I had cataracts taken off. And I can see good now at night, don't bother me at all. Before I could see two lights, you know.

By expressing concern over a parent's ability to drive safely, middle-aged children directly threaten the positive face of the parent. In essence, the child is questioning the parent's competence. If the children follow this expression of concern with advice, they also threaten the parent's negative face by suggesting a particular course of action.

Decision Making: Suggested Communication Strategies

How can adult children and parents successfully negotiate their conflicting needs for autonomy and paternalism while maintaining the face of all parties? Should children exert their paternalism by making decisions for their parents, or should they acknowledge parents' needs for autonomy by refraining from discussing the problem areas at all? Should parents demand complete autonomy or accept assistance and advice from their children?

A Strategy to Avoid. While there may be some contention over the best decision-making strategies, the research to date suggests that the worst strategy (in most instances) is for children to take complete control and make all the decisions for their parents (Morgan & Hummert, 2000; Schulz & Heckhausen, 1999; Silverstone, & Horowitz, 1992). Although this strategy may be the most efficient and most likely to achieve the adult child's instrumental goals and paternalism needs, it also has the most potential for harm. Research on aging and control suggests that alleviating opportunities for older adults to make decisions—and thus to have control over important life domains—has negative impacts on both psychological and physical well being (Langer & Rodin, 1976; Rodin & Langer, 1977; Schulz, 1976; Schulz & Hanusa, 1978; Schulz & Heckhausen, 1999). For instance, low perceived control is associated with depression for institutionalized older persons (Schulz, 1976), and with increased mortality and hospitalizations for old-old individuals (Menec & Chipperfield, 1997)

Young, middle-aged, and older participants in an experimental investigation of family conversational control strategies (Morgan & Hummert, 2000) appeared to be aware of the dangers of a middle-aged family member assuming complete control over a decision for an older parent. Participants evaluated three different conversations in which middle-aged women confronted either daughters in their mid-twenties or mothers in their mid-seventies about a problem behavior (unpaid bills, dirty apartment, fainting). In the conversations, the middle-aged women used one of three control strategies: direct control (complete paternalism), indirect control (expression of concern and availability for assistance), or no control (complete autonomy for the other family member). Participants of all ages rated the direct control strategy as less respectful, nurturing and appropriate, and as less likely to lead to conversational satisfaction (for either person in the conversation), than either the indirect or no control strategies. However, participants did rate the direct control strategy as more appropriate and the no control strategy as less appropriate when the target of control was a mother in her 70s than when she was a daughter in her 20s. Together, these results indicate that, in general, individuals prefer to let other family members make their own decisions, but they believe that intervening in decisions of older family members may be more legitimate than intervening in those of young family members.

The Ideal Decision-Making Process.   Some guidelines for families can be found in interview accounts (Hummert & Morgan, 1999) of the way family decisions were made or of the way in which participants wish they had been made. Whether the decision involved moving from a private home to a congregate living facility in the same community, giving up driving, moving to a new city to be near children, or forgoing treatment for a terminal disease, we found that the most positive accounts shared three characteristics: (a) the parent or parents made the primary decision before a crisis developed; (b) children supported the decision, providing emotional and instrumental support as the decision was implemented; and (c) all family members were able to frame the decision as positive evidence of the closeness of their family and the core competence of the parent. For instance, the 94-year-old woman (Hummert & Morgan, Interview 3) who described how difficult it was to give up driving and to be dependent on others for transportation also said of her decision: "It's been a positive thing. Cause I really made up my mind that that's what I want to do." Likewise her daughter (Hummert & Morgan, Interview 1), who provides most of this woman's transportation, acknowledged the difficulties of aging, but also emphasized her mother's competence: "Age and dependency, selling the car, the physical um, part of arthritis. But umm she's on top of making appointments. . . . And, you know, and she's, she's up on her insurances and takes care of her own business and her own bills and all that stuff. . . . You just think that aging ah, you know, we think it is not coming to us, you know. Aging and death come to all. (laughs) Whether we think about it or not. And ah, I think she's done it very well. . . ."

Other interviewees in the same study (Hummert & Morgan, 1999) emphasized the importance of older persons making decisions before they found themselves in the midst of a health crisis. One woman (Hummert & Morgan, Interview 4) said of her mother who had fractured several verte- brae, "And so, she, she was very strong um, you know, physically and men- tally and emotionally and so, um, it wasn't until she developed this that she became a little more frail and more unsure in making decisions. Ah, they just seemed a little bigger to her when she didn't feel well." An 86-year-old man (Hummert & Morgan, Interview 5) who had moved from a farm to an apartment in a small town offered this advice to others: "Well, don't wait too long. . . . Yeah. If I'd have waited much longer, you know, it might have been more of an effort to move, but, uh, opportunities come along, the kids moved me in, moved the stuff in and that turned out. The older you get, the more you get set in your ways and, uh, you're not as active." The woman (Hummert & Morgan, Interview 6) quoted earlier whose mother had had a stroke asserted that ". . . it actually would have been better if she would have gotten rid of her house maybe five, ten years ago, you know, before she had the stroke. And gone into . . . an independent living section of a retirement place. . . . If she had made a move to a facility like that ten years ago, or so, it probably would have been an easier, easier decision for her, um, when she was healthier to have made that choice, rather than the choice sort of now being forced upon her due to circumstances with her health . . ."

In reviewing this evidence, we suggested that one reason the inter- viewees showed such a strong preference for the parents making the deci- sion on their own, prior to a health crisis, was that it maintained tradi- tional parent–child roles for the parties. Adult children do not wish to make decisions for their parents if they can avoid making them. In fact, when we manipulated conversational control in the experimental study (Morgan & Hummert, in press), participants indicated that the middle- aged woman would be most satisfied with the no control conversation in which she left any decisions entirely to her mother (or to her young adult daughter). More importantly, however, by making decisions themselves, older individuals are exercising their autonomy and maintaining the per- sonal sense of control necessary for psychological and physical health (Schulz & Heckhausen, 1999).

Decision Making in a Crisis Situation.   Many families, however, find themselves facing decisions precipitated by a parent's health crisis or, as an interviewee in the Hummert and Morgan (1999) study stated, "a help cri- sis." In some cases, the parent may not be able to handle the decision process alone. How can families best approach this type of decision-making situation, one that may be the rule rather than the exception? We suggest four principles to guide families: (a) Children must play an active role as *researchers* on behalf of their parents; (b) parents must exercise their autonomy to make the final decision (to the extent that their health permits); (c) the entire sibling group must be involved in the decision-making and implementation process; and (d) parents must develop their secondary control strategies through delegating the information-gathering and implementation tasks of decision making to their children. If family members can follow these principles, they may be as successful as those in the ideal situation, ultimately framing their handling of the crisis as a testament to the family's closeness and the core competence of the parent.

The goal of the four principles is to enhance the parent's personal control and to relieve the children of the burden of paternalism. Parents who have experienced health crises such as strokes, heart attacks, etc., may find their decision-making ability compromised because their physical and emotional states constrain their ability to gather and evaluate information. Children can assume those aspects of the decision-making process for their parents, researching the types of assistance available and critically evaluating the quality of that assistance. By sharing that information with their parents, children reinforce the parents' position as arbiters of the final decision. As Coupland and Coupland (see chap. 6, this volume) show in their analysis of interactions between physicians, older patients, and patients' children, adult children can play an important supportive role to parents as intermediaries and translators in physician consultations.

Parents in a weakened state must guard against assigning complete control over decision making to their children. Yet they must be willing to delegate some of the instrumental tasks associated with implementing the decision to their children. In other words, parents may not be able to exert primary control, "those behaviors that generate effects in the external world" (Schulz & Heckhausen, 1999, p. 142), but must depend on the children to exert that control as their proxies. On the other hand, parents must engage in adaptive or secondary control strategies to preserve their personal sense of competence (Heckhausen & Schulz, 1995; Schulz & Heckhausen, 1999). According to Schulz and Heckhausen (1999), secondary control refers to "individuals' abilities to shape their own emotions, motivational states, and cognitions about themselves and the world around them" (p. 142). For example, secondary control for older parents may involve devaluing a prior goal (e.g., staying in one's own home) and substituting an alternative goal (e.g., choosing the retirement home apartment with the best view and services).

Involvement of the entire sibling group in the decision-making process is important in ensuring that the parent receives the appropriate help in implementation, as well as in diminishing subsequent family conflicts. Lieberman and Fisher (1999) investigated the role of multigenerational family members in the care for an elder with dementia. They found that families with a focused family decision-making style (shared decision making with much discussion) and a positive family conflict resolution style (e.g., compromise) provided more help to their dementing relative than did other families.

One couple (husband aged 85 and wife aged 83) in our interview study (Hummert & Morgan, 1999) provided an example of these principles in action. The couple had moved from their farm to an assisted living apartment a few months prior to the interview. The move was precipitated by a health crisis: the wife had a leg amputated after other treatments for a severe infection had failed. The couple had two daughters and two sons ranging in age from 42 to 61, with all but one son residing in the same community as the parents. When the issue of a move arose, the wife was in the hospital. As the husband said, "Well we knew we was going to have to go somewhere and, uh, cause I couldn't, well she'd need a lot of care. We'd have to sell the farm." The parents at first considered the only two facilities they were familiar with, large complexes with graduated levels of care in a larger city about 20 miles from their home community. They described how their children were instrumental in finding their current apartment:

Interview 8, Excerpt 2

1	Husband:	We didn't think we'd want to do that (move to the larger city), so we, uh, it was S's (their youngest daughter's) idea. She said, oh, she'd come over here and she's heard of this, uh,
2	Wife:	Retirement home.
3	Husband:	I'd never been here before. I knew it was here, but I never was . . .
4	Wife:	I never paid any attention.
5	Husband:	So she came out one day and we went around and looked and at that time there was either two available. See, they're pretty well filled up.
6	Interviewer:	Yeah.
7	Wife:	There was a waiting list.
8	Husband:	A waiting list. And we, uh, uh, we like this one better because I liked the view here. See, you can look out here, at times, and they just

have flowers everywhere out in there. A big flower bed right here
and, uh, at the other place you just look at a blank wall.

9   Interviewer: Yeah.

10 Husband: And I could see people when they come in. If you were on the other
side, you couldn't see anything.

As the husband's description makes clear, their daughter provided
essential help in first gathering information about the retirement home in
their community (turn 1) and then taking her father to tour the available
apartments (turn 5). The decision to move to this complex and to this
particular apartment, however, was the parents (turn 8). As the interview
continued, the couple provided more details of their children's involvement in the move.

Interview 8, Excerpt 3

1   Interviewer: Do you remember, though, did you talk at all with your kids?
2   Wife: [Oh my yes]
3   Husband: [Oh yes]
4   Interviewer: Oh my yes?
5   Wife: They all come to the hospital and talk [and talk].
6   Husband: [and talk].
. . . (talk continues about the exact order of events)
7   Wife: I'll tell her that.
8   Interviewer: Okay.
9   Husband: All right, all right, tell her.
10 Wife: They (the daughters) assured me that I would like it, because I would
just be like I was home. And when I walked in here . . .
11 Interviewer: Yeah.
12 Wife: And seen ((laugh)) all these things that they put out of each room,
they took something, well, you can tell. They just took something and
just made it look like home. And it really was.
13 Interviewer: So, it felt pretty good then?
14 Wife: Um hmm. Um hmm.
15 Interviewer: So, they were, it sounds like your daughters were pretty, um, uh . . .
16 Wife: I have got the best daughters of anybody.

In the first part of this excerpt, the wife and husband confirm that the
move was discussed in depth with their children (turns 1–6). Although
the repetition of "and talk" by both spouses may be evidence that the parents felt the talk was excessive and one-sided (i.e., the children did the

talking and the parents the listening), the remainder of this excerpt and the tone of the interview in general indicate that the parents appreciated the input of their children (turn 16). In the second part of this excerpt, the wife describes how her daughters not only handled the logistics of the move to reduce the physical stress on their parents, but also worked to reduce the psychological stress of the transition from the family home—where the couple had lived for over 60 years—to the retirement apartment. The children were sensitive to the emotional implications of the move, and carefully selected items so that the apartment would "look like home" (turn 12).

As with any new place of residence, this apartment had a flaw: The old carpet buckled and caused problems for the wife's walker and wheel chair. The logistics of replacing the carpet while they were living there seemed overwhelming to the couple, but their children and grandchildren engineered a strategy to accomplish this with minimal stress to their parents. This involved arranging for the couple to spend a week-end at the home of a relative, the husband's brother. Then, as the couple described it:

Interview 8, Excerpt 4

1	Wife:	. . . So, about 20 of our kids, grandchildren, and neighbors come. Moved all of our furniture down this hallway to the end one (apartment) [that was for rent to]
2	Husband:	[It was empty.]
3	Interviewer:	This was empty?
4	Wife:	It was empty and they was going to put a new carpet in it anyway. They moved all of our furniture down there. And the boys come in here on a Sunday afternoon, tore up the old carpet—they told the carpet man they was going to do it—cleaned it all up for them and they (the carpet layers) said they'd never had that done for them before. . . . And on Monday morning the carpet layers were here, put down the new carpet, the kids come again, moved everything back in here, rearranged things ((laughs)).
5	Interviewer:	It was like coming home again.
6	Wife:	Yeah, right, right. Because they moved the furniture around quite a bit.

(Talk continues about the former locations of some pieces of furniture)

7	Wife:	So, we told them that just as soon as everybody could get together, you know, all at one time, we'd go down to R__ R__ (a steakhouse franchise) and have supper and we did that in [just a couple of]
8	Husband:	[About a week] or something.
9	Interviewer:	Uh huh.

10	Wife:	We had K. and M., you know where we stayed, and all the kids (who) helped. And there were 25 of us went down.
11	Interviewer:	Oh my gosh.
12	Husband:	I started them out and told them to order what they want and I paid the bill then. A _____ dollars, I believe it was.
13	Interviewer:	Wow.
14	Husband:	But they all had plenty.
15	Interviewer:	Oh yeah.
16	Wife:	And, you know, they knew we was thankful.

This excerpt illustrates again the important instrumental aid provided by the couple's extended family. As with the move into the apartment, the aid was designed to implement a decision that the couple had made. This excerpt also shows how this couple has developed secondary control strategies (Heckhausen & Schulz, 1995; Schulz & Heckhausen, 1999) that enable them to accept the help of their family while maintaining their personal sense of competence. First, the wife notes with a laugh that the "boys" rearranged the furniture when they moved it back into the apartment (turns 4 and 6). In a way, she seems to be saying, "Yes, they're wonderful and accomplish much, but they're still my children and though I love them, they're not perfect." Second, the couple was able to provide a service to their family to thank them for their help: They treated all family members involved to a dinner at a restaurant (turns 7–12). This dinner served to reinforce the couple's role as the matriarch and patriarch of the family, demonstrating that despite their physical limitations they were financially able to provide for their children and grandchildren. As the husband said (turn 14), "But they all had plenty." The couple's description of this dinner communicates that they see the dinner as a testimony to their continued autonomy, even though they sometimes require assistance from their children.

This couple and their children were successful in negotiating the parents' transition from their private residence to a retirement complex. They accomplished this by enacting the four principles we outlined earlier. First, they ensured that the children's help involved gathering information so that the parents could make an informed decision, and then, second, providing the physical assistance necessary to implement the decision. Third, the entire family group was involved in the discussions surrounding the move ("They all come to the hospital and talked and talked," Interview 8, Excerpt 3, turn 5). Fourth, the parents coped with the move's inherent challenges to their self-esteem by maintaining primary control over decisions and adopting secondary control strategies allowing them to accept assistance. These strategies enabled them to maintain their personal sense of competence and their parental identities, even when the children challenged that competence as when the daughters questioned their father's driving ability (Interview 8, Excerpt 1).

As a result, this couple was able to frame the move and the assistance of their children as evidence of their strength as a family. As the wife said, one of the best things about the discussions regarding the move was that "they [the children] wanted us to be closer to them." This statement addresses geographical closeness ("closer to them") in a way that connects it with psychological closeness ("they wanted"; Hummert & Morgan, 1999). When asked to describe how the move had affected her relationship with her children, the wife stated this directly: "I think it's drawn us closer."

CONCLUSIONS

We have attempted to outline some of the challenges to family communication associated with parents' decision making about age-related lifestyle changes. We have also tried to outline some communication guidelines so that families can respond effectively to these challenges. Our guidelines provide only a partial answer, however. Important questions remain to be addressed in future research.

For example, one goal of future research should be the identification of practices that parents and children can use to begin dialogues on sensitive issues such as driving, moving from one's private home to a congregate living facility, and so on. The decision-making process begins with one of the individuals addressing the problematic situation. Yet both parties may avoid initiating such discussions because they are uncertain about how to approach these sensitive issues and perhaps because they are frightened of the implications of the problem for the parent's mortality. As one interviewee (Hummert & Morgan, 1999, Interview 10) stated, "It would be wonderful if a person had really open things, open discussion about them way before it was ever much of an issue. But how much of a discussion? I mean I'm going to be 60 before too many more years. That spooks my kids any time you talk about. . . . And I understand that. I've been there. And I didn't want to talk about it either. . . ." This desire to avoid these topics may be accompanied by a wish to avoid family conflict according to Cicirelli (1993). As a result, even when families discuss these issues they may rush to a solution before all options are considered, resulting in a less than optimal decision.

Other research should address long-term communication patterns within families as they relate to decision making. Pecchioni's (1999) research, for instance, suggested that decision-making processes in crisis may reflect standard practices in noncrisis situations. As we discussed earlier, even though the mothers in her study were currently healthy and the mother–daughter dialogue was on a hypothetical problem, some daughters assumed a highly directive decision-making style and their mothers accepted that style. Given other research that shows a relationship between decision making within families and the provision of care to ailing parents (Lieberman & Fisher, 1999), and between personal control and the health of older individuals (Schulz & Heckhausen, 1999), identifying how family decision-making patterns develop and change over time is essential.

We also see a need for research that considers factors that complicate the decision-making process for some families. These include the challenges of making decisions when parents and children reside in different cities, states, or even countries, and of negotiating within blended families that may include more than one set of siblings and parents. In addition, single older persons or childless married couples may rely on nieces and nephews (or more distant relatives) as their partners in the decision process (Hummert & Morgan, 1999). These relationships may pose somewhat different problems—and benefits—for both younger and older participants than does the parent–child relationship.

A final focus for future research is how to approach decision making when the older family member is incapable of participating in that process or is unwilling to participate. Two questions are central to this issue: (a) Under what circumstances is it appropriate for a child to assume decision-making power for a parent or for a parent to assign that power to a child? and (b) What is the optimal decision process in these situations?

Even in the best of circumstances, the types of decisions we have addressed in this chapter are made with much reluctance on the part of parents and children (Cicirelli, 1993; Hummert & Morgan, 1999; Lieberman & Fisher, 1999; Pecchioni, 1999). Unfortunately, these decisions are often an inevitable consequence of living longer, and more and more families will be challenged by the dilemmas inherent in reaching these decisions. On the other hand, increased dependence for the parent need not be an inevitable consequence of the process. As Baltes (1996) suggested, "dependency due to decline in old age is in large part the outcome of society's negative attitudes toward old age. It is more a self-fulfilling prophecy than a reflection of the true competence level of the elderly" (p. 1). The goal for parents and children must be to avoid this self-fulfilling prophecy, negotiating decisions in a way that balances dependence with independence, shared control with personal control, and familial love with mutual respect.

ACKNOWLEDGMENTS

Preparation of this chapter was supported by National Institute on Aging/National Institutes of Health Grant 1 R01 AG16352, and by a sabbatical leave provided by the University of Kansas to Dr. Hummert.

REFERENCES

Aldous, J. (1987). New views on the family life of the elderly and near-elderly. *Journal of Marriage and the Family, 49*, 227–234.

Amota, P. R., & Booth, A. (1991). Consequences of parental divorce and marital unhappiness for adult well-being. *Social Forces, 69*, 895–914.

Aquilino, W. S. (1994). Impact of childhood family disruption on young adult's relationships with parents. *Journal of Marriage and Family, 56*, 295–313.

Baltes, M. M. (1996). *The many faces of dependency in old age*. New York: Cambridge University Press.

Blenker, M. (1965). Social work and family relationships in later life with some thoughts on filial maturity. In E. Shanas & G. F. Streib (Eds.), *Social structure and the family: Generational relations* (pp. 46–59). Englewood Cliffs, NJ: Prentice-Hall.

Brown, P., & Levinson, S. (1987). *Politeness: Some universals in language usage*. Cambridge, England: Cambridge University Press.

Cicirelli, V. (1983). Adult children's attachment and helping behavior to elderly parents: A path model. *Journal of Marriage and the Family, 45*, 815–826.

Cicirelli, V. G. (1981). *Helping elderly parents: The role of adult children*. Boston: Auburn.

Cicirelli, V. G. (1989). *A measure of family members' belief in autonomy and paternalism in relation to caregiving practices toward elderly parents* (Final report to the Retirement Research Foundation). West Lafayette, IN: Purdue University, Department of Psychological Sciences.

Cicirelli, V. G. (1992). *Family caregiving: Autonomous and paternalistic decision making*. Newbury Park, CA: Sage.

Cicirelli, V. G. (1993). Intergenerational communication in the mother–daughter dyad regarding caregiving decision. In N. Coupland & J. F. Nussbaum (Eds.), *Discourse and lifespan identity* (pp. 215–236). Newbury Park, CA: Sage.

Clark, M. (1969). Cultural values and dependency in later life. In R. A. Kalish (Ed.), *The dependencies of old people* (pp. 59–72). Ann Arbor: Institute of Gerontology, University of Michigan.

Coupland, N., Wiemann, J. M., & Giles, H. (1991). Talk as "problem" and communication as "miscommunication": An integrative analysis. In N. Coupland, H. Giles, & J. M. Wiemann (Eds.), *"Miscommunication" and problematic talk* (pp. 1–17). Newbury Park, CA: Sage.

Fitzpatrick, M. A., & Badzinski, D. M. (1994). All in the family: Interpersonal communication in kin relationships. In M. L. Knapp & G. R. Miller (Eds.), *Handbook of interpersonal communication* (pp. 726–771). Thousand Oaks, CA: Sage.

Giles, H., Coupland, N., & Coupland, J. (1991). (Eds.), *Contexts of accommodation: Developments in applied sociolinguistics*. Cambridge, England: Cambridge University Press.

Heckhausen, J., & Schulz, R. (1995). A life-span theory of control. *Psychological Review, 102,* 284–304.

Horowitz, A., Silverstone, B. M,. & Reinhardt, J. P. (1991). A conceptual and empirical exploration of personal autonomy issues within family caregiving relationships. *The Gerontologist, 31,* 23–31.

Hummert, M. L., & Morgan, M. (1999, May). *Personal and familial identity in later life: Decision-making about lifestyle changes*. Paper presented at the annual meeting of the International Communication Association, San Francisco.

Hummert, M. L., & Ryan, E. B. (1996). Toward understanding variations in patronizing talk addressed to older adults: Psycholinguistic features of care and control. *International Journal of Psycholinguistics, 12,* 149–169.

Hummert, M. L., & Ryan, E. B. (in press). Patronizing communication. In W. P. Robinson & H. Giles (Eds.), *The handbook of language and social psychology* (2nd ed.). Chichester, UK: Wiley.

Hummert, M. L., Shaner, J. L., Garstka, T. A., & Henry, C. (1998). Communication with older adults: The influence of age stereotypes, context, and communicator age. *Human Communication Research, 25,* 124–152.

Langer, E. J., & Rodin, J. (1976). The effects of choice and enhanced personal responsibility for the aged: A field experiment in an institutional setting. *Journal of Personality and Social Psychology, 34,* 191–198.

Lawton, L., Silverstein, M., Bengston, V. L. (1994). Solidarity between generations in families. In V. L. Bengston & R. A. Harootyan (Eds.), *Intergenerational linkages: Hidden connections in American society* (pp. 19–42) New York: Springer.

Lieberman, M. A., & Fisher, L. (1999). The effects of family conflict resolution and decision making on the provision of help for an elder with Alzheimer's disease. *The Gerontologist, 39,* 159–166.

Lustbader, W., & Hooyman, N. R. (1994). *Taking care of aging family members: A practical guide*. New York: Macmillan.

Lye, D. N. (1996). Adult child–parent relationships. *Annual Review of Sociology, 22,* 79–102.

Mancini, J. A. (Ed.). (1989). *Aging parents and adult children*. Lexington, MA: Lexington Books.

Mancini, J. A., & Blieszner, R. (1989). Aging parents and adult children: Research themes in intergenerational relations. *Journal of Marriage and the Family, 51,* 275–290.

Menec, V. H., & Chipperfield, J. G. (1997). The interactive effect of perceived control and functional status on health and mortality among young-old and old-old adults. *Journal of Gerontology: Social Sciences, 52B,* S118–S126.

Morgan, M., & Hummert, M. L. (2000). Perceptions of communicative control strategies in mother–daughter dyads across the lifespan. *Journal of Communication, 56*(3), 48–64.

Norris, J. E., Powell, V. & Ryan, E. B. (1996, May). *Family communication predicaments: Balancing a sense of responsibility with respect for older persons' autonomy*. Paper presented at the Third International Communication, Aging and Health Conference, Kansas City, MO.

Norris, J. E., & Tindale, J. A. (1994). *Among generations: The cycle of adult relationships*. New York: Freeman.

Nussbaum, J. F., Thompson, T., & Robinson, J. D. (1989). *Communication and aging*. New York: Harper & Row.

Olson, D. H., & Wilson, M. (1982). Family satisfaction. In D. H. Olson, H. I. McCubbin, H. Barnes, A. Larson, M. Muxen, & M. Wilson (Eds.), *Family inventories* (pp. 97–118). St. Paul: University of Minnesota Press.

Pecchioni, L. L. (1999, May). *The older mother–daughter relationship: Three interaction styles.* Paper presented at the annual meeting of the International Communication Association, San Francisco.

Persson, D. (1993). The elderly driver: Deciding when to stop. *The Gerontologist, 33,* 88–91.

Pratt, C. C., & Jones-Aust, L. (1993). Decision-making influence strategies of caregiving daughters and their elderly mothers. *Family Relations, 42,* 376–383.

Rodin, J., & Langer, E. J. (1977). Long-term effects of a control-relevant intervention with the institutionalized aged. *Journal of Personality and Social Psychology, 35,* 897–903.

Rossi, A. S., & Rossi, P. H. (1990). *Of human bonding: Parent–child relations across the life course.* New York: Aldine de Gruyter.

Ryan, E. B., Giles, H., Bartolucci, G., & Henwood, K. (1986). Psycholinguistic and social psychological components of communication by and with the elderly. *Language and Communication, 6,* 1–24.

Ryan, E. B., Hummert, M. L., & Boich, L. H. (1995). Communication predicaments of aging: Patronizing behavior towards older adults. *Journal of Language and Social Psychology, 14,* 144–166.

Silverstone, B. M., & Horowitz, A. (1992). The role of families. *Generations, 16,* 27–31.

Schulz, R. (1976). Effects of control and predictability on the physical and psychological well-being of the institutionalized aged. *Journal of Personality and Social Psychology, 33,* 563–573.

Schulz, R., & Hanusa, B. H. (1978). Long-term effects of predictability and control enhancing interventions: Findings and ethical issues. *Journal of Personality and Social Psychology, 36,* 1194–1201.

Schulz, R., & Heckhausen, J. (1999). Aging, culture and control: Setting a new research agenda. *Journal of Gerontology, 54B,* P139–P145.

Troll, L. E., Miller, S. J., & Atchley, R. J. (1979). *Families in later life.* Belmont, CA: Wadsworth.

Umberson, D. (1992). Relationship between adult children and their parents: Psychological consequences for both generations. *Journal of Marriage and the Family, 54,* 664–674.

Weigel, D. J., & Weigel, R. R. (1993). Intergenerational family communication: Generational differences in rural families. *Journal of Social and Personal Relationships, 10,* 467–473.

Weigel, D. J., Weigel, R. R., & Blundall, J. (1987). Stress, coping, and satisfaction: Generational differences in farm families. *Family Relations, 36,* 45–48.

9

Family Caregiving, Communication, and the Health of Care Receivers

Helen Edwards
Queensland University of Technology, Australia

The year 1999 was designated the International Year of Older Persons to recognize the importance and contribution of people aged 65 years and over. Not only are the numbers of older people increasing but they will live longer and be more active, healthier, and independent than ever before (Australian Institute of Health and Welfare [AIHW], 1997). Although this concept of healthy aging does exist, frailty for some older adults cannot be ignored. Sometimes, in spite of medical treatment and their own determination, older people need to receive assistance and care. Because of concurrent trends in social, economic, and health policies, families are assuming more responsibility for the care of their older family members and now represent the primary source of long-term care for frail older people (AIHW, 1997; Blasinsky, 1998).

Family caregiving for older people has received much attention in the literature, especially from the perspective of the caregiver. To bridge the gap between research and practice, many intervention programs and policies have been developed to help family caregivers manage the burden and psychological distress they experience from caregiving (e.g., Braithwaite, 1990; Miller, McFall, & Montgomery, 1991). From the research and practice perspective, two issues of relevance to family caregiving have received little attention. Firstly, few studies have examined family caregiving from the care recipient's viewpoint, that is, carereceiving. Secondly, outcomes of caregiving experiences have focused predominantly on burden and psychological distress for carers such that only a limited number of studies have examined the interactional processes of care or the quality of the care provided (e.g., Phillips et al., 1995). This chapter describes a portion of a much larger project of older people and their family carers and examines family caregiving from the perspective of the care receiver and the relationship between care processes and the mental well-being of the older care receiver. In recognition of the differences in family relationships, data are presented for families where spouses are the carers and families where the sons and daughters are the carers. Based on the findings presented, suggestions for practice are offered.

The Other Side of Caregiving—Carereceiving

Implicit in the family caregiving literature is the assumption that older care receivers will benefit from the care they receive. Costs associated with carereceiving have, however, been identified and include depression (Thompson & Sobolew-Shubin, 1993), helplessness (Walker, Martin, & Jones, 1992), increased negative behaviors (Vitaliano, Young, Russo, Romano, & Magana-Amato, 1993), and declines in morale (Stoller, 1984), relational quality (Johnson & Catalano, 1983), and future outlook (Rakowski & Clark, 1985). These studies support the idea that receiving care might not always be beneficial for the care receiver and that variables important in explaining outcomes are different for carers and care receivers. Research by Lawton, Moss, and Duhamel (1995) focused attention on older care receivers and suggested that the quality of life of older persons receiving in-home care could be enhanced by providing a more enriching environment. As many of the reported costs of carereceiving are related to psychological well-being, this chapter examines older care receivers' psychological well-being and its relationship to a number of factors inherent in the process of care.

Psychological Well-Being of Older Care Receivers

Psychological well-being in older people can be conceptualized along a range of dimensions, including distressing psychological symptoms, current emotional states, and cognitive judgments about life over time (Lawton, 1983). In the study reported in this chapter, these three aspects of psychological well-being were examined using measures of anxiety/depression, affect balance, and life satisfaction.

Consistent with the multidimensionality of psychological well-being, the determinants of well-being are equally likely to involve a variety of sources. Previous research suggested that the quality of social support and interpersonal relationships are likely to be important determinants of well-being in older people being cared for by family members. Research in the area of chronic disability has shown that high levels of well-being for care receivers are associated with high levels of social support and, in particular, support from a primary carer (Schulz & Decker, 1985). In addition, support from spouse, friends, and adult children has been shown to ameliorate depressive symptoms in older people (Dean, Kolody, & Wood, 1990). More specifically, the quality of relationships with members of the support group is likely to influence care receivers' well-being. Studies have examined the carer–care receiver relationship and found that affection, attachment, intimacy, conflict, reciprocity and communication are important for the well-being of older people, family relationships, and quality of life (Braithwaite, 1998; Carruth, Tate, Moffett, & Hill, 1997; Edwards & Noller, 1998; Ferris & Bramston, 1994; Neufeld & Harrison, 1998; Walker et al., 1992; Whitbeck, Hoyt, & Huck, 1994).

The importance of health status to the well-being of older people has also been demonstrated. In Bowling and Browne's (1991) study, health status was found to be a better predictor of emotional well-being in old people than social network or support variables. Walker et al. (1992) found that although mothers with poorer health reported feeling more helpless, they also reported feeling more loved. The findings of such studies highlight the need to include health status as a determinant of well-being.

The well-being of the carer is another possible determinant of well-being for care receivers. Schulz, Tompkins, Wood, and Decker (1987) reported a strong relationship between burden reported by carers and care receiver depression. In this study, however, the care receiver's depression had been rated by the carer and it is therefore possible that the carer's perceptions were distorted by their own affective state. Studies that have collected data from both carer and care receiver are rare, thereby limiting work in this area. Exploration of the links between carer and care receiver well-being was possible in the study discussed here as self-report measures from both parties were obtained.

Researchers have developed models to explain the stresses associated with caregiving (e.g., Pearlin, Mullan, Semple, & Skaff, 1990). Coping is regarded as a principal mediator within these models and therefore is important to the process of care. Braithwaite (1990) found that family carers used coping strategies that were either problem-focused (e.g., getting assistance [taking control]; going away for a few days [withdrawing]) or emotion-focused (e.g., telling yourself that things could be worse [rein-

terpreting/reframing]; reading a book [avoidance]). The use of these coping strategies did not prevent burden, but appeared to be a response to
burden. After controlling for burden, the use of coping strategies predicted minor psychiatric symptomatology. Control and withdrawal were associated with fewer psychiatric symptoms, whereas reinterpretation/refram-
ing was associated with more symptoms. While the use of certain coping
strategies in response to burden can reduce or increase carers' symptomatology, it is not known what impact carers' coping strategies have on care
receivers. The study discussed in this chapter examined the relationship
between carers' coping strategies and the well-being of care receivers.

The caregiving literature shows that spouse and filial carers can be distinguished by the type and extent of care they provide (Montgomery &
Kosloski, 1994). Although both groups of carers experience considerable
burden and distress, factors influencing their experiences have been
shown to differ between spouse and filial carers (Miller et al., 1991). The
effect of gender of carer on caregiving has also been examined, and female
carers have been found to be more distressed than male carers (Miller &
Cafasso, 1992). In recognition that males are increasingly providing care,
and of the impact of gender on caregiving, studies including caregiving
husbands (Kramer, 1997; Lutzky & Knight, 1994) and sons (Harris, 1998;
Mui, 1995) have become more common.

As Young and Kahana (1989) noted, simultaneous investigations of
gender and kinship are rare. Spouse and filial carers are sometimes con-
trasted, but the gender within the groups is rarely examined. A study by
Barber and Pasley (1995) simultaneously examined the effects of gender
of carer and kinship between carer and care receiver and found that the
impact of caregiving varied according to gender and kinship. Female carers experienced greater strain in their family relationships and greater
decline in their health. Spousal carers reported greater restriction to their
social activities. As female carers are most negatively affected by caregiving, it is likely that their care receivers will also be more negatively affected by carereceiving than will care receivers cared for by males.

THE CAREGIVING–CARERECEIVING STUDY

Unlike most studies of family caregiving, the study discussed here drew on
the experiences of the carer and the older care receiver. The purpose of
the study was to systematically examine well-being in older adults being
cared for by a spouse or adult child. Possible factors contributing to well-
being included health status, social support, relational quality, carer well-

being, and carer coping strategies. The effect of gender of carer was also examined. The following questions were addressed:

1. What is the level of psychological well-being in older people being cared for by a spouse or adult child?
2. How important are factors such as social support, health status, relational quality, carer well-being, gender, and coping as determinants of well-being in older care receivers?

The participants in the study were 93 elderly people (i.e., over 60 years of age) and their primary carers. All lived in the community and the carers resided with the elderly care receiver. The care receivers had adequate sight and hearing (i.e., able to see and hear a television set), spoke and understood English, and had no diagnosis or history of dementia, confusion, or depression. Carers were either the husband or wife or daughter or son of the care receiver, were the primary provider of care, and resided with the care receiver. All carers were receiving the Domiciliary Nursing Care Benefit, a benefit paid by the government to people who provide care for a family member.

The study involved four groups: 27 wives cared for by husbands, 26 husbands cared for by wives, 28 mothers cared for by daughters, and 12 mothers cared for by sons. The following section describes the care receivers and carers who participated.

Care Receivers

The age of care receivers ranged from 62 to 95 years and care receivers cared for by adult children were older than those cared for by a spouse. The majority were born in Australia with the others having been born in the United Kingdom or Europe. Level of education differed across the groups with male care receivers being better educated than female care receivers. Most had previously been employed as laborers, clerks or trades persons. Approximately two thirds of care receivers said that they had "just enough" money to live on, while one third said they were "quite comfortable."

Care receivers being cared for by their spouses had been married to their caregiving spouses for an average of 51 years. The majority of mothers being cared for by an adult child were widowed. About half of the mothers still lived in their own home. Sons were more likely than daughters to be living in their mothers' homes.

Approximately three fourths of the sample said their health was "fair" or "good." In contrast, the majority said that, for a great deal of the time, their health problems prevented them from doing things they wanted to do. During the previous year, about half the sample had suffered from arthritis and approximately one third had experienced a variety of cardiovascular problems. Because care receivers with a diagnosis of dementia, confusion, or depression were excluded from the study, the incidence of mental illness in the sample was low with only 1% reporting they had experienced a mental health problem in the previous year.

Carers

The average age for the sample of carers was 65 years. Age differed across the groups with filial carers younger than caregiving spouses and caregiving wives younger than caregiving husbands. The number of people residing in the household also differed across the groups with fewer people residing in the homes of spousal carers than in the homes of filial carers.

The majority of carers were born in Australia with the rest being born in the United Kingdom or Europe. Just over three fourths of the sample had completed primary school and had attended high school. A higher percentage of caregiving wives and sons than husbands and daughters had never been employed. A higher percentage of filial carers were currently employed than spousal carers. The type of work undertaken by carers did not differ across the groups with most working, or having worked, as clerks, laborers or trades people. Income differed across the groups with a higher percentage of filial carers having an income greater than $20,000 than was true for spousal carers. It is interesting to note that caregiving sons had the highest percentage of income less than $10,000. Half of the filial carers said that they had helped their mother financially and one third said that their mother had helped them financially.

With regard to the filial carers, about one third had never been married. Daughters were more likely to have been married than sons. Of those who had been married, the majority were still married; one third were divorced or separated. Only a small proportion were widowed. About half of the filial carers said there was no one else who could have taken on the role as caregiver.

The carers reported caring for their spouse or mother for an average of 7 years. Wives had been carers for longer than husbands, sons, or daughters. Spousal carers were more likely to have become carers because of a specific health problem, whereas filial carers were more likely to be involved because of gradual deteriorating health.

Most carers described their health as "good" or "fair." One third said they suffered from arthritis or had some muscular-skeletal problem, and just under one third had experienced a cardiovascular problem. Problems of a mental health or psychiatric nature were reported by 16% of carers.

Data Collection

A group of care receivers and carers was recruited from various senior citizens centres, church organizations, community care agencies, and day respite centers. Initial contact was made with the dyads by telephone and for those who agreed to participate, a mutually convenient time was arranged for the interviewers to visit the dyads in their home. Only 6% of dyads who were contacted refused to participate. Participants were assured of confidentiality and anonymity. Two interviewers visited the dyad, one to interview the care receiver and one to interview the carer.

The interview consisted of a number of questions related to the caregiving–carereceiving experience and the participant's individual response to his or her situation. Both carers and care receivers were asked about their psychological well-being, that is, symptoms of anxiety and depression, the amount of negative and positive mood or affect they experienced, and their general life satisfaction. In addition, the carers were asked about the degree of burden they experienced as a result of caregiving.

The interview also included other areas that were considered likely to impact on the well-being of the care receiver. Therefore questions concerning the care receiver's health, the quality of the past and present carer–care receiver relationship, the amount of social support received by the care receiver, and the coping strategies used by the carer were included.

FINDINGS OF THE STUDY

Level of Well-Being of Care Receivers

The different groups of care receivers had similar levels of psychological well-being. The levels of anxiety and depression reported by the care receivers suggested that they were on the point of pathological disturbance; that is, their levels were just beyond that expected as part of everyday living. They were also at a pivotal point with their mood or affect, with approximately equal levels of positive and negative affect being reported. One third of the care receivers reported poor life satisfaction.

In comparison to other groups of older people living in the community (Stacy & Gatz, 1991), the level of well-being reported by the care receivers was low enough to be of concern as a public health issue. The findings also confirm previous research that receiving care involves emotional costs for the care receiver. The level of well-being reported by these care receivers could be the "norm," or expected level, for older people who require care and remain in the community. There is, however, evidence to suggest that the levels reported by this group of care receivers is lower than that reported from nursing home residents (Parmelee, Katz, & Lawton, 1989). This finding is of concern as an assumption underlying current home and community health funding and programs is the belief that care in a home environment is more beneficial than institutional care. Although more studies are needed to examine the level of well-being for older people receiving care in the community, the levels reported in this study support a finding by Lawton et al. (1995) that it should not automatically be assumed that home life is beneficial for those receiving care.

Predicting Care Receiver Well-Being

From the other information that was collected from carers and care receivers, it was possible to examine which factors were likely to predict low levels of psychological well-being for care receivers. As expected, care receiver health, social interaction, and relational quality, and carer well-being, coping, and gender were important determinants of care receivers' psychological well-being. Even after accounting for care receivers' health status, the other factors could predict care receiver well-being. Different factors emerged as being important for the spousal and filial dyads, and these two groups are discussed separately.

Important Factors Explaining Well-Being of Carereceiving Spouses

The health status of the carereceiving spouses was an important predictor of their anxiety and depression (see Table 9.1). As expected, carereceiving spouses with poor physical health were more likely to report feeling anxious and depressed. Further, as shown in Table 9.1, caring spouses' life satisfaction and care receivers' reports of conflict in the relationship were important predictors of negative mood in carereceiving spouses. Low affect balance in carereceiving spouses was more likely to occur

TABLE 9.1
Hierarchical Regression Analyses for Carereceiver Well-Being (Spousal Sample)

Predictor Variables	β	R^2	R^2 change
Anxiety/Depression			
Step 1		.13*	.13*
Cr Health[a]	−.38**		
Step 2		.25	.12
Cr Health[a]	−.27		
Cg Gender	−.01		
Conflict[a]	.24		
ASIS[a]	−.14		
Withdrawal[b]	.01		
LSIA[b]	.19		
Affect Balance			
Step 1		.04	.04
Cr Health[a]	.25		
Step 2		.42**	.38**
Cr Health[a]	.07		
Cg Gender	−.09		
Conflict[a]	−.34*		
ASIS[a]	.19		
Withdrawal[b]	.01		
LSIA[b]	−.46**		
Life Satisfaction			
Step 1		.01	.01
Cr Health[a]	.13		
Step 2		.37**	.36**
Cr Health[a]	−.02		
Cg Gender	.19		
Conflict[a]	−.31*		
ASIS[a]	.22		
Withdrawal[b]	−.34*		
LSIA[b]	−.23		

Note. Gender was coded as male = 0, female = 1. LSIA = Life Satisfaction; ASIS = Availability of Social Interaction Scale. Cg = Carer; Cr = Care receiver.

[a] Rated by care receiver. [b] Rated by carer.

* $p < .05$. ** $p < .01$.

when they reported high levels of conflict in the relationship or their carers reported high life satisfaction. Finally, the use of withdrawal as a coping strategy by carers and the conflict reported by the care receivers were important predictors of life satisfaction for carereceiving spouses (see Table 9.1). Low life satisfaction in carereceiving spouses was more likely their carer used withdrawal as a coping strategy and there was high levels of conflict in the relationship.

The importance of conflict is underscored as it contributed to two of the well-being measures, namely, affect balance and life satisfaction. Conflict contributed, as expected, and confirmed previous research that poor quality relationships can have a negative impact on the well-being of older care receivers (Rakowski & Clark, 1985; Talbott, 1990; Walker et al., 1992). As noted by Hansson and Carpenter (1994), it is not surprising that conflict arises, given that caregiving is frequently undertaken under difficult conditions and, often, with no end in sight. Although the data confirm strong relationships between conflict and care receiver well-being, causal inferences cannot be made. Conflict between the dyad may lead to reduced well-being for the care receiver, or alternatively, poor well-being in care receivers may create tensions in the relationship. In reality, the links are more likely to be circular than linear. Regardless of causality, the findings suggest that the outcomes of care for both carer and care receiver are likely to improve if the quality of the relationship is addressed.

Carers' life satisfaction and use of withdrawal as a coping strategy did not contribute to well-being in carereceiving spouses in the ways that had been expected. Low affect balance and life satisfaction in these care receivers was associated with high, not low, life satisfaction in carers. Perhaps the care receivers' feelings represent a reaction to being dependent on a spouse who appears to be satisfied and happy with life. It may be a case of one person being happy and satisfied from assuming the caring more protective role, whereas the other is unhappy and dissatisfied at having to adopt the dependent role, as well as having to witness the partner's satisfaction. Having one's spouse feeling good about him or herself may worsen the care receivers' feelings about some of the results of being dependent, having diminished control, and enduring invasions of privacy and overprotectiveness (Hansson & Carpenter, 1994). Another explanation for this finding could be that carers look after their own needs more than the needs of their care receivers. Given the demands of caregiving, this explanation is feasible and needs to be followed up in future research.

Braithwaite (1990) suggested that withdrawal is a positive and problem-focused coping strategy, as it involves physical separation, gives the carer time to rest and relax, and has been shown to improve mental well-being in carers. As a problem-focused and therefore positively orientated strategy, withdrawal was expected to be positively related to care receiver well-being. It was found, however, to be negatively correlated with care receiver life satisfaction. Although withdrawal may be problem-focused and beneficial for carers, the care receivers may perceive the need for their carers to get away from them as disinterest in, or dislike of, providing care, or as a form of rejection. Such negative perceptions are likely to have a negative effect on the well-being of care receivers. The use of withdrawal by spousal carers is likely to be of great concern to their care-receiving partners because of the normative expectations of the marital bond (e.g., "for better, for worse").

Important Factors Explaining Well-Being in Carereceiving Mothers

The factors that predicted care receiver well-being in the filial sample were: the mothers' health and degree of available social interaction, and the carers' gender and use of reinterpretation/reframing as a coping strategy (see Table 9.2). Consistent with previous research (e.g., Bowling & Browne, 1991; Walker et al., 1992), poor health in the mothers was the strongest predictor of their reporting symptoms of anxiety and depression. The mothers were probably concerned not only about their poor health, but the impact it was having on their children and their families.

As shown in Table 9.2, symptoms of anxiety and depression were also more likely to be reported by mothers cared for by their daughters. Consistent with previous research, the daughters in this study reported higher levels of burden and more symptoms of anxiety/depression than did the caregiving sons. These negative effects of caregiving on daughters may be associated with negative outcomes for their mothers. If carers are feeling burdened and anxious, it is likely to be difficult for them to have pleasant interactions with their care receivers. Through their daily interactions, the mothers are likely to sense their daughters' negative feelings which, in turn, may arouse their anxieties.

The data presented in Table 9.2 also show that low reports of anxiety and depression and high affect balance in carereceiving mothers were more likely when the sons and daughters used reinterpretation/reframing as a coping strategy. The use of reinterpretation/reframing is seen as an

TABLE 9.2
Hierarchical Regression Analyses for Carereceiver Well-Being (Filial Sample)

Predictor Variables	β	R^2	R^2 change
Anxiety/Depression			
Step 1		.17*	.17*
Cr Health[a]	−.41*		
Step 2		.40*	.23
Cr Health[a]	−.51*		
Cg Gender	.40*		
Conflict[a]	.02		
ASIS[a]	−.11		
Reinterpretation[b]	−.34*		
Burden[b]	−.16		
Affect Balance			
Step 1		.16*	.16*
Cr Health[a]	.39*		
Step 2		.46**	.30**
Cr Health[a]	.11		
Cg Gender	.02		
Conflict[a]	−.29		
ASIS[a]	.22		
Reinterpretation[b]	.39*		
Burden[b]	−.25		
Life Satisfaction			
Step 1		.19**	.19**
Cr Health[a]	.44**		
Step 2		.40*	.21
Cr Health[a]	.23		
Cg Gender	−.25		
Conflict[a]	−.26		
ASIS[a]	.32*		
Reinterpretation[b]	.16		
Burden[b]	.01		

Note. Gender was coded as male = 0, female = 1. LSIA = Life Satisfaction; ASIS = Availability of Social Interaction Scale. Cg = Carer; Cr = Care receiver.

[a] Rated by care receiver. [b] Rated by carer.

* $p < .05$. ** $p < .01$.

emotion-focused coping strategy, and because it may not help carers directly deal with their problems, it seems to be associated with greater symptomatology in carers (Braithwaite, 1990). Consequently, frequent use of this strategy by carers was expected to adversely affect care receivers. In contrast, in this study, the mothers of carers who frequently used reinterpretation/reframing reported high levels of well-being. This finding suggests that, although cognitive coping strategies may not help carers deal with their problems or improve their well-being, the use of such strategies by carers could be beneficial for the well-being of the care receivers.

Finally, low life satisfaction for the carereceiving mothers was more likely when they had limited access to a social network (see Table 9.2). As Hansson and Carpenter (1994) noted, regardless of how social inter-action is measured, or what exact function it performs, social functioning is integral to human functioning. Older people are just as likely to face crises as young people, and at such times, personal relationships and the support that develops through social interaction can become critical to the older person's adaptation and well-being. This finding suggests that access to social partners and social support needs to be maintained for mothers cared for by their adult children. Caregiving sons and daughters are usually very busy with the demands of their own family and may, at times, forget the importance of social support for their mothers.

Comparing the Spousal and Filial Dyads

For the spousal sample, the coping strategy of withdrawal was important to care receiver well-being, whereas the strategy of reinterpretation/ reframing was important for care receiver well-being in the filial sample. The use of withdrawal by carers is more likely to be of concern to carere-ceiving spouses than to carereceiving mothers because of the normative expectations of the marital relationship. Although different types of cop-ing strategies were important to the two samples, the carers' coping strate-gies were strong predictors of care receiver well-being in both samples. Interestingly, the two coping strategies were not related to care receiver well-being in the directions predicted. Whereas withdrawal has been associated with improved well-being in carers, its use in this study was associated with reduced well-being for care receivers. Reinterpretation/ reframing has been associated with reduced well-being in carers, but in this study it was associated with high levels of well-being in care receivers. These findings have important clinical significance, as they demonstrate that strategies beneficial to one member of a caring dyad may not be beneficial to the other member. Carers may need assistance to find ways to deal with the burden of caregiving that is beneficial both to them and to their care receivers. More importantly, as providing care can be viewed as a communicative act (Giles, Coupland, & Weimann, 1990), many of the carers' coping strategies are likely to be enacted through their interactions with their care receivers (e.g., avoiding certain topics, expressing feelings), suggesting the need for detailed examination of these processes.

Carer well-being was important for spousal care receivers' well-being, but not mothers' well-being. While both groups of carers may experience burden associated with caregiving, the adult children are more likely to have avenues outside the caregiving context by which they can bolster their overall well-being. In contrast, well-being for the caregiving spouses is more likely to be influenced by the caregiving context, as spousal carers are known to be more immersed and committed to caregiving (Young & Kahana, 1989), and more enmeshed with the relationship (Johnson & Catalano, 1983).

The lesser importance of conflict in the relationship for the filial sample may be due to the self-selected nature of living with, and providing care for, a parent. If there was already conflict between a child and their parent who required care, both parties may seek alternative arrangements. Therefore adult children who live with and care for their parents may have strong positive emotional bonds and less conflictual relationships. Spouses who are required to care for their partners may not seek alternative arrangements, even if they have conflictual relationships. Longitudinal studies could examine the role of conflict at the commencement of caregiving and its development over time.

As female carers in the current study were more affected by caregiving than males carers, the gender of carer in the spouse sample was expected to be related to care receiver well-being for the spouse sample, as well as for the filial sample. Perhaps over the life time of the marriage the wives have become "masters" at hiding their distress from their husbands, or perhaps because of their coping strategy of withdrawing, their husbands are not aware of the full extent of their distress. Alternatively, even if the husbands do recognize the distress in their wives, it may not have such a negative impact on their well-being because of the normative expectations of marriage and the stability of their relationship over a long period.

The older age of the care receivers in the filial sample could explain the importance of health for the carereceiving mothers, although there were no differences in functional status between the samples. The link between poor health and well-being for the mothers may reflect their concerns about being a burden to their children and going beyond the bounds of the expected parent–child relationship. Poor health in carereceiving spouses may not engender the same concerns because of the expectations that marital partners will care for their spouses.

Social interaction could be more important to carereceiving mothers than carereceiving spouses because the mothers are likely to have a different social network from the carer. In contrast, spousal dyads are more likely to have similar social networks. Carereceiving spouses may be content to draw their social support from within their relationship, whereas the carereceiving mothers may wish to seek support from a broader network.

APPLICATION TO PRACTICE

The findings of the study discussed in this chapter have several important applications for the care of older people cared for by families. First, the low levels of psychological well-being reported by the older care receivers need to be seriously considered by practitioners as family caregiving may be detrimental to the health of both carer and care receiver. The emotional costs of being a care receiver are just as serious a public health issue as the burden experienced by carers. This finding challenges practitioners to carefully assess the family caregiving context and not to assume that "home" is "best" nor to pressure families into caregiving. The needs of the older person and the family who is to provide care should be assessed and matched with the most appropriate model of care. Practitioners need to be aware that the needs of carers and care receivers can be quite different as can the needs of spousal and filial dyads. In addition, assessment needs to be ongoing, as over long periods of caregiving, the needs of carers and care receivers are likely to change. Practitioners working in this field need to be very skilled at assessment and need to consider the dyad as the focus of their work as opposed to focusing on the individual carer and care receiver.

Second, community and home care programs and interventions to assist older people and their carers should be critically reviewed by practitioners. Since home care for older people has become a "preferred" option, many programs have been developed to provide families with the knowledge and skills on how to provide the physical care required. In addition, many programs have been designed to assist carers with the burden and distress they can experience with caregiving. Such programs include respite, day, or more long term, and visitor schemes. Although many programs provide physical care and rehabilitation services for the older person, most programs have as their primary aim relief for the carer. Based on the research evidence about carer burden, these programs can be justified. However, programs to address care receiver "burden" need to be considered. The aim of any program should include the improvement of the well-being of older care receivers. This is not to suggest that programs for carers should cease but to ensure that assistance is given to the care receivers who may be just as burdened as the carers. Such programs could include counseling, coaching in coping skills, and interpersonal skills, and access to social networks. As caregiving daughters and mothers cared for by daughters appear to be the most at risk in terms of emotional distress, special programs for these groups could be considered and might include increased respite and individual and dyadic counseling.

Third, practitioners need to be prepared to assist caring dyads with relationship issues. It is interesting to note that several programs dealing with family relationships have been well accepted and provided by health professionals. Such programs include marriage guidance, parent effectiveness training, and positive parenting instruction. Programs for dealing with relationship issues for older people and their family do not appear to be a high priority. There is an opportunity here for practitioners to develop specific programs to assist carers and care receivers with their relationship and interpersonal issues. The findings of the research discussed in this chapter highlight the impact of conflict on the well-being of older care receivers. Unresolved conflict can only be detrimental to ongoing relationships (Roloff & Cloven, 1990) and consequently the well-being of both carer and care receiver. Other data collected in the larger caregiving study (Edwards, 1996) but not reported in this chapter, suggest that caring dyads, particularly spousal dyads, do not discuss issues of conflict although both members of the dyad would like to discuss issues of concern to them. Practitioners could facilitate the dyad to discuss the issues which concern them and encourage the dyad to work towards resolution. Conflict management skills are not just the domain of the "younger" generation but could be used by practitioners to reduce conflict in caregiving relationships.

Fourth, as an extension of the interpersonal focus, practitioners could facilitate discussions between caring dyads to determine how the coping strategies used by carers are perceived by care receivers. The data from this study show how a coping strategy, which may be used effectively by one member of the dyad, can have a negative effect on the other member of the dyad. Practitioners could encourage carers and care receivers to talk about their coping strategies and the perceptions they might have of each other's strategies. Carers may need assistance to find ways to deal with the burden of caregiving that are beneficial both to them and to their care receivers. Assisting the dyad to understand and accept each other's views in positive and constructive ways would also be beneficial for the caregiving relationship. In addition, carers and care receivers could be encouraged to use a range of coping strategies that includes problem-focused and emotional focused strategies.

To facilitate the suggestion that caring dyads should talk about their concerns more, specific strategies for carers and care receivers are offered. At least once a month, time should be allocated for the carers and care receivers to talk specifically about the caregiving situation. This time should be free from distractions and at a time when the carer and care receiver are both comfortable and relaxed as possible. Equal time needs to be given to the carer and the carereceiver. Carers may need to be reminded that, even though their care receiver may be dependent is some aspects of care, communication is maximized when it is two way and based on equality. To avoid controlling communication with their care receivers, carers should be encouraged to:

- allow their care receiver to introduce and change topics for discussion;
- provide interest and encouragement (back-channeling) when care receivers introduce topics;
- allow care receivers to continue discussing topics introduced by themselves or their carer;
- avoid interrupting or talking over their care receiver;
- avoid ignoring or deflecting topics introduced by their care receiver;
- introduce topics by asking an open question of their care receiver (when a question is used, there is an expectation that it will be answered and the topic can be developed: however, when a statement is used, it can be taken up or ignored);
- use "differences" as a way of talking through issues and not expect their care receivers to share their (the carer's) viewpoint on caregiving issues or to agree with them;
- strive for a balance between asking for information and suggestions and giving information and opinion;
- express their feelings of affection and care as well as their frustrations and tensions.

To promote effective carer–care receiver communication, care receivers should be encouraged to:

- initiate topics of concern to them;
- continue to discuss topics with their carer and not to "give the floor" to their carer;
- provide interest and encouragement (back-channeling) when their carer is talking;
- avoid interrupting or talking over their carer;
- avoid deflecting or ignoring topics introduced by their carer;
- respond to questions and statements from their carer;
- express their points of view even if they differ from those of their carer and to be prepared to discuss these differences;
- ask their carer for their suggestions and opinions regarding issues of concern;
- express their feelings of frustration and helplessness as well as their feelings of gratefulness, affection, and admiration.

Although these principles of communication for carers and care receivers will not solve every caregiving issue, they will promote a positive communication environment. In such an environment, the dyad can explore how the caregiving context is affecting each person.

Finally, practitioners need to be prepared to intervene in specific ways for different caring dyads. When working with spousal dyads, practitioners need to acknowledge that although the well-being of one spouse is closely related to the well-being of the other spouse, the relationship may not be as expected. As a positive experience by a spouse can have a negative effect on their partner, it would be beneficial for practitioners to explore with spousal dyads their perceptions and reactions about their own role and the role of their spouse. These reactions and perceptions need to be discussed within the caregiving dyad so that shared meanings can be understood and clarified. Again practitioners can play a pivotal role in facilitating such discussions.

When working with filial dyads, practitioners need to ensure that not only is everything being done to improve the health status of carereceiving mothers but to be prepared with strategies to reduce anxiety/depression in mothers cared for by adult children. In addition, practitioners need to monitor the degree and type of social contact available to carereceiving mothers and, if necessary, use respite, community activities and community visitor schemes to maintain social networks.

The differing needs of spousal and filial dyads are examples of why practitioners need to assess, plan, and intervene for specific families. The generic programs that are commonly used for family carers will not address the emotional needs of older care receivers. A challenge for practitioners will be to develop programs that are beneficial to both carers and carereceivers.

CONCLUSIONS

The study discussed in this chapter is intended to challenge and stimulate researchers and practitioners who work in the area of family caregiving for older people. As noted in the introduction, much of the family caregiving literature to date has focused on the well-being of the carer and the process of caregiving. In direct contrast, this chapter has focused on the well-being of the care receiver and the processes of carereceiving. When working with caregiving families, it is critical that practitioners work with both members of the dyad. Given the complexities of family relationships and caregiving, this is certainly a challenge for practitioners.

As the study has shown, the well-being of older carereceivers receiving family care can be low enough to be of concern and may, in fact, be no better than residents of long-term care facilities. This emphasizes that the well-being of care receivers is just as serious an issue as the well-being of family carers. Just as importantly, it should encourage practitioners to question the assumption that home care is "better" than institutional care. At a general level, home care could still be argued to be "better" in terms of familiarity, consistency of carer, access to family, and certainly better for governments in financial terms. At the individual family level, however, the general assumption may not hold up. Practitioners, therefore, have an important role in assessing the situation and the needs of carers and care receivers before they make any recommendations regarding ongoing care for older people.

Also reported in this chapter are the factors that are likely to predict reduced well-being in care receivers. Again, these findings can assist practitioners to assess the caregiving and carereceiving context and to design interventions appropriate to improving the well-being of both carers and carereceivers. As the study shows, some factors can affect the carers and care receivers differently and this challenges practitioners to work closely with the dyad so that any interventions will have maximum, mutual benefits to both partners of the dyad. The study also confirms that practitioners need to be aware of differences between spousal and filial caregiving and carereceiving and to design interventions appropriate to the relationships involved.

Family caregiving is necessary for the ongoing care of many older people. Family relationships are complex and need to be supported in times of increased pressure. Practitioners have a challenge to ensure that family caregiving will be of benefit to the older people who require it. This chapter provides practitioners with some challenges for assessment and interventions to promote the mental well-being of older care receivers.

ACKNOWLEDGMENT

The study reported in this chapter was supported by Research and Development Grant HS 252 from the Research and Development Advisory Committee, Department of Health, Housing, and Community Service, Australia.

REFERENCES

Australian Institute of Health and Welfare. (1997). *Older Australia at a glance*. Canberra, Australia: Author.

Barber, C. E., & Pasley, B. K. (1995). Family care of Alzheimer's patients: The role of gender and generational relationship on carer outcomes. *Journal of Applied Gerontology, 14*, 172–192.

Blasinsky, M. (1998). Family dynamics: Influencing care of the older adult. *Activities, Adaption and Aging, 22*(4), 65–72.

Bowling, A., & Browne, P. D. (1991). Social networks, health and emotional well-being among the oldest old in London. *Journal of Gerontology: Social Sciences, 46*, S20–S32.

Braithwaite, V. (1990). *Bound to care*. Sydney, Australia: Allen & Unwin.

Braithwaite, V. (1998). Institutional respite care: Breaking chores or breaking social bonds. *The Gerontologist, 38*(5), 610–617.

Carruth, A., Tate, U., Moffett, B., & Hill, K. (1997). Reciprocity, emotional well-being, and family functioning as determinants of satisfaction in caregivers of elderly parents. *Nursing Research, 46*(2), 93–100.

Dean, A., Kolody, B., & Wood, P. (1990). Effects of social support from various sources on depression in elderly persons. *Journal of Health and Social Behaviour, 31*, 148–161.

Edwards, H. (1996). *Communication between older people and their family carers*. Unpublished doctoral dissertation, University of Queensland, Australia.

Edwards, H., & Noller, P. (1998). Factors influencing caregiver–carereceiver communication and its impact on the well-being of older care receivers. *Health Communication, 10*(4), 317–341.

Ferris, C., & Bramston, P. (1994). Quality of life in the elderly: A contribution to its understanding. *Australian Journal on Ageing, 13*, 120–122.

Giles, H., Coupland, N., & Wiemann, J. (Eds.). (1990). Communication, health and the elderly (pp. i–iv). *Fulbright International Colloquium, 8.* Manchester, England: Manchester University Press.

Hansson, R. O., & Carpenter, B. N. (1994). *Relationships in old age: Coping with the challenge of transition.* New York: Guilford.

Harris, P. (1998). Listening to caregiving sons: Misunderstood realities. *The Gerontologist, 38*(3), 342–352.

Johnson, C. L., & Catalano, D. J. (1983). A longitudinal study of family supports to impaired elderly. *The Gerontologist, 23,* 612–618.

Kramer, B. (1997). Differential predictors of strain and gain among husbands caring for wives with dementia. *The Gerontologist, 37*(2), 239–249.

Lawton, M. P. (1983). Environment and other determinants of well-being in older people. *The Gerontologist, 23,* 349–357.

Lawton, M. P., Moss, M., & Duhamel, L. M. (1995). The quality of daily life among elderly care receivers. *Journal of Applied Gerontology, 14,* 150–171.

Lutzky, S. M., & Knight, B. G. (1994). Explaining gender differences in carer distress: The roles of emotional attentiveness and coping styles. *Psychology and Aging, 9,* 513–519.

Miller, B., & Cafasso, L. (1992). Gender differences in caregiving: Fact or artifact? *The Gerontologist, 32,* 498–507.

Miller, B., McFall, S., & Montgomery, A. (1991). The impact of elder health, carer involvement, and global stress on two dimensions of carer burden. *Journal of Gerontology: Social Sciences, 46,* S9–19.

Montgomery, R. J., & Kosloski, K. (1994). A longitudinal analysis of nursing home placement for dependent elders cared for by spouses vs. adult children. *Journal of Gerontology: Social Sciences, 49,* S62–S74.

Mui, A. C. (1995). Caring for frail elderly parents: A comparison of adult sons and daughters. *The Gerontologist, 35,* 86–93.

Neufeld, A., & Harrison, M. (1998). Men as caregivers: Reciprocal relationships or obligation? *Journal of Advance Nursing, 28*(5), 959–968.

Parmelee, P. A., Katz, I. R., & Lawton, M. P. (1989). Depression among institutionalised aged: Assessment and prevalence estimation. *Journal of Gerontology: Medical Sciences, 44,* M22–M29.

Pearlin, L., Mullan, J., Semple, S., & Skaff, M. (1990). Caregiving and the stress process: An overview of concepts and their measures. *The Gerontologist, 30,* 583–594.

Phillips, L., Morrison, E., Steffl, B., Chae, Y., Cromwell, S., & Russell, C. (1995). Effects of the situational context and interactional process on the quality of family caregiving. *Research in Nursing, 18,* 205–216.

Rakowski, W., & Clark, N. M. (1985). Future outlook, caregiving, and care-receiving in the family context. *The Gerontologist, 25,* 618–623.

Roloff, M., & Cloven, D. H. (1990). The chilling effect in interpersonal relationships: The reluctance to speak one's mind. In D. D. Cahn (Ed.), *Intimates in conflict: A communication perspective* (pp. 49–76). Hillsdale, NJ: Lawrence Erlbaum Associates.

Schulz, R., & Decker, S. (1985). Long-term adjustment to physical disability: The role of social support, perceived control and self-blame. *Journal of Personality and Social Psychology, 48,* 1162–1172.

Schulz, R., Tompkins, C. A., Wood, D., & Decker, S. (1987). The social psychology of caregiving: Physical and psychological costs of providing support for the disabled. *Journal of Applied Social Psychology, 17,* 401–428.

Stacey, C. A., & Gatz, M. (1991). Cross-sectional age differences and longitudinal change on the Bradburn affect balance scale. *Journal of Gerontology: Psychological Sciences, 46,* P76–P78.

Stoller, E. P. (1984). Self-assessments of health by the elderly: The impact of informal assistance. *Journal of Health and Social Behaviour, 25*, 260–270.

Talbott, M. M. (1990). The negative side of the relationship between older widows and their adult children: The mothers' perspective. *The Gerontologist, 30*, 595–603.

Thompson, S. C., & Sobolew-Shubin, A. (1993). Overprotective relationships: A nonsupportive side of social networks. *Basic and Applied Social Psychology, 14*, 363–383.

Vitaliano, P., Young, H., Russo, J., Romano, J., & Magana-Amato, A. (1993). Does expressed emotion in spouses predict subsequent problems among care recipients with Alzheimer's disease? *Journal of Gerontology: Psychological Sciences, 48*, P202–209.

Walker, A. J., Martin, S. S., & Jones, L. L. (1992). The benefits and costs of caregiving and care receiving for daughters and mothers. *Journal of Gerontology: Social Sciences, 47*, S130–S139.

Whitbeck, L., Hoyt, D. R., & Huck, S. M. (1994). Early family relationships, intergenerational solidarity and support provided to parents by their adult children. *Journal of Gerontology: Social Sciences, 49*, S85–S94.

Young, R. F., & Kahana, E. (1989). Specifying carer outcomes: Gender and relationship aspects of caregiving strain. *The Gerontologist, 29*, 660–666.

10

Family Caregivers, Communication, and Alzheimer's Disease

J. B. Orange
University of Western Ontario, Canada

The acquired syndrome of dementia emerges in adults and older adults after decades of subtle but eventually cataclysmic deterioration in thinking and behavior. It is increasing in prevalence among older adults, especially among adults over the age of 85 years where it is estimated to occur in approximately 35% of the cohort (Canadian Study of Health and Aging, 1994). The most frequent form of dementia is Alzheimer's disease (AD), accounting for approximately 60% to 65% of all types (Canadian Study of Health and Aging, 1994). AD presents initially with persistent and progressive declines in cognition, particularly in memory systems and processes (American Psychiatric Association, 1994). Changes in language and communication also emerge early in the course of AD, most often in the form of word-finding difficulties and problems with social communication (e.g., day-to-day contacts with family and friends; Bayles & Kaszniak, 1987).

AD is reasonably well described in terms of brain pathology and behavioral profiles for each of the three clinical stages of the disease (i.e., early/mild, middle/moderate, and late/severe). Researchers and clinicians are becoming more aware of the multiple effects of AD on those diagnosed with the illness. However, the disease is by no means isolated to the individuals with AD. Family, friends, neighbors, and formal care providers are affected deeply by its comprehensive pervasiveness and its relentless progression. Individuals with AD and their care providers, most frequently family members, are at great risk of suffering significant negative health, social, emotional, psychological, and financial consequences

225

(Gwyther, 1998; Welleford, Harkins, & Taylor, 1994). In particular, family members are faced with the prospect of becoming increasingly isolated from their relative with AD as a result of declines in language and communication. In order to battle successfully against these problems and the social isolation that often accompanies AD, family members are forced to take on new roles as facilitators of communication and social interaction. These added responsibilities are in addition to the other health, social, emotional, financial, and daily care responsibilities they must shoulder as part of caring for their relative. The accumulated responsibilities of caregiving can lead to significant levels of physical and emotional stress and burden among family members.

With these considerations in mind, this chapter addresses the following issues. First, language and communication changes associated with AD and its three clinical stages are presented. This information is intended to act as a foundation for the ideas presented in the other three themes in the chapter. Next, family members' perspectives of caregiving, communication and AD, and the impact of communication changes associated with AD are reviewed. Third, patterns of communication between family caregivers and their relative with AD are presented. These patterns are derived primarily from the literature on conversational analyses of family caregiver–AD dyads. Finally, the chapter concludes with comments on current intervention approaches designed to enhance and optimize communication and a discussion of considerations for future interventions.

LANGUAGE AND COMMUNICATION IN AD

The hallmark feature of spoken and written language during the early clinical stage of AD is word-finding problems (i.e., anomia) for people, places, objects, and actions (Appell, Kertesz, & Fisman, 1982). Early stage individuals use clichés and stereotyped phrases, and produce incomplete sentences, primarily as a result of their anomia (Bayles & Kaszniak, 1987). Individuals may repeat words, sentences, and ideas, and digress temporarily from the topic of conversations. These features are believed to occur as a result of deteriorations in working memory, cohesion problems, and declines in pragmatic competence (Garcia & Joanette, 1997; Mentis, Briggs-Whittaker, & Gramigna, 1995). Early stage individuals often will participate in and help maintain conversations, although they may exhibit shorter and more frequent conversational turns (Hutchinson & Jensen, 1980; Ripich & Terrell, 1988). Spontaneous writing (e.g., letters and cards) may be abandoned (Rapcsak, Arthur, Bliklen, & Rubens, 1989). Generally, early stage individuals with AD understand most spoken and written language unless it contains complex grammar, syntax, figurative elements (e.g., metaphors, analogies, proverbs, etc.), or a complex story structure (Kempler, Van Lancker, & Read, 1988).

Middle clinical stage individuals with AD show a pronounced anomia. Their expressive language carries little meaning because it contains few content words (Nicholas, Obler, Albert, & Helm-Estabrooks, 1985). In addition, middle stage AD individuals may not identify clearly to whom or to what they are referring, creating further ambiguity for their communication partners (Ripich & Terrell, 1988). They frequently repeat words, utterances, and ideas much to the dismay of their family and formal care providers (Orange, 1991b). Middle stage individuals frequently use stereotyped social greetings and phrases in conversations although they continue to engage in and maintain conversations (Mentis et al., 1995; Ripich & Terrell, 1988). They may make socially inappropriate comments, suggesting poor sensitivity to where (i.e., social contexts) and with whom they are communicating (Bayles & Kaszniak, 1987). They often cannot tell or write a coherent story because they focus more on secondary than primary details. They often digress off the topic of conversation and suffer substantial anomia (Garcia & Joanette, 1997; Kempler, 1991; Ulatowska et al., 1988). Despite these obvious problems, middle stage AD individuals monitor and frequently correct their own speaking errors and the errors made by their conversational partner (Hamilton, 1994; McNamara, Obler, Au, Durso, & Albert, 1992; Orange, Lubinski, & Higginbotham, 1996; Watson, Chenery, & Carter, 1999). Moreover, they let their partners know when they do not understand what is said to them (Orange et al., 1996; Watson et al., 1999). Middle stage AD individuals normally answer single, grammatically and syntactically simple questions moderately well but experience greater problems with multistep commands (Bayles & Kaszniak, 1987). They show greater problems in the everyday functional aspects of communication. They may be lost in multipartner conversations (Alberoni, Baddeley, Della Salla, Logie, & Spinnler, 1992). Reading comprehension is often limited to frequently occurring words such as those in newspaper headlines (Cummings, Houlihan, & Hill, 1986).

Late clinical stage AD individuals show wide variability in expressive language and pragmatic performances ranging from mutism to continuous spoken streams of nonsense words and utterances (i.e., jargon; Causino Lamar, Obler, Knoefel, & Albert, 1994). Some late stage individuals may

produce isolated and meaningful words or utterances after lengthy periods of not talking (Bayles & Kaszniak, 1987; Causino Lamar et al., 1994).
They also may repeat themselves and what others say (Cummings & Benson, 1992). Writing is nonfunctional (Kempler, 1991). Late stage AD
individuals rely predominantly on pitch changes in speech, syllable and
word stress patterns, and the emotional tone and the familiarity of voices and music to comprehend what is going on around them. In addition,
they rely heavily on touch, facial expressions, simple gestures, and other
aspects of nonverbal communication (Kempler, 1991).

FAMILY PERCEPTIONS OF CAREGIVING
AND COMMUNICATION

There is a large body of literature on caregivers' perspectives of caring for
family members with AD including qualitative studies on the views of
husbands, wives, adult children, and adolescents (Beach, 1997; Kuhn,
1998; Parsons, 1997; Siriopoulos, Brown, & Wright, 1999; Urquhart,
1997). These perspectives and expectations of care often change with different stages of the disease and the changing emotions of family members
(Abraham, Onega, Chalifoux, & Maas, 1994; Kuhn, 1998). Many of the
qualitative studies show that caregivers describe both negative and positive consequences of providing care for their relative with AD (Beach,
1997). For example, caring for individuals with AD often results in high
levels of psychological, emotional, social, and physical stress and burden
for family members (Kramer, 1997). Depression is common among family caregivers of individuals with AD (Cohen & Eisdorfer, 1988; Haley
1997). Caregiver burden is correlated directly with the personality and
behavioral changes of individuals with AD (Gwyther, 1998). Gender,
education, social participation, the health of caregivers, and coping
strategies help differentiate the stress and burden levels in family caregivers, although there is a multidimensional structure of caregivers' subjective appraisals of the experience of caregiving (Beach, 1997). For
example, burden, caregiving satisfaction, and caregiver mastery are correlated with the extent of memory and behavioral problems, caregivers'
coping styles, the locus of control, self-esteem, ego strength, level of
depression, and perceived emotional support (Talkington-Boyer & Snyder, 1994). Positive consequences of caregiving include seeking positive
affirmations of the work, looking for better staff communication, seeking
permission from family or formal health care authorities to withdraw from
the caregiving role, and giving to others (Bonnel, 1996).

Recurring themes of caregiving emerge from the commentaries of spouses and other family members of individuals with AD. These include the loss of the family member as a partner (including the loss of communication), high levels of caregiver burden, the need to develop coping methods, and the need to change lifestyles (Kuhn, 1998; Siriopoulos et al., 1999). The following examples illustrate several of these themes:

Example 1

The basic challenge is trying to be patient because he asks me questions repeatedly. We can go over the same thing over and over and over. In our marriage, when we had an issue that had to be worked, well, we would work it out. But now it's all undone an hour later or the next day. And we have to go through the same issue again, and sometimes I get angry with him. Yet, I know he can't help it, but I get tired. Sometimes I'm okay and sometimes I could just wring his neck, but I won't. So that's the hardest part. (Kuhn, 1998, p. 193)

Example 2

The experience as a caregiver is most frustrating is probably the only way I can describe it. The fact that her complete loss, or almost, of remembering things, it's very hard for a caregiver to remember some of these things and you could be at times a little sharp or impatient. (Siriopoulos et al., 1999, p. 82)

Family members note deteriorations in the quality of their relationship especially with respect to the communication changes of AD, the overall effects of AD and its impact on their own health, the need for health and social support systems, concerns for the future, financial worries, increasing conflicts among family members, a sense of enduring, the need for increased vigilance of the individual with AD, and a need to search for and discover information concerning AD (Kuhn, 1998; Parsons, 1997; Siriopoulos et al., 1999; Urquhart, 1997). The following examples illustrate some of these themes:

Example 3

In other words, we never had anybody to talk to anymore . . . He was there physically, but he wasn't there . . . He didn't recognize who I was, I sort of lost that thing, the father–son relationship, and it was hard (Parsons, 1997, p. 398)

Example 4

I had to curtail my social life, things I wanted to do. . . . It's almost better if a person were dead because it is final. (Parsons, 1997, p. 398)

Example 5

Every Tuesday my sister comes down and helps me with laundry, does her hair, and whatever. Without the relatives, I don't know how I would manage. . . . You need help from other people and your children, if you can, to give you sort of a break from your routine, and start you off fresh again. . . . It is helpful to have home care, have her go to the senior citizens' day care or have someone come in to stay with her when I'm away. . . . The centre is a Godsend and she goes four times a week. I have a cleaning lady here that comes in once every two weeks. She's sort of a nurse and that sort of gives me an extra day. (Siriopoulos et al., 1999, p. 83)

Example 6

Well, you're really tied down. The wife can't be left alone. Twice she has wandered around looking for me in the neighbourhood and it's going to get worse. You've got to keep her in sight at all times. (Siriopoulos et al., 1999, p. 83)

Studies that consider the contribution of communication problems to caregiver stress show that communication breakdown is perceived by caregivers to be a primary problem in their ability to cope with the disease (Clark, 1991). Among the most stressful behaviors identified by family members of individuals with dementia are their relative's language and cognitive-communication problems (e.g., repeating questions; Quayhagen & Quayhagen, 1988). Rabins, Mace, and Lucas (1982) noted that 74% of families report communication difficulties cause frustration and catastrophic reactions in their relatives with dementia. The deterioration of communication skills of individuals with AD can lead to personal isolation and frustration for family members (Bayles & Tomoeda, 1991; Orange, 1991b; Powell, Hale, & Bayer 1995). Family members in Orange's study (1991b) made the following comments regarding the impact of their AD relative's communication problems:

Example 7

Well, yes, in that we don't have the good . . . rapport. I feel lonely sometimes because it's not the same. There is nothing coming back in the way of conversation . . . but it's the talking I miss. I miss the conversation. I miss discussing the why's and wherefore's and trying to figure out why those people did that or what's gonna happened down there. I miss that a whole lot. (p. 184)

Example 8

I think it has maybe a bit, when you're in the house with a person and you can't talk to them, not that . . . it really doesn't bother me, I guess, but it's difficult when you haven't got somebody to talk to that understands what you're trying to say. We can go with the crowd (at church social functions) but the thing is, I find him sitting back in a corner not interacting. I feel rotten. I feel guilty. I think, now there he's sitting in the corner by himself, I should be sitting there too, but then, I mean I don't. . . . (p. 184)

To date, there are few published studies that examine the exact nature of the relationship between language and communication problems of AD and levels of caregiver burden and stress. However, in the development of the *Screen for Caregiver Burden*, researchers found that communication problems are among the most prevalent and most stressful for families with an individual who has AD (Vitaliano, Russo, Young, Becker, & Maiuro, 1991). Other scales of caregiver stress and burden attempt to quantify the relationship between family members' level of stress and the communication problems experienced by their relative with AD. These scales include Poulshock and Deimling's (1984) scale of caregiver burden: Given, Collins, and Given's (1988) *Caregiver Assessment*; and Zarit, Reever, and Bach-Peterson's *Burden Interview* (1980), which makes reference to communication problems between individuals with dementia and their family members.

More recently, Orange, Lubinski, Ryan, Dvorsky, and Harkness (1999) advanced the development of an evaluative, self-report questionnaire of language and communication that is completed by family members of individuals with AD. The Perception of Communication–dementia of the Alzheimer's type (PCI–DAT) is intended to provide researchers and clinicians with valuable information concerning the nature of AD individuals' language and communication problems. The questionnaire also is designed to document the social and emotional effects of communication problems on family caregivers. Most importantly, however, the PCI–DAT is intended to provide information on strategies used by AD individuals and their family members to correct communication problems. To date, data have been collected from over 100 family members and over 50 experienced speech-language pathologists. Caregivers' responses show that communication problems are of paramount concern and have far reaching effects on their social and emotional well-being and that of their relatives with AD. Clinicians believe that the PCI–DAT will help unravel the complex interplay between the language and communication problems in AD and the amount of caregiver stress and burden that they create. Future studies are planned to explore whether and how much the language and communication problems in AD affect caregiver stress and burden, especially following caregivers' participation in communication education and training programs.

The development and use of questionnaires that address language and communication in AD and caregiver stress and burden stem from several suggestions in the literature that family members are frequently the first to recognize symptoms, such as communication problems, in relatives with dementia (Bayles & Tomoeda, 1991; Ory et al., 1985) and that family members' perceptions are critical elements in understanding stress related to caring for a relative with dementia (Poulshock & Deimling, 1984). Studies that consider communication-related stress show that communication breakdown is perceived by caregivers to be a primary problem in coping with the disease and that communication problems increase the risk of early institutionalization of the individual with AD (Clark, 1995; Gurland, Toner, Wilder, Chen, & Lantigua, 1994; Orange, 1991b; Richter, Roberto, & Bottenberg, 1995; Williamson & Schulz, 1993).

COMMUNICATION BETWEEN FAMILY CAREGIVERS AND INDIVIDUALS WITH AD

The majority of work on the language and communication of individuals with AD includes analyses of performance across its three clinical stages and the profiles that distinguish the different types of dementia and other neurological conditions (e.g., AD vs. aphasia, multiinfarct dementia, frontotemporal lobe dementia, Pick's disease, primary progressive aphasia, etc.; Appell et al., 1982; Bayles, Boone, Tomoeda, Slauson, & Kaszniak, 1989; Illes, 1989; Nicholas et al., 1985). A large body of literature also exists on the discourse and conversational performances of individuals with AD, consisting primarily of narrative and picture-description discourse tasks, and conversations with unfamiliar, nonfamily partners (Bayles, Tomoeda, & Trösset, 1992; Garcia & Joanette, 1997; Hamilton, 1994; Mentis et al., 1995; Ramanathan, 1997; Ripich & Terrell, 1988; Tomoeda & Bayles, 1993; Ulatowska et al., 1988). A companion collection of studies addresses interactive aspects of communication between professional caregivers (e.g., nurses and health care aides) and institutionalized adults with AD, particularly those residents identified as verbally disruptive or abusive (Hallberg & Norberg, 1990; Lai, 1999). However, a smaller and more recently emerging group of studies consist of objective conversational data that reflect family members' communication with a relative diagnosed with AD. These studies examine communication breakdown and repair behaviors, responses to requests, and the relationships between communication patterns and caregiver depression in conversations between family caregivers and their relatives with AD.

Goldfein (1990), Orange (1991a), Orange et al. (1996), and Orange, Van Gennep, Miller, and Johnson (1998) were among the first to document conversational patterns involving family members of individuals with AD. The work of these researchers focused primarily on communication breakdown and repair strategies and the success of repair strategies in their spontaneous conversations.

Goldfein (1990) examined repair patterns in the conversations of four husband–wife AD dyads in which the wife suffered from mild–moderate AD. Goldfein found that the husbands signaled more often the need for their wives to correct or repair misunderstandings in the conversations. She also noted that the husbands often corrected the errors made by their wives with AD.

Orange et al. (1996, 1998) examined this pattern of caregiver repair signaling in more detail. In a systematic, lag-sequential analysis of communication breakdown and repair patterns in early (n = 5) and middle (n = 5) stage AD dyads, Orange (1991a) found unique, stage-dependent profiles of repair signaling and repair activity among family members and their relative with AD. Orange observed that in early stage dyads, family members more often created miscommunications, requiring their AD relative to signal the need for repair. In turn, the family member more often repaired the misunderstanding. This pattern was particularly evident in complex, consecutive strings of utterances comprising multiple repair signals by the AD individual and repair attempts by the family member. Orange hypothesized that family members of early stage AD individuals did not adjust the semantic and morphosyntactic complexity of their utterances to match the level of the deteriorating language and cognitive systems of their AD relative.

The following example illustrates this pattern. In Example 9, the early stage AD individual (ED) asks repeatedly for clarification of the status of the new home care aide following the family member's (FP) repeated attempts to correct the misunderstanding.

Example 9

FP: I think you have a new girl tomorrow.
ED: Is that right?
ED: Permanent you mean or just temporary.
FP: No just one day a week.
ED: Oh.
ED: In addition like you mean?
FP: No just a different girl for the one day.
ED: Yeah.
FP: She's gonna do uh . . .
ED: (interrupts) Is this for something special?
ED: Something special or something?
FP: We'll just do special interest things with you instead of just walking.
ED: Oh.

(Orange et al., 1996)

The pattern of repair described above and observed in early stage AD dyads was flipped in middle stage AD dyads. In these instances, the middle stage AD individual more often created the misunderstanding while the family partner signaled the need for repair. Orange (1991a) hypothesized that this pattern resulted from the deteriorating semantic and cognitive systems associated with disease progression that limited the content and accuracy of AD individuals' spoken language. In Example 10, a middle stage AD individual (MD) creates the communication problem and attempts to repair the misunderstanding after the multiple signals produced by the family member (FP).

Example 10

MD: Maybe she maybe she to tell you you know.
FP: Say that again.
FP: Maybe what?
MD: Well when I talked to her she said I said I have to go.
FP: Mmhm.
MD: An she said well you uhm you go uh with what you wanna do you know uhm with regard to . . .
MD: I said oh that'd be a good good idea of of ah Aunt Mary that if take uhm Mary Aunt Mary . . .
FP: I don't know what you mean.
FP: We do what we wanna do.

FP: What what do we wanna do?
MD: Well no she's she thought I think that . . .
FP: (attempts to complete sentence) you were gonna phone her?
MD: Yeah.

(Orange et al., 1996)

Overall, Orange (1991a) found that both the family members and the AD individuals participated in the generation, signaling, and repair of misunderstandings, but that the roles of partners changed with disease progression. Detailed analyses of repair activity in Orange's cross-sectional data (1991b) can be found in Orange et al. (1996), and more detailed sequential analyses of the patterns of repair can be found in Orange, Higginbotham, and Lubinski (1999). Current sequential analyses of patterns of conversational repair are underway on a longitudinal data base involving spousal AD dyads first described in Orange et al. (1998). Of particular interest to the current analyses is the anecdotal observation by Mathew (1994) in which she noted that sequences of utterances comprising communication breakdown and repair episodes occur more frequently at junctures in the conversation where new topics are introduced. Detailed analyses of this pattern on a longitudinal database are also underway.

More recently, Hendryx-Bedalov (1999) examined mealtime conversations of three community dwelling, moderate–severe AD and three non-AD spousal dyads with the purpose of identifying the effect of communication style of family caregivers on the outcome of the conversations. Analyses showed the AD individuals were less successful in providing relevant and expected responses to requests by their family caregiver than the non-AD individuals. The use of repetitive directives and critical comments by one AD spouse, the lack of responsiveness by one AD individual, and the use of requests and referents that were not related to the immediate environment and content of the interaction contributed to the poor communication success rates.

In a related study, Speice, Shields, and Blieszner (1998) explored the relationship between family communication patterns and AD family caregiver depression. They found that when family caregivers and their relative with middle stage AD do not share the same focus in conversations (i.e., competing-talk), the caregivers are more depressed. That is to say, family caregivers who talk about the illness of AD rather than maintaining or expanding on the statements and topics introduced by their AD relative are more likely to suffer from depression. Speice et al. believe that cooperative, joint-talking between family caregivers and their relative with AD is associated with lower caregiver depression.

What these studies of the patterns of AD family caregiver communication share in common is that they point to a strong relationship between the occurrence of communication problems and negative emotional responses of caregivers. Findings suggest that unambiguous requests posed in relation to events in the immediate context of the interaction and on the same or related topic being discussed results in successful interactions and lower levels of caregiver depression.

ENHANCED COMMUNICATION: STRATEGIES AND EDUCATION AND TRAINING

Several recent studies of family caregiver–AD individual communication education and training identified unique profiles of communication, including conversation breakdown and repair, pre- and postintervention (Bourgeois, Burgio, Schulz, Beach, & Palmer, 1997; Orange & Colton-Hudson, 1998). Findings from these and related communication education and training programs suggest that the negative influence of communication difficulties may be reduced when caregivers possess adequate knowledge of the nature of communication changes over the course of AD (Buckwalter, Cusack, Kruckberg, & Shoemaker, 1991; Shulman & Mandel, 1988). Moreover, when given specific detailed strategies derived from observed conversational interactions, family members may be more apt to deal positively with the challenges posed by the language and communication changes in AD. For example, Bourgeois et al. (1997) successfully reduced the number of times AD individuals verbally repeat the same statement or question by instructing family caregivers to use memory cuing strategies, such as a memory notebook or having the AD individual read prepared responses off index cards or memo-boards.

Orange and Colton-Hudson (1998) examined the usefulness of a communication intervention for a spousal caregiver of a middle stage individual with AD. Twice weekly education and training sessions were provided over 12 weeks in the caregiver's home. The first weekly session was designed as an education session. It included approximately 90 min of discussion between the speech-language pathologist and the spousal caregiver of the language, communication, cognitive, and behavioral features of AD, and changes that occur over the course of the disease. The second weekly session included language and communication training exercises designed specifically for the spouse and her husband. Activities and strategies were developed based on the extensive language, discourse, and conversational analyses conducted pre-intervention. Role-playing, video playback, and handouts were used extensively. The husband with AD participated in this second weekly session. Following completion of the education and training program, the percentage of problematic communication dropped from nearly one third to one fifth of the total amount of communication. In addition, ratings of the spouses' negative emotional reactions to challenging behaviors, including communication problems, fell following completion of the program.

Buckwalter et al. (1991) conducted a 15-month study that examined the usefulness of family member involvement in an individualized speech therapy enhancement program (labeled STEP) for residents in a nursing home care unit in a U.S. Veteran's Administrative Medical Center. A speech-language pathologist developed individualized interventions for family and nursing staff based on content analyses of video- or audio-recorded interactions between family members and their relatives. Nursing staff implemented the strategies for 10 min daily during the routine activities of day and evening shifts. Families also developed video and audiotapes of their relative's important life events and provided pictures and photographs for reminiscence during periods when they were unable to visit. Family member involvement also included person-to-person reminiscences during their visit. The taped, photographic, and live aspects of reminiscence provided verbal and visual reinforcement for enhanced, individualized communication. Buckwalter et al. found that family members' satisfaction of care for their language and cognitively impaired relatives increased significantly, compared to a control group whose relative received traditional speech-language therapy biweekly. The increase in caregiver satisfaction among the experimental group occurred despite minimal improvement in their relatives' communication ability. The investigators believe that the increase in ratings resulted from the direct participation of family members and nursing staff, and the use of personally relevant memorabilia, pictures, photographs, and audio and video recordings.

There is strong consensus among researchers and clinicians that enhanced communication in AD is best achieved within the context of individualized assessment and programming based on real needs (Orange, Ryan, Meredith, & MacLean, 1995) rather than stereotyped and negative misperceptions of older adults (Ryan, Meredith, MacLean, & Orange, 1995). Moreover, communication interventions are optimized when family caregivers learn to change their own behaviors or develop specific ways to change the behaviors of their relative (Bourgeois, 1997). Studies to date show clearly that individualized communication strategies work best. This is particularly important as the communication needs and skills of individuals with AD and their caregivers change over the clinical stages of the illness. Caregivers must be prepared to use strategies that target their relative's skill set and not to follow blindly nonspecific strategies. Strategies that target individual needs will help minimize communication-related caregiver stress and burden and will help reduce the tension that arises from using ineffective, generalized strategies. In addition, communication can be enhanced when family caregivers facilitate their relatives' access to preserved skills and memories. For example, reminiscence therapy helps adults with AD undergo life review through access to memories that are better preserved in their autobiographical memory (Harris, 1997).

Considerations for enhancing family members' communication with their relative with AD are presented in Tables 10.1 through 10.6. These strategies are adapted from Orange and Ryan (2000). Most are derived from the scientific literature that supports their usefulness. The strategies listed in the tables are by no means exhaustive or complete. Nor are they meant to be formulaic. That is, they should not be used in a prescriptive way by all caregivers of individuals with AD. Some strategies will work well with some AD individuals. Others may be less useful at particular time-points in the progression of the disease. It is critical to keep in mind that communication must be shaped to meet individual needs and skills. The strategies presented in the tables are examples of how family caregivers might wish to tailor their interactions to meet the individual communication needs of their relative with AD.

Language, Cognition, and Conversation Strategies

There is an inextricable link between language and cognition. This strong relationship is particularly important for caregivers of individuals with AD. Language and cognitive disturbances in AD are hallmark, early emerging features that manifest themselves in communication. Caregivers, therefore, must be cognizant of the words that they use (i.e., vocabulary), how the words are organized within and between sentences (i.e., syntax and grammar), how the words and ideas map onto their relative's previous knowledge (i.e., memory systems), and whether their relative is attending to them (e.g., sustained attention). The strategies presented in Table 10.1 reflect, among other objectives, the importance of using personally relevant vocabulary, using directly worded statements and questions, obtaining and maintaining a person's attention, capitaliz-

TABLE 10.1
Language, Cognitions, and Conversation Strategies

Language

- Use directly worded, simple active declarative sentences (e.g., "You and I are going for a walk outside.").
- Use yes–no questions or closed ended questions that help identify the target word(s) (e.g., "Are you hungry?" or "Do you want tomato soup or a grilled cheese sandwich?").
- Place modifiers after nouns (e.g., "Do you want soup, tomato or vegetable?").
- Provide the word(s) the person is having difficulty recalling; there is no need to test the person or to make him or her recall it without your help.
- Avoid ambiguous and indefinite terms and nonspecific pronouns (e.g., thing, that, there, those, this); use the names of people, places and objects.
- Avoid figurative language because the person may interpret them literally (e.g., "He gave you the cold shoulder?").
- Talk primarily in face-to-face situations rather than from another room; avoid giving instructions or important information over the phone as this eliminates nonverbal aspects of communication (e.g., facial expressions, gestures, body posture, etc.).
- Multilingual family members can act as sources of valuable information or as translators for a person who speaks languages other than English.

Cognition

- Be the memory trigger for the person; provide options from the person's personal long-term memory that helps them recall personally relevant information and that helps start and extend communication (e.g., "Tell me about the time you and your wife Marg were on holidays in Scotland.").
- Minimize effects of poor memory on communication:
  - Give instructions in writing and in single steps.
  - Give ample time for person to respond; do not interrupt.
  - Use memory notebooks containing personally relevant pictures and photographs.
- Do not test or confront a person who makes up stories; reality orientation does not work.

Conversation

- Communication takes time; if you do not have the time, you should not attempt to hold a conversation.
- Focus on information exchange rather than the person's accurate use of words; do not test a person when you know the word(s) the person is unable to say or write.
- Talk to the person about the general activities you are doing as you do them (e.g., washing dishes, cleaning or changing clothes, preparing a meal) even if the person does not talk back; explain what you are doing as you are doing it.
- Use statements that maintain and extend the topic of conversation (e.g., "That sounds very interesting. Tell me more about ___.").
- Tell a person when you are changing the topic (e.g., "Now let's talk about ___."), however, do not change the topic too often or too quickly; it may confuse the person.
- Tell the person exactly what you misunderstood (e.g., "I don't understand what ___ means?") or provide a possible understanding (e.g., "Do you mean ___?").
- If after repeated attempts you are unable to understand what the person is saying or the person does not understand what you are saying, acknowledge the problem, say you will get back to it in a moment, or change the topic.

TABLE 10.2
Speech and Nonverbal Strategies

Speech

- Use pauses and stress syllables and words to highlight important information.
- Speak clearly at a slightly low pitch and at a slightly louder volume.
- A calm, soothing speech in conjunction with nonverbal behaviors captures and maintains attention.
- Make obvious pitch changes in your voice that signal clearly a question, a statement, or a very important statement (i.e., imperative).

Nonverbal

- Use calm facial expressions, body movements and posture; becoming angry or over-excited may alarm and confuse a person.
- Use slow and deliberate movements; quick ones can appear threatening.
- Get a person's attention first before talking (e.g., call out the person's name, crouching for a person in a wheelchair).
- Get close (but not too close!) before speaking; closeness helps minimize distractions and focuses attention.
- Touch lightly on hand to (re)gain attention and to reassure; *do not* touch until your presence is known.
- You do not always have to talk to communicate; for example, gestures, touch, facial expressions, and responses written on cards can communicate reassurance, help minimize anxiety and fear, and reduce repetition of statements.
- Maintain eye contact when communicating, but be aware of cultural and sex differences.
- Watch your use of body language that signals restlessness, lack of commitment or rejection during interaction (e.g., crossed arms, frowns, poor eye contact, clock watching, turning away, hurry-up postures such as foot tapping, sighing, etc.).

ing on preserved memories to start and extend conversations, and providing unambiguous feedback that clearly identifies the nature of communicative misunderstandings.

Speech and Nonverbal Strategies

The rate and volume at which a person speaks, the stress placed on selected words and syllables to highlight meaning and importance of ideas, and the use of nonverbal behaviors (e.g., facial expressions, gestures, body posture, etc.) to gain and maintain attention and to augment the meaning of what is said, are thought to optimize communication. These issues are especially important for late clinical stage AD individuals (see Table 10.2). There is emerging scientific evidence that documents the important roles of various adjustments in speech production and nonverbal behaviors on communicative success with individuals with AD.

Sensory-Based Communication Strategies

The overwhelming majority of older adults experience age-related hearing and vision problems. However, these problems are varied and manifest in different ways. Among individuals with AD, the presence of sensory problems, including hearing and visual acuity difficulties, exacerbate underlying language and cognitive disturbances, and, in turn, negatively influence communication. Hearing and vision testing of individuals with AD is imperative. Prescription of hearing aids and glasses and successful use of them are becoming more common among individuals with AD. The other strategies outlined in Table 10.3 will help caregivers identify additional, relatively better preserved input channels for communication.

Communication Environments

Much has been written about communication impaired environments and their influence on the behaviors of individuals with AD (Lubinski, 1991). The considerations presented in Table 10.4 highlight the importance of structuring physical and psychosocial environments to support communication and the desire to communicate by individuals with AD and their caregivers.

Medications

The use of multiple medications by older adults, commonly referred to as polypharmacy, is well documented. Caregivers must be aware of the primary and secondary effects of medications on language, cognition, speech, motor control, and the emotions of individuals with AD. More importantly, caregivers in consultation with physicians and pharmacists

TABLE 10.3
Hearing, Vision, Tactile, and Other Sensory Strategies

Sensory

- Minimize competing background noise (i.e., sights, sounds, smells); may be too confusing.
- Use other senses to facilitate talking and understanding:
  - Pictures, photos or videos of family, relatives, vacations, pets.
  - Familiar music or audio-recorded conversations of family and friends.
  - Different aromas of foods or spices.
- Speak slightly louder than normal and at a lower pitch to accommodate hearing problems; if too loud, voice is distorted.

TABLE 10.4
Communication Environment Strategies

Environments (physical and psychosocial)

- Limit conversations to a small number of familiar people.
- Private and quiet locations (e.g., bedrooms, gardens, etc.) will enhance communication and help minimize distractions.
- Provide opportunities for communication with relatives and friends through social programs and outings.
- Promote the person as an active participant rather than a passive recipient during communication.
- Beware that fatigue may make communication more difficult and less rewarding.

TABLE 10.5
Strategies for Medications That Influence Communication

- Several groups of drugs interfere with speech, language, and cognition in persons with dementia:
    - Sedatives, antidepressants, anxiolytics, antipsychotics, anticoagulants, antihypertensives, narcotic-based analgesics.
- Consult with physicians, pharmacists, and well-recognized scientific literature to establish effects of medications on speech, language, and cognition.

---

should explore the effects of drug interactions among multiple medications (See Table 10.5).

Emotions, Interactive Style, Roles and Relationships, and Perceptions and Attitudes

Presented in Table 10.6 is a range of considerations that address important, but sometimes overlooked, issues that influence communication in AD. Studies that examined the importance of communication to family caregivers of individuals with AD found that emotional attachments, as established, maintained, or lost through communication, are especially crucial. Just as important is how caregivers adjust their communicative roles and relationships with their AD relative in light of deteriorating language, cognition, and communicative performances. Further, the importance of caregivers' positive perceptions and attitudes to older adults is well known. Negative perceptions and attitudes toward individuals with AD, as manifest in a patronizing, elderspeak form of communication (Kemper, Anagnopoulos, Lyons, & Heberlein, 1994), undermines their personal integrity.

TABLE 10.6
Strategies for Emotions, Interactive Style, Roles and Relationships,
and Perceptions and Attitudes

Emotions

- Acknowledge the person's emotions (e.g., isolation, fear, and loneliness; "I understand you feel frustrated. I would feel frustrated too if ___.").
- An empathetic tone of voice and responses signal that you understand the person's feelings of loneliness, anxiety, helplessness, etc.
- Respond to the person's message not the words; words may give one message (e.g., anger) but the real meaning may be one of fear or frustration.
- Ignore a person's sudden verbal outbursts; do not respond in an agitated manner.

Style

- Communication is a fundamental aspect of being human; it shapes personal identity (i.e., personality) and establishes self-worth and dignity.
- Adopt a style that is respectful and signals caring.

Roles and Relationships

- Roles change with aging (i.e., retirement, no longer parent but possibly grandparent, fewer social responsibilities), influence number and type of social activities, and the place of older adults within society.
- Support a role of independent communicator for the persons (e.g., do not complete sentences when person is unable to find the right word, ask a person to tell you more about the topic of conversation, etc.).
- Communication establishes and maintains relationships; use communication to expand the integrity of your relationship and to maintain the person's identity of "self."

Perceptions and Attitudes

- Minimize your actions which support communication dependence (i.e., speaking on person's behalf).
- Provide unconditional positive regard; see the person as having unconditional self-worth.
- Eliminate use of "elderspeak" and patronizing talk (e.g., exaggerated pitch, shrill tone, loud voice, terms of endearment such as "Sweetie," "Dearie," nicknames or pet names, and nonverbal behaviors that suggest incompetence, dependency, or lack of respect).
- Do not overaccommodate your language and communication to a person based on negative perceptions, attitudes, and stereotypes of older adults (e.g., "Persons with AD don't understand much of what goes on around them so it's okay to talk about them in front of them.").

CONCLUSIONS

In the new millennium, speech-language pathologists and other health and social care clinicians must be prepared to help develop and implement empirically sound caregiver communication enhancement education and training programs. These programs must address a number of issues including: (a) how best to optimize residual communication abilities of individuals with AD; (b) how to capitalize on communication strengths and problem-solving skills of family caregivers; (c) targeting challenging behaviors of individuals with AD that are related to language and communication problems and that may be contributing to increased levels of caregiver stress, burden, and depression; and (d) responding to changes in language, communication, and cognition over the course of AD. There is strong evidence that family and peer-support groups, respite services, training coping strategies, and education and training programs, among other types of interventions, that focus on problem-focused coping rather than emotion-based coping, are particularly helpful for family caregivers (Gwyther, 1998; Haley, 1997; Kramer, 1997). In the meantime, researchers, clinicians, and family and formal caregivers can look to a developing body of literature that outlines a series of helpful strategies that, while not all have been established empirically, serve to support communication with AD individuals (Bayles & Tomoeda, 1993; Bourgeois, 1991; Clark 1995; Clark & Witte, 1991; Lubinski, 1991; Orange & Ryan, 1999; Rau, 1993).

REFERENCES

Abraham, I., Onega, L., Chalifoux, Z., & Maas, M. (1994). Care environments for patients with Alzheimer's disease. *Nursing Clinics of North America, 29,* 157–172.

Alberoni, M., Baddeley, A., Della Salla, S., Logie, R., & Spinnler, H. (1992). Keeping track of a conversation: Impairments in Alzheimer's disease. *International Journal of Geriatric Psychiatry, 7,* 639–642.

American Psychiatric Association. (1994). *Diagnostics and statistical manual of mental disorders* (4th ed.). Washington, DC: Author.

Appell, J., Kertesz, A., & Fisman, M. (1982). A study of language functioning in Alzheimer patients. *Brain and Language, 17,* 73–91.

Bayles, K. A., Boone, D. R., Tomoeda, C. K., Slauson, T. J., & Kaszniak, A. W. (1989). Differentiating Alzheimer's patients from the normal elderly and stroke patients with aphasia. *Journal of Speech and Hearing Disorders, 54,* 74–87.

Bayles, K. A., & Kaszniak, A. W. (1987). *Communication and cognition in normal aging and dementia.* Boston, MA: College-Hill Little Brown.

Bayles, K. A., & Tomoeda, C. K. (1991). Caregiver report of prevalence and appearance order of linguistic symptoms in Alzheimer's patients. *The Gerontologist, 31,* 210–216.

Bayles, K. A., & Tomoeda, C. K. (1993). *The ABC's of dementia.* Tucson, AZ: Canyonlands.

Bayles, K. A., & Tomoeda, C. K., & Trösset, M. W. (1992). Relation of linguistic communication abilities of Alzheimer's disease patients to stage of disease. *Brain and Language, 42,* 454–472.

Beach, D. L. (1997). Family caregiving: The positive impact on adolescent relationships. *The Gerontologist, 37*(2), 233–238.

Bonnel, W. B. (1996). Not gone and not forgotten: A spouse's experience of late-stage Alzheimer's disease. *Journal of Psychosocial Nursing and Mental Health, 34*(8), 23–27.

Bourgeois, M. S. (1991). Communication treatment for adults with dementia. *Journal of Speech and Hearing Research, 34,* 831–844.

Bourgeois, M. S. (1997). Families caring for elders at home: Caregiver training. In B. B. Shadden & M. A. Toner (Eds.), *Aging and communication: For clinicians by clinicians* (pp. 227–249). Austin, TX: Pro-Ed.

Bourgeois, M. S., Burgio, L. D., Schulz, R., Beach, S. & Palmer, B. (1997). Modifying repetitive verbalizations of community dwelling patients with AD. *The Gerontologist, 37*(1), 30–39.

Buckwalter, K. C., Cusack, D., Kruckeberg, T., & Shoemaker, A. (1991). Family involvement with communication-impaired residents in long-term-care settings. *Applied Nursing Research, 4,* 77–84.

Canadian Study of Health and Aging Working Group. (1994). Canadian study of health and ageing: Study methods and prevalence of dementia. *Canadian Medical Association Journal, 50,* 899–913.

Causino Lamar, M. A., Obler, L. K., Knoefel, J. E., & Albert, M. L. (1994). Communication patterns in end-stage Alzheimer's disease: Pragmatic analyses. In R. L. Bloom, L. K. Obler, S. De Santi, & J. S. Ehrlich (Eds.), *Discourse analysis and applications: Studies in adult clinical populations* (pp. 217–235). Hillsdale, NJ: Lawrence Erlbaum Associates.

Clark, L. W. (1991). Caregiver stress and communication management in Alzheimer's disease. In D. N. Ripich (Ed.), *Handbook of geriatric communication disorders* (pp. 127–141). Austin, TX: Pro-Ed.

Clark, L. W. (1995). Interventions for persons with Alzheimer's disease: Strategies for maintaining and enhancing communicative success. *Topics in Language Disorders, 15*(2), 47–66.

Clark, L. W., & Witte, K. (1991). Nature and efficacy of communication treatment with dementia. In R. Lubinski (Ed.), *Dementia and communication* (pp. 238–256), Philadelphia: Mosby.

Cohen, D., & Eisdorfer, C. (1988). Depression in family members caring for a relative with Alzheimer's disease. *Journal of the American Geriatrics Society, 36,* 885–889.

Cummings, J. L., & Benson, D. F. (1992). *Dementia: A clinical approach* (2nd ed.). Boston, MA: Butterworth-Heinemann.

Cummings, J. L., Houlihan, J., & Hill, M. A. (1986). The pattern of reading deterioration in dementia of the Alzheimer type: Observations and implications. *Brain and Language, 29,* 315–323.

Garcia, L., & Joanette, Y. (1997). Analysis of conversational topic shift: a multiple case study. *Brain and Language, 58,* 92–114.

Given, C. W., Collins, C. E., & Given, B. A. (1988). Sources of stress among families caring for relatives with Alzheimer's disease. *Nursing Clinics of North America, 23,* 69–82.

Goldfein, S. (1990). *The use of conversational repair in the presence of Alzheimer's disease.* Unpublished doctoral dissertation, Columbia University, NY.

Gurland, B., Toner, J., Wilder, D., Chen, J., & Lantigua, R. (1994). Impairment of communication and adaptive functioning in community-residing elderly with advanced dementia. *Alzheimer's Disease and Associated Disorders, 8,* 230–241.

Gwyther, L. (1998). Social issues of the Alzheimer's patient and family. *The American Journal of Medicine, 104*(4A), 17S–21S.

Haley, W. E. (1997). The family caregiver's role in Alzheimer's disease. *Neurology, 48*(Suppl. 6), S25–S29.

Hallberg, I. R., & Norberg, A. (1990). Staffs' interpretation of the experience behind vocally disruptive behavior in severely demented patients and their feelings about it: An exploratory study. *International Journal of Aging and Human Development, 31*(4), 295–305.

Hamilton, H. E. (1994). Requests for clarification as evidence of pragmatic comprehension difficulty: The case of Alzheimer's disease. In R. L. Bloom, L. K. Obler, S. De Santi, & J. S.

Ehrlich (Eds.), *Discourse analysis and applications: Studies in adult clinical populations* (pp. 185–199). Hillsdale, NJ: Lawrence Erlbaum Associates.

Harris, J. L. (1997). Reminiscence: A culturally and developmentally appropriate language intervention for older adults. *American Journal of Speech-Language Pathology*, 6(3), 19–26.

Hendryx-Bedalov, P. M. (1999). Effects of caregiver communication on the outcomes of requests in spouses with dementia of the Alzheimer's type. *International Journal of Aging and Human Development*, 49(2), 127–148.

Hutchinson, J. M., & Jensen, M. (1980). A pragmatic evaluation of discourse communication in normal and senile elderly in a nursing home. In L. Obler & M. L. Albert (Eds.), *Language and communication in the elderly* (pp. 59–73). Lexington, MA: Lexington.

Illes, J. (1989). Neurolinguistic features of spontaneous language production dissociate three forms of neurodegenerative disease: Alzheimer's, Huntington's, and Parkinson's. *Brain and Language*, 37, 628–642.

Kempler, D. (1991). Language changes in dementia of the Alzheimer type. In R. Lubinski (Ed.), *Dementia and communication* (pp. 98–115). Philadelphia: Mosby.

Kempler, D., Van Lancker, D., & Read, S. (1988). Proverb and idiom interpretation in Alzheimer disease. *Alzheimer Disease and Associated Disorders*, 2, 38–49.

Kemper, S., Anagnopoulos, C., Lyons, K., & Heberlein, W. (1994). Speech accommodations to dementia. *Journal of Gerontology: Psychological Sciences*, 49(5), P223–P229.

Kramer, B. J. (1997). Differential predictors of strain and gain among husbands caring for wives with dementia. *The Gerontologist*, 37(2), 239–249.

Kuhn, D. R. (1998). Caring for relatives with early stage Alzheimer's disease: An exploratory study. *American Journal of Alzheimer's Disease*, 13(4), 189–196.

Lai, C. K. Y. (1999). Vocally disruptive behaviors in people with cognitive impairment: Current knowledge and future research directions. *American Journal of Alzheimer's Disease*, 14(3), 172–180.

Lubinski, R. (1991). Environmental considerations for elderly patients. In R. Lubinski (Ed.), *Dementia and communication* (pp. 257–278). Philadelphia: Mosby.

Mathew, M. G. (1994). *A longitudinal study of repair initiator variables in conversations of the elderly and individuals with dementia of the Alzheimer's type.* Unpublished manuscript, University of Western Ontario, Canada.

McNamara, P., Obler, L. K., Au, R., Durso, R., & Albert, M. L. (1992). Speech monitoring skills in Alzheimer's disease, Parkinson's disease, and normal aging. *Brain and Language*, 42, 38–51.

Mentis, M., Briggs-Whittaker, J., & Gramigna, G. D. (1995). Discourse topic management in senile dementia of the Alzheimer's type. *Journal of Speech and Hearing Research*, 38(5), 1054–1066.

Nicholas, M., Obler, L., Albert, M. L., & Helm-Estabrooks, N. (1985). Empty speech in Alzheimer's disease and fluent aphasia. *Journal of Speech and Hearing Research*, 28, 405–410.

Orange, J. B. (1991a). *Analysis of troublesource-repair variables in conversations of the elderly and individuals with dementia of the Alzheimer's type.* Unpublished doctoral dissertation, State University of New York, Buffalo.

Orange, J. B. (1991b). Perspectives of family members regarding communication changes. In R. Lubinski (Ed.), *Dementia and communication* (pp. 168–186). Philadelphia: Mosby.

Orange, J. B., & Colton-Hudson, A. (1998). Enhancing communication in dementia of the Alzheimer's type: Caregiver education and training. *Topics in Geriatric Rehabilitation*, 14(2), 56–75.

Orange, J. B., Higginbotham, D. J., & Lubinski, R. (1999). *Sequential analysis of conversational repair in dementia of the Alzheimer's type.* Unpublished manuscript, University of Western Ontario, Canada.

Orange, J. B., Lubinski, R., & Higginbotham, D. J. (1996). Conversational repair by individuals with dementia of the Alzheimer's type. *Journal of Speech and Hearing Research, 39,* 881–895.

Orange, J. B., Lubinski, R., Ryan, S., Dvorsky, A., & Harkness, D. (1999). *Item selection, reduction, formatting, and pre-testing of the Perception of Conversation Index—dementia of the Alzheimer's type.* Unpublished manuscript, University of Western Ontario, Canada.

Orange, J. B., & Ryan, E. B. (2000). Alzheimer's disease and other dementias and patient–physician communication. In R. Adelman & M. Greene (Eds.), *Clinics in geriatric medicine: Communication between older adults and their physicians* (Vol. 16, pp. 153–173). Philadelphia, PA: W. B. Saunders.

Orange, J. B., Ryan, E. B., Meredith, S. D., & MacLean, M. J. (1995). Application of the communication enhancement model for long-term care residents with Alzheimer's disease. *Topics in Language Disorders, 15*(2), 20–35.

Orange, J. B., Van Gennep, K. M., Miller, L., & Johnson, A. (1998). Resolution of communication breakdown in dementia of the Alzheimer's type: A longitudinal study. *Journal of Applied Communication Research, 26*(1), 120–138.

Ory, M. G., Williams, T. F., Emr, M., Lebowitz, B., Rabins, P., Salloway, J., Sluss-Radbaugh, T., Wolff, E., & Zarit, S. (1985). Families, informal supports, and Alzheimer's disease. *Research in Aging, 7,* 623–644.

Parsons, K. (1997). The male experience of caregiving for a family member with Alzheimer's disease. *Qualitative Health Research, 7*(3), 391–407.

Poulshock, S. W., & Deimling, G. T. (1984). Families caring for elders in residence: Issues in the measurement of burden. *Journal of Gerontology, 39,* 230–239.

Powell, J. A., Hale, M. A., & Bayer, A. J. (1995). Symptoms of communication breakdown in dementia: Carers' perceptions. *European Journal of Disorders of Communication, 30,* 65–75.

Quayhagen, M., & Quayhagen, M. (1988). Alzheimer's stress: Coping with the caregiving role. *The Gerontologist, 28,* 391–396.

Rabins, P., Mace, N., & Lucas, M. (1982). The impact of dementia on the family. *Journal of the American Medical Association, 248,* 333–335.

Ramanathan, V. (1997). *Alzheimer discourse: Some sociolinguistic dimensions.* Mahwah, NJ: Lawrence Erlbaum Associates.

Rapcsak, S. Z., Arthur, S. A., Bliklen, D. A., Rubens, A. B. (1989). Lexical agraphia in Alzheimer's disease. *Archives of Neurology, 46,* 65–68.

Rau, M. T. (1993). *Coping with communication challenges in Alzheimer's disease.* San Diego, CA: Singular.

Richter, J. M., Roberto, K. A., & Bottenberg, D. J. (1995). Communicating with persons with Alzheimer's disease: Experiences of family and formal caregivers. *Archives of Psychiatric Nursing, 9*(5), 279–285.

Ripich, D., & Terrell, S. (1988). Patterns of discourse cohesion and coherence in Alzheimer's disease. *Journal of Speech and Hearing Disorders, 53,* 8–15.

Ryan, E. B., Meredith, S. D., MacLean, M. J., & Orange, J. B. (1995). Changing the way we talk with elders: Promoting health using the Communication Enhancement Model. *International Journal of Aging and Human Development, 41,* 87–105.

Shulman, M., & Mandel, E. (1988). Communication training of relatives and friends of institutionalized elderly. *The Gerontologist, 28*(6), 797–799.

Siriopoulos, G., Brown, Y., & Wright, K. (1999). Caregivers of wives diagnosed with Alzheimer's disease: Husbands' perspectives. *American Journal of Alzheimer's Disease, 14*(2), 79–87.

Speice, J., Shields, C. G., & Blieszner, R. (1998). The effects of family communication patterns during middle-phase Alzheimer's disease. *Family, Systems, & Health, 16*(3), 233–248.

Talkington-Boyer, S., & Snyder, D. K. (1994). Assessing impact on family caregivers to Alzheimer's disease patients. *The American Journal of Family Therapy, 22*(1), 57–66.

Tomoeda, C. K., & Bayles, K. A. (1993). Longitudinal effects of Alzheimer's disease on discourse production. *Alzheimer's Disease and Associated Disorders, 7*, 223–236.

Ulatowska, H. K., Allard, L., Donnell, A., Bristow, J., Haynes, S. M., Flower, A., & North, A. J. (1988). Discourse performance in subjects with dementia of the Alzheimer type. In H. Whitaker (Ed.), *Neuropsychological studies of nonfocal brain damage: Dementia and trauma* (pp. 108–131). New York: Springer-Verlag.

Urquhart, C. (1997). *Caregiving experiences of spouses of individuals with Alzheimer's diseases.* Unpublished manuscript, University of Western Ontario, Canada.

Vitaliano, P. P., Russo, J., Young, H. M., Becker, J., & Maiuro, R. D. (1991). The Screen for Caregiver Burden. *The Gerontologist, 31*(1), 76–83.

Watson, C. M., Chenery, H. J., & Carter, M. S. (1999). An analysis of trouble and repair in the natural conversations of people with dementia of the Alzheimer's type. *Aphasiology, 13*(3), 195–218.

Welleford, E. A., Harkins, S. W., & Taylor, J. R. (1994). Personality changes in dementia of the Alzheimer's type: Relations to caregiver personality and burden. *Experimental Aging Research, 21*, 295–314.

Williamson, G. M., & Schulz, R. (1993). Coping with specific stressors in Alzheimer's disease caregiving. *The Gerontologist, 33*, 747–755.

Zarit, S. H., Reever, K. E., & Bach-Peterson, J. (1980). Relatives of the impaired elderly: Correlates of feelings of burden. *The Gerontologist, 20*, 649–655.

11

Intergenerational Communication and Psychological Adjustment: A Cross-Cultural Examination of Hong Kong and Australian Adults

Kimberly A. Noels
University of Saskatchewan, Canada

Howard Giles
University of California, Santa Barbara

Cynthia Gallois
The University of Queensland, Australia

Sik Hung Ng
Victoria University of Wellington, New Zealand

According to the National Institute on Aging (Global Aging, 1996), the proportion of adults over age 65 is growing in many nations, such that the older population in most countries is growing faster than the population as a whole. This demographic shift necessitates better understanding of older populations and communication across generations. At the same time that the world is growing older, it is also often maintained that the world is getting smaller. As the opportunity for contact with people from other cultures increases, it becomes more important to understand cultural influences on intergenerational relationships and communication. This chapter describes an ongoing program of research that approaches intergenerational communication from an intergroup perspective. In addition, our program examines how relations between age groups are related to subjective health. Moreover, it looks at these issues in light of the cultural context in which the intergenerational relations take place, illustrating cross-cultural similarities and differences with some recent data from Hong Kong and Australia.

INTERGENERATIONAL COMMUNICATION: A COMMUNICATION ACCOMMODATION PERSPECTIVE

The theoretical framework guiding this research is communication accommodation theory (CAT; see Giles, Coupland, Coupland, Williams, & Nussbaum, 1992; Fox & Giles, 1993). Researchers working on communication across the lifespan in the framework of CAT maintain that an intergroup approach is useful for understanding intergenerational communication. From such a perspective (see Harwood, Giles, & Ryan, 1995), it is argued that when individuals encounter others from another social group, such as another age group, they tend to treat them as members of that social category, rather than as individuals. Communicating with other people as members of a social group generally implies that there is a tendency for individuals to deal with others in a manner that reflects the stereotypes held with regard to that group (see also Hummert, 1994). Very often, stereotypes of outgroup members (i.e., people who do not belong to our own social group) are less positive than those pertaining to ingroup members (i.e., people who do belong to our own social group). For instance, although young people hold some positive stereotypes about older people (see, e.g., Hummert, 1990), considerable research has suggested that their stereotypes are quite negative, perceiving them as grouchy (Dillard, Henwood, Giles, Coupland, & Coupland, 1990); unhealthy, unattractive, unhappy, and miserly (Kite & Johnson, 1998); feeble, egocentric, incompetent, abrasive, frail, and vulnerable (Williams & Giles, 1996).

According to CAT, communication behavior with people from other groups reflects the stereotypes held about those groups. Thus, corresponding with the negative stereotypes about old age, research indicates that younger people may "overaccommodate" to older adults, in the sense that they are excessively concerned with ensuring that their message is clear and simple, as characterized through louder and slower speech, simplified grammar and vocabulary, and repetition (Giles & Coupland, 1991). Such a communication style may be perceived as demeaning and patronizing

(Ryan, Hummert, & Boich, 1995), particularly by socially and cognitively active older people.

Like other intergroup theories, CAT proposes that the decision to treat others as individuals or according to stereotypes about their social groups (e.g., their age group) is based largely in the sociohistorical relations between the groups (Gallois & Giles, 1998; Giles & Coupland, 1991). In particular, contexts of social inequality or structural power differences are likely to produce intergroup, stereotype-based communication. Intergenerational contexts involve complex and paradoxical power inequalities (see Gallois, 1994), and this may be the only intergroup context where most individuals pass through many levels of the power hierarchy. Intergenerational relations are influenced first by the power difference between parents and children; as we discuss later, this difference is greater and more formalized in some cultures than others. As children grow up, their social power increases, and at a certain moment they may begin to see their own age group as more influential than that of their parents. Our previous research has found cultural differences in the perceived power of young adults relative to older ones (see following). In all the cultures we have studied, however, middle-aged people were perceived as the age group with the most social power. This is the age group to which the parents of young adults belong, and it is also the group these young adults will be in when their own parents are elderly. It is important, therefore, to keep the perceived power relations between age groups in mind when explaining intergroup communication moves.

Intergenerational Communication
in East Asian Nations

Although research conducted with CAT has usually upheld its central tenets, this framework, and related others in the study of communication and aging, was developed in North America and Europe (Paoletti, 1998; Viladot & Giles, 1998; Ytsma & Giles, 1997) and, thus, is likely to reflect a Western bias on intergenerational relations (see Ng, Weatherall, Liu, & Loong, 1998). Indeed, there is good reason to think that intergenerational relations may not be the same in other parts of the world. We have been particularly interested in examining intergenerational relations in Pacific Rim countries, because many East Asian cultures endorse the Confucian-rooted ethic of *filial piety* (Kiefer, 1992; Kim, 1994; Kim & Yamaguchi, 1994; Palmore, 1975; Yum, 1988). According to Ho (1994), filial piety (or to use the Chinese word, *xiao*) is more than simply obeying and honoring one's parents; it includes an elaborate series of relations and obligations between parents and children and, beyond that, to the larger community and preceding and succeeding generations. Filial piety describes formal obligations that protect the power of parents relative to their children throughout their lives, and which carry concomitant obligations on parents to play significant social roles within the family (Chow, 1996).

In addition to other obligations, filial piety includes attention by children to the material and psychological well-being of aged parents, honoring ancestors, and conducting oneself in a manner that will maintain the honor of the family name. These attributes, moreover, may generalize to authority relationships beyond the family; other nonfamily elders may also have high social status and be accorded respect. In line with this ethic, the Hong Kong Government (1965, p. 5, cited in Chow, 1983) stated that the family has a "moral responsibility to care for the aged or infirm." This ethic of filial piety is evident in several East Asian nations, including Korea (Kim, Kim, & Hurh, 1991), China (Turkoski, 1975), Japan (Tobin, 1987), Taiwan (Lee, Parish, & Willis, 1994), and Hong Kong (Ikels, 1975) as well as in The Philippines (with the Filipino term, *utang na loob*) and Thailand (*bunkun*). Given that many individuals raised in East Asian countries are exposed to this value of appreciation for older age, it might be expected that there would be more positive relations, along with more accommodative communication, between older and younger generations in East Asian nations than in the Western nations.

This vision of honored elders may, however, only reflect what Tobin (1987) has called the "American idealization of old age" in East Asian cultures. Several authors suggested that a particularly positive conception of older adults in East Asia may be a myth at worst, or diluted feature of the past at best (Koyano, 1989; Tien-Hyatt, 1987; for Hong Kong in particular, see Fei, 1985). Using focus group data from younger and older adults in four Asian nations (The Philippines, Singapore, Taiwan, and Thailand), Ingersoll-Dayton and Saengtienchai (1999) identified five ways in which respect was still accorded older people these days. They include (a) an array of gestures and politeness forms (e.g., placing hands together, bowing); (b) material tokens (e.g., food and money); (c) customs and rituals (e.g., staying apart from elders at social gatherings until invited to join); (d) advice (e.g., about buying large purchases, anniversaries); and (e) obedience (e.g., accepting a scolding). The respondents also indicated that there had been some erosion of communicating respect in all these categories, and especially with regard to obedience. They also attributed the cause of this process to significant changes in family structure (i.e., away from the extended network to the nuclear structure), relative increases in educational and income differentials between younger and older people, and modernization.

Related to this, Chow (1999) presented quantitative data from younger and older adults in Hong that underscore the above changes. He reports:

> ... while the elders are still respected, both within the family, and in society, they are no longer regarded as the head of the household and are certainly no longer entrusted with the responsibility to make the final decisions. . . . [their] role has now been confined to such limited areas, like helping in household chores and looking after the grandchildren. . . . And since . . . [these] . . . functions are generally replaceable by the employment of domestic maids, the contributions of the elders in these areas is not much valued. (pp. 75–76)

This is not to say that beliefs and practices of respecting older people are not apparent in more individualistic societies, even though there is no readily available term (like *filial piety*) for it. Gallois et al. (1999) found that Canadian, Californian, Australian, and New Zealand students (especially females) self-reported very high levels of respect toward elderly family and nonfamily members in providing physical and communicative support. These Western students claimed they would provide more of the latter (e.g., listening, keeping in contact) than Eastern students (from The Philippines, Korea, Japan, and Hong Kong). The latter in their turn intended to provide more tangible support in terms of finances and physical care. It is to such cross-cultural research and issues that we now turn.

Cultural Differences in Intergenerational Relations and Communication. Some of our research to date suggests that intergenerational relationships in certain urban areas of East Asia may be more problematic, relative to some Western societies, than the previous discussion indicates. For instance, we found that stereotypes toward older persons among young people were more positive in California than in Hong Kong (Giles, Harwood, Pierson, Clément, & Fox, 1998). Indeed, we found that not only do Hong Kong students have particularly negative images of older persons in terms of their wisdom, activity, generosity, and so forth (Harwood, et al., 1996), but we are finding (with as yet unpublished data) that older people there also endorse these images themselves. Such application of negative stereotypes to one's own group often reflects inequalities of social power. In the case of intergenerational relations, it may also reflect the fact that youthful stereotypes endure as one passes into older age groups.

In another study (Ota, Giles, & Gallois, 2000), we found that whereas Australian and Japanese students viewed their same-aged peers similarly, the former were significantly more favorably inclined to middle-aged and older adults than the latter. Similarly, Harwood, Giles, Pierson, Clément, and Fox (1994) examined the perceived vitality of younger, middle-aged, and older age groups, and found that elderly people were generally viewed as having less status and institutional support in Hong Kong than in California. In a more ambitious study examining seven Eastern nations versus four Western ones (Giles, Noels, et al., in press), the foregoing pattern was confirmed, with Westerners attributing significantly more favorable ratings to middle-aged and elderly targets than their Eastern counterparts. That said, we should point out that data emerging from Georgian and Turkish elderly suggest more positive patterns of vitality among rural than urban informants. Even in this case, however, the vitalities of older people do not approach that accorded young, and particularly middle-aged, targets.

In sum, the results of these studies suggest consistent trends that run counter to the traditional expectation that older people would be revered in Eastern relative to Western societies. In other words, the erosion of filial piety in the East may have resulted in an evaluative backlash toward older persons, such that social perceptions of older adults are now less favorable there than in western societies. It is possible, given recent signs of older people finding their less powerful status in society to be illegitimate and vocally exercising their rights in such domains as workplace discrimination, that this downward spiral in East Asia contrasts with an upward spiral of respect for older people in the West. As no longitudinal data exist, these ideas must remain speculations for the moment.

The Pacific Rim Enterprise

In collaboration with many colleagues around the Pacific Rim, we have been examining cross-cultural variations in perceptions of communication with people of different age groups. In an initial study, Williams et al. (1997) asked young adults in Canada, the United States, Australia, and New Zealand, as well as in The Philippines, Hong Kong, the People's Republic of China, Korea, and Japan to give their perceptions of older people with regard to how accommodative (e.g., supportive, attentive, interesting) and nonaccommodative (e.g., complaining, self-centered, and patronizing) they were. These two categories of perceptions have been shown in previous research to characterize satisfying and dissatisfying communications with older people (Williams & Giles, 1996). Williams et al. also asked the young participants whether they felt an obligation to be deferential toward older people and whether they felt the interactions were satisfactory. Their results suggested that older adults (especially the frail elderly, as Harwood and Williams, 1998, showed) were viewed as less accommodating, and interactions with them were less satisfying, in Eastern than Western cultures, although there was considerable variability in the East Asian cultures. In a follow-up study, Giles et al. (2000) asked young people across six of these nations to evaluate their own age group in addition to older people. The results replicated the cross-national differences found by Williams et al., as did a study comparing Californian and Taiwanese students (Giles, Liang, Noels, & McCann, in press). Giles et al. (2000) also found that older nonfamily adults were perceived less positively than same-age peers on several dimensions (see also Ng, Lui, Weatherall, & Loong, 1997). That young adults report more communicative problems with elderly people (albeit less with family elderly) than peers was again accentuated in East Asia. Koreans and Japanese reported the least positive emotions with nonfamily elderly. Interestingly, and again counter to conventional wisdom, Western students reported more satisfaction in communicating with family elders than Easterners.

Perceptions Attributed to and by Older Adults. Given the premise of CAT that one tends to communicate with members of negatively stereotyped outgroups in negative ways, it might be expected that older people would use some negative strategies in interactions with younger adults. Consistent with this premise, Giles and Williams (1994) found that young people claim that older people are underaccommodative, in that they use an authoritarian or dismissive style that is suggestive of being inattentive, "closed-minded," and "out-of-touch." At the same time, older adults in satisfying intergenerational communications are characterized as supportive, attentive, complimentary, and interesting (Williams & Giles, 1996). This evidence, however, relies on the perceptions of younger adults; there has been very little research on older adults' perceptions of intergenerational communication. Moreover, what research there is on older people's perceptions of intergenerational communication has been conducted mainly in Western nations (e.g., Coupland, Coupland, & Giles, 1991; Giles & Ryan, 1986).

Noels, Giles, Cai, and Turay (1999) examined younger and older adults' perceptions of intra- and intergenerational communication. They found that both age groups favored their own group, for example by describing their group as more accommodative. This ingroup bias was accentuated for younger people, who were also more avoidant of older people and who described them as more nonaccommodating (i.e., more self-centered, controlling, and patronizing; see Table 11.1) than vice versa; the older sample did not differentiate older from younger people along these lines.

Some recent studies, however, indicate that the intergenerational perceptions of older adults in East Asian nations may be complex. For instance, research by Cai et al. (1998; see also Noels et al., 1999) with older adults from the People's Republic of China showed that older participants perceived their same-age peers to be more nonaccommodative than younger adults. We consistently found this outgroup bias with other Eastern samples, such as Thai elderly, who felt more obligation to be deferential towards same-aged peers than towards younger adults. At the same time, younger adults who were not family members were perceived as less accommodative than younger adults who were family members or than same-age peers. Thus, while younger outgroup members may not be positively perceived on some dimensions, they may nevertheless be more positively perceived than same-age, ingroup members on other dimensions.

INTERGENERATIONAL COMMUNICATION
AND PSYCHOLOGICAL WELL-BEING

Understanding intergenerational relations is not only relevant to promoting harmony in interpersonal interactions, but may also have direct implications for psychological health of older people. This assumption is clearly articulated in the Communication Predicament of Aging Model (CPA; Ryan, Giles, Bartolucci, & Henwood, 1986; Ryan, Hummert, & Boich, 1995; see Ryan & Norris, chap. 12, this volume). Ryan and her colleagues argue that young people's negative stereotypes regarding older people may dispose them to communicate with older people in a manner that reflects their negative perceptions. For instance, they may regard older people as feeble and incompetent, and hence speak to them in a patronizing tone. Repeated interactions of this type may eventually lead older people to wonder if they truly are as incompetent as the behavior of the younger person suggests. As a result, they may assume some of the characteristics implied by the younger person's communication style.

TABLE 11.1
Items From the Perceptions of Communication Subscales

During conversations with people who are *not* family—or I do *not* regard as close friends, almost like family—I found, *in general* . . .

Accommodation
  . . . they told interesting stories.
  . . . they were supportive.
  . . . they were attentive.
  . . . they were polite.
  . . . they discussed socially acceptable topics.
  . . . they discussed topics of mutual interest.
  . . . they gave respect.

Nonaccommodation
  . . . they were "closed-minded."
  . . . they were "out-of-touch."
  . . . they forced their attention on me.
  . . . they made angry complaints.
  . . . they complained about their health.
  . . . they complained about life circumstances.
  . . . they negatively stereotyped young people.
  . . . they talked down to me.
  . . . they treated me like a child.
  . . . they gave unwanted advice.
  . . . they were overly caring.
  . . . they were controlling.
  . . . they were patronizing.
  . . . they were self-centered.
  . . . they were overly polite.
  . . . they were overly positive when speaking to me.
  . . . they tried too hard.

Respect/Obligation
  . . . I felt obliged to be polite.
  . . . I showed respect for their age.
  . . . I made allowances for their age.
  . . . I talked about the topics they enjoy.
  . . . I spoke slower.
  . . . I spoke louder.
  . . . I did not act like myself.
  . . . I used simplified vocabulary.

Avoidant Communication
  . . . I had to "bite my tongue."
  . . . I did not know what to say.
  . . . I avoided certain topics.
  . . . I looked for ways to end the conversation.

They may act more dependent and deferential toward the younger person, when in fact they are quite competent and independent individuals. Over time, acting in such a manner, older people may come to believe that they really are less competent. This poor self-perception may be linked with a lessened sense of self-worth and decreased sense of well-being. Such a psychological state, often exacerbated by socio-structural factors, such as income, can have profound effects on an elder's psychosocial functioning (see Chau-Kin, Jik-Joen, & Cheung-Ming, 1994; Krause, 1996; Roscow, 1976).

To examine the validity of the CPA cross-culturally, and keeping in mind that self-interest and individuals' goals may have been overlooked in the literature on collectivistic societies where social harmony has been the guiding ethos (Chang & Holt, 1991), Noels et al. (1999; see also Cai et al., 1998) collected data from older adults in the People's Republic of China and the United States. They compared American and Chinese elderly adults on their perceptions of communication with same-age peers and with younger adults. For the Americans, the results were in line with the CPA model. The more older American adults felt they had to be deferential to younger people, and the more they avoided communication with younger people, the lower was their self-esteem and life satisfaction. The same pattern was not found with older Chinese adults, however. In fact, interactions with nonfamily, younger adults were not associated with psychological well-being at all, although a poor communicative climate with younger family members was predictive of depression. Based on these findings, Noels et al. suggested that the CPA model may be more specific to Western contexts, perhaps because of the cultural value associated with youthfulness in American culture. For older Americans, feeling distance and perhaps discrimination from a relatively high-status group may be detrimental to mental health. For older Chinese, who may perceive themselves as a high-status group (as reflected in the ethic of filial piety), interactions with a lower status group may not have as much bearing on well-being.

In this study, for both Chinese and American groups intragenerational communication was related to well-being. The more same-age peers were perceived as being accommodative (i.e., supportive and attentive toward the participant), the better was participants' psychological well-being. Noels et al. (1999) argued that peers may be important sources of social support when individuals face the strains of daily life and indeed major life events (e.g., health, family, mortality issues, etc.). Peers may be much more understanding of the specific issues faced by older adults, and hence provide stronger support than can younger adults. Hence, having same-age friends may prove beneficial for well-being.

These findings, of course, are restricted in that they compare only one Western and one East Asian nation. To increase confidence that cultural values figure in intergenerational relations and psychological health, additional nations from each cultural block should be examined. The remainder of this chapter discusses such an analysis, involving Australian and Hong Kong younger and older adults. This analysis is unique in its investigation of both young and older respondents' perceptions of intra- and intergenerational communication in a single study.

A CROSS-CULTURAL EXAMINATION OF THE RELATIONS BETWEEN COMMUNICATION AND ADJUSTMENT

We asked people from Australia (a Western nation) and Hong Kong (an East Asian nation) to fill out our questionnaire. The Australian group included 60 adults aged 65 years and older (M = 71.83 years, SD = 5.04) and 60 adults between the ages of 17 and 29 years (M = 18.45 years, SD = 2.48). The Hong Kong group included 62 adults aged 65 years or older (M = 70.40 years, SD = 4.96) and 61 adults between the ages of 19 and 24 years (M = 20.13 years, SD = 1.18). The older Australian group included 35% males, and the younger Australian group included 15% males. The older Hong Kong group included 52% males and the younger Hong Kong group included 49.2% males.

The questionnaire was based on the instrument developed by Cai et al. (1998). It included scales to assess perceptions of communication and indices of psychological adjustment.[1] The communication instruments included scales to assess perceptions of Accommodation, Nonaccommodation, Respect/Obligation, and Avoidant Communication. As can be seen in Table 11.1, Accommodation items refer to the perception that the person with whom one is interacting is positive, other-centered, and interesting. Nonaccommodation items refer to the perception that the person with whom one is interacting is negative, self-centered, and critical. Respect/Obligation items include the self-perception of an obligation to be deferential toward the person with whom one is interacting, and Avoidant Communication involves the self-perception that one desires to withdraw from the interaction. Participants were first asked to com-

---

[1]The Cronbach alpha indices of internal consistency ranged from .44 to .87, with a mean of .65 for the Hong Kong group and ranged from .63 to .94, with a mean of .80 for the Australian group.

plete these items with regards to interactions with people between the ages of 17 and 30 years and then with regard to interactions with people 65 years and older. The scales to assess psychological adjustment were Antonovsky's (1987) Sense of Coherence scale, which determined participants' sense that their lives were meaningful, managable, and comprehensible, and an adaptation of Rosenberg's (1965) Self-Esteem scale, which included four positively worded items that assessed participants' feelings of self-worth. For all of the instruments, the participants rated the extent to which they agreed or disagreed with each statement. The mean score for each variable could range from 1 (*disagree completely*) through 4 (*neither agree or disagree*) to 7 (*agree completely*). (See Table 11.1.)

Do Older and Younger People From Hong Kong and Australia Differ in how They Perceive Same-Age and Other-Age People?

The first question we addressed was whether there were differences between younger and older Australian and Hong Kong respondents in how they viewed interactions with their own age group and the other age group on each communication variable. The results, using ANOVA procedures, suggested that the age of the participant (young or old), country of origin (Hong Kong or Australia), and age of the target person (same-age group or ingroup; other-age group or outgroup) interact in influencing communication perceptions.

Perceptions of Others' Communication Behavior. For Accommodation[2] (see Table 11.2), Australians rated both age groups as more accommodative than did the Hong Kong people, with the exception that younger Australians saw their same-age peers to be as accommodative as young Hong Kong respondents perceived their same-age peers. The two Australian age groups showed few differences in their perceptions of same- and other-age groups. In contrast, younger Hong Kong adults perceived their same-age peers as more accommodative than the other-age

---

[2]With regard to Accommodation, both the *Target Age*, $F(1, 239) = 18.73$, $p < .001$, $eta^2 = .07$, and the *Nation*, $F(1, 120) = 5.61$, $p < .001$, $eta^2 = .32$, main effects were significant, but the *Age Group* effect was not, $F(1, 239) = 3.48$, $p = .06$, $eta^2 = .014$. The Target Age by Nation effect was significant, $F(1, 239) = 7.40$, $p < .01$, $eta^2 = .03$. The Target Age by Age Group interaction was not significant, $F(1, 239) = 0.224$, $p = .64$, $eta^2 = .01$, nor was the Age Group by Nation effect, $F(1, 239) = 1.35$, $p = .25$, $eta^2 = .01$. Finally, the three-way interaction effect was significant, $F(1, 239) = 9.65$, $p = .002$, $eta^2 = .04$.

TABLE 11.2
Means (M) and Standard Deviations (SD) of Communication Variables
as a Function of Target Age, Age Group, and Nation

	Perceptions of Same-Age Group		Perceptions of Other-Age Group	
	M	SD	M	SD
Australia				
Younger (*N* = 60)				
Accommodation	5.21	0.91	5.28	0.88
Nonaccommodation	3.43	0.69	3.81	0.75
Respect/obligation	3.69	0.81	4.87	0.86
Avoidant communication	3.94	1.37	4.43	1.25
Older (*N* = 60)				
Accommodation	5.64	0.95	5.35	0.97
Nonaccommodation	3.34	0.87	3.24	1.28
Respect/obligation	4.02	1.02	3.69	1.21
Avoidant communication	3.28	1.34	3.39	1.69
Hong Kong				
Younger (*N* = 61)				
Accommodation	4.86	0.57	4.12	0.64
Nonaccommodation	3.36	0.54	4.37	0.72
Respect/obligation	3.75	0.80	5.28	0.65
Avoidant communication	3.70	1.01	4.78	0.95
Older (*N* = 62)				
Accommodation	4.67	0.84	4.42	0.89
Nonaccommodation	4.06	0.56	3.71	0.71
Respect/obligation	4.66	0.74	4.09	0.72
Avoidant communication	3.91	1.05	4.28	1.51

Note. For all variables, the scale range is 1–7. Higher means indicate perceptions in the direction of the variable label (e.g., more accommodative, more respect/obligation, etc.).

group, but older Hong Kong adults perceived the two groups as equally accommodative.

For Nonaccommodation[3] (see Table 11.2), Hong Kong people perceived both age groups as more nonaccommodative than did Australians, with the exception that young Hong Kong people saw their same-age peers to be as accommodative as young Australians perceived their same-age peers.

---

[3]For Nonaccommodation, the Target Age main effect, $F(1, 239) = 16.46, p < .001, eta^2 = .06$, and the *Nation*, $F(1, 239) = 24.65 \, p < .001, eta^2 = .09$, were significant, but the *Age Group*, $F(1, 239) = 3.55, p = .06, eta^2 = .02$, was not significant. The Target Age by Age Group effect was significant, $F(1, 239) = 65.53, p < .001, eta^2 = .22$, as was the Age Group by Nation effect, $F(1, 239) = 4.30, p = .04, eta^2 = .02$, but the Target Age by Nation effect was not, $F(1, 239) = 2.77, p = .10, eta^2 = .01$. The three-way interaction was also significant, $F(1, 239) = 15.02, p < .001, eta^2 = .06$.

Young people in both places perceived older people to be more nonaccommodative than younger people. Older Australians made little distinction between the two age groups, but older people from Hong Kong felt that their own-age group was *more* nonaccommodative than the younger group. Younger and older people in Australia were similar in their perceptions of how nonaccommodative their own-age group was, but young Australians perceived the other-age group to be more nonaccommodative than older Australians did. In a similar manner, young Hong Kong respondents perceived the other-age group to be more nonaccommodative than older Hong Kong respondents did. Curiously, older Hong Kong respondents perceived their peers to be more nonaccommodative than younger people.

Self-Perceptions of Communication Behavior. With regard to Avoidant Communication,[4] whereas Australians did not differentiate between same-age peers and other-age people (M = 3.61, SD = 1.36; and M = 3.91, SD = 1.47, respectively), people in Hong Kong were more avoidant of other-age people than same-age peers (M = 4.53, SD = 1.23; and M = 3.81, SD = 1.03, respectively). Older people made little distinction between how avoidant they were of same-age peers and other-age people (M = 3.60, SD = 1.20; and M = 3.84, SD = 1.60, respectively), but younger people tended to be more avoidant of other-age people than of same-age peers (M = 4.61, SD = 1.11; and M = 3.82, SD = 1.19, respectively). Finally, in Hong Kong, participants did not differ across ages in how avoidant they were of others generally (younger: M = 4.24, SD = .98; older: M = 4.10, SD = 1.28). In Australia, however, older people were considerably less avoidant of communication with others generally than were younger people (M = 3.34, SD = 1.52; and M = 4.19, SD = 1.31, respectively), and indeed much less avoidant than their same-age peers in Hong Kong. In other words, older people in Australia were less avoidant of other people in general than any other group examined.

Lastly, with regard to Respect/Obligation[5] (see Table 11.2), there was a tendency for both young groups to have greater sense of respect for their

---

[4]Concerning Avoidant Communication, all main effects were significant, Target Group: $F(1, 239) = 24.97, p < .001, eta^2 = .10$; Age Group: $F(1, 239) = 14.53, p = .001, eta^2 = .06$; Nation: $F(1, 239) = 9.84, p = .002, eta^2 = .04$, as were all the two-way interaction effects, Age Group by Nation: $F(1, 239) = 7.31, p = .007, eta^2 = .03$; Target Age by Age Group: $F(1, 239) = 7.04, p = .008, eta^2 = .029$; Target Age by Nation: $F(1, 239) = 4.21, p = .04, eta^2 = .02$. The three-way interaction effect was not significant, $F(1, 239) = 0.65, p = .42, eta^2 = .003$.

[5]With regard to Respect/Obligation, all main effects were significant, Target Age: $F(1, 239) = 42.55, p < .001, eta^2 = .15$; Nation: $F(1, 239) = 19.01, p < .001, eta^2 = .07$; Age Group: $F(1, 239) = 10.67, p = .001, eta^2 = .04$. Neither the Age Group by Nation interaction effect, $F(1, 239) = 2.82$,

elders than for their same-age group, although this tendency was somewhat stronger in Hong Kong than in Australia. At the same time, older adults in Australia did not differentiate between the two groups, but older adults in Hong Kong indicated that they felt more obligated to be respectful of older than of younger people. Young and older people in Australia reported the same obligation to be respectful to same-age peers, but young Australians felt more obligation to be respectful of other-age adults than did older Australians. Likewise, young Hong Kong respondents felt more obligation to be respectful of other-age adults than older Hong Kong people did. Older Hong Kong adults felt more obligation to be respectful to their own age group than younger Hong Kong adults did.

These results broadly suggest that young people in both countries perceive elders to be negative and complaining relative to same-age peers, although this tendency is stronger in Hong Kong; moreover, young Hong Kong people perceive older adults to be less supportive and interesting. This pattern of less positive ratings by young people is consistent with the position that intergenerational relationships are particularly problematic for younger adults. In line with the predictions of CAT, these findings also reflect a bias to view outgroups less positively than ingroups. It may also be, however, that young people generally adopt a norm of respect for elders (and perhaps more so in East Asian nations, where this ethic is more fully articulated) because they view older people as being of high status and deserving of respect. If this ethic implies that an older person's needs and desires are attended to without concern for the needs and desires of the younger person, the interaction may be dissatisfying for the younger person and may make the younger person feel powerless and victimized.

Although this explanation is tenable, it is important to note that we cannot at this point conclude with certainty that young people, especially in Hong Kong, find the nature of intergenerational interactions to be dissatisfying. It may be that the nonaccommodative nature of intergenerational communication is expected, given the degree of power distance (cf. Hofstede, 1980; see also Singelis, Triandis, Bhawuk, & Gelfand, 1995) between higher status elders and lower status young adults. In the sense that these interactions meet normative expectations, they may be perfectly acceptable. To violate this cultural norm by interacting with others from

---

$p = .09$, $eta^2 = .01$, nor the Target Age by Nation effect, $F(1, 239) = 0.21$, $p = .65$, $eta^2 < .01$, was significant, but the Target Age by Age Group interaction effect was, $F(1, 239) = 168.86$, $p < .001$, $eta^2 = .41$. The three-way interaction effect was significant, $F(1, 239) = 4.42$, $p = .04$, $eta^2 = .02$.

a higher status on a more intimate or informal basis may be considered highly inappropriate and be emotionally upsetting. That said, Chang (2000) has shown how, in the context of Chinese conversations, "social harmony, as a cultural performance, is conducted by Chinese only at the surface level, with turbulence . . . [and aggressiveness sometimes] . . . concealed beneath the superficial politeness" (see also Chang, 1999). This idea is compatible with our earlier results, which revealed negative attitudes toward elders by young adults in East Asia (and especially in Hong Kong) than in Western Pacific Rim countries. Although the present study considered communication perceptions on several dimensions that might be suggestive of dissatisfaction (e.g., perceptions of nonaccommodation and the desire to avoid communication), it did not explicitly consider how people evaluate these interactions in terms of how enjoyable and/or normatively appropriate they are. It will be important to consider this issue more directly in future research before concluding, for instance, that perceptions of nonaccommodation are necessarily associated with dissatisfaction with the interaction. At least for Chinese in New Zealand, available data from a study of 100 families show no significant correlation between nonaccommodation and dissatisfaction with the interaction, in contrast to a significant positive correlation between perceived accommodation and interaction satisfaction (Ng, Liu, Loong, & Weatherall, 1999).

The examination of older adults' perceptions indicated that there is a tendency for older adults in Hong Kong to agree with younger Hong Kong people's perception that older adults are more complaining and self-centered in their interactions than younger people (although not necessarily as less supportive and interesting). Also consistent with their younger cohorts, older Hong Kong respondents viewed interactions even with their same-age peers as requiring more respect and obligation than interactions with younger people. These findings are similar to those of Noels et al. (1999) with regard to older respondents from the People's Republic of China. As Noels and her colleagues argue, a heightened sense of obligation for politeness and accommodation toward the older group is consistent with a sense of value for older people, perhaps related to the bias to favor the ingroup (in line with CAT) and/or the norm of respect for older people (in line with the ethic of filial piety). The tendency for some negativity toward the ingroup may also be related to East Asian cultural beliefs about the nature of relationships: Many people in East Asian nations tend to see more asymmetry and hierarchy in relationships, such that the status of social categories plays an important role in how individuals relate to each other (see Gallois et al., 1999). Older Hong Kong respondents may view interactions with nonfamily members, even those of the same age group, as outgroup interactions. Perceptions of nonaccommodation from others and avoidance of these kinds of interactions may reflect the tendency for people from collectivistic cultures to make relatively sharp ingroup–outgroup distinctions (Yum, 1988).

In contrast with the older Hong Kong group, which seems to have a slightly negative view of their own-age group, older Australians seem to have a more positive view of communication with the two age groups, evaluating the groups fairly equivalently on all dimensions. This finding is similar to that reported by Noels et al. (1999), who found that older Americans construed others as less nonaccommodating and were less avoidant of communication with others than younger Americans or older Chinese. It is also consistent with the findings of Paltridge and Giles (1984), who found that elderly listener-judges were evaluatively more tolerant of speakers with different speech styles than younger raters. Two explanations might account for this tendency. First, this pattern of findings may be related to Western societies' tendency to see relationships as symmetrical and reciprocal (in contrast to East Asian societies, as previously described), making less sharp distinctions between ingroups and outgroups. Younger Western adults may not yet have such an egalitarian perspective because of the concurrent norm of respect for elders. An alternative explanation is that the reason for the equivalence is linked to the positive perception of youth in Western culture. It is desirable to be youthful, and so interactions with young people are perceived relatively positively. At the same time, older adults may hold a positive perception of their ingroup (as suggested, in part, by CAT), so that both groups are valued positively, but for different reasons.

Do Communication Variables Predict Psychological Adjustment?

Our second set of questions pertained to the CPA model, and particularly the suggestion that younger people's communication behavior might be associated with older people's psychological adjustment. In other words, we wanted to determine whether perceptions of communication with younger people predicted life satisfaction and self-esteem in older adults, above and beyond perceptions of communication with other older people.

To look at the relationship between communication variables and psychological adjustment variables, a series of standard multiple regression equations was calculated. Standard multiple regression equations allow the researcher to determine how well each predictor variable independently predicts an outcome variable (cf. Tabachnick & Fidell, 1996). In the present case, we were interested in how well the communication variables pertaining to older and younger people predicted each adjustment variable (i.e., life satisfaction and self-esteem). This procedure was done separately for each nation, resulting in eight analyses for each nation (i.e., four communication variables examined for each of two adjustment variables; see Table 11.3 for a summary).

Results indicated that for older Australians, the more one felt avoidant of communication with younger people, the lower were feelings of life satisfaction. In addition, the more accommodative younger people were perceived to be, the greater was the sense of satisfaction in life and per-

TABLE 11.3

Standard Multiple Regression Analyses With Older Hong Kong and Australian Adults: Predicting Psychological Adjustment From Communication Variables

	R^2	F	Perceptions of Same-Age Adults Beta	Perceptions of Other-Age Adults Beta
Life Satisfaction				
Australia				
Accommodation	.22	7.82*	−.04	.46*
Nonaccommodation	.10	3.03	−.12	−.24
Respect/Obligation	.14	4.80*	−.24	−.23
Avoidant Communication	.13	4.39*	−.02	−.36*
Hong Kong				
Accommodation	.00	0.05	−.01	.05
Nonaccommodation	.01	0.42	.09	−.12
Respect/Obligation	.02	0.63	−.04	.15
Avoidant Communication	.03	1.04	.08	.16
Self-Esteem				
Australia				
Accommodation	.20	6.97*	−.01	.44*
Nonaccommodation	.04	1.20	−.09	.22
Respect/Obligation	.12	3.99*	−.30*	.29*
Avoidant Communication	.03	0.90	−.12	.17
Hong Kong				
Accommodation	.16	5.64*	.30*	.18
Nonaccommodation	.03	0.99	.19	−.05
Respect/Obligation	.10	3.25*	.29*	.07
Avoidant Communication	.00	0.09	.05	.02

* This communication variable significantly predicts the psychological variable at $p < .05$.

sonal self-esteem. In addition, the more personal self-esteem was enhanced, the more one felt compelled to be deferential to younger people and less deferential to older people. The ratings of older people in Hong Kong, however, indicated that increased life satisfaction was not associated with any of the communication variables examined here. Greater personal self-esteem was associated with perceptions of accommodation from older people and the sentiment that one should be respectful and polite with other elders.

In sum, these results suggest that, for older Australians, life satisfaction and self-esteem were linked primarily to positive communication with young people, although interactions with same-age peers were also important for self-esteem. In Hong Kong, communication variables were not particularly strongly or consistently linked with life satisfaction, although relations with same-age peers did have implications for self-esteem. Consistent with the results reported by Noels et al. (1999), these results suggest different implications for ingroup and outgroup relations, depending on the culture of origin. Chinese participants indicated that accommodation from same-age peers enhances self-esteem, suggesting that satisfactory, supportive interactions with peers is a culturally universal predictor of psychological health. For Hong Kong people, a sense of respect and deference toward older people is indicative of better psychological health, whereas for Australians, the less one feels deferential toward one's peers, the better is psychological health. With reference to the Chinese participants whom they studied, Noels et al. (1999) suggested that in collectivistic societies, self-esteem may derive, at least in part, from adhering to the norm of respect for other elders more than in a more individualistic Western society, where age is not accorded such high status.

Also consistent with the Noels' et al. (1999) findings, the Eastern and Western groups differed in terms of how important interactions with younger adults were for well-being. Although perceptions of communication with younger people were associated with life satisfaction and self-esteem for the Australian group, they were irrelevant for the Hong Kong group. This finding bolsters the argument forwarded by Noels et al., that the psychological, behavioral, and health implications of the interaction pattern described in the CPA model may be culture specific. It is arguable that the CPA model's patterns are more important in Western societies because of a strong cultural belief that youth is more active, vital, and independent than older age (see Cai et al., 1998; see also Edwards & Giles, 1998; Gallois et al., 1999). Hence, where youth is highly valued, older adults who feel distanced from younger adults may also experience a lessened sense of self-worth and life satisfaction. It should be noted that these results do not bear one way or the other on the CPA's proposal that it is the communication of younger people that starts the negative cycle leading to low self-esteem and a sense of helplessness among older people. Instead, they are equally compatible with the proposal that negative stereotypes held by older people about their own group (relative to younger adults) may start the unhealthy spiral. While some experimental research has addressed this issue (see Hummert & Ryan, 1996), future research should examine it more systematically and in more than one culture.

CONCLUSIONS

The findings of this study suggest that younger people perceive intergenerational communication less positively than older people do, and that this pattern is stronger in some respects in Hong Kong. The results do not suggest that intergenerational communication is particularly problematic for older adults. Rather, the pattern of findings differs depending on the nation of origin. Whereas intergenerational relations seemed to be rated as highly as intragenerational relations by older Australians, interactions with same-age peers were perceived more negatively on some dimensions by older Hong Kong Chinese. These findings suggest that, whereas there may be some cross-cultural validity to CAT (most evidently with younger people), cultural norms and values with regards to aging, particularly with older adults, are also highly salient.

Communication variables are important correlates of psychological adjustment, but again there may be some limitations to the Western-conceptualized CPA model. Whereas positive communication with younger people and a sense of respect for younger adults, combined with a lessened sense of deference (and possibly less social distance) toward same-age peers, is important for older Australians, positive interactions and respect for other elders is more important for Hong Kong older adults. This cross-cultural difference suggests that it is important to consider the cultural values associated with aging and the social power these values entail, in developing models of intergenerational communication. Clearly, as we argued elsewhere (Edwards & Giles, 1998), current models such as the CPA need to be infused not only with culturally mediating mechanisms (e.g., filial piety and the like), but also require attention to intragenerational concerns. In addition, following Williams and Coupland (1998), we ought to focus on the communicative climates of those who are not just the felt victims of discrimination and demise, but also on the many who manage their personal and social activities where age does not intervene in any debilitating manner. Finally, we must build theory that takes into account the fact that in some contexts, older adults still hold more social and personal power (or they are perceived to do so) than their younger interlocutors. In other words, intergenerational communication must be considered from the perspective of both young and older people, within the sociostructural relations that cultural values and norms imply.

There are, of course, many limitations to this study. First, the small number of participants, from only two cultural groups, can hardly be thought to represent complete nations or regions of the world. Although some of the present results are quite similar to those reported by Noels et al. (1999) with regard to groups from the United States and the People's Republic of China, it is necessary to examine communication perceptions in other East Asian and Western nations to determine the extent of these patterns; programmatic work toward this end with our associates is already underway. Moreover, a complete cross-cultural understanding of intergenerational communication requires attention to other corners of the globe, where cultural values relevant to aging may relate to intergenerational communication perceptions in different ways. As this program of research develops across the Pacific Rim, into Central and South America, and into the realm of intergenerational communication in the workplace, it will be necessary to ensure that the survey items designed to tap the issues at hand have cross-cultural, cross-linguistic, and cross-generational validity. Indeed, the social and psychological routes to life satisfaction may well vary between individualistic and collectivistic societies (Oishi, Diener, Lucas, & Suh, 1999). Although the research to date has utilized the insights of informants and translators from the national and age groups surveyed, ascertaining the validity of the constructs and the instruments used remains an ongoing issue. Furthermore, we must be careful with older respondents not to assume subjective peerhood where none exists. Put another way, asking elderly informants to rate their interactions with "older people" may induce them to think not of those of their age (psychological or chronological), but rather of frail, much older individuals from whom they wish to differentiate themselves (see Paoletti, 1998).

Second, other studies conducted in the context of this program of research have illustrated that intergenerational communication with nonfamily members may be perceived quite differently from intergenerational communication with family members (e.g., Cai et al., 1998; Giles et al., 2000; Ng et al., 1997). It is interesting to note that the literature relating communication to life satisfaction has been equivocal (e.g., Strain & Chappell, 1982; Nussbaum, 1985). A more complete understanding of intergenerational communication, then, requires more complex distinctions in terms of older and younger people's family, work, and social relationships. Moreover, the crossing of age categories with other social categories, such as sex and ethnicity (see Paoletti, 1998), may reveal very different patterns of perceptions of inter- and intragenerational communication.

Finally, this research program has focussed thus far on people's beliefs or perceptions about intergenerational and intragenerational communication. In future research, it will be essential to examine actual communicative episodes of people from different age groups to determine the correspondence between perceptions and actual behavior during the process of communication. In addition, as noted earlier, an explicit evaluation of the affect experienced in the encounter and the normative appropriateness of each person's behavior would more directly assess satisfaction with the encounter. Such an analysis would have to include a longitudinal aspect to determine the validity of the hypothesis that aspects of communication cause variations in psychological adjustment (as opposed to the other way around), and also more objective indices of psychosocial functioning than the limited measures we have thus far adopted. Clearly, many important social demographic and sociopsychological variables, such as marital status, income, physical and psychological health, perceived social support and usefulness, and competency (to name but a few), have been found to mediate both older people's self-esteem (e.g., Lai & McDonald, 1995; Reitzes, Mutran, & Fernandez, 1994) and life satisfaction (e.g., George, Okun, & Landerman, 1995; Ranzijn, Keeves, Luszcz, & Feather, 1998), let alone the complex relations between them and other related variables (see Krause & Borawski-Clark, 1994) that can vary cross-culturally (Diener & Diener, 1995). Future work should also include, within the same design, these foregoing outcome measures in order to ascertain the relative weight of our, and others', communication variables in predicting older persons' psychological adjustment.

Practical Implications

Given these limitations, some practical implications for enhancing intergenerational communication, based on the issues raised in this study, might be suggested. The results indicate that there may be some support to the prediction of CAT that when we define a situation as intergroup, we tend to categorize people into groups and to view our ingroup more positively relative to outgroups. In their review of intercultural communication training, Cargile and Giles' (1996) discussion of how this bias can be attenuated might usefully be applied to intergenerational communication. They suggest that it is important to consciously monitor automatically activated stereotypes about people from the other group and to resist the ease with which these cognitive and motivational processes affect perceptions of others. By decreasing the salience or importance of group boundaries, perhaps by reframing the situation as an interpersonal one or by recategorizing individuals in terms of a superordinate group (such that participants become ingroup members with respect to each other), intergroup bias may be reduced (see also Gallois & Giles, 1998; Hajek & Giles, in press). To the extent that this strategy is possible, one may be able to evaluate others more in terms of their personal characteristics, as opposed to group-based stereotypes. Devine (1989) emphasized that trying to "break the habit" of relying on automatic, stereotyped information may meet with mixed success initially, but with practice people can make progress in reaching their nonprejudiced standards. In achieving this goal, it may also be possible to reduce the negative impact of poor intergenerational communication on older adults' psychological well-being.

In a similar vein, Ryan, Meredith, MacLean, and Orange (1995) have elaborated the Communication Enhancement of Aging model (see Ryan & Norris, chap. 12, this volume). This model underscores the importance of intergenerational encounters in which older adults are treated as individuals with idiosyncratic competencies, rather than as members of a group with that group's stereotypical characteristics. This individualization would be accomplished by training younger people about the normal aging process and encouraging them to adopt a more consultative and participatory interactive style with older adults. It should be noted that this strategy also pays dividends in terms of trainees' own self-stereotypes as they age. A more appropriate communication style would support the older adult's sense of competence and autonomy, and ultimately feelings of self-worth, well-being, and empowerment (Cusack, 1999; Minkler, 1996). In turn, the older adult would be a model of positive aging, and presumably be more likely to elicit more appropriate behavior from others.

A second practical implication might be suggested based on the finding that intragenerational communication may be as important as intergenerational communication for psychological adjustment, if not more important in some cultural contexts. We are not alone (see e.g., Auslander & Litwin, 1991; Krause, Liang, & Keith, 1990; Krause, Liang, & Yatomi, 1989; Ryff & Seltzer, 1996) in the observation that supportive interactions with same-age peers may provide an important resource for older adults. Programs for successful aging could well emphasize opportunities to develop these important social support networks in addition to positive cross-generational relations. This is particularly the case given that strong family ties can result in over-caring and a loss of autonomy on occasion and, hence, may not be the welcome haven some older folk anticipate (Nussbaum, 1985). As Patterson, Bettini, and Nussbaum (1992) pointed out, "despite the central role of friendship, it appears that friends may be in short supply for older persons" (p. 146). Indeed, it has been found that elder best friends (usually of the same gender) are those who live some distance away and are conceptualized more in the minds of elders than are readily available for contact (e.g., Rawlins, 1992). Hence, it is essential for well-being that the communicative climate is supportive when intragenerational contact exists. If we find that positive ingroup communication among elderly peers is wanting (as was shown in our data with respect to Asian elderly in particular), then health costs can ensue. Data from Patterson and Bettini (1993) show that "interaction alone is not likely to generate well-being" (p. 167) and that a healthy emotional exchange protects against depression. As Rawlins (1995) concluded, "despite their limitations, friends usually play vital roles in sustaining older persons' feelings of wellbeing and life satisfaction. Friends are uniquely valued to talk, reminisce, and judge with, and to keep confidence. They relieve loneliness . . . [itself a prime mediator of physical health, see Fees, Martin, & Poon, 1999] . . . help with incidental needs, connect individuals to larger communities, and foster their ongoing enjoyment of life" (p. 252). Relatedly, Gibb (1999) also discussed the value of peer–elderly conversations in terms of what she calls "working out." This refers to successful intragenerational communication leading to the "resolution and integration of life experiences into expressive value about life itself."

    A final practical implication of this program of research is that, in addition to cognitive and motivational biases in how we treat people from other groups, how we think about our own-age group and other-age groups is affected by cultural values regarding aging. Moreover, these values also seem to play into the extent to which interactions with other-age groups are related to psychological adjustment. The importance of attending to cultural values in aging was underscored in a recent presentation given by one of the authors of this chapter. An audience member stated that, although this research program was theoretically interesting, she was training to become a health caregiver in a Western society. Why was it important to understand how other cultures conceptualize aging and intergenerational communication? From our point of view, given that many Western nations, especially those considered in the present program of research (i.e., Australia, Canada, New Zealand, and the United States) are so-called "immigrant nations," there is a strong possibility that Western health professionals will encounter people from many different cultures in their career. Providing the optimum levels of service involves effective communication between generations, and this may also involve effective communication across cultural divides. Understanding the diversity of expectations, beliefs, and values that clients hold may be an essential first step toward such high quality care.

ACKNOWLEDGMENTS

Howard Giles acknowledges the University of California Pacific Rim Agency for, in part, supporting the research reported in this chapter. Sik Hung Ng wishes to thank Gwendolin Wong, for her assistance with collecting the Hong Kong elders' data, and the Department of Psychology of the Chinese University of Hong Kong, for hosting his research and study leave. Finally, we are very grateful to Mary Lee Hummert and Jon Nussbaum for their very thoughtful and meticulous feedback on previous drafts of this chapter.

REFERENCES

Antonovsky, A. (1987). *Unraveling the mystery of health: How people manage stress and stay well.* San Francisco: Jossey Bass.

Auslander, G. K., & Litwin, H. (1991). Social networks, social support, and self-ratings of health among older persons. *Journal of Aging and Health, 3,* 493–510.

Cai, D., Giles, H., & Noels, K. A. (1998). Elderly perceptions of communication with older and younger adults in China: Implications for mental health. *Journal of Applied Communication Research, 26,* 32–51.

Cargile, A. C., & Giles, H. (1996). Intercultural communication training: Review, critique, and a new theoretical framework. In B. R. Burleson (Eds.), *Communication yearbook 19* (pp. 385–423). Thousand Oaks, CA: Sage.

Chang, H.-C. (1999). The "well-defined" is "ambiguous"—Indeterminacy in Chinese conversation. *Journal of Pragmatics, 31,* 535–556.

Chang, H.-C. (2000). *Harmony as performance: The turbulence under Chinese interpersonal communication.* Manuscript submitted for publication.

Chang, H.-C., & Holt, G. R. (1991). More than relationship: Chinese interaction and the principle of *Kuan-Hsi. Communication Quarterly, 39,* 251–271.

Chau-Kiu, C., Jik-Joen, L., & Cheung-Ming, C. (1994). Self-esteem and perceptions of older persons. *Social Behavior and Personality, 22,* 279–290.

Chow, N. (1983). The Chinese family and support of older persons in Hong Kong. *The Gerontologist, 23,* 584–588.

Chow, N. (1996). Filial piety in Asian Chinese communities. *Hong Kong Journal of Gerontology, 10* (Suppl.), 115–117.

Chow, N. (1999). Diminishing filial piety and the changing role and status of the elders in Hong Kong. *Hallym International Journal of Aging, 1,* 67–77.

Coupland, N., Coupland, J., & Giles, H. (1991). *Language, society and the elderly: Discourse, identity, and aging.* Oxford, England: Blackwell.

Cusack, S. (1999). Critical educational gerontology and the imperative to empower. *Education and Ageing, 14,* 21–38.

Devine, P. G. (1989). Prejudice and outgroup perception. In A. Tesser (Ed.), *Advanced social psychology* (pp. 467–524). New York: McGraw-Hill.

Diener, E., & Diener, M. (1995). Cross-cultural correlates of life satisfaction and self-esteem. *Journal of Personality and Social Psychology, 68,* 653–663.

Dillard, J. P., Henwood, K., Giles, H., Coupland, N., & Coupland, J. (1990). Compliance gaining young and old: Beliefs about influence in different age groups. *Communication Reports, 3,* 84–91.

Edwards, H., & Giles, H. (1998). Prologue on two dimensions: The risk and management of intergenerational miscommunication. *Applied Communication Research, 26*(1), 1–12.

Fees, B. S., & Martin, P., & Poon, L. W. (1999). A model of loneliness in older adults. *Journal of Gerontology: Psychological Sciences, 54B,* P231–P239.

Fei, X. (1985). The caring of the old in families undergoing structural changes. In C. Chia (Ed.), *Proceedings of the conference on modernization and Chinese culture* (pp. 121–132). Hong Kong: Faculty of the Social Sciences and Institute of Social Studies, The Chinese University of Hong Kong, Shatin.

Fox, S., & Giles, H. (1993). Accommodating intergenerational contact: A critique and theoretical model. *Journal of Aging Studies, 7,* 423–451.

Gallois, C. (1994). Group membership, social rules, and power: A social-psychological perspective on emotional communication. *Journal of Pragmatics, 22,* 301–324.

Gallois, C., & Giles, H. (1998). Accommodating mutual influence in intergroup encounters. In M. T. Palmer & G. A. Barnett (Eds.), *Mutual influence in interpersonal communication: Theory and research in cognition, affect and behavior* (pp. 130–162). New York: Ablex.

Gallois, C., Giles, H., Ota, H., Pierson, H. D., Ng, S. H., Lim, T.-S., Maher, J., Somera, L., Ryan, E. B., & Harwood, J. (1999). Intergenerational communication across the Pacific Rim: The impact of filial piety. In J.-C. Lasry et al. (Eds.), *Proceedings of the 13th Conference of the International Association of Cross-Cultural Psychology* (pp. 192–211). Amsterdam: Swets & Zeitlinger.

George, L. K., Okun, M. A., & Landerman, R. (1985). Age as a moderator of the determinants of life satisfaction. *Research on Aging, 7,* 209–233.

Gibb, H. (1999, July). *Understanding older people's perspectives.* Keynote Address delivered at the 4th International Conference on Communication, Ageing, and Health, Gold Coast, Queensland, Australia.

Giles, H., & Coupland, N. (1991). Language attitudes: Discursive, contextual and gerontological considerations. In A. G. Reynolds (Ed.), *McGill Conference on Bilingualism, Multiculturalism and Second Language Learning: A tribute to Wallace E. Lambert* (pp. 21–42). Hillside, NJ: Lawrence Erlbaum Associates.

Giles, H., Coupland, N., Coupland, J., Williams, A., & Nussbaum, J. (1992). Intergenerational talk and communication with older people. *International Journal of Aging and Human Development, 34,* 271–297.

Giles, H., Harwood, J., Pierson, H. D., Clément, R., & Fox, S. (1998). Stereotypes of older persons and evaluations of patronizing speech: A cross-cultural foray. In R. K. Agnihotri, A. L. Khanna, & I. Sachdev (Eds.), *Social psychological perspectives on second language learning* (pp. 151–186). New Delhi: Sage.

Giles, H., Liang, B., Noels, K., & McCann, R. (in press). Communicating across and within generations: Taiwanese, Chinese-Americans, and Euro-Americans' perceptions of communication. *Journal of Asian Pacific Communication.*

Giles, H., Noels, K. A., Ota, H., Ng, S. H., Gallois, C., Ryan, E. B., Williams, A., Lim, T.-S., Somera, L., Tao, H., & Sachdev, I. (in press). Age vitality in eleven nations. *Journal of Multilingual and Multicultural Development.*

Giles, H., Noels, K. A., Williams, A., Lim, T.-S, Ng, S. H., Ryan, E. B., Somera, L., & Ota, H. (2000). *Intergenerational communication across cultures: Young people's perceptions of conversation with family elders, non-family elders, and same-age peers.* Manuscript submitted for publication.

Giles, H., & Ryan, E. B. (Eds.). (1986). Language, communication, and the elderly. *Language and Communication, 6.*

Giles, H., & Williams, A. (1994). Patronizing the young: Forms and evaluations. *International Journal of Aging and Human Development, 39,* 33–53.

Global aging into the 21st century. (1996). *Wallchart of the U.S. Census Bureau and National Institute of Aging.* Washington, DC.

Hajek, C., & Giles, H. (in press). Intercultural communication competence: An alternative position. In B. Burleson & J. Greene (Eds.), *Handbook of social skills and communicative competence.* Mahwah, NJ: Lawrence Erlbaum Associates.

Harwood, J., Giles, H., Ota, H., Pierson, H. D., Gallois, C., Ng, S-H., Lim, T-S., & Somera, L.-B. (1996). College students' trait ratings of three age groups around the Pacific Rim. *Cross-Cultural Gerontology, 11,* 307–317.

Harwood, J., Giles, H., Pierson, H. D., Clément, R., & Fox, S. (1994). Vitality perceptions of age categories in California and Hong Kong. *Journal of Multilingual and Multicultural Development, 15,* 311–318.

Harwood, J., Giles, H., & Ryan, E. B. (1995). Aging, communication, and intergroup theory: Social identity and intergenerational communication. In J. F. Nussbaum & J. Coupland (Eds.), *Handbook of communication and aging research* (pp. 133–160). Mahwah, NJ: Lawrence Erlbaum Associates.

Harwood, J., & Williams, A. (1998). Expectations for communication with positive and negative subtypes of older adults. *International Journal of Aging and Human Development, 47,* 11–33.

Ho, D. Y.-F. (1994). Filial piety, authoritarian moralism, and cognitive conservatism in Chinese societies. *Genetic, Social and General Psychology Monographs, 120,* 347–365.

Hofstede, G. (1980). *Culture's consequences: International differences in work-related values.* Beverly Hills, CA: Sage.

Hummert, M. L. (1990). Multiple stereotypes of older persons and young adults: A comparison of structure and evaluations. *Psychology and Aging, 5,* 182–193.

Hummert, M. L. (1994). Stereotypes of older persons and patronizing speech. In M. L. Hummert, J. M. Wiemann, & J. F. Nussbaum (Eds.), *Interpersonal communication in older adulthood: Interdisciplinary research* (pp. 162–184). Newbury Park, CA: Sage.

Hummert, M. L., & Ryan, E. B. (1996). Toward understanding variations in patronizing talk addressed to older adults: Psycholinguistic features of care and control. *International Journal of Psycholinguistics 12*, 149–170.

Ikels, C. (1975). Old age in Hong Kong. *The Gerontologist, 15*, 230–235.

Ingersoll-Dayton, B., & Saengtienchai, C. (1999). Respect for older persons in Asia: Stability and change. *International Journal of Aging and Human Development, 48*, 113–130.

Kiefer, C. W. (1992). Aging in Eastern cultures: A historical overview. In T. R. Cole, D. D. Van Tassel, & R. Kastenbaum (Eds.), *Handbook of the humanities and aging* (pp. 96–123). New York: Springer.

Kim, K. C., Kim, S., & Hurh, W. M. (1991). Filial piety and intergenerational relationships in Korean immigrant families. *International Journal of Aging and Human Development, 33*, 233–245.

Kim, U. (1994). Individualism and collectivism: Conceptual clarification and elaboration. In U. Kim, H. C. Triandis, C. Kagitçibasi, S.-C. Choi, & G. Yoon (Eds.), *Individualism and collectivism: Theory, method, and applications* (pp. 19–40). Thousand Oaks, CA: Sage.

Kim, U., & Yamaguchi, S. (1994). Cross-cultural research methodology and approach: Implications for the advancement of Japanese social psychology. *Research in Social Psychology, 10*, 168–179.

Kite, M. E., & Johnson, B. T. (1998). Attitudes towards older and younger adults: A meta-analysis. *Psychology and Aging, 3*, 233–244.

Koyano, W. (1989). Japanese attitudes toward older persons: A review of research findings. *Journal of Cross-Cultural Gerontology, 4*, 335–345.

Krause, N. (1996). Welfare participation and self-esteem in later life. *Gerontologist, 36*, 665–673.

Krause, N., & Borawski-Clark, E. (1994). Clarifying the functions of social support in later life. *Research on Aging, 16*, 251–279.

Krause, N., Liang, J., & Keith, V. (1990). Personality, social support, and psychological distress in later life. *Psychology and Aging, 5*, 315–326.

Krause, N., Liang, J., & Yatomi, N. (1989). Satisfaction with social support and depressive symptoms: A panel analysis. *Psychology and Aging, 4*, 88–97.

Lai, D. W. L., & McDonald, J. R. (1995). Life satisfaction of Chinese elderly immigrants in Calgary. *Canadian Journal on Aging, 14*, 536–552.

Lee, Y.-J., Parish, W. L., & Willis, R. J. (1994). Sons, daughters and intergenerational support in Taiwan. *American Journal of Sociology, 99*, 1010–1041.

Minkler, M. (1996). Critical perspectives on ageing: New challenges for gerontology. *Ageing and Society, 16*, 467–487.

Ng, S. H., Liu, J. H., Loong, S. C. F., & Weatherall, A. (1999). *Links across generations among New Zealand Chinese.* Unpublished report, School of Psychology, Victoria University of Wellington, New Zealand.

Ng, S. H., Liu, J. H., Weatherall, A., & Loong, C. S. F. (1997). Younger adults' communication experiences and contact with elders and peers. *Human Communication Research, 24*, 82–108.

Ng, S. H., Weatherall, A., Liu, J. H., & Loong, S. F. C. (1998) *Ages ahead: Promoting inter-generational relationships.* Wellington, New Zealand: Victoria University Press.

Noels, K. A., Giles, H., Cai, D., & Turay, L. (1999). Perceptions of inter- and intra-generational communication in the United States of America and the People's Republic of China: Implications for self-esteem and life satisfaction. *South Pacific Journal of Psychology, 10*, 120–135.

Nussbaum, J. F. (1985). Successful aging: A communication model. *Communication Quarterly, 33*, 262–269.

Oishi, S., Diener, E. E., Lucas, R. E., & Suh, E. M. (1999). Cross-cultural variation in predictors of life satisfaction from needs and values. *Personality and Social Psychology Bulletin, 25,* 980–990.

Ota, H., Giles, H., & Gallois, C. (2000). *Age stereotypes and vitality in Australia and Japan.* Manuscript in preparation.

Palmore, E. (1975). *The honorable elders: A cross-cultural analysis of ageing in Japan.* Durham, NC: Duke University Press.

Paltridge, J., & Giles, H. (1984). Attitudes towards speakers of regional accents of French: Effects of regionality, age, sex of listeners. *Linguistische Berichte, 90,* 71–85.

Paoletti, I. (1998). *Being an older woman: A case study in the social production of identity.* Mahwah, NJ: Lawrence Erlbaum Associates.

Patterson, B. R., & Bettini, L. A. (1993). Age, depression, and friendship: Development of a general friendship inventory. *Communication Research Reports, 10,* 161–170.

Patterson, B. R., Bettini, L. A., & Nussbaum, J. F. (1992). The meaning of friendship across the lifespan: Two studies. *Communication Quarterly, 41,* 145–160.

Ranzijn, R., Keeves, J., Luszcz, M., & Feather, N. (1998). The role of self-perceived usefulness and competence in the self-esteem of elderly adults: Confirmatory factor analyses of the Bachman revision of Rosenberg's Self-Esteem Scale. *Journal of Gerontology: Psychological and Social Sciences, 55B,* P96–P104.

Rawlins, W. K. (1992). *Friendship matters: Communication, dialectics, and the life course.* New York: Aldine DeGruyter.

Rawlins, W. K. (1995). Friendship in later life. In J. F. Nussbaum & J. Coupland (Eds.), *Handbook of communication and aging research* (pp. 227–258). Mahwah, NJ: Lawrence Erlbaum Associates.

Reitzes, A., Mutran, E. J., & Fernandez, M. (1994). Middle-aged working men and women: Similar and different paths to self-esteem. *Research on Aging, 16,* 355–374.

Roscow, I. (1976). Status and role change through the life span. In R. H. Binstock & E. Shanas (Eds.), *Handbook of aging and the social science* (pp. 457–482). New York: Van Nostrand-Reinhold.

Rosenberg, M. (1965). *Society and the adolescent self-image.* Princeton, NJ: Princeton University Press.

Ryan, E. B., Giles, H., Bartolucci, G., & Henwood, K. (1986). Psycholinguistic and social psychological components of communication by and with older persons. *Language and Communication, 6,* 1–24.

Ryan, E. B., Hummert, M. L., & Boich, L. (1995). Communication predicaments of aging: Patronizing behavior toward older adults. *Journal of Language and Social Psychology, 13,* 144–166.

Ryan, E. B., Meredith, S. D., MacLean, M. J., & Orange, J. B. (1995). Changing the way we talk with elders: Promoting health using the Communication Enhancement Model. *International Journal of Aging and Human Development, 41,* 87–105.

Ryff, C. D., & Seltzer, M. M. (1996). *The parental experience of midlife.* Chicago: University of Chicago.

Singelis, T. M., Triandis, H. C., Bhawuk, D., & Gelfand, M. (1995). Horizontal and vertical dimensions of individualism and collectivism: A theoretical and measurement refinement. *Cross-Cultural Research, 29,* 240–275.

Strain, L. A., & Chappell, N. L. (1982). Confidants: Do they make a difference in quality of life? *Research on Aging, 4,* 479–502.

Tabachnick, B. G., & Fidell, L. S. (1996). *Using multivariate statistics.* New York: HarperCollins.

Tien-Hyatt, J. L. (1987). Self-perceptions of aging across cultures: Myth or reality? *International Journal of Aging and Human Development, 24,* 129–148.

Tobin, J. J. (1987). The American idealization of old age in Japan. *The Gerontologist, 27,* 53–58.

Turkoski, B. (1975). Growing old in China. *Journal of Gerontological Nursing, 11,* 32–34.

Viladot, M. A., & Giles, H. (1998). Habla condescendiente y ancianidad: Evaluaciones intergeneracionales en Cataluña [Condescending speech and aging: Intergenerational evaluations in Catalonia]. *Revista de Psicologia Social Aplicada, 8,* 29–60.

Williams, A., & Coupland, N. (1998). Epilogue: The socio-political framing of communication and aging. *Journal of Applied Communication Research, 26,* 139–154.

Williams, A., & Giles, H. (1996). Intergenerational conversations: Young adults' retrospective accounts. *Human Communication Research, 23,* 220–250.

Williams, A., Ota, H., Giles, H., Pierson, H. D., Gallois, C., Ng, S.-H., Lim, T.-S., Ryan, E. B., Somera, L.-B, Maher, J., Cai, D., & Harwood, J. (1997). Young people's beliefs about intergenerational communication: An initial cross-cultural comparison. *Communication Research, 24,* 370–393.

Ytsma, J., & Giles, H. (1997). Reactions to patronizing talk: Some Dutch data. *Journal of Sociolinguistics, 1,* 259–268.

Yum, J. O. (1988). The impact of Confucianism on interpersonal relations and communication patterns in East Asia. *Communication Monographs, 55,* 374–388.

Epilogue

Communication, Aging, and Health: The Interface Between Research and Practice

Ellen Bouchard Ryan
McMaster University, Canada

Joan E. Norris
University of Guelph, Canada

This epilogue serves two main purposes. First, we provide an integration of some of the key ideas from all the contributions in terms of two models of communication in aging. Second, we take a step back and apply the two communication models to the activity of conducting research in aging. We discuss the sources of communication gaps between researchers and practitioners in the field of aging and identify a central role for communication experts in facilitating the interface between these two groups.

COMMUNICATION CHALLENGES FOR OLDER ADULTS AND THE HEALTH PRACTITIONERS SERVING THEM

The chapters in this book contribute in many diverse ways to our emerging understanding of communication issues in aging and health. We highlight selected points from these chapters within the contexts of our model of the communication predicaments experienced by older adults, especially in health care contexts, and a second model intended to stimulate communication enhancement strategies to minimize such communication predicaments.

Communication Predicaments of Older Adults

The Communication Predicament Model of Aging (Ryan, Giles, Bartolucci, & Henwood, 1986; Ryan, Hummert, & Boich, 1995) offers a framework for understanding the ways in which health providers may often inhibit the ability of older clients to display their competence and limit the success of their own interventions. The model, depicted in modified form in Fig. 1, portrays a negative feedback loop that operates most fully in first encounters but typifies some repeated interactions in health care settings where the provider never gets to know the person receiving care. Upon encountering an older person, the provider forms impressions based on old age cues. These can include chronological age information, physical cues (e.g., facial appearance, stature, and voice), behavioral cues (e.g., forgetfulness, requests for repetition, complaints), and sociocultural cues (e.g., retiree status, senior center member, nursing home resident). The impressions based on these age cues tend to be stereotyped expectations rather than reactions to the individual. Stereotypes of older adults are demonstrably negative in terms of health, vitality, competence, dependence, and memory (see Harwood et al., 1996; Kite & Johnson, 1988; Ryan, 1992). The crux of the feedback loop is that stereotyped expectations lead to modified communication styles that elicit age-stereotyped behaviors from the older person and reduce opportunities for satisfying communication. The communication modifications are highly varied across circumstances, but include the following possibilities: slow speech, loud speech, high pitch, exaggerated intonation, childish forms of address, short simple sentences, simplified vocabulary, repetition, omission of politeness forms, avoidance of communication, restriction in topic selection, and abrupt gestures (Caporael, 1981; Hummert & Ryan, 1996; Hummert, Shaner, Garstka, & Henry, 1998; Kemper & Harden, 1999). Repeated exposure to such communication can lead to reduced self-esteem, loss of a sense of personal control, reduced activity, entry into more age-accommodated settings linked with stereotypes, and eventually to increased cues to old age and infirmity (see Rodin & Langer, 1980).

Communication predicaments can be exacerbated by the health problems of older adults, by the demands of particular relationships, by the constraints of particular settings such as nursing homes, and by environmental factors.

Two specific health conditions were addressed by chapters in this volume: dementia and hearing impairment. Norberg (chap. 7, this volume)

Communication Predicament Model

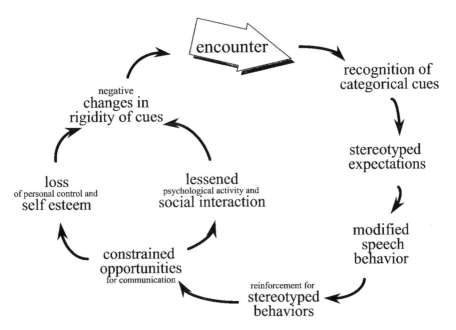

FIG. 1. Communication Predicament Model (Ryan, Meredith, MacLean, & Orange, 1995; modified to fit intergenerational communication and other stereotype-based interactions).

identified the excess disability suffered by individuals with dementia through degrading communication when they are treated as nonpersons. During this self-threatening disease, they are especially vulnerable to messages that disconfirm their sense of self. Older adults with hearing impairment (Pichora-Fuller & Carson, chap. 3, this volume) are reluctant to use hearing aids, partly because of the associated stigma, and they need to learn to cope with inappropriate strategies (e.g., shouting) by communication partners.

The three important communication relationships dealt with in this text comprise family, intergenerational, and physician–patient. Negotiating health decisions within the family can pose risks for older adults. This can happen in terms of unnecessary loss of autonomy through adult children's paternalistic overemphasis on protection of the parents' well-being (Hummert & Morgan, chap. 8, this volume). Edwards (chap. 9, this volume) highlighted the predicaments of the older adult in the care receiver role. Older care receivers are dependent on family caregivers not only for physical care, but also for their mental and social health. Their well-being depends on their relationship with the caregiver, the caregiver's psychological well-being, and the caregiver's coping strategies. Orange (chap. 10, this volume) discussed the impact of communication changes associated with Alzheimer's disease on communication patterns of family caregivers as well as on the caregiver burden experienced. The new role as facilitator of communication can add considerably to the responsibilities of already burdened family members. Moving to a cross-cultural context, Noels, Giles, Gallois, and Ng (chap. 11, this volume) examined intergenerational communication between young and old from an intergroup perspective. With data from Hong Kong and Australia to illustrate East/West similarities and differences, they assessed negative and positive aspects of communication between the generations and showed some associations between negative views among older adults in the West and their poor psychological health.

The physician–patient relationship is central to the maintenance of health for older adults. Nussbaum, Pecchioni, and Crowell (chap. 2, this volume) examined new opportunities and threats associated with this relationship from emerging changes in health care systems in the United States and elsewhere. Managed care systems emphasize the role of primary care physician as case manager and hence, underline the importance of a fruitful relationship with older patients. Yet, at the same time, developing and maintaining such a relationship may well be more difficult when both physician and patient are small units within a complex system often focused more on financial management than health management. According to Greene and Adelman (chap. 5, this volume), ageist features that have been observed in physician–patient interactions include less physician responsiveness to older patients, less concordance on major goals, less joint decision making, and less respectful and optimistic manner. One age-associated situation that may put older patients at risk is the frequent accompaniment on doctor visits by a companion (Coupland & Coupland, chap. 6, this volume; Nussbaum et al., chap. 2, this volume). Despite the benefits of a companion, the older person's autonomy may be threatened if the companion speaks for, with, or about them. Finally, the increasingly widespread use of computer mediated technology in health care may have some negative consequences for older adults: inappropriate assumptions about acceptability, unequal access, likelihood of greater reliance on stereotypes for communication at a distance, and difficulty of making appropriate modifications where communication problems exist (Whitten & Gregg, chap. 1, this volume).

Communication Enhancement Strategies

The Communication Enhancement Model was developed as a framework for communication interventions intended to reverse the operation of the negative feedback Predicament loop (Baltes, Neumann, & Zank, 1994; Orange, Ryan, Meredith, & MacLean, 1995; Ryan, Meredith, MacLean, & Orange, 1995). This framework, shown in modified form in Fig. 2, emerged from a consideration of health promotion strategies that focus on the roles of self-care, mutual aid, and social support.

The success of a dyadic interaction between care provider and an older client is seen to depend on multiple environmental influences well beyond the interaction itself. One can improve the chances for a satisfactory encounter by dealing with some of those environmental factors (e.g., average time allowed per encounter, institutional philosophy, sound and lighting conditions, training level of personnel, financial issues). The key to an initial encounter is to assess cues about the older client in an individual-

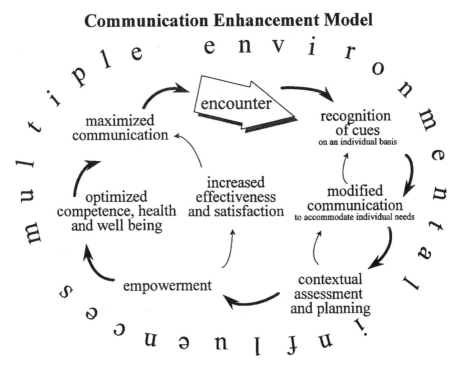

FIG. 2. Communication Enhancement Model (Ryan, Meredith, MacLean, & Orange, 1995; modified to fit intergenerational communication and other stereotype-based interactions).

ized, contextualized manner. If some communication modification appears needed because of limited English as a second language or a hearing impairment, for example, adult-focused modifications are attempted and feedback regarding their appropriateness is sought. The provider is well aware of the tendency to overgeneralize impairments and to overdo communication modifications in response to particular communication difficulties and is constantly monitoring the mode and content of the communication. The assessment and development of a treatment plan for the client are as individualized as possible and as collaborative with the client as feasible. The care provider attempts to empower the client, to help them identify the issues, and participate in their resolution. The strengths of the client are an important part of the assessment and treatment planned; the client's sense of control is thereby supported. The client experiences enhanced competence, health, and control.

The provider has a high probability of achieving a satisfactory encounter, and the treatment plan has a better chance of success. With repeated exposure, clients grow in their ability to collaborate with the provider in seeking their own health, and both client and provider may become more able to influence environmental constraints on healthy communication.

In her chapter on communication with severely demented individuals, Norberg (chap. 7, this volume) discussed various aspects of integrity promoting care that exemplify the communication enhancement approach. Consoling nurses were able to be in communion with their patients, and their enabling manner appeared to maximize periods of lucidity. Their interpretations of conversation about past time and places as messages about current emotions led to a sense of satisfying communication for both parties. Strikingly, if the patient was seen as a valuable person, a positive feedback loop was reinforced whereby the caregiver was also seen as a valuable person.

Pichora-Fuller and Carson (chap. 3, this volume) provided an overview of several comprehensive rehabilitation interventions for hearing-impaired older adults. These interventions, designed within an ecological health promotion framework, emphasize behavioral interventions with the hearing impaired persons along with broader interventions in the environments for communication and with potential communication partners.

In terms of family relationships, Garstka, McCallion, and Toseland (chap. 4, this volume) showed the value of support groups for enhancing family caregiver health. Edwards (chap. 9, this volume) argued that such community programs to support caregiving in the home should attend to the care receiver as well as the caregiver. She also pointed out the need to focus on the relationship between the two and facilitate healthy relationships and outlets for social support for both the caregiver and care receiver. In line with this emphasis, Orange (chap. 10, this volume) briefly reviewed current and future intervention approaches designed to optimize communication between individuals with dementia and their family caregivers to buttress the relationship threatened by communication impairment. Hummert and Morgan (chap. 8, this volume) made some useful suggestions regarding communication strategies between older parents and adult children to promote an appropriate balance between independence and dependence as the parents' health declines.

With respect to physician–patient relationships, Greene and Adelman (chap. 5, this volume) highlighted contributions of both the physician and the patient for enhancing communication. For example, the physician should acknowledge the personhood of the older patient (including life review), attend to the patient's agenda, confront difficult-to-talk-about subjects, and deal sensitively with sensory and other functional limitations. Correspondingly, the patient should contribute to improving the relationship by using a list to ensure that important issues are addressed, taking notes during the visit, asking the physician for educational materials, informing the physician of special needs regarding communication, and even switching doctors if the first few visits are not satisfactory. Coupland and Coupland (chap. 6, this volume) argued for the importance of the physician attending to relational and identity goals in addition to the instrumental goals of medical care. This is particularly important when a companion is part of the visit because problems can arise even in the clinic with an official policy indicating the patient's right to be addressed in the second person and to make their own health decisions.

In summary, we have discussed the chapters of this volume in terms of their contributions to understanding the communication predicaments of older adults and possible communication-enhancing interventions with older adults, their communication partners, and/or the communication environments.

COMMUNICATION ISSUES FOR GERONTOLOGICAL RESEARCHERS AND PRACTITIONERS

In this section of the chapter, we move from the communication challenges facing older adults and those who interact with them, and consider how our models might be applied to interactions among those who study aging-related phenomena.

Disciplinary Challenges for Gerontology

Gerontology is a multidisciplinary field, drawing expertise from all aspects of scientific and clinical endeavor. A glance at the typical undergraduate curriculum reveals courses in literature and aging, the physiology of aging, social gerontology, and adult development and aging. Despite the breadth of these topics, however, gerontology is not fundamentally interdisciplinary with each discipline collaborating fully to understand aging and the concerns of older people. Instead, there are many camps of scholars and practitioners often bound by the socialization and expertise of their own specialized fields. As knowledge about aging grows in depth and complexity, such factions have increased in number, often abandoning generalist organizations and publications for those which are discipline specific. The crossover of even related subspecialities has become less likely. Consider, for example, the move to divide the *Journals of Gerontology* into two: one journal for the biological sciences and one for the social and psychological sciences. In the past, the eye of a sociologist needed to trip over a geneticist's article on her way to a piece on caregiving, insuring at least a glimpse of both titles. Now, that geneticist's writings are not even likely to be on her shelf.

Given this rigid and powerful disciplinarity, it is little wonder that older adults and their families feel challenged and frustrated by their interactions with health care professionals. We, and other gerontologists, have written about the communication difficulties encountered by those on either side of the client–practitioner relationship (e.g., Clark, 1996, 1997; Elliott, 1993; Orange & Ryan, 1995). This literature describes older clients' complaints that practitioners do not understand their perspective or their needs, but notes their reluctance to challenge the suggestions of care providers (Beisecker, 1991). Practitioners have countered that clients do not understand their need to decontextualize a problem; that is, to remove it from the specific life circumstances of the older person and place it within the broader system of clinical knowledge (Clark, 1996). Both groups have found it difficult to break out of their communication predicament (Ryan, Meredith, et al., 1995).

There have been efforts in many health care organizations to improve the coordination and delivery of care to older adults, and to create equal partnerships between providers and clients. The most common approach to this coordination is through multidisciplinary teams (see Nussbaum et al., chap. 2, this volume). Ideally, practitioners from a variety of disciplines should be able to cross boundaries and facilitate communication among themselves and with the client. In practice, this may not happen. Disciplinary allegiances and power differentials are frequently too difficult to overcome (Byrne, 1991). Drinka and Streim (1994) have described the "purgatory" of membership in geriatric teams which are characterized by a lack of knowledge, uncertain outcomes of treatment plans, and continually changing personnel. When the geriatric team is also low in power and status, relative to other specialties within the health care organization, functioning may spiral further downward.

Interdisciplinarity has also not fared well within academic ranks. Universities are still organized around single discipline departments, often leaving an area of study, such as aging, with no one structure to house it and no one unit to nurture its development. Instead, interdisciplinary pursuits are regarded with suspicion or dismissed outright (Nissani, 1997). This is not just a problem for gerontologists seeking tenure, but, as Katz (1996) noted, disciplinarity in gerontological scholarship has a powerful effect on older people as well, constructing a dominant discourse which "determines the ways in which the people who inhabit it can be known, studied, calculated, trained, helped, punished, and liberated" (p. 2).

Practitioner–Researcher Collaboration in an Interdisciplinary Setting

Given the potential internal conflicts that affect both groups of researchers and groups of practitioners, what happens when researchers and practitioners attempt to collaborate? This issue has been widely discussed in other fields of social science, and major obstacles to communication and collaboration noted. Parloff (1998), for example, described the current state of relationships between clinical and research psychologists as one of "assault and nattery" with researchers denigrating the value of therapists' clinical skills and therapists only reluctantly considering the conclusions of researchers' outcome studies. Other authors have echoed this concern, noting that the failure of researcher–clinician collaboration has hindered the development of effective psychological intervention for diverse target groups (Brown et al., 1997; Holland, 1998; Kuster & Poburka, 1998).

The situation is much the same when the focus is on aging and older adults. Practitioners, researchers, and older people may not share the same goals. Bieman-Copland, Ryan, and Cassano (1998), for example, noted in their review of research on memory interventions that whereas researchers might be most interested in improving the memory of older adults, these adults are likely to care more about metamemory, that is, how to improve their understanding of memory processes and how to feel more confident about the working of their own memories. If practitioners ally themselves with the concerns of older clients, but cannot convince researchers that this is the best approach, joint attempts at intervention and understanding are likely to fail.

Communication Predicaments of Gerontological Researchers and Practitioners in Aging

There are at least two major reasons for this researcher–practitioner gap. The first relates to the scientific method; the second to the separate epistemologies of researchers and practitioners. Both create stereotypes that can impede communication and cooperation. Traditionally, the relationship between science and practice has been top-down and unidirectional (Fey & Johnson, 1998; Wilcox, Hadley, & Bacon, 1998). Basic researchers are charged with the responsibility of discovery, finding new information that can shed light on a specific phenomenon. Applied researchers are expected to take this basic information and assess its utility in mundane settings or in interventions with clients. At the bottom of this hierarchy is the clinician, expected to apply the findings of the other two groups in immediate, clinical settings.

The links in this chain of dissemination are weak. As Wilcox et al. (1998) noted, information of use to practitioners may never reach them, either because the work is published in journals likely to be read only by researchers or because practitioners have too little time and too few resources available to engage in any professional development. Even when research is accessed by those who might use it, it may be perceived as remote and irrelevant. The description of a tightly controlled, quantitatively oriented, experimental study with a homogeneous sample may seem a long way from the diverse and vaguely defined problems that a clinician encounters in clients' narratives.

Differences in the system of knowledge employed by researchers and clinicians may also impede collaboration. Some authors have argued that researchers and clinicians operate from epistemologies that are profoundly different in their foundation and perspective (e.g., Byrne, 1991). Others believe that the differences are more a function of semantics. Herr (1996), for example, wrote that the disjunction between theory and practice is at least an overstatement, if not an outright myth. Following his line of reasoning, researchers and clinicians have difficulty communicating because the former anchor their thinking abstractly, whereas the latter think more concretely about the real circumstances of real individuals in a particular social context. According to Herr, some effort at translation between the two modes of thinking would go a long way in facilitating mutual understanding. As part of this translation process he also recommends that researchers give up their quest for a grand, unifying theory of human behavior and focus on more contextually bound "segmental" theories. These would be of more immediate use to practitioners and eventually would advance the cause of science as well.

Differences in perspective between researchers and practitioners can have an immediate impact on their communication. The Communication Predicament Model (see Fig. 1) can be taken to illustrate the potential pitfalls of incomplete information and stereotyping in researcher–practitioner interaction. Consider this situation: A geriatric social worker, Mary Sabry, is asked by her long-term care facility to meet with a researcher from the local university, John Kawash, to develop a means of evaluating the facility's music therapy program. Each recognizes superficial differences in the other (e.g., the social worker's white coat; the researcher's honorific Dr.), which create stereotyped expectations for their relationship. Dr. Kawash believes Ms. Sabry is concerned only with assessing clinical goals that have immediate impact. He further feels that she will want to use only anecdotal methods to assess the program, and will care little for an eventual publication of their results. At the same time, Ms. Sabry has formed her own impression: Dr. Kawash is there only to consider how music therapy programs, in general, may affect older adults. She fears he will overstress her clients and fail to understand the clinical situation in which she operates.

In their initial encounter, the stereotypes are engaged rapidly and speech patterns modified to fit perceptions of the situation: The researcher calls Ms. Sabry by her first name, she responds with his title and last name, and a power differential is reinforced. At this point, the social worker may be feeling resentful and thus unlikely to share fully the details of the music program. In turn, the researcher may be annoyed at having to meet with someone whom he perceives is not his equal and who seems unwilling to be fully cooperative. Opportunities for further communication are constrained, as the figure illustrates, and both parties may begin to feel threats to their self-esteem and a desire to curtail further interactions. Future meetings may be even more stilted as both parties operate from the perspective of their stereotyped view of each other—a view which is likely to be confirmed by behaviors brought about by their problematic first encounter. Dr. Kawash appears more officious and aloof, Ms. Sabry more deferential and sullen.

Communication Enhancement for Gerontological Researchers and Practitioners

The Communication Predicament Model represents a cycle of mutually reinforcing attitudes and behaviors leading to progressively poorer outcomes. Conceptualizing the process in this way provides us with a variety of sites for intervention and change. Our overall strategy is to help the actors understand that positive interaction is a product of multiple environmental influences, some part of the larger social, temporal, and historical context and some part of the individual circumstances of a single exchange.

Operating from a communication enhancement perspective, a social actor is sensitive to the characteristics of another but avoids a stereotypic response. Instead, modifications to communication may be attempted while information about appropriateness of such modifications is solicited. In the aforementioned case, it is important for the two professionals to determine the relevance of the social cues they first notice and then to proceed with their business agenda. If both parties begin by using last names, for example, they can provide feedback to one another about their preferred form of address in future interactions. An attitude open to learning about the context and the individual is an essential first step to communication enhancement.

Sensitivity to social cues is a significant component of social competence in any setting (Norris & Rubin, 1984; Pratt & Norris, 1999; Rest & Navraez, 1994). Appropriately tailored behaviors must follow, however, for a successful encounter to occur. We believe that there are four essential components to communication skill that facilitate interaction. The first of these is the ability to listen and remain silent as others express their views. In our aforementioned hypothetical case, it is critical that both parties explain their perspective and their goals for the project, avoiding jargon and adopting a respectful approach from the initial form of address. Active and attentive listening has been shown to be a critical feature of successful communication in a wide variety of settings (e.g., within the physician–patient encounter; Lepper, Martin, & DiMatteo, 1995).

The second general skill involves the ability to seek common ground, however small this patch of turf might appear initially. As Petronio, Ellemers, Giles, and Gallois (1998) argued in their recent review, boundaries of many kinds must be understood and managed for successful communication to occur. If Ms. Sabry and Dr. Kawash can focus on their overall reason for meeting in the first place, that is, to provide high quality care for older institutionalized adults, and not on their differences in approach or philosophy, then communication will be enhanced. Negotiation from a common position is much easier than struggling for control from apparently disparate perspectives.

Negotiating shared goals and roles for the project is therefore the third important component within the enhancement framework. As Dees and Cramton (1999), among others, noted, successful negotiation involves an honest discussion of individual goals and preferences. Arriving at a general common objective, perhaps to maintain funding for nonmedical programs in the case of our two professionals, is a good place to start. From this stance, stakeholders can work toward compromises on issues such as the time taken to complete the task and the ultimate use of the information. For Ms. Sabry, who wants quick information about the effectiveness of her program, this may mean designing an ongoing process evaluation; for Dr. Kawash who is more interested in the long-term impact, this may mean that a significant component of the evaluation will be its outcome measures.

Finally, the fourth communication skill important in this process is making appropriate accommodations to the needs and circumstances of other actors. Norris, Davey, and Kuiack (1994) noted that stakeholders in aging-related evaluation research may communicate from inflexible and defensive stances, even when they recognize and understand each other's perspective. For effective working relationships, these individuals must be prepared to adjust their interactions in appreciation of their partners' characteristics. As Ryan and others noted, sensitive accommodation can increase the probability of rewarding interaction (Orange et al., 1995; Ratzan, 1996; Ryan et al., 1995). Ms. Sabry, for example, might put aside—at least temporarily—her desire for immediate feedback and offer to discuss Dr. Kawash's plans for a publication. For his part, Dr. Kawash might offer Ms. Sabry more recognition as an important part of the research team, perhaps a co-authorship on the publication.

Referring again to Fig. 2, we see that communication modified to accommodate individual needs, combined with an assessment of the specific context for that communication, can lead to feelings of empowerment for all members of the interaction. In turn, increased feelings of self-efficacy and personal competence can facilitate further improvements in communication, which carry over to subsequent encounters.

Cultural Brokers: Communication Experts
in Aging and Health Research

Communication experts have a special responsibility to enhance interaction among gerontologists. By becoming aware of both the culture of
practitioners and the culture of researchers, they can function as cultural
brokers, mediating the relationship between the two groups, and improving communication. As a result, practitioners and researchers may
become more open to each other's perspectives and willing to accommodate these perspectives in their shared research programs.

There are at least four prime opportunities for communication brokers
in aging research. First, there are many avenues for community-based
health promotion research. Pichora-Fuller and Carson's work with hard-
of-hearing seniors (chap. 3, this volume; Carson & Pichora-Fuller, 1997)
is an excellent example of this approach.

As our earlier hypothetical example suggested, there are also opportunities for collaborative program evaluations. Norris, Davey, Davey, and
Weiler (1995), for example, undertook an evaluation of an educational
and supportive program for caregivers run by a local community health
agency. As we noted elsewhere (Norris et al., 1994), enhanced communication was the biggest challenge in this endeavor. All parties to the
evaluation (researchers, graduate students, agency director, program staff,
funders, clients) struggled to overcome easy stereotypes and inappropriate
accommodation in order to listen sincerely to other perspectives and
negotiate joint goals and procedures.

Clinical investigators can be powerful communication allies in collaborative investigations within academia (e.g., see Greene & Adelman,
chap. 5, this volume). The scientist–practitioner model, however, needs
special support to remain viable within university settings. Particular
recognition of the extra hours devoted to practice and to improving communication among colleagues must be made at the level of tenure and
promotion reviews. Further, recognition must be given to differences in
the scholarship of the scientist–practitioner versus the traditional academic. Original research may be replaced by reflective reviews, single
case analyses, or workshops on collaboration and communication offered
for colleagues.

Finally, there are many roles for retirees that have been overlooked in
research collaborations. A wealth of experience and communication
expertise exists among retired researchers and practitioners. For example,
our own universities have programs that involve older adults as mentors

in undergraduate gerontology classes. These older people are truly cultural brokers, commenting with wisdom and a broad historical perspective on the information much younger students are acquiring. Many granting agencies require community partnerships with people like our senior volunteers in an effort to give voice to all stakeholders in the research enterprise. When these partnerships are established with communication enhancement in mind, they can be extremely effective (see, e.g., Tindale's, 1993, study of a mental health promotion program for older adults). In this regard, we can also point to the central involvement of retirees as discussants in the Third International Conference on Communication, Aging, and Health, the conference leading to this published volume.

Health Promotion Strategies for Brokers

Communication experts also have a responsibility to promote and maintain in themselves those health protective strategies that they attempt to foster in others. We believe that there are three general strategies that these experts, and all who learn from them, can use to make the enhancement model work for them.

First, self-care is critical. Gerontological researchers know that expert performance is maintained only when practiced, whether this performance relates to typing, chess-playing, or social skill (see Pratt & Norris, 1994). Communication experts can collaborate with each other to share insights and challenges, and to carry out research on communication challenges. In particular, information about how to engage in appropriate accommodation with colleagues and clients can benefit even those most well-versed in communication techniques. In quick encounters within busy lives, even those who know better may resort to stereotyped behaviors.

A related strategy is that of formal mutual aid. A conference such as the one which resulted in the chapters in this book—the International Conference on Communication, Aging and Health—and, indeed, the book itself, can promote visibility and respect for communication experts. In addition, interest groups within professional and gerontological associations allow the sharing of new ideas and mutual support within the larger context of our multidisciplinary field. For those who cannot easily attend professional conferences, e-mail can become a kind of "scholarly skywriting" (Kuster & Poburka, 1998), where ideas are exchanged between practitioners and researchers in a thoughtful and public forum.

Finally, as we have noted above, healthy work environments are created and maintained by enhanced communication. Researchers and practitioners might facilitate this communication through the cross-fertilization of ideas and strategies. Collaborative research projects are an obvious vehicle for this cross-fertilization. Such projects may be designed to investigate communication issues between professionals and their clients or to look within the community of professionals to understand systemic stereotyping and inappropriate accommodation.

It would also enhance researcher–practitioner interaction if each was able to interact with the other's environment in a meaningful fashion. Some innovative programs to further this goal have been established throughout North America: For example, clinical investigators have been trained jointly by universities and health care institutions through the establishment of research institutes (Cohen-Mansfield, Lawton, & Riskin, 1990). Other researchers have held funded research positions in community or clinical settings (Lipsitz, 1995–1996). Still others have received clinical and research training within teaching nursing homes (Lipsitz, 1995–1996; Shaughnessy, Kramer, Hittle, & Steiner, 1995). The demonstrated success of all of these initiatives suggest that they deserve broader application.

CONCLUSIONS

We had two major goals in writing this chapter. We considered the other contributions to this volume within the framework of our two models of communication in aging: the Communication Predicament and Communication Enhancement models. Using these models, we identified the challenges and rewards of communication among generations.

Our second goal was to extend the applicability of the communication models to the researcher–practitioner relationship. It is clear that many communication problems affecting older people also affect those who provide services for them, whether those services are professional, supportive, or scientific. By understanding the pitfalls of stereotyping and overaccommodation, gerontologists are in a better position to collaborate fully on areas of joint interest. Using the Communication Predicament and Enhancement models, we can gain insight into the specific causes of problematic interaction, and suggest sites and avenues of intervention. This book is an excellent example of how communication can be enhanced through the interaction of people, and their ideas, from a broad variety of disciplines. It is our hope that both contributors and readers will take away from these interactions fresh ideas that will be applied fruitfully in many aging-related settings.

ACKNOWLEDGMENTS

The authors acknowledge support from grants from the Social Sciences and Humanities Research Council of Canada. We would also like to thank Jessica Trim and Ann Anas for their help in preparing this chapter.

REFERENCES

Baltes, M. M., Neumann, E.M., & Zank, S. (1994). Maintenance and rehabilitation of independence in old age: An intervention program for staff. *Psychology and Aging, 9*, 179–188.

Beisecker, A. E. (1991). Aging and the desire for information and input in medical decisions: Patient consumerism in medical encounters. *Gerontologist, 28*(3), 330–335.

Bieman-Copland, S., Ryan, E. B., & Cassano, J. (1998). Responding to the challenges of late life: Strategies for maintaining and enhancing competence. In D. Pushkar, W. M. Bukowski, A. E. Schwartzman, D. M. Stack, & D. R. White (Eds.), *Improving competence across the lifespan: Building interventions based on theory and research* (pp. 141–157). New York: Plenum.

Brown, T. L., Swenson, C. C., Cunningham, P. B., Henggeler, S. W., Schoenwald, S. K., & Rowland, M. D. (1997). Multisystemic treatment of violent and chronic juvenile offenders: Bridging the gap between research and practice. *Administration and Policy in Mental Health, 25*(2), 221–238.

Byrne, C. (1991, Fall). Interdisciplinary education in undergraduate health sciences. *Pedagogue: Perspectives on Health Sciences Education, 3*(3), 3–8.

Caporael, L. R. (1981). The paralanguage of caregiving: Baby-talk to the institutionalized aged. *Journal of Personality and Social Psychology, 40*, 867–884.

Carson, A., & Pichora-Fuller, K. (1997). Health promotion and audiology: The community–clinic link. *Journal of the Academy of Rehabilitative Audiology, 30*, 29–51.

Clark, P. G. (1996). Communication between provider and patient: Values, biography, and empowerment in clinical practice. *Ageing and Society, 16*, 747–777.

Clark, P. G. (1997). Values in health care professional socialization: Implications for geriatric education in interdisciplinary teamwork. *Gerontologist, 37*(4), 441–451.

Cohen-Mansfield, J., Lawton, M. P., & Riskin, C. (1990). Research institutes affiliated with nursing homes: Strengths and developmental issues. *Gerontologist, 30*, 411–16.

Dees, J. G., & Cramton, P. C. (1999). Shrewd bargaining on the moral frontier: Toward a theory of morality in practice. In R. J. Lewicki, D. M. Saunders, & J. W. Minton (Eds.), *Negotiation: Readings, exercises, and cases* (3rd ed., pp. 234–258). Boston, MA: Irwin/McGraw-Hill.

Drinka, T. J. K., & Streim, J. E. (1994). Case studies from purgatory: Maladaptive behavior within geriatrics health care teams. *Gerontologist, 34*(4), 541–547.

Elliott, C. (1993). Meaning what you say. *The Journal of Clinical Ethics, 4*, 61–62.

Fey, M. E., & Johnson, B. W. (1998). Research to practice (and back again) in speech-language intervention. *Topics in Language Disorders, 18*(92), 23–34.

Harwood, J., Giles, H., Ota, H., Pierson, H. D., Gallois, C., Ng, S. H., Lim, T.-S., & Somera, L. (1996). College students' trait ratings of three age groups around the Pacific Rim. *Journal of Cross-Cultural Gerontology, 11*, 307–317.

Herr, E. L. (1996). Toward the convergence of career theory and practice: Mythology, issues, and possibilities. In M. L. Savickas & W. B. Walsh (Eds.), *Handbook of career counseling theory and practice* (pp. 13–35). Palo Alto, CA: Davies-Black.

Holland, A. L. (1998). Some guidelines for bridging the research–practice gap in adult neurogenic communication disorders. *Topics in Language Disorder, 18*(2), 49–57.

Hummert, M. L., & Ryan, E. B. (1996). Toward understanding variations in patronizing talk addressed to older adults: Psycholinguistic features of care and control. *International Journal of Psycholinguistics, 12,* 149–170.

Hummert, M. L., Shaner, J. L., Garstka, T. A., & Henry, C. (1998). Communication with older adults: The influence of age stereotypes, context, and communicator age. *Human Communication Research, 25,* 124–151.

Katz, S. (1996). *Disciplining old age: The formation of gerontological knowledge.* Charlottesville & London: University Press of Virginia.

Kemper, S., & Harden, T. (1999). Experimentally disentangling what's beneficial about elderspeak from what's not. *Psychology and Aging, 14*(4), 656–670.

Kite, M. E., & Johnson, B. T. (1988). Attitudes toward older and younger adults: A meta-analysis. *Psychology and Aging, 3,* 233–244.

Kuster, J. M., & Poburka, B. J. (1998). The Internet: A bridge between research and practice. *Topics in Language Disorders, 18*(2), 71–87.

Lepper, H. W., Martin, L. R., & DiMatteo, M. R. (1995). A model of nonverbal exchange in physician–patient expectations for patient involvement. *Journal of Nonverbal Behavior, 19*(4), 207–222.

Lipsitz, L. A. (1995–1996). The teaching nursing home: Past accomplishments and future directions. *Generations, Winter,* 47–51.

Nissani, M. (1997). Ten cheers for interdisciplinarity: The case for interdisciplinary knowledge and research. *The Social Science Journal, 34*(2), 201–216.

Norris, J. E., Davey, A., Davey, S., & Weiler, J. (1995). "Healthy Alternatives/Healthy Choices": Considering the usefulness of a support group for caregivers. *Canadian Journal of Community Mental Health, 14*(2), 132–146.

Norris, J. E., Davey, A., & Kuiack, S. (1994). Evaluating self-help and mutual aid programs for older Canadians: Traps and tips. In G. M. Gutman & A. W. Wister (Eds.), *Health promotion for older Canadians: Knowledge gaps and research needs.* Vancouver, BC: Gerontology Research Centre and Program, Simon Fraser University.

Norris, J. E., & Rubin, K. (1984). Peer interaction and communication: A life span perspective. In P. Baltes & O. G. Brim, Jr. (Eds.), *Life span development and behavior* (Vol. 6). New York: Academic.

Orange, J. B., & Ryan, E. B. (1995). Effective communication. In B. Pickles, A. Compton, J. Simpson, C. A. Cott, & A. Vandervoort (Eds.), *Physiotherapy with older people* (pp. 119–137). London: W. B. Saunders.

Orange, J. B., Ryan, E. B., Meredith, S. D., & MacLean, M. (1995). Application of the Communication Enhancement Model for longterm care residents with Alzheimer's disease. *Topics in Language Disorder, 15*(2), 20–35.

Parloff, M. B. (1998). Is psychotherapy more than manual labor? *Clinical psychology: Science and practice, 5*(3), 376–381.

Petronio, S., Ellemers, N., Giles, H., & Gallois, C. (1998). (Mis)communicating across boundaries: Interpersonal and intergroup considerations. *Communication Research, 25*(6), 571–595.

Pratt, M. W., & Norris, J. E. (1994). *The social psychology of aging: A cognitive perspective.* Cambridge, MA: Blackwell.

Pratt, M. W., & Norris, J. E. (1999). Moral development in maturity: Lifespan perspectives on the processes of successful aging. In T. Hess & F. Blanchard-Fields (Eds.), *Social cognition and aging* (pp. 291–317). New York: Academic.

Ratzan, S. C. (1996). Effective decision-making: A negotiation perspective for health psychology and health communication. *Journal of Health Psychology, 1*(3), 323–333.

Rest, J., & Narvaez, D. (1994). *Moral development in the professions: Psychology and applied ethics.* Hillsdale, NJ: Lawrence Erlbaum Associates.

Rodin, J., & Langer, E. J. (1980). Aging labels: The decline of control and the fall of self-esteem. *Journal of Social Issues, 36*, 12–29.

Ryan, E. (1992). Beliefs about memory changes across the adult life span. *Journal of Gerontology: Psychological Sciences, 47*, P41–P46.

Ryan, E. B., Giles, H., Bartolucci, G., & Henwood, K. (1986). Psycholinguistic and social psychological components of communication by and with the elderly. *Language and Communication, 6*, 1–24.

Ryan, E. B., Hummert, M. L., & Boich, L. H. (1995). Communication predicaments of aging: Patronizing behavior toward older adults. *Journal of Language and Social Psychology, 13*, 144–166.

Ryan, E. B., Meredith, S. D., MacLean, M. J., & Orange, J. B. (1995). Changing the way we talk with elders: Promoting health using the communication enhancement model. *International Journal of Aging and Human Development, 41*(2), 89–107.

Shaughnessy, P. W., Kramer, A. M., Hittle, D. F., & Steiner, J. F. (1995). Quality of care in teaching nursing homes: Findings and implications. *Health Care Financing Review, 16*(4), 55–83.

Tindale, J. A. (1993). Participant observation as a method for evaluating a mental health promotion program with older persons. *Canadian Journal on Aging, 12*(2), 200–215.

Wilcox, M. J., Hadley, P. A., & Bacon, C. K. (1998). Linking science and practice in management of childhood language disorders: Models and problem-solving strategies. *Topics in Language Disorders, 18*(2), 10–22.

Author Index

A

Abraham, I., 228, *244*
Abrahamson, J., 57, *69*
Acton, H., 5, *21*
Adams, S. W., 55, *72*
Adelman, R., xiii, xv, xvi, *xix*, 26, 27, 28, 36, *41*, 102, 104, 105, 107, 108, 110, 111, 115, 116, *118*, *119*, 121, *154*
Administration on Aging, xii, *xviii*
Adolfsson, R., 161, 162, *170*, *173*
Affleck, D. C., 5, *22*
Aguilar, C., 53, *72*
Akao, C., 13, *22*
Alberoni, M., 227, *244*
Albert, M. L., 227, 228, 232, *245*, *246*
Aldous, J., 178, *199*
Alemayehu, E., 61, *72*
Allard, L., 227, 232, *248*
Allen, A., 4, 5, 6, 8, 10, 15, 16, 18, *20*, *21*, *22*
Ambinder, A., 86, *96*
American Academy of Physician Assistants, 30, *41*
American Association of Health Plans, 25, *41*
American Psychiatric Association, 162, *170*, 225, *244*
Amota, P. R., 178, *199*
Anagnopoulos, C., 242, *246*
Anderson R., 78, *96*

Anthony, C., 82, 86, *98*
Antonovsky, A., 260, *273*
Antonucci, T. C., 79, *94*
Aponte, J. F., 89, *93*
Appell, J., 226, 232, *244*
Aquilino, W. S., 178, *199*
Aquino, G., 89, 90, *96*
Arthur, S. A., 227, *247*
Ashworth, J., 75, *93*
Aspinwall, L. G., 80, *97*
Asplund, K., 160, 161, 162, 163, 164, 165, 166, 167, 168, 169, *170*, *171*, *172*, *173*
Atchley, R. J., 178, *201*
Athlin, E., 161, 165, 166, 167, 168, *170*, *172*
Atkinson, J., 127, *154*
Atkinson, S. J., 76, *93*
Au, R., 227, *246*
Auslander, G. K., 272, *273*
Austin, J. L., xii, *xviii*
Australian Institute of Health and Welfare, 203, *222*

B

Babbs, C. F., 10, *22*
Bach-Peterson, J., 231, *248*
Bacon, C. K., 288, *297*
Baddeley, A., 227, *244*

299

Newton, H., 7, *22*
Ng, S. H., xiii, xv, xvii, 253, 254, 255, 264,
    267, 269, *274, 275, 276, 278,* 280, *295*
Nicholas, M., 227, 232, *246*
Nissani, M., 287, *296*
Noble, W., 43, 57, *72*
Noels, K. A., xiii, xv, xvii, 254, 255, 256, 258,
    259, 264, 265, 267, 269, *273, 275, 276*
Noller, P., 205, *222*
Norberg, A., xiv, xv, xvii, 157, 159, 160, 161,
    162, 163, 164, 165, 166, 167, 168,
    169, *170, 171, 172, 173,* 233, *245*
Nordmark Sandgren, Å., 164, *171*
Normann, K., 161, 164, 166, *172, 173*
Norris, J. E., xiv, xv, xviii, 178, 179, 180,
    181, *200,* 290, 291, 292, *296, 297*
North, A. J., 227, 232, *248*
Northouse, L. L., 38, *42*
Northouse, P. G., 38, *42*
Nurse Practitioner Central, 30, *42*
Nussbaum, J. F., xiii, xv, xvii, *xix,* 27, 40, *42,*
    123, *155,* 178, *200,* 250, 270, 272,
    275, 276, 277

O

Obler, L. K., 227, 228, 232, *245, 246*
Oishi, S., 269, *277*
O'Keefe, B. J., xii, *xviii*
O'Keefe, D. J., xii, *xviii*
Okun, M. A., 270, *274*
Olson, D. H., 179, *200*
Onega, L., 228, *244*
Orange, J. B., xiv, xv, xvii, xviii, *xix,* 227,
    230, 231, 232, 233, 234, 235, 236,
    237, 238, 244, 246, 247, 271, *277,*
    281, 283, 286, 291, *296, 297*
Ordway, L., 78, *97*
Ory, M. G., 27, 28, *41,* 110, *120,* 232, *247*
Osgood, N. J., 11, *21*
Ota, H., 253, 254, 264, 267, *274, 275, 277,*
    278, 280, *295*

P

Paccioretti, D., 58, *71*
Palmer, B., 236, *245*
Palmer, C. V., 55, *72*

Palmore, E., 251, *277*
Paltridge, J., 265, *277*
Paoletti, I., 251, 269, 270, *277*
Papousek, M., 166, *171*
Parham, I. A., 11, *21*
Parish, W. L., 252, *276*
Parloff, M. B., 287, *296*
Parmelee, P. A., 210, *223*
Parsons, K., 228, 229, 230, *247*
Parsons, T., 101, *120*
Parving, A., 63, *72*
Pasley, B. K., 206, *222*
Patel, U. H., 10, *22*
Patterson, B. R., 272, *277*
Patterson, J., 18, *22*
Patterson, M. B., 160, *173*
Pawlby, S. J., 167, *173*
Peak, T., 76, 78, 81, 82, 83, 84, 85, 86, 93,
    95, 96, *97*
Pearce, W. B., xii, *xviii*
Pearlin, L., 205, *223*
Pearlman, D. A., 75, *96*
Pecchioni, L. L., xiii, xv, xvi, *xix,* 179, 187,
    198, *201*
Pedersen, S., 16, *22*
Perednia, D. A., 4, 5, 6, 18, *22*
Persson, D., 187, *201*
Peters, C., 44, *72*
Petronio, S., 290, *296*
Phillip, B., 63, *72*
Phillips, D. P., 49, *72*
Phillips, L., 204, *223*
Pichora-Fuller, M. K., xiv, xv, xvi, *xviii,* 45,
    46, 50, 51, 53, 55, 56, 57, 58, 63, 64,
    65, 66, 67, 68, 69, *71, 72, 73,* 292, *295*
Pierson, H. D., 253, 254, 264, 267, *274, 275,*
    278, 280, *295*
Pillemer, K., 80, *96*
Piquard, J. F., 12, *22*
Plomp, R., 52, *72*
Poburka, B. J., 287, 293, *296*
Poon, L. W., 272, *274*
Potter, J., 44, *72*
Potts, S., 16, *20*
Poulshock, S. W., 231, 232, *247*
Powell, J. A., 230, *247*
Powell, V., 179, 180, 181, *200*
Power, P., 75, *97*
Pratt, C. C., 186, *201*

Subject Index